COLD WAR
CAPITALISM

Richard B. Day

COLD WAR CAPITALISM

THE VIEW FROM MOSCOW
1945–1975

M.E. Sharpe

Armonk, New York
London, England

Library of Congress Cataloging-in-Publication Data

Day, Richard B., 1942–   .
Cold War capitalism : the view from Moscow, 1945–1975 / by Richard B. Day.
p.   cm.
Includes bibliographical references and index.
ISBN 1-56324-660-0 (alk. paper).—ISBN 1-56324-661-9 (pbk. alk. paper)
1. Soviet Union—Economic policy.
2. Economic history—1945–
3. Cold War.
I. title.
HC333.D39   1995
338.947—dc20
95-9029
CIP
10064 7896X
Printed in the United States of America

The paper used in this publication meets the minimum requirements of
American National Standard for Information Sciences—
Permanence of Paper for Printed Library Materials,
ANSI Z 39.48-1984.

BM (c)   10   9   8   7   6   5   4   3   2   1
BM (p)   10   9   8   7   6   5   4   3   2   1

In Memory of Dot and Stan

CONTENTS

INTRODUCTION

The collapse of the Soviet Union in December 1991 followed nearly seven and one-half decades of Communist Party rule and more than four decades of Cold War. Viewing the Cold War from the perspective of the mid-1990s, it seems difficult to believe that Soviet power and influence for so long represented a challenge to the capitalist system. The astonishing events of the recent past provoke questions that few observers expected to be addressing. Instead of speculating as to how the Cold War might end, we must now inquire how and why it lasted as long as it did. Why did Soviet leaders exhaust both their economy and the patience of their people in a struggle that, in retrospect, was doomed to fail?

My thesis in this book is that a study of Soviet political economy helps to explain both the perceptual origins of the conflict and the tenacity with which it was waged. The conclusion I reach is that by the mid-1970s Soviet leaders were convinced that they were gaining the upper hand. During the brief period of detente, America was acknowledged to be the dominant force in the capitalist world, but its relative strength appeared to be in decline. Humiliated in Vietnam, racked by student disaffection, divided by racial strife and stunned by Watergate and political assassinations, the United States was portrayed in the Soviet press as a decadent imperialist center. Soviet leaders, in contrast, anticipated continuous expansion of Communist influence not only in the third world but also in Western Europe.

By analyzing the perceptions that shaped Soviet attitudes to the Cold War, this study departs from traditional concerns with military strategy, localized conflicts, third-world rivalries, and the role of statecraft in determining relations between NATO and the Soviet bloc. The question I ask is this: How did Soviet specialists on the capitalist countries interpret western developments to Soviet political leaders? Since William Zimmerman's *Soviet Perspectives on International Relations 1956-1967*, several books have been written on how Soviet perceptions may have influenced Moscow's foreign policy.[1] I know of no previous monograph, however, that has studied Soviet interpretations of postwar capitalism specifically from the standpoint of political economy. This book represents an effort to fill that gap.

My work on this project originated with *The 'Crisis' and the 'Crash': Soviet Studies of the West (1917-1939)*, which I originally intended to be the first of two volumes. The project has now grown: the current volume covers three decades from 1945 to the mid-1970s; a third will include the period from the mid-1970s to the end of Boris Yeltsin's first term as president of the new Russian state. While doing research for this second volume, I quickly found that Soviet debates after 1945 were incomprehensible without reference to the literature of the 1920s and the 1930s. Interpretations of postwar capitalism were profoundly influenced by the Great Depression, Roosevelt's New Deal, and the rise of Nazi Germany. In thematic as well as chronological terms, *Cold War Capitalism* has turned out to be a direct sequel to *The 'Crisis' and the 'Crash.'*

The continuity between these two periods demonstrates that ideology, while obviously not the sole determinant of Soviet attitudes to the outside world, was nevertheless a factor of considerable importance. In *Ideology and Power in Soviet Politics*, Zbigniew K. Brzezinski cautioned against two extremes in interpreting the role of Marxism-Leninism during the Cold War: one involved "the simplistic conclusion that Soviet ideology is merely a cynical sham, consciously manipulated by the Soviet leaders"; the other, an equally simplistic view "that the Soviet approach to reality can be understood merely by consulting a Marxist handbook." Brzezinski characterized ideology as "an autonomously existing factor, conditioning behavior through the selection of the various policy alternatives that may exist at any particular moment."[2] This book begins with a similar premise; namely, that ideology filters what political observers see and therefore plays a unique role in constituting their particular "reality."

A study of Cold War capitalism, as seen from Moscow, requires facility in three languages: Russian is obviously needed to research Soviet sources, but there is also a requirement of familiarity with the unique "languages" of Marxist and western political economy. One of my tasks has been to bridge this language barrier and to translate Soviet literature into terms that will have meaning for western readers. I have tried to do this in two ways: first, I have situated the work of Soviet economists within the context of Marx's *Capital* and later theories of imperialism; second, I have related the themes of Soviet postwar debates to the rise of Keynesianism and the capitalist welfare state.

Because the idiom of Soviet political economy invariably sounds propagandistic, the impression is created that the literature itself must be tainted through Communist Party supervision. While party control was real and ever-present, my research indicates that there are no grounds for concluding that economic analyses were uniformly orchestrated. Economists typically began or ended their publications with references to the "authorities"—Marx, Engels, Lenin, Stalin, Khrushchev, Brezhnev, or the like—but in the main text of their work (and, when necessary, in the subtext), they engaged in vigorous debate concerning both current events and basic questions of theory. The range of debate widened and narrowed over time, depending upon the proximity of contentious issues to immediate concerns of the party leadership, but it was rarely within the power of the apparatus, even in Stalin's time, to suppress dissent entirely. The extent and persistence of disagreements among Soviet writers will strike many readers as one of the most surprising findings of this study.

Economists maintained a greater degree of autonomy than scholars in many other areas for one obvious reason: party leaders depended upon them for information concerning both current events and future prospects in the capitalist countries. In speeches on world affairs, Soviet leaders commonly cited sources and data first discovered and interpreted by one or another economist. A researcher such as Evgeny Samuilovich Varga, whose work figures prominently in this book, was at various times either a consultant to the highest political authorities or a stubborn critic of the particular line they were seeking to promote. Even when he was disciplined for overstepping the boundaries of received doctrine, Varga's ideas returned to alter the views of a subsequent generation. Varga was the most conspicuous among Soviet economists in this regard, but he was certainly not alone.

The importance that the Soviet government attached to studies of capitalist economies was indicated by the fact that such research enjoyed the status of a distinct subdiscipline within economics over a period of more than six decades. During the interwar years this work was organized by the Institute of World Economy and World Politics under the leadership of Varga. Although Varga and many of his colleagues continued to be active after 1945, Stalin considered their field so politically sensitive that in the late 1940s he purged the Institute of World Economy and merged it with the more conservative Institute of Economics. During the 1950s subdisciplinary autonomy was reestablished in a new Institute of World Economy and International Relations, joined in the late 1960s by the Institute of the USA (renamed in 1974 the Institute of the USA and Canada).[3]

That Soviet leaders had a need for economic interpretations of the capitalist countries is intuitively obvious. Strategic decisions concerning foreign policy and the international communist movement would have been impossible without knowledge of what was happening abroad and some sense of why. Less evident, perhaps, is the connection between interpretations of the west and Soviet domestic policy. In my previous volume I showed how western instability in the interwar years heightened fears of aggression, which Stalin used to justify strict priority for heavy industry and armaments in the five-year plans. After 1945 many economists expected that a more active role on the part of capitalist governments might bring a period of economic stabilization in the west, reduction of international tensions, and thus a prospect of gradual reform within the Soviet Union itself. The Cold War thwarted these hopes. By 1947 Stalin was determined to reinforce internal controls and to consolidate Soviet domination of Eastern Europe.

If, as Stalin suspected, imperialists were actively preparing for war against the Soviet Union, it seemed that the economy of the USSR must also be preserved on a war footing. To rationalize his own Cold War policies, Stalin denied the prospect of capitalist stabilization and penalized academic dissenters. The official interpretation of Keynesian economic policies portrayed countercyclical expenditures by capitalist governments as income transfers, through taxation, from the "toilers" to the most reactionary and aggressive imperialist monopolies. "Military Keynesianism," according to Stalinist doctrine, could only make economic crises more severe by curtailing mass purchasing power in order to finance war preparations. Since capitalist countries were assumed to respond to such crises through imperialist aggression, the Stalinist view held that war would remain a threat so long as capitalism existed.

By the late 1950s this Stalinist interpretation of "state-monopoly capitalism" met with growing criticism. As the salutary potential of government policies in the west became clearer, Soviet analysts again thought economic stabilization might reduce international tensions and facilitate domestic reform through the de-Stalinization program of Nikita Khrushchev. Whereas Stalin's repression had been rationalized in terms of the alleged inevitability of imperialist wars, Khrushchev explained his own innovations by insisting upon the need for peaceful coexistence and economic cooperation. The Khrushchev years brought relaxation of political constraints on economic researchers and made possible far-reaching reassessments both of postwar capitalism and of many traditional tenets of Marxist theory.

By the time of Khrushchev's own forced retirement in 1964, economists were reaching conclusions exactly the opposite of those that prevailed under Stalin. During the mid-1960s they believed not only that the capitalist state could prevent (or at least significantly moderate) cyclical fluctuations, but also that the role of the state was dramatically changing in conditions of full employment. With organized labor driving up wages at the expense of profits, it appeared that the state itself was becoming the principal *architect and initiator* of economic slowdowns, deliberately using monetary and fiscal restraint to curtail wage demands and restore profit margins as the long postwar expansion in the west began to decelerate.

This reversal of doctrine had implications both for Soviet expectations of the world economy and also for the international communist movement. If the modern state was able to "regulate" or even "program" economic development, Soviet writers concluded that politics must be assuming priority over economics in the class struggle. From the Khrushchev period onward, the political strategies of western communist parties were based on the premise that a popular, antimonopoly coalition of left-wing forces might capture the institutions of the capitalist state and transform the system from within, using many of the same instruments said to be employed by monopolies in "planning" a capitalist economy. The strategy of peaceful transition to socialism required West European communists to adopt essentially social-democratic programs of gradual reform.

Keynesian economics appeared to demonstrate the effectiveness of each state within its own boundaries, but the late 1960s also brought unexpected complications. The inflationary effects of war in Vietnam weakened the dollar's role as a world currency, prompting a belief that the contradictions of capitalism—now (partially) suppressed *within nation-state economies*—had been deflected instead into the *international financial system*. By the early 1970s the financial institutions created after World War II were in disarray, and Soviet researchers advised Leonid Brezhnev that the forces of "peace and socialism" had gained ascendancy in economic competition with the west.

Richard Nixon's pursuit of detente was interpreted as evidence of a weakened America's need for peace, markets, and new sources of energy. When Nixon traveled to Moscow in 1972, Soviet specialists on American affairs enthusiastically proclaimed that the USSR was emerging as the victor in the global struggle that had begun a quarter of a century earlier. This book will tell the story of that struggle through the eyes of Soviet economists as they looked west from Moscow. In my projected third volume, I hope to recount the concluding chapters of this story— from failure of detente in the 1970s to collapse of the Soviet Union and Boris Yeltsin's subsequent efforts to reintegrate Russia into the world capitalist economy.

COLD WAR CAPITALISM

CHAPTER 1

ORIGINS OF POSTWAR SOVIET DEBATES

Soviet studies of the west in the years 1945-75 began with the role of the state in national economies and subsequently turned to global contradictions of the world capitalist system. A parallel development occurred in Marxist thought from publication of the first volume of *Capital* in 1867 to the Russian revolution in 1917. In *Capital* Marx abstracted from foreign trade and investment to define the "laws of motion" leading to cyclical economic crises within a self-contained capitalist system. His analysis indicated that periodic fluctuations of market economies would become increasingly severe and culminate in proletarian revolution. When revolution was delayed long beyond the time expected, later Marxists turned from internal contradictions of capitalist economies to theories of the world economy and imperialism.

The spread of capital into precapitalist areas was commonly thought to have sustained the rate of profit in the leading capitalist countries and to have postponed the revolutionary crisis. In this interpretation not only did foreign trade and investment assume a far more prominent role than in *Capital*, but in many writings on imperialism the role of the state in organizing, regulating, and even planning economic affairs also took on new salience. Marxist theories of imperialism provide the historian with an important point of entry into Soviet debates during the decades that preceded World War II as well as during those that followed.

Immediately after the Russian revolution, Soviet Marxists were so preoccupied with imperialism—especially with its implications for the Soviet Union within the "capitalist encirclement"—that Marx's original concern with business cycles faded into the background. In *The 'Crisis' and the 'Crash'* I demonstrated how this atrophy of business-cycle theory complicated subsequent assessments of the Great Depression. Economists found themselves wrestling with the question of whether the catastrophe of 1929-33 was merely another *cyclical crisis*, such as the capitalist

3

countries had experienced for more than a century, or the *final crash* of the imperialist system as a whole.

By the late 1940s the official Stalinist view held that the Great Depression had initiated a period of terminal decline from which no sustained recovery was possible. Economists who opposed this interpretation, expecting stabilization in the west, likewise drew upon experience of the Great Depression. Impressed by the innovative role of government under Hitler and Roosevelt, they believed that modern capitalism had displayed a new potential for mitigating cyclical fluctuations. The most important question, from this point of view, appeared to be whether the state would serve the aggressive intentions of militant reactionaries, as in the case of the Nazis, or contribute to progressive democratic reforms such as Roosevelt had initiated in America.

Preoccupation of post-1945 Soviet debates with the new economic role of the state coincided with a similar focus in western thought due to the prevalence of Keynesian doctrines. It also represented a significant departure from the work of Marx, who considered political institutions to be of secondary importance compared to the objective laws that governed the cyclical pattern of capitalist development. Marx's most unique contribution to economic theory lay in his analysis of recurrent contradictions giving rise to capitalist cycles. To establish the context for Soviet debates after 1945, I shall therefore begin this study with a brief review of Marx's *Capital* and its relation to subsequent theories of imperialism and the Great Depression.

1. Marx on the Cyclical Pattern of Capitalist Development

In *Capitalism, Socialism and Democracy*, Joseph Schumpeter praised Marx as one of the founders of modern research into the business cycle. With reference to *Capital*, Schumpeter wrote that "We find practically all the elements that ever entered into any serious analysis of business cycles, and on the whole with very little error."[1] Whereas economic crises had previously been attributed to fortuitous circumstances, Marx compared the movement of industrial production to the orbits of the planets: "[Just] as the heavenly bodies, once thrown into a certain definite motion, always repeat this, so it is with social production as soon as it is thrown into this movement of alternate expansion and contraction."[2]

Marx's study of capitalism's "laws of motion" began with the concepts of *value* and *surplus value*. Selling their labor power to capitalists, industrial workers were said to receive a wage equal in value to the cost of maintaining themselves and their dependents at the prevailing level of subsistence. When capitalists sold the resulting commodities, they realized both their costs of production and profit. The secret of profit, according to Marx, was unpaid labor. During part of the day, workers created commodities of sufficient value to cover the costs of production, including their own wages; for the remainder of the day they created surplus value. The market *law of value* compelled every capitalist to attempt to increase the rate of profit by raising the rate of surplus value (or exploitation). Marx thought each employer must try to introduce labor-saving technology in order to increase productivity and reduce costs. "The battle of competition," he wrote, "is fought by cheapening of commodities."[3] As some capitalists prevailed in the competitive struggle and others went bankrupt, two consequences followed: existing capital tended to become more centralized through bankruptcies, and accumulation of new capital tended to be concentrated in fewer but larger firms. The *law of the centralization and concentration of industrial capital* followed inevitably from competition.

Because living labor was the sole source of surplus value, however, the struggle for private profit had contradictory implications for the system as a whole. Continuous introduction of new technology caused relative displacement of workers by machinery, or what Marx called a rise in the *organic composition of capital*. The result was that each capitalist, in attempting to raise his *individual* rate of profit, contributed to a gradual lowering of the *social average* rate. The *law of the falling rate of profit* suggested that capitalist production must eventually give way to socialism. Socialist planning would replace investments for the sake of private profit with technological advances designed to shorten the working day, lighten the burden of social labor, and extend opportunities for human self-development.

In capitalist society, on the contrary, accumulation of private capital presupposed recurring impoverishment of workers. Marx argued that each wave of competitive investments depended upon a reserve army of the unemployed who could be absorbed into new production at relatively low wages with a corresponding potential for a high rate of profit. The result was a uniquely capitalist *law of population* that required labor periodically to become "relatively superfluous":[4]

> The course characteristic of modern industry, viz., a decennial cycle (interrupted by smaller oscillations), of periods of average

activity, production at high pressure, crisis and stagnation, depends on the constant formation, the greater or less absorption, and the re-formation of the industrial reserve army or surplus population. In their turn, the varying phases of the industrial cycle [first] recruit the surplus population and [then] become . . . the most energetic agents of its reproduction.[5]

Marx believed that cyclical growth of production, through its effects upon employment and wages, determined the absorptive capacity of markets. By investing in new production facilities, capitalists reemployed workers who had lost their jobs in the previous cyclical contraction, expanded output, and created a new market for commodities through increasing wage expenditures. At a later point in the cycle, however, they just as predictably curtailed production in response to rising wages and falling profit rates, thus contracting markets and precipitating a general crisis of overproduction. A fundamental contradiction of the capitalist system was that in order to expand the forces of production, it must periodically destroy a part of the existing capital through bankruptcy of the weakest firms.

Marx referred to "the poverty and restricted consumption of the masses"[6] as the final cause of industrial crises, but he did not subscribe to the theory of (chronic) underconsumption that prevailed in the thinking of many later Marxists. In volume II of *Capital* he wrote:

> It is sheer tautology to say that crises are caused by the scarcity of effective consumption. . . . [I]f one were to attempt to give this tautology the semblance of a profounder justification by saying that the working class receives too small a portion of its own product and [that] the evil would be remedied as soon as it receives a larger share of it and its wages increase in consequence, one could only remark that *crises are always prepared by precisely a period in which wages rise generally and the working class actually gets a larger share of that part of the annual product which is intended for consumption.*[7]

Marx believed that the capitalist system of income distribution was flawed by the contradiction between social labor and private appropriation of the product: the limit to social consumption became apparent in the capitalists' response to a temporary increase of wages at the expense of profits when a cyclical expansion approached its peak. Full employment provided a market for the sale of commodities, but it also created a "disproportion between capital and exploitable labour power,"[8] or a scarcity of cheap wage labor, signifying the need to restore profitability through re-creating the industrial reserve army of the unemployed. Capitalist production created the market, but the market could not continuously grow because social income depended upon the fluctuating demand for labor:

> Taking them as a whole, the general movements of wages are exclusively regulated by the expansion and contraction of the industrial reserve army, and these again correspond to the periodic changes of the industrial cycle. They are, therefore, . . . determined by . . . the varying proportions in which the working class is divided into the active and reserve army, by the increase or diminution in the relative . . . surplus population, by the extent to which it is now absorbed [into production], now set free.[9]

In volume II of *Capital* Marx expanded the concepts of proportionality and disproportionality to consider the macroeconomic conditions required for reproduction of social capital as a whole. He began by dividing industry into two Departments. Department I produced means of production, or "constant" capital, which in turn was divided into "fixed" and "circulating" capital (equipment and materials respectively). Department II was responsible for output of consumer goods. Marx demonstrated that in order to guarantee a stable level of total output—or maintenance of current consumption and simple replacement of resources used in production—the flow of values between these two Departments must be equal.

Department II produced consumer goods by purchasing means of production from Department I. Department I, in turn, provided for consumption by its own capitalists and workers by purchasing consumer goods from Department II. Were Department II to spend more on machinery and materials than it received from Department I in payment for consumer goods, a cyclical expansion would begin. The flow of social purchasing power would increase as capitalists in the consumer goods sector invested their accumulated savings in new means of production. Prices for the means of production supplied by Department I would rise as a consequence of this new demand from Department II, and growing investments would then occur in the capital goods industries as well.

The same analysis applied in reverse. If Department II curtailed purchases of materials and equipment from Department I, or if Department I overexpanded relative to the long-run requirements of Department II, the necessary result would be an economic crisis.[10] Production would decline in the capital goods sector; the resulting unemployment would then spread back into Department II through reduced purchases of consumer goods. With this model of the two Departments, Marx claimed to demonstrate both the *theoretical* ability of the capitalist system to maintain a constant level of production—through equal exchanges between the two Departments—and also the inevitability of crises arising from spontaneous inter-Departmental disproportions.

Marx was convinced that *unevenness* of investment, or continual fluctuations in the rate of replacement and expansion of fixed capital, created the "material basis" of the economic cycle.[11] "[P]remature renewals of factory equipment on a rather large social scale," he wrote, "are mainly enforced by catastrophes or crises."[12] In the struggle for economic survival, every capitalist made individual investment decisions with no knowledge of the plans of his rivals. This lack of coordination would lead to new disproportions between and within the two Departments, resulting in relative shortages in some branches and relative overproduction in others. These disproportions would then have to be resolved by another cyclical crisis, which would eliminate redundant capital in industries that had overexpanded and stimulate new investments in those experiencing shortages.

Marx described this pattern by saying that "proportionality of the individual branches of production springs as a continual process from disproportionality."[13] Uninterrupted growth would require all sectors of the economy to expand "*simultaneously*, and *at once in the same proportion*"; in the absence of comprehensive planning, "departure from the given proportion in one branch of production drives all of them out of it, and in unequal proportions."[14] Dependence of production and investment on spontaneously changing prices meant that objective requirements could only be determined *after* resources had already been committed. In capitalist society, Marx observed, "social reason asserts itself only *post festum.*"[15] Socialism would rationally guarantee proportionality in advance by planning both investments and inventories. Market prices determined capitalist production through signaling relative scarcities; socialism would eliminate the need for such signals by planning for "continuous relative overproduction" in conditions beyond all scarcity.[16]

Marx regarded economic cycles as a permanent feature of capitalism, but he also saw historical limits to this pattern. The laws of the system's overall movement suggested that economic contradictions would intensify social conflict, leading eventually to proletarian revolution. Capitalist relations of production were already becoming a "fetter" upon development of the productive forces. Private property was objectively moving in the direction of socialization, even within the existing system, through ever-increasing dominance of the largest firms. Marx concluded that "Centralisation of the means of production and socialisation of labour at last reach a point where they become incompatible with their capitalist integument. This integument is burst asunder. The knell of capitalist private property sounds. The expropriators are expropriated."[17]

2. Interpretations of Marx Prior to the Russian Revolution

By interpreting capitalism as an historical mode of production, subject to change through its own internal contradictions, Marx implied that the process of cyclical movement would alter with the approach of socialist revolution. Intensification of economic contradictions would compel workers to organize for political struggle. After Marx's death in 1883, however, Engels considered another possibility: centralization and concentration of capital might also permit capitalists to make significant improvements in economic organization. Editing volume III of *Capital*, Engels observed that centralization and concentration were already causing the productive forces to "outgrow the control of the laws of the capitalist mode of commodity exchange."[18]

In Marx's analysis the traditional cycle was driven by spontaneous competition in production and investments. Engels emphasized instead the growth of protectionism and industrial trusts, "which regulate production, and thus prices and profits."[19] To the extent that new forms of commercial and industrial organization suppressed spontaneous market forces, they appeared to be eliminating "most of the old breeding grounds of crises and opportunities for their development."[20] This interpretation led directly to the question of how the proletarian revolution might still be expected to occur. If traditional cycles were in doubt, did this not suggest that the system might endure far longer than Marx had expected?

Engels answered that maintenance of high market prices by trusts and cartels also restricted domestic sales, implying that "chronic stagnation would necessarily become the normal condition of modern industry, with only insignificant fluctuations."[21] In response to this threat, capital had been driven to find alternative outlets for commodities in foreign markets. Monopolistic barriers to new domestic competition also led to growing exports of capital in search of more profitable ventures elsewhere. The taming of contradictions within national economies merely deflected the problems analyzed by Marx into the world economy. Engels anticipated later theories of imperialism when he predicted that capitalist organization of national economies pointed in the direction of an "ultimate general industrial war which shall decide who has supremacy on the world market. Thus every factor which works against a repetition of the old crises carries within itself the germ of a far more powerful future crisis."[22]

Marx had demonstrated that capitalism both creates and destroys its own internal markets through cyclical expansions and contractions. Engels thought that unless capital enjoyed the opportunity for continuous expansion into new foreign markets, modern forms of organization would pose a threat of "general chronic overproduction."[23] Two years after Marx's death, Engels wrote of a "continued chronic depression [that] must prepare a crash of a violence and extent such as we have never known before."[24] Engels' references to chronic depression caused many later Marxists to infer that effective demand on the part of workers and capitalists could *never* absorb the entire output of modern industry.

The first comprehensive theory of capitalism's chronic dependence upon "third-party" markets—or new sources of demand in addition to that of capitalists and workers—came in Rosa Luxemburg's book *The Accumulation of Capital*, published in 1913. Luxemburg maintained that Marx's analysis of reproduction, as set out in the model of two Departments, was merely a theoretical construction which "cannot explain the actual and historical course of accumulation."[25] Only in noncapitalist markets was it possible to realize the surplus value that capitalists must accumulate for purposes of new investment: "The decisive fact is that the surplus value cannot be realised by sale either to workers or to capitalists, but only if it is sold to such social organisations or strata whose own mode of production is not capitalistic."[26] In *The 'Crisis' and the 'Crash'* I showed that this type of argument played a dominant role in shaping Soviet assessments of capitalism during the 1920s and the 1930s. Since theories of the *problem of markets* continued to prevail in Stalinist literature after 1945, it is important to review Luxemburg's argument here.

We have seen that Marx's reproduction schemes demonstrated both capitalism's *theoretical* capacity to create its own markets and also the practical impossibility of continuous growth due to unplanned investments and inter-Departmental disproportions. The model of the two Departments assumed "pure capitalism" in the sense that all social purchasing power originated with expenditures by the capitalist class. Apart from capitalists, the only other class consisted of wage laborers. In terms of value, Marx divided the total social product into three categories: expenditures on equipment (fixed capital) and materials (circulating capital); expenditures on labor power in the form of wages (variable capital); and surplus value as the source of profits and new accumulation.

Marx showed that in order merely to continue production at the same level, capitalists had no alternative but to spend a portion of their revenues to replace equipment and materials used up in current operations. This part of total social revenue would be spent predictably. Because wages were taken to be at, or close to, the level of subsistence (depending upon the phase of the industrial cycle), workers were also assumed to spend their incomes in a predictable manner. This pattern of necessary expenditures meant that values embodied in at least two component parts of the social product would be realized: commodities needed for replacing worn-out means of production and for sustaining workers' consumption would be sold.

If the capitalists themselves purchased and consumed the remaining portion of social output, then all values would be accounted for—but Luxemburg also contended that there could be no accumulation of *new capital* for industrial expansion. Accumulation required capitalists to forgo consuming part of their surplus value and to sell the corresponding commodities elsewhere in order to generate the money capital needed to finance new investments. Luxemburg's question was: Who will buy these commodities? The workers obviously could not do so, for all wages were assumed in advance to be spent on consumption. But if this responsibility must fall to the capitalists themselves, they would merely be involved in the futile endeavor of trying to accumulate new capital from their own pockets.

According to Luxemburg, "so long as we retain the assumption that there are no other classes but capitalists and workers, . . . there is no way that the capitalists as a class can . . . accumulate capital."[27] This argument appeared to indicate that the capitalist system could not possibly expand in the absence of noncapitalist markets both among domestic producers and in precapitalist countries: "there must develop right from the start an exchange relationship between capitalist production and the non-capitalist milieu, where capital . . . finds the possibility of realizing surplus value in hard cash for further capitalization."[28] Luxemburg believed that the "pure capitalism" of Marx's model faced a chronic problem of markets.

The fact is that Marx had suggested an answer to this apparent dilemma when dealing with saving and investment in *Capital*. Discussing the *unevenness* of investment, he observed that at any given time *some* capitalists would be accumulating money capital for future replacement of equipment or new additions, while *others* would be spending their past savings on current investments. If current expenditures from accumulation funds exceeded revenues being set aside, the response to Luxemburg's objection would be perfectly clear: the capitalist class—or at least those capitalists presently spending past savings—would indeed finance expansion of the domestic market and realization of surplus value, and they would do so for the purely conventional reason of adding to production capacity in pursuit of profit.[29]

Marx did not deny either the empirical significance of foreign trade or the possibility of more profitable sales and investments in noncapitalist markets. His analysis of market creation did indicate, however, at least the theoretical possibility of expanded reproduction—or continuing investments in new equipment and a growing social output—without any necessary reliance upon third-party, or noncapitalist, markets. During the 1890s Lenin interpreted Marx in exactly this manner. In a debate with the Narodniks (Russian agrarian socialists), who argued that Russia could not pass through the capitalist stage because peasant impoverishment would create a problem of markets, Lenin answered that "the limits of the development of the market . . . are set by the limits of the specialisation of social labour. But this specialisation, by its very nature, is as infinite as technical developments."[30]

Lenin thought that market expansion, as Marx had argued, depended on capitalist installation of new technology. Once commodity production was established, each article would be broken into its component parts and made the object of specialized manufacturing and new investments. In Lenin's view, "Marx proved . . . that capitalist production is quite conceivable without foreign markets, with the growing accumulation of wealth, and without any 'third parties.'"[31] Rejecting both the problem of markets in general and theories of chronic underconsumption in particular, Lenin agreed with Marx that "it is precisely in the periods which precede crises that the workers' consumption rises."[32]

In his own explanation of foreign trade, Lenin spoke of the need for proportionality between branches of industry. Whereas Marx had pointed to disproportionality as the source of cyclical crises, Lenin added that foreign trade was one means typically employed by capitalists both to earn a higher rate of profit and to correct domestic disproportions:

> The various branches of industry, which serve as "markets" for one another, do not develop evenly, but outstrip one another, and the more developed industry seeks a foreign market. This does not mean at all "the impossibility of the capitalist nation realising surplus-value." . . . It merely indicates the lack of proportion in the development of the different industries.[33]

Lenin's contribution to this question was forgotten by the late 1920s, when Soviet Marxists resurrected the problem of markets in a protracted dispute over capitalist "stabilization," or the possibility of avoiding crises through internal market creation regulated by the state. As in the case of imperialism, the theory of stabilization could be traced to Engels' reinterpretation of Marx. In 1878 Engels had predicted that the objective process of socialization would ultimately lead beyond trusts and cartels to circumstances in which the state would become "the ideal collective body of all capitalists."[34]

Engels thought the steadily rising organic composition of capital would make investments so costly that they would increasingly have to be financed out of resources amassed by the state: "The more productive forces . . . [the state] takes over, the more it becomes the real collective body of all the capitalists, the more citizens it exploits."[35] State-financed investments would ultimately transform capitalist entrepreneurs into a rentier class, whose members would no longer have any social role "save the pocketing of revenues, the clipping of coupons and gambling on the Stock Exchange, where the different capitalists fleece each other of their capital."[36]

The Austrian Marxist Rudolf Hilferding was the first to undertake a thorough study of capitalism's changing organizational structure in his book *Finance Capital*, published in 1910. Stressing the importance of institutional changes, as opposed to an alleged chronic problem of markets, Hilferding introduced the new concept of *finance capital* as the mediating link between large-scale industry and big banks. The role of banks was to combine the resources of individual capitalists in order to finance investments that were beyond the reach even of the largest joint-stock companies. "I call bank capital," Hilferding wrote, "that is, capital in money form which is actually transformed . . . into industrial capital, finance capital. . . . An ever-increasing proportion of the capital used in industry is finance capital, capital at the disposition of the banks which is used by the industrialists."[37]

Marx had associated the rising organic composition of capital with a falling rate of profit, but here Hilferding added another qualification. The purpose of industrial cartels and trusts, each relying upon support from its bankers to finance inventories and control prices during economic fluctuations, was to maintain the rate of profit of organized capital at the expense of unorganized, small-scale producers. Cartel profit represented "participation in, or appropriation of, the profit of other branches of industry."[38] Hilferding's theory of organized capitalism examined new sources of economic stability, but he also believed that *Capital* continued to provide the explanation for periodic crises. The organization of particular branches of industry, independently of each other, could never guarantee proportionality between their respective private plans. As Hilferding remarked,

> Partial regulation . . . has absolutely no influence upon the proportional relations in industry as a whole. . . . Planned production and anarchic production are not quantitative opposites such that by tacking on more and more "planning" conscious organization will emerge out of anarchy. Such a transformation can only take place . . . by subordinating the whole of production to conscious control.[39]

Hilferding believed, like Marx, that real economic planning was "a question of power."[40] It was *economically* conceivable that capitalism might achieve comprehensive planning through a "general cartel" embracing the whole of industry, but what was economically conceivable was also "impossible" in social and political terms. The objective limit to capitalist organization was the class struggle of the workers against exploitation, which Hilferding thought would end with an electoral victory of the Social-Democratic party:

> Once finance capital has brought the most important branches of production under its control, it is enough for society, through its conscious executive organ—the State conquered by the working class—to seize finance capital in order to gain immediate control

of these branches. . . . [T]aking possession of six large Berlin banks would mean taking possession of the most important spheres of large-scale industry, and would greatly facilitate the initial phases of socialist policy . . . when capitalist accounting might still prove useful.[41]

During the First World War, Nikolai Bukharin's theory of imperialism drew heavily upon Hilferding's *Finance Capital*. Bukharin believed that imperialist war economies, particularly the war economy of Germany, had transformed Hilferding's speculative universal cartel into an historical reality. Although Hilferding had seen a continuing contradiction between organized and unorganized capital, with the former accumulating surplus value at the expense of the latter, Bukharin referred instead to the rise of "collective capitalism" and "a collective, joint capitalist" in the form of the state, much as Engels had originally predicted.[42]

"Statification" of capitalist means of production, according to Bukharin, had imparted greater internal unity to the system than ever before in its history. In place of Marx's spontaneous law of value, or the endless rivalry between individual capitalists over accumulation of surplus value, Bukharin argued that it was now the state that regulated prices, allocated materials, controlled trade, and determined production priorities. "As a result, the anarchic commodity market to a large degree is replaced by the organized distribution of the product, in which the supreme authority is . . . the state power."[43]

The modern state was the primary organizing institution in Bukharin's view of imperialism, but following Hilferding he also assigned a central role to finance capital under the supervision of the state bank. Selling securities in order to transform private accumulation into public expenditures needed to prosecute the war, the bank had converted individual capitalists into shareholders of a single "state-capitalist trust." Bukharin's theory of capitalism's internal organization reaffirmed Engels' prediction that domestic contradictions would be diverted into the international sphere. According to Bukharin, imperialist wars of aggression would now tend to replace the cyclical economic crises that Marx described in *Capital:*

> the reorganization of finance-capitalist relations of production has followed a path toward universal state-capitalist organization, involving the elimination of the commodity market, the conver-

> sion of money into a unit of account, the organization of produc-
> tion on a state-wide scale, and the subordination of the entire
> "national-economic" mechanism to the goals of international
> competition; in other words, mainly to war.[44]

Lenin's theory of imperialism was also influenced by Hilferding's
account of new capitalist institutions, but Lenin never went so far as
Bukharin in attributing a unifying role to the state. Lenin thought the
claim that cartels could abolish the business cycle was merely "a fable
spread by bourgeois economists."[45] Excessive emphasis upon trusts,
cartels and central banking, he argued, ignored the continuing contradictions between organized and unorganized capital, or

> the contradiction between monopoly and free competition which
> exists side by side with it, between the gigantic "operations"
> (and gigantic profits) of finance capital and "honest" trade in the
> free market, the contradiction between cartels and trusts on the
> one hand, and non-cartelised industry on the other, etc.[46]

Despite Lenin's reservations concerning theories both of "organized
capitalism" and of chronic dependence upon third-party markets, the
approaches of Bukharin and Luxemburg dominated Soviet economic
discussions throughout the 1920s. These new theories also led to use of
the term "crisis" in a sense different from Marx's original meaning.
Marx referred to *cyclical crises* required to restore interbranch proportionality. Luxemburg's chronic problem of markets, in contrast,
implied the inevitability of imperialist wars and *systemic collapse* once
third-party markets no longer existed. Bukharin's reinterpretation of
Hilferding similarly omitted cyclical crises and indicated that imperialist
warfare would culminate in the *final crash* of the world capitalist system.

3. Soviet Marxism in the 1920s

The problem after World War I was to reconcile these new theories of
imperialism with the survival of capitalism and to explain the anomalous
role of the Soviet state within the economic encirclement imposed by the
victorious powers. In 1917 Russian Marxists unanimously expected the
Soviet state to be supported by proletarian revolution in the west.
Opinions varied as to how and when European workers would seize
power, but no party leader doubted that the final collapse of capitalism

had begun. The war was followed, however, by an economic boom in Britain and America that continued until the crisis of 1920-21. When the third congress of the Communist International met in 1921, the task of reorienting Marxist theory fell to Leon Trotsky.

Trotsky's account of the "curve of capitalist development" represented the first effort by a Soviet Marxist to reintegrate the concepts of cyclical and systemic crisis. Contrary to Bukharin's emphasis upon the organizational capacity of the imperialist state, Trotsky argued that new capitalist institutions had not ended the traditional cyclical movement: "So long as capitalism is not overthrown by the proletarian revolution, it will continue to live in cycles, swinging up and down. Crises and booms were inherent in capitalism at its very birth; they will accompany it to its grave."[47] The real issue, for Trotsky, was to determine how postwar changes in the cycle might affect long-run prospects for capitalism's survival as a world system.

The business cycle was the "pulse" of the capitalist "organism," and Trotsky thought a comparative study of cycles would provide a measure of the system's health and possible longevity.[48] Historical data, he claimed, showed that the slope of capitalism's overall curve (or graph) of development depended upon the peculiar character of cyclical movement in different historical periods: "In periods of rapid capitalist development the crises are brief and superficial . . . while the booms are long-lasting and far-reaching. In periods of capitalist decline the crises are . . . prolonged . . . while the booms are fleeting, superficial, and speculative. In periods of stagnation the fluctuations occur upon one and the same level."[49]

Trotsky believed that development of capitalism as a whole could be understood in terms of this changing pattern. Until the mid-nineteenth century the system had gradually expanded; the year 1848 inaugurated an interval of more rapid growth lasting until 1873; from 1873 until 1894 a period of depression prevailed; from 1894 until the eve of war there was a sustained boom. The year 1914 appeared to mark the beginning of "the period of the destruction of capitalist economy."[50] The aggregate curve of development would turn downward in the 1920s through a succession of weak recoveries and protracted setbacks. World capitalism appeared to have been crippled by the war and destruction of the *international division of labor*.

Marx had related cyclical crises to disproportions between sectors; Trotsky took a similar approach in assessing the world economy. The crisis of 1920-21, he claimed, indicated that America would face "a prolonged epoch of depression" because its production capacity had expanded disproportionately in order to serve European wartime demand that no longer existed.[51] Unable to redress its own postwar disproportions with imports from America, Europe would meanwhile experience economic "levelling out in reverse," or general contraction dictated by curtailment of production in "the most ruined areas and branches of industry."[52] Trotsky acknowledged that if the revolution were delayed for another fifteen or twenty-five years, there was a theoretical possibility that capitalism might enter a new period of "equilibrium." For the immediate future, however, he thought that America would languish and Europe would be "thrown violently into reverse gear."[53]

Although this assessment corresponded in most respects with Marx's approach, Trotsky's reference to the possibility of a new equilibrium was potentially misleading. Marx had emphasized that capitalism was a moving system of contradictions. For him equilibrium referred not to an historical period but only to the brief interlude of paralysis occasioned by each successive industrial crisis. "The crises," he declared, "are always but *momentary* and forcible solutions of the existing contradictions."[54] The fundamental import of capitalism's internal contradictions was that lasting equilibrium was impossible.

Professor N.D. Kondrat'ev, a prominent "bourgeois" participant in early Soviet debates, proposed instead that capitalism be thought of as *a system of moving equilibrium*. In *The World Economy and its Conjunctures*, published in 1922, Kondrat'ev maintained that the purpose of each cyclical crisis was to restore the pattern of moving equilibrium: "In its most general form the essence of an economic crisis lies in the fact that *the national economies of separate countries and the world economy as a whole, taken as a moving system of elements, loses its equilibrium and experiences an acute, painful process of transition to the condition of a new moving equilibrium.*"[55]

Kondrat'ev believed that capitalism involved not one cycle but two: a short cycle of approximately ten years—the one analyzed by Marx—and a longer cycle lasting up to fifty years or more. The long cycle, in turn, was divided into a rising wave and a declining wave, each lasting approximately twenty-five years. The appearance of regularity in these long cycles suggested an underlying *historical continuity*, which Kondrat'ev thought Trotsky had mistakenly interpreted as separate and distinct *historical periods*. Kondrat'ev conceded that world capitalism had now entered the falling wave of a long cycle, but the obvious implication of his theory was that a new wave of prosperity must follow.[56]

Kondrat'ev's attempt to reconcile Marx's theory of cyclical contradictions with the concept of equilibrium resulted in conclusions that most
Russian Marxists regarded as clearly counterrevolutionary. The exception
came when Bukharin undertook to reformulate his own prewar theory of
imperialism by incorporating the concept of equilibrium. In 1919 Lenin
had repudiated Bukharin's work, arguing that it confused Marx's ana-
lytical model of pure capitalism with the reality of modern imperialism.
By excluding internal contradictions, Bukharin had misrepresented "state-
capitalist trusts" as a new historical form of "pure imperialism." Lenin
claimed that "Pure imperialism, without the fundamental basis of [com-
petitive] capitalism, has never existed, does not exist anywhere, and
never will exist. This is an incorrect generalisation of everything that was
said of the syndicates, cartels, trusts and finance capitalism, when finance
capitalism was depicted as though it had none of the foundations of the
old capitalism under it."[57]

Bukharin's response came in a new book, *The Economics of the Transition Period*, published in 1920. He acknowledged that despite the
organizational potential of imperialist economies, protracted warfare had,
indeed, thwarted the prospect of planned capitalism by undermining what
he now termed the system's "dynamic equilibrium." Economic growth
required expanding investments in equipment and materials, but
armaments production had transformed real productive forces into weapons that were destroyed on the battlefields. The result was to reverse
Marx's description of the normal process of accumulation. Reconsidering
"state-monopoly capitalism" in terms of Marx's model of reproduction,
Bukharin now thought a war economy meant that

> the real basis of social production narrows with each turnover of
> the social capital. Here we have neither expanded reproduction
> nor even simple reproduction, but a growing *underproduction*.
> Such a process can be designated as *expanded negative reproduc-
> tion*. That is what war means . . . from the economic point of
> view.[58]

Bukharin still believed in 1920 that "elements of dissolution and
revolutionary breakdown" were advancing from month to month in all
the leading capitalist countries.[59] Within a year, however, this conclusion too was obviously mistaken, causing him to reflect further on
capitalism's "law of mobile equilibrium." In *Historical Materialism* he
suggested that the unique experience of wartime capitalism could only be

understood in terms of a general theory of equilibrium. Expanded negative reproduction was described as a form of equilibrium "with a negative indication," but two other variants were possible: simple reproduction, or "constant re-establishment of equilibrium . . . on the old basis"; and expanded reproduction, or "unstable equilibrium with a positive indication."[60]

Once Bukharin adopted a general theory of equilibrium, he soon found himself agreeing with Kondrat'ev that the predicted "general crisis" and revolutionary "crash" of the world capitalist system had in fact turned out to be merely a "creeping crisis"[61] tending toward "a certain stabilization."[62] In *Imperialism and the Accumulation of Capital*, he disputed Luxemburg's theory of third-party markets and explained stabilization by again referring to state capitalism:

> Let us imagine . . . the *collective-capitalist social order* (state capitalism), in which the capitalist class is a unified trust. . . . Is accumulation possible here? Of course it is. Constant capital grows, the consumption of the capitalists grows, new branches of production continually arise in response to new needs, the consumption of the workers grows even though it is confined within definite limits. *Despite* this "underconsumption" of the masses, crises do not occur because the demand of *each branch of production in relation to the others* . . . is determined in advance (there is no "anarchy of production", but a rational plan from the viewpoint of capital). . . . Thus *no crisis of overproduction can occur here*. The course of production, in general, is planned.[63]

By the mid-1920s Bukharin thought that stabilization represented an entirely "new phase of capitalist development."[64] Modern industry had inaugurated a wave of technological innovations that were "qualitatively modifying" production.[65] Entire new branches of industry were emerging, including the growing use of electrical energy, new methods in metallurgy, development of liquid fuels, and use of chemistry to produce various synthetic materials. In other words, the "trust form of capital" continued to prevail and was organizing creation of new domestic markets through investments that Bukharin described in 1928 as nothing less than a new "technological revolution."[66]

Bukharin's reassessment of capitalist prospects had important implications for his views concerning the Soviet economy. He hoped that stabilization in the west would create a suitable environment for domestic stabilization through the New Economic Policy. In particular, he was anxious to avoid a clash with the peasantry over use of forced saving, or what Trotsky and his supporters called "primitive socialist accumulation," as a means of financing Soviet industrialization. Once Trotsky was politically defeated, however, Bukharin quickly discovered that his current ally, Stalin, was an even more serious threat to the hope for a peaceful and gradual transition to socialist planning.

From the mid-1920s onward, Stalin determined to industrialize the Soviet Union as rapidly as possible. Whereas Bukharin saw beneficial consequences flowing from capitalist stabilization, Stalin insisted that the postwar world had been divided into two hostile camps: "the camp of capitalism, headed by Anglo-American capital, and the camp of socialism, headed by the Soviet Union."[67] Precisely because the Soviet Union had dropped out of the world capitalist system, narrowing international markets and curtailing imperialist access to cheap labor and raw materials, Stalin thought that stabilization was becoming precarious and "rotten."[68] "Is it difficult to understand," he asked, "that the growth of capitalism's productive potentialities, coupled with the limited capacity of the world market . . . intensifies the struggle for markets and deepens the crisis of capitalism?"[69]

Once assessments of capitalist prospects became linked with the political conflict between Bukharin and Stalin over domestic policies, a number of professional party economists quickly became involved. By this time the most important Soviet analyst of western economic developments was E.S. Varga. Since 1921 he had been an adviser to the Communist International, and from the mid-1920s he presided over a growing body of researchers at the new Institute of World Economy and World Politics. Varga sided with Stalin, believing that Europe was plunging into a "stabilization crisis." He argued that American assistance to Germany, through the Dawes Plan, was causing production to expand and the struggle over export markets to intensify.

Bukharin saw new investments as the cause of market expansion in the west; Varga thought, on the contrary, that competition for markets had resulted in cost-cutting industrial rationalization and widespread unemployment. German industry used American loans to undercut imperialist rivals by replacing living labor with new technology. In Varga's opinion, "all prophecies regarding a fresh revival of European capitalism" were "idle predictions" and "counter-revolutionary apologetics."[70] Europe would continue to experience "rapidly recurring and lengthy crises, interspersed with brief intervals of better conditions [and] . . . acutely revolutionary situations."[71]

Varga shared Luxemburg's view that modern capitalism suffered from a chronic problem of markets, or what he termed a contradiction between production capacity and social "consuming power." Competition forced the capitalists "always to apply the latest means of production . . . , to raise the organic composition of capital, [and] to expand the total productive power beyond the consuming power of society."[72] This claim appeared to be illustrated by American data in 1928: for the first time in the history of capitalism, the number of productive workers (those creating surplus value) seemed to have declined during a period of normal cyclical expansion. Varga concluded that increased productivity was causing industrial unemployment because agriculture in America had become fully capitalist, thus eliminating the domestic noncapitalist (or third-party) market:

> The actual development of the USA is approaching the condition of "pure" capitalism, and in this regard the question arises—or more correctly, could be raised by the supporters of Rosa Luxemburg's theory—as to whether obstacles now emerge to the further accumulation and realization of surplus value.[73]

Varga believed that in theory surplus value could be realized; in practice it could not. A solution to the problem of markets would require a *transfer of income* from capitalists to workers, "But only Social Democrats can seriously believe that the capitalists will raise wages in order to find buyers for their surplus commodities. This would be senseless, for it would mean that the capitalist class as a whole would voluntarily grant the working class a part of the surplus value."[74] In *The Accumulation of Capital,* Rosa Luxemburg had similarly argued that "maintenance of an ever-larger army of workers" could not be "the ultimate purpose of the continuous accumulation of capital."[75] The last concern of the capitalist class was the prosperity of workers.

The conflict over Bukharin's theory of stabilization came to a climax in 1928 at the sixth congress of the Communist International. Bukharin asserted that the further state capitalism developed, the less likely would economic crises become: "Under [full] state capitalism . . . crises would be impossible, although the 'share' of the workers may steadily decline. This diminishing share would be taken into account in the plan."[76] When critics denounced him for adopting the views of Rudolf Hilferding, who by this time was regarded as a social-democratic traitor to the proletarian revolution, Bukharin denied that his arguments involved a "Social-Democratic 'Hilferding tinge.'"[77] In any case, he declared that he was willing "to come to the defence of 'poor' Hilferding" and "to take the 'prewar' Hilferding under my protection."[78] As for Varga's comments on America, Bukharin described them as "the Luxemburgist theory" in a new guise and announced his absolute disagreement with the suggestion that "the internal possibilities of American capitalism have been 'exhausted'. They have not yet been exhausted and . . . I am on principle opposed to this point of view. It is wrong both in theory and practice . . . it is a reiteration of Rosa Luxemburg's theory."[79]

In response to Bukharin, Varga repeated the main themes of his recent work. Pointing to "a new kind of unemployment, what I call structural unemployment," he asked: "What does this development signify? . . . It means that technological progress, the progress in the productivity and intensity of labour, has surpassed the capacity of the market. . . . Today we find that the expansion of the market no longer suffices to provide . . . for those who have . . . been thrown out of work in the imperialist countries." In the leading capitalist countries, third-party markets in precommercial farming had been eliminated. Since colonial markets were already divided between the major imperialist powers, Varga agreed with Stalin that "the struggle for markets is going to become more and more acute in the near future."[80]

Varga's views lent support to Stalin's claim that the end of "rotten stabilization" would precipitate a new historical period of wars and proletarian revolutions. His dismal projections of the capitalist future assisted Stalin in easing Bukharin out of political power and in rationalizing the First Five-Year Plan. If the international struggle over markets pointed to a renewal of imperialist wars, forced collectivization could also be justified in order to provide the resources needed to build Soviet heavy industry. The magnitude of Bukharin's "errors," both theoretical and political, appeared to be confirmed by the Great Depression. After 1929 further debate over stabilization was pointless.

4. Soviet Interpretations of the Great Depression

As the capitalist world economy collapsed in 1929-33, it seemed that Engels' and Luxemburg's predictions of chronic overproduction were at last being fulfilled. In his introduction to the English-language edition of the first volume of *Capital*, Engels had written in 1886 that "The decennial cycle of stagnation, prosperity, over-production and crisis, ever recurrent from 1825 to 1867, seems indeed to have run its course; but only to land us in . . . a permanent and chronic depression."[81] In 1930 Varga came to exactly the same conclusion: "The alternation of the phases of crisis, depression, expansion, a high conjuncture, and a new crisis—which was characteristic of progressive capitalism—no longer exists for large parts of the world economy; now periods of chronic depression and more acute phases of crisis follow one another."[82] Modern capitalism appeared to have passed beyond the cyclical movement analyzed in *Capital*, revealing a new "tendency toward a *chronic* disproportion between productive and consuming capacity."[83]

In June 1930 Stalin gave the sixteenth party congress his own interpretation of recent events. "Things have turned out," he boasted, "exactly as the Bolsheviks said they would." Hymns of capitalist "prosperity," "panegyrics in honor of the new technology," and proclamations of "the unshakeable firmness of capitalist stabilization"—all had given way to universal collapse.[84] The current crisis demonstrated that capitalism was following "a *descending* curve,"[85] which Stalin attributed to "the contradiction between the social character of production and the capitalist form of appropriation." Explaining this contradiction, Stalin ignored Marx's theory of cyclical disproportions and, like Varga, adopted a view similar to that of Rosa Luxemburg:

> An expression of this fundamental contradiction of capitalism is the contradiction between the colossal *growth* of capitalism's potentialities of production . . . and the relative *reduction* of the effective demand of the vast masses of the working people, whose standard of living the capitalists always try to keep at the *minimum* level. To be successful in competition and to squeeze out the utmost profit, the capitalists are compelled to develop their technical equipment, to introduce rationalization, to intensify the exploitation of the workers . . . all the capitalists are compelled, in one way or another, to take this path of furiously developing production potentialities. The home and foreign market, however . . . remain on a low level. Hence overproduction crises.[86]

If Bukharin had exaggerated the economic role of the state, Stalin went to the opposite extreme of ignoring it. On January 30, 1933, Adolf Hitler became chancellor of the German Reich. With the Nazis promising to use state power to organize recovery, the problem of the state and its economic potential immediately returned to the center of debate. For the remainder of the 1930s the overriding concern of Soviet economists was whether the political superstructure of capitalist society could affect real levels of economic activity. Economists had to avoid the theoretical "errors" of Bukharin, but they also had to deal with increasingly troublesome evidence.

In a first attempt to explain what was happening in Germany, Varga cast Hitler in an ambiguous role: on the one hand, he was a creature of the big monopolies; on the other hand, he aspired to be an arbitrator between them. As "champion of the interests of monopolist capital," Hitler was "bound in the near future to effect a further reduction of wages and salaries. . . . The Hitler movement has been financed, fostered, and placed in authority only in order that it may enhance the exploitation of the working class and attempt to get the better of the crisis at the expense of the proletariat."[87]

Varga believed that Hitler's success would depend upon his ability to mobilize small shopkeepers and farmers in support of policies designed to terrorize the working class. The outcome of this strategy seemed problematic at best, for the petty bourgeoisie could have no material interest in the Nazis' real economic program, which was to promote the interests of monopoly capital. Monopolies had first claim in the *redistribution* of existing national income, and Varga thought that any *increase* of national income could be ruled out in advance because chronically redundant production capacity would paralyze new investments.

Marx had shown, however, that the counterpart of idle physical capital is idle money capital in the depreciation accounts of large firms. Hjalmar Schacht, Hitler's president of the Reichsbank, recognized that the key to cyclical recovery lay in expansionary government spending to restore effective demand in the market. By borrowing idle money capital and spending it back into circulation, or using tomorrow's tax revenues today, Schacht demonstrated the ability of government to contribute to market creation in much the same way as private investments had done in Marx's analysis of the business cycle. With Schacht in control of economic policy, all the German recovery required from the Nazis was imposition of political and social order.

In May 1933 the Nazis restored "labor peace" by destroying the social-democratic trade union movement. In September they passed the Hereditary Farm Law to win the support of farmers. The law provided that small farms could not be sold, divided, or mortgaged. To protect the Junker estates, small farmers were diverted from grain production into other crops for which the government increased prices. Varga saw a parallel between Nazi agricultural policies and Roosevelt's attempts to raise grain prices in America. "German fascism," he wrote, "is being driven . . . along the path which Roosevelt has had to take—compulsory restriction of output. The rottenness of the whole capitalist system is revealed here in its crassest form."[88] Roosevelt's Agricultural Adjustment Act signified "fascisation of government methods in the United States";[89] his National Recovery Act was "fascism disguised as 'planned state capitalism.'"[90]

Varga portrayed both Hitler and Roosevelt as servants of monopoly capital: "German fascism . . . supports the big monopolies with all possible means. Roosevelt's laws to enforce 'fair competition' also resolve themselves . . . into open support of the cartels."[91] But in spite of government policies in Germany and America, Varga persisted in his belief that real economic recovery was impossible. There could be "no question of overcoming the crisis in the old way" because excessive production capacity created insurmountable barriers to new investments.[92] When industrial production finally did begin to grow, Varga and other Soviet economists dismissed the change as a purely temporary and artificial "military-inflationary boom."

In the Soviet interpretation, Marx's traditional cycle was understood to move through four phases: contraction of output in the *crisis*; momentary paralysis in the *depression*; new investments in the *recovery*; and growth of output beyond the peak of the previous cycle during the *expansion*. Acting "on the advice of Comrade Stalin," Varga explained why this classical pattern could no longer be repeated:

> We are not talking of a normal depression, but of one that is unique. . . . The main difference between the current depression and those of prewar times is to be found in the fact that the current depression does not represent a stable foundation for the transition to recovery and expansion. . . . *The retarding influence of the general crisis of capitalism—the chronic excess of fixed capital . . . the chronic agrarian crisis*, the enormous *chronic unemployment*, the resulting contraction of the domestic market, and so forth—*will appear much more forcefully in this cycle than before*, because the economic crisis has deepened the

general crisis of the capitalist system. We are talking of a "depression" *in conditions of the end of capitalist stabilization.*[93]

In January 1934 Stalin warned delegates to the seventeenth party congress that signs of modest improvement in the west should not lead to overestimating the ability of the capitalist state to mitigate the crisis: "Evidently what we are witnessing is a transition from the lowest point of decline of industry, from the lowest point of the industrial crisis, to a depression—not an ordinary depression, but a depression of a special kind, which does not lead to a new upswing and flourishing of industry, but which, on the other hand, does not force industry back to the lowest point of decline."[94] From 1934 until the mid-1950s the theory of *depression of a special kind* would remain the hallmark of Stalinist doctrine in denying the possibility of any return of classical business cycles.

Almost immediately after Stalin defined the official party position, however, Varga realized that the Nazis were forcing various "sections and groups" of the German ruling class to bury their differences. Hitler was "violently forcing unity upon them under the leadership of finance capital."[95] The objective basis of this new unity within the capitalist class, as Varga now understood, was not merely *transfer of income* from the toilers to monopoly capital but rather *national income expansion.* It was clear that the German experiment had demonstrated the ability of the capitalist state to expand production and markets even in the absence of traditional "third parties." The next obvious question was how far economic growth might proceed as a result of rearmament expenditures. Varga's response demonstrated his uncertainty:

It is very difficult to calculate how far the [consumer] capacity of society is increased as a result of increased war expenditure. The latter problem depends above all upon the manner in which the expenditure is financed. If this expenditure is financed chiefly from taxation, then there is no effect upon the [consumer] capacity of society because the population receives back from war expenditure only that sum which was previously taken away from it in taxation. However, if war expenditure is financed by the floating of loans, that is to say, if idle loan-capital is brought into action, then the result is a temporary enlivenment of industrial activity. . . .[96]

Despite the availability of financial resources to support state expenditures, Varga still thought that a war economy could at best generate a brief recovery. Like Bukharin in his analysis of "expanded negative reproduction" during the First World War, he thought that commitment of all available resources to armaments ignored the need for maintenance and replacement of existing fixed capital in other industries. The eventual result would be capital consumption and steadily declining activity in the nonmilitary branches.

Although this reasoning seemed to apply to Nazi Germany, American developments were more problematic. Not only was America not rearming, but Roosevelt had also failed to win the confidence of the ruling class, most of whom opposed budget deficits and provisions for labor unionization in the National Recovery Act. Varga explained that Roosevelt, unlike Hitler, had failed to impose unity on the ruling class: "The main reason [for Roosevelt's failure] is that in view of the strong antagonisms between the various sections and groups of the bourgeoisie, arising as a result of their struggle for the limited market, it is not possible to pursue a policy which would satisfy all these sections and groups at the same time."[97]

When the NRA was judged unconstitutional by the Supreme Court in 1935, Varga attributed Roosevelt's defeat to sabotage of the New Deal by the most reactionary groups of American capitalists. Given this short-sightedness on the part of militant reactionaries, Roosevelt then undertook what Soviet economists regarded as a "left maneuver." To save the ruling class from its own folly, he introduced new programs of relief and public works, secured passage of a Wealth Tax Act, and extended the rights of trade unions under the Wagner Act. In the most comprehensive Soviet study of the New Deal, Sergei A. Dalin described the significance of Roosevelt's policies this way:

> The downfall of capitalist "planning" [the Court decision against the NRA] . . . will not bring an end of state intervention in economic life. Capitalism finds itself at such a stage of decay that the action of its internal spontaneous forces has become impaired and no longer leads either to a speedy overcoming of economic crises or to a new flourishing of the capitalist economy. The so-called automatic nature of the capitalist economy has been disrupted. . . . Hence an attempt to reinforce the action of capitalism's internal forces with artificial state measures. . . . [I]ntervention in general cannot be halted.[98]

By 1935 there could no longer be any doubt that "artificial" measures, deliberately undertaken by the state, were principally responsible for economic improvements both in Germany and in the United States. The tenuous nature of the American recovery, however, sustained hope that another relapse would soon occur. In 1937 Varga thought he saw new evidence to support the theory of "depression of a special kind." What appeared to be occurring in America was an expansion "of a special kind":[99] although orders for machinery were twice as high as in 1929, the surge of demand was "mainly restricted to the renewal of equipment in *existing enterprises*" with no significant new industrial construction.[100] Once again it seemed that major investments had been blocked by chronically redundant fixed capital, which Varga continued to regard as the outstanding characteristic of "the general crisis of capitalism."

When industrial production declined in the United States by the end of 1937, Varga predicted that a new crisis in 1938 would be "just as deep as that of 1929."[101] Despite all the artificial measures undertaken by Roosevelt, it appeared that the "depression of a special kind" still could not grow over into a genuine expansion. In *Capitalism and Socialism After Twenty Years*, Varga claimed that it was nonsense to suggest that capitalism might create its own markets: "*in the most highly developed countries a tendency can be observed towards an absolute decline in the number of productive workers.*"[102] Chronic unemployment and a chronic crisis were inevitable because the "depeasantizing" process had ended and agriculture was now itself capitalist. Without access to new third-party markets, either at home or abroad, resumption of capital accumulation was impossible due to the chronically limited "consuming power" of society.[103]

In Varga's major publications of 1937, however, one important change did appear in the unique significance that he assigned to investments in transportation. In previous decades, railway construction was said to have alleviated the problem of markets. Railways differed from other types of capital construction in one essential respect: they were intended "only for the shipment of commodities, not for their production. This means that they do not increase the mass of commodities being produced, unlike means of production in the narrow sense of the word. For this reason they are not a source of overproduction."[104]

Once Varga made this discovery, vast possibilities opened up. It seemed that any form of investment that raised the level of employment without simultaneously producing a new flow of traditional commodities might help to alleviate the supposed problem of markets. Ironically, Rosa

Luxemburg had anticipated this very conclusion. In *The Accumulation of Capital* she had observed that military production is "a pre-eminent means for the realisation of surplus value; it is in itself a province of accumulation."[105] By 1938 Varga too saw new significance in rearmament: "In rich countries, such as the United States and Great Britain, where there is a surplus of capital, . . . armaments expenditures [can be financed] chiefly by floating loans. . . . [They] represent an extension of the capitalist market and, as a result, encourage economic recovery and diminish the unfavourable effects of the economic crisis."[106]

In terms of the theory of capital accumulation, armaments expenditures could play the same role as railways: they could create a new market by reemploying workers—and they could do so without contributing directly to industrial overproduction. When Stalin told the eighteenth party congress in 1939 that a "serious economic crisis" was continuing in the capitalist countries,[107] Varga knew better. In America, production was steadily growing because "the purchasing power of the working masses" was being "reinforced by great government expenditures on public works, unemployment support, and so on."[108] In Britain, rearmament was having "a stimulating effect upon . . . all branches of industry without exception."[109] Varga thought the major lesson of the 1930s was that "government expenditures . . . for armaments and public works influence and modify the cyclical development of reproduction, which is based upon the internal laws of capitalist society."[110]

In *The General Theory of Employment, Interest and Money*, published in 1936, John Maynard Keynes reached similar conclusions. Although Keynes came from an entirely different tradition of economics and took pride in his ignorance of Marx, his practical recommendations for preventing a recurrence of the Great Depression were almost identical to Varga's. In an economy where physical means of production were idled by excessive saving and lack of private investment, Keynes called for ambitious programs of public spending, financed through borrowing and reactivating idle monetary resources. For Keynes it was not the object of public expenditures that mattered but the volume: "Pyramid-building, earthquakes, even wars may serve to increase wealth, if the education of our statesmen on the principles of classical economics stands in the way of anything better."[111]

By the late 1930s western and Soviet economists were converging on a new appreciation of the role of the capitalist state. Although Varga had yet to clarify the full implications, he clearly sensed that the problems posed by Rosa Luxemburg's critique of *Capital* might now be answered:

the state itself was the third party potentially able to regulate the capitalist market economy. The remaining issue was whether state expenditures would serve peaceful reconstruction after World War II or preparations for new hostilities against the Soviet Union. In Marx's analysis, capitalism had been governed by objective laws that made cyclical fluctuations inevitable. No such certainty was possible when it came to assessing how the capitalist class would use the state apparatus. In these circumstances Varga's economic analysis of capitalism came into conflict after 1945 with Stalin's political assessment of capitalist intentions in the Cold War.

CHAPTER 2

POSTWAR CAPITALISM:
FASCISM OR A NEW DEAL?

Soviet studies of capitalism in the 1930s created two possible approaches for interpreting developments after the Second World War. The first involved the concept of a fascist war economy, exemplified by Nazi Germany; the second anticipated a more enlightened and democratic capitalism of the kind associated with Franklin Delano Roosevelt and the New Deal. Although Varga had identified Roosevelt's New Deal with Nazi policies at the height of the depression, a decade later the differences were obvious. During World War II, Roosevelt had become a hero in Soviet Russia through his partnership with Stalin and Churchill in the struggle against Hitler. Most Soviet observers expected that after the war Roosevelt would resume New Deal reforms while promoting a peaceful and cooperative international order.

Roosevelt was respected in the Soviet Union as one of the political giants of the twentieth century. Representing the most progressive bourgeois forces in America, he was thought to have triumphed over reactionary capitalists by using the state apparatus to promote democratic change. Although he continued *objectively* to be a servant of capital, he also made important concessions to workers in order to preserve the existing order during the Great Depression. In *The Communist Manifesto,* Marx had described the executive of the modern state as "a committee for managing the common affairs of the whole bourgeoisie."[1] Varga believed that the Roosevelt administration provided a convincing illustration of Marx's thesis by sacrificing the interests of individual capitalists in order to protect those of the ruling class as a whole.

Stalin was more skeptical. In a 1934 interview with H.G. Wells, he acknowledged Roosevelt's "talent and courage" and described him as "one of the strongest figures among all the captains of the contemporary capitalist world." But Roosevelt's personal strength did not mean that he could single-handedly reorganize American capitalism or overcome "anarchy in production." Roosevelt proposed to eliminate unemployment; Stalin told Wells that "no capitalist would ever agree to . . . abolition of the reserve army of unemployed." Roosevelt might make some progress in applying what Stalin called "the principle of regulation in [the] national economy," but ultimately he would fail: "Without getting rid of the capitalists, without abolishing the principle of private property, . . . it is impossible to create planned economy." Unlike Varga, Stalin believed that the political superstructure of capitalist society was merely an apparatus of repression serving the needs of capital: "The capitalist State does not deal much with [the] economy in the strict sense of the word, the latter is not in the hands of the State. On the contrary, the State is in the hands of [the] capitalist economy."[2]

This interpretation had to be modified when World War II caused every capitalist government to establish extensive controls over production and distribution. Because Soviet Russia was allied with the United States, a distinction also had to be made between fascist and democratic forms of regulation. Varga saw the defining characteristic of a fascist economy in its total commitment, even in peacetime, to arms production and militarization. The result was neglect of fixed-capital replacement in other branches of industry, strict suppression of civilian consumption, and the resulting need for political terror to destroy working-class resistance. Judging by these criteria, the economy of the United States was the polar opposite of Germany's. Not only had the Americans been slow to rearm, but they had also entered the war with both a democratic government and significant reserves of idle labor and capital left over from the 1930s.

During the war years, American industry grew at an unprecedented rate. Varga thought that after 1945 this vast new production capacity could be redirected to satisfying postponed demand for consumer durables. Far from facing an immediate postwar problem of markets, America might enjoy a period of relative stability. This forecast led to a return of many of the issues debated in the interwar period. Hitler and Roosevelt had demonstrated the state's capacity to act as an *economic* third party in market creation, but Stalinists told Varga that this did not imply *political* neutrality; the purposes for which state power was employed would ultimately depend upon *who was in control*. Roosevelt's death in 1945 created immediate reservations concerning the intentions of his successor, Harry S. Truman. When Truman appeared to abandon the New Deal, Varga found himself as isolated as Bukharin had been when the Great Depression shattered earlier predictions of stabilization.

1. Assessing the Capitalist War Economies

Varga's postwar "errors" were linked by critics to his mistaken appraisals of the German war economy and to his alleged tendency to give
technical economic analysis priority over "party-mindedness." Varga
thought that Germany had entered the war with a process of economic
"impoverishment" already under way.[3] Capital consumption in nonmilitary branches was said to have begun in the late 1930s; by the
beginning of 1942, two-thirds of current industrial output was going
directly to the war effort, causing "rapid wear of fixed capital,
exhaustion of material supplies, and general impoverishment of the
country."[4] According to Varga, Hitler had adopted a *blitzkrieg* strategy
because manpower was scarce, labor productivity was falling, and
workers faced "chronic hunger."[5]

Predictions of Nazi Germany's economic disintegration were common
in Soviet literature as early as 1940, when S.M. Vishnev published *The
Economic Resources of Germany*.[6] Vishnev compared the inevitable
decline of German production with the completely different circumstances of the Allies, who had only begun to deploy their "inexhaustible
human and material resources."[7] A. Leont'ev spoke of a protracted "war
of reserves" that Hitler could not possibly win.[8] The historian I.M.
Lemin thought that German production peaked in mid-1941.[9] Impressed
by the advice of his economists, in November 1941 Stalin himself
predicted that Germany might collapse within a few months.[10] Six
months later Stalin acknowledged that the end of the war was not yet in
sight, but he still thought that German reserves of manpower, oil, and
materials were approaching exhaustion.[11] By November 1942 the battle
of Stalingrad was in progress, and Stalin complained that Hitler had been
supported by delay of the second front in Europe, which permitted all
remaining German resources to be redirected to the east.[12]

Once Stalin revised his expectations, economists became more circum-
spect in predicting Germany's collapse. Vishnev admitted that "Three
years of war have clearly demonstrated that the economic exhaustion of
fascism alone will not yield final victory."[13] In January 1943, Vishnev
repudiated "crudely simplified" interpretations of the role of economic
exhaustion in determining the war's outcome.[14] Later in the same year,
Varga and several other members of the Institute of World Economy
published *The Exhaustion of the Economic Resources of Fascist Germany*.
Varga conceded that economic factors would not "automatically" bring
about Germany's collapse. Attributing depletion of German resources to

heroic blows struck by the Red Army, he noted that the struggle would have progressed much more rapidly had the second front not been delayed in Europe.[15]

In view of America's dramatic wartime expansion, it was understandable for Soviet writers to be perplexed concerning the timing of the second front. In 1941 alone, the Americans reabsorbed three million workers into production, causing heavy industrial output to expand by 25 percent and production of machine tools to double. Never before in history had there been such a rapid increase of military production. By 1942 the Allies established naval and air superiority over Germany. U.S. armaments output, including 5,000 aircraft per month and two ships per day, exceeded that of the entire fascist bloc.[16] With 1935-39 as the base, the American index of industrial production soared to 203 by April 1943.[17] Soviet economists attributed this unprecedented growth to state regulation of the American war economy.

In an article on "The War Economy of the United States," E. Gurvich remarked that war orders had contributed to rapid "concentration and centralization of American production and capital and a strengthening of its ties with the state."[18] In 1942, 80 percent of American construction was state-financed[19] and every sphere of the economy was "subject to the influence of regulatory measures and a growing intervention by the government."[20] I.A. Trakhtenberg, a specialist on western finances at the Institute of World Economy, referred to accelerated development of "state-monopoly capitalism" in all the belligerent countries.[21] Quoting Lenin, Varga similarly characterized the new forms of organization as "war-monopoly state capitalism."[22]

As a general proposition, Varga believed that "The big bourgeoisie uses . . . [the state] apparatus in every possible way to strengthen its domination of the toilers and to secure its profits."[23] He also believed, however, that state power had been used to subordinate immediate capitalist interests to the common goal of winning the war. Individual capitalists looked for unprecedented profits from free market prices, but in wartime the market would allocate scarce goods to the wealthy and cause labor productivity to plummet. Success in war required accumulation of private capital to be socially regulated: "For this reason," Varga wrote, "the big bourgeoisie is interested in distributing scarce consumer goods in an organized manner . . . and at prices established by the state."[24]

Varga expected the war economies to provide important precedents for postwar reconstruction. Rationing and price controls represented an objectively necessary class compromise in which government played the mediating role of third party. The claims of workers and employers had been balanced during the war by coopting representatives of both groups into state administration.[25] The fact that war economies required workers' representatives to play a role *within the state apparatus* raised the question of whether, after 1945, workers' parties and trade unions might successfully continue their pressure for further reforms of the kind associated with Roosevelt's New Deal.

2. Prospects for Postwar Capitalist Reforms

Varga's first assessment of American postwar prospects came in 1946 with *Changes in the Economic Structure of Capitalism as a Result of the Second World War*. His central theme—that in a war economy the state always plays a role of "decisive importance"[26]—picked up where he had left off at the close of the 1930s. "War-monopoly state capitalism" created a guaranteed market in which the kind of crisis predicted by Rosa Luxemburg could no longer occur:

> In peacetime, the most difficult problem for capital is the question of realizing the value of the commodity, or the conversion [of capital] from the commodity form into the monetary form. The problem of realization, or in other words, the problem of the market . . . does not exist in time of war. . . . [T]he state enters the market as a purchaser with unlimited buying power.[27]

At the beginning of the war, American capitalists had feared the problem of markets and resisted adding to production capacity in the expectation that new fixed capital would prove redundant once the conflict ended. The state had absorbed this risk by investing $16 billion in new factories that were then leased at nominal expense to private operators.[28] Profits from these public investments were privately appropriated, and monopolies were promised the opportunity to buy the facilities on generous terms after the conclusion of peace. With rapidly growing war contracts, major technological innovations—which Soviet observers believed had been suppressed in the 1930s—were implemented with no risk of devaluing existing capital. Whole new industries sprang up in response to state purchases. Since war orders were allocated mainly to the largest monopolies, which then subcontracted to smaller firms, the war economy also dramatically accelerated the centralization and concentration of capital. American industry as a whole became more highly specialized, standardized, and automated.[29]

Varga thought the most important question in 1945-46 was whether America's expanded production capacity might continue in full operation. He predicted that, for at least two or three years, America would experience a "high conjuncture of a special kind," resulting from postponed civilian purchases of automobiles, houses, appliances, and other consumer durables.[30] How long this demand would persist, however, ultimately depended upon further expansion of the market through continuing investments. Here prospects were less certain. Because new technologies had increased productivity, there was a possibility that consumer needs might be satisfied relatively quickly. The disproportionate wartime expansion of industries producing means of production, or what Marx called Department I, meant that unemployment might begin in this sector and then spread to the rest of the economy. If fear of unemployment caused workers to hesitate in spending their savings, the result might also be to hasten a crisis of overproduction.[31]

As in his studies of the Great Depression, Varga thought that "the basic factor determining the development of the industrial cycle after the war will remain . . . the general surplus of fixed capital. . . ."[32] One way to employ productive potential and expand markets at the same time would be to increase capital exports. After the First World War, Trotsky had expected the American economy to contract due to loss of sales in Europe. Varga noted that in 1946 continental Europe was again collapsing in a crisis of "underproduction" while America faced the opposite difficulty of converting wartime industries to peacetime requirements. Whereas Trotsky had predicted in 1921 that both America and Europe would suffer for a decade from war-induced disproportions, Varga suspected that the Americans would now repeat the experience of the Dawes Plan by financing Europe's reconstruction: "The enormous resources of the USA not only permit large-scale exports of capital to Europe . . . but will also—given the danger of [American] overproduction . . . and the threat of mass unemployment—make such exports extremely attractive."[33]

Exports of American capital to Europe would address both of the issues that had dominated prewar Soviet debates: international *disproportions* would be reduced through international *market creation*. Varga still expected, though, that conversion of the American economy to peacetime production would contribute by 1947-48 to a new crisis of overproduction, possibly even on the scale of 1929-33. Capitalism's continuing "general crisis" might result in a new "depression of a special kind" with a return of chronically underused production capacity and chronic unemployment.[34] In the late 1930s, however, Varga had realized that railway construction and even armaments production could create a market without flooding it at the same time with commodities. In *Changes in the Economic Structure of Capitalism*, he indicated that postwar fluctuations might similarly be moderated by public expenditures intended to stabilize the "consuming power" of society, provided these measures did not contribute to industrial overproduction.

Just as armaments had served this purpose in the 1930s, public works might play the same role in the postwar period: "in those cases where the state uses labor power for nonproductive purposes, such as construction of schools, hospitals, charitable accommodation for the aged, etc., 'make-work measures' will not displace labor power elsewhere."[35] Allowing for this possibility, Varga qualified his prediction of a postwar "depression of a special kind." If "nonproductive" market-creating expenditures were financed by taxing wages normally spent on consumption, they would be ineffective: one type of expenditure would simply replace another. But "if the state draws resources from that part of the surplus value that otherwise would go to accumulation of [idle] money capital, . . . [then] state measures to provide work will lead to a genuine reduction of unemployment."[36]

Varga's reasoning seemed to be no different from the Keynesian doctrines being embraced after 1945 by social-democratic parties in the west. The difficulty was that social democrats endorsed Keynesianism as an *alternative to socialist revolution*. Varga paid no regard to these political considerations. He believed that capitalism's political "super-structure" could no longer be interpreted in the Stalinist manner. There was no doubt that the state continued to represent "the interests of the whole bourgeoisie as a class," but this formulation also implied divergent interests within the ruling class. Lenin had pointed to such divisions when disputing Bukharin's theory of unified "state-capitalist trusts." Varga took a similar approach when he described struggles between monopolies to place their own representatives in controlling positions within state agencies. The monopolies continued to be "decisive" within these organs,[37] but rivalries between capitalists also explained the ability of political leaders such as Roosevelt to use the state as a third party, acting on behalf of the capitalist class as a whole.

Conceiving of the state in these terms, Varga inadvertently invited comparison of his own work with Rudolf Hilferding's *Finance Capital*.

Hilferding had suggested that once capitalism became organized through new regulatory institutions, those same institutions—in Hilferding's example, the six largest Berlin banks—might be captured by a democratically elected socialist government and set to work creating a planned economy. Marx had also predicted socialization within "the capitalist integument." This theme reappeared in Varga's *Changes in the Economic Structure of Capitalism* when he asserted that state regulation created a real possibility of working-class influence upon public policy. In a state-regulated economy, economic issues would become political issues; opposing classes, like the capitalist monopolies, would struggle for influence *within the state system*. At the close of his book, Varga summarized this prospect:

> *In future the role of the state will remain more important than before the war.* The question of greater or lesser participation in management of the state will be the main content of the political struggle between the two basic classes of capitalist society: the bourgeoisie and the proletariat. The polarization of bourgeois society is increasing . . . [T]he relative importance *(udel'nyi ves)* of the proletariat will grow.[38]

3. The Labour Government and British "Socialism"

A practical illustration of how working-class parties might use capitalist institutions for their own purposes appeared with the postwar Labour government of Britain. Many Soviet economists thought that Labour, like Roosevelt with the New Deal, might "manage" the economy while also promoting social and economic reforms. Varga spoke of the Labour government's "progress in the direction of democracy of a new type."[39] M.N. Smit wrote that Labour's plans for nationalization and full employment pointed in the direction of a new and "progressive democracy."[40] D.Yu. Zorina thought that nationalization "strengthens the position of the working class."[41] L.A. Mendel'son considered public ownership to be a "progressive undertaking" that would help to create the "material preconditions for transition to socialism."[42]

One of the leading authors in defining the Soviet view of postwar Britain was L.Ya. Eventov, who in 1946 published *The War Economy of England*. Eventov claimed that state controls had led to a "merger" *(sliyanie)*[43] between administrative organs and monopoly capital in which the major benefits went to the monopolies.[44] Like Varga in his assessment of America, however, Eventov also thought that the British war economy had involved "a temporary compromise between the main classes of the country"[45] and a growing political influence on the part of "democratic organizations."[46] Labour's election victory in 1945 seemed to be a continuation of progressive tendencies already apparent during the war.

Although many Soviet commentators viewed the Labour government as progressive, this opinion was far from unanimous. Sh.B. Lif protested that the capitalist character of the state had not changed: the "nationalized" branches of industry had merely become "the common property of the class of capitalists." Workers were being exploited "not by individual capitalists, but by the aggregate capitalist in the form of the state."[47] Nationalizing coal, steel, transportation, and other industries, Labour was said to be reequipping them at public expense in order to subsidize goods and services sold to private monopolies. Labour's Keynesian prescriptions for full employment appeared even more dubious. Recalling Stalin's comment to H.G. Wells that the capitalists would never agree to elimination of unemployment, E. Shifrin contended that Keynesianism ignored class contradictions.[48] V.A. Cheprakov described Keynesian economics as an "illustration of the impotence and futility of contemporary bourgeois economic science."[49]

Soviet economists thought Keynesian theory was fundamentally flawed by its substitution of alleged "psychological laws" for objective economic forces. Keynes believed that individuals have a disposition to save part of their income once conventional expectations of an appropriate living standard are met. If these savings failed to be offset by investments, causing a decline of aggregate demand, it was the responsibility of government to restore full employment by increasing public expenditures and redistributing purchasing power to those with lower personal incomes and a higher "propensity to consume."

Despite his sympathies with Labour, Eventov thought such income transfers had nothing to do with real market creation: if governments tried to increase aggregate demand through expenditures based on taxation, they would merely appropriate incomes otherwise spent by individuals; if they resorted instead to borrowing, they would curtail savings otherwise available for private investments.[50] In neither case would there be any new demand. I.A. Trakhtenberg likewise believed that income redistribution was an "unrealizable utopia" until capitalist property relations were eliminated.[51] L.A. Mendel'son wrote that Keynes had mistakenly attributed instability of demand to a psychological disposition to save rather than to working-class impoverishment:

> The instability of demand . . . is rooted not in the peculiarities of human psychology . . . but in the antagonistic relations of capitalist production and distribution. . . . Sharp fluctuations of demand . . . are not a cause, but the result and form of expression of approaching crises and the threat of unemployment.[52]

I.G. Blyumin, a senior authority on western economic theory, claimed that Keynes' "eternal psychological laws," which bourgeois economists understood to be "independent of the given social-economic system,"[53] deliberately obscured the fact that income distribution in capitalist society was objectively determined by private ownership of the means of production. Blyumin explained the appeal of Keynesianism, to capitalists and social democrats alike, in terms of its promise that "socialization of demand" would eliminate the need for "socialization of production."[54] As for the Labour government's nationalization program, he considered it nothing more than a response to American competition in the global struggle for markets. The purpose of nationalized industries was to provide private monopolies with low-cost energy, materials, and transportation. The "socialism" of the Labour Party was only another means for reducing the price of exports and defending the traditional interests of British imperialism.[55]

Those economists who were unimpressed by the British experiment located the only real hope for socialism in communist parties loyal to Moscow. In Italy, Belgium, France, and other West European countries, communists were expected to increase their electoral support because of their prominent role in the underground antifascist struggle.[56] In Eastern Europe, Soviet power had led to creation after 1945 of democracies "of a new type,"[57] where state regulation was intended eventually to grow over into socialism and proletarian dictatorship. Whatever happened in Europe, though, it was clear that events in America would determine the ultimate shape of the postwar world. Varga's expectations of America appeared to be refuted by new developments even at the time when he was completing his book.

4. Who Controls the State?

Varga had taken American capitalism in the Roosevelt era as his model for postwar democratic reform. Although Soviet writers held Roosevelt in high esteem, they were far less impressed by Truman, the former haberdasher from Missouri. Shortly after Roosevelt's death, Truman's decisions raised serious doubts concerning the underlying assumptions of Varga's work. By mid-1945, M.I. Rubinshtein noted growing opposition to Roosevelt's policy of using the state budget to preserve full employment. Anticipating the dislocations that would come from converting military to peacetime production, the *New York Times* had protested that government responsibility for full employment would require state regulation on a scale unprecedented in American history.[58]

In December 1945, V.I. Lan spoke of the possible consequences of abandoning the New Deal: "authoritative" economists were predicting in the *American Economic Review* that up to 30 million workers would be unemployed in the next economic crisis.[59] Lan agreed with Varga that the New Deal had proved the state's ability to support employment through public works: "President Roosevelt demonstrated that the state can reduce the numbers of unemployed in the USA. He organized public works . . . at the cost of increasing the state debt."[60] But Lan did not think such possibilities would be acted upon. Leading banks and employers' associations were already indicating their intention to use unemployment in order to eliminate trade unionization and other gains "won by the American proletariat under President Roosevelt."[61]

By the end of 1946, Lan saw growing evidence to confirm these suspicions. Roosevelt's supporters still believed that "in the interests of the capitalists themselves, government must pay a certain degree of attention to the toilers,"[62] but the Truman administration had removed from office most of the leading personalities associated with the New Deal. The most enlightened representatives of American capitalism had been replaced by a government "clearly to the right of center."[63] Reactionary capitalist elements, headed by the Morgans, Rockefellers, Du Ponts, Mellons, and Cleveland industrial interests, had compelled Truman "openly and definitively to repudiate the legacy of Roosevelt."[64] Price and wage controls had been lifted, allowing inflation to erase workers' savings; real wages were falling; and more than four million workers had responded by striking during the first eleven months of 1946.[65]

In November 1946, N. Sergeeva expressed the misgivings of many Soviet writers when interpreting losses by the Democratic Party in congressional elections. Truman and the Democrats, she claimed, had forfeited popular support because of their "uninterrupted concessions to reaction."[66] The masses voted for Republicans not because they supported reaction, but in protest against Truman's departure from

Roosevelt's policy of making "certain concessions to the most essential demands of the workers."[67] "In both American and foreign circles," Sergeeva wrote, "the defeat of the Democratic Party is being explained by the fact that it abandoned the policy of Roosevelt. . . ."[68] By December 1946, Stalin endorsed this interpretation in an interview with Roosevelt's son. "It seems to me," Stalin remarked, "that the elections demonstrate that the present government has squandered the moral and political capital created by the late president, and thus it facilitated the victory of the Republicans."[69]

In February 1947, A. Georgiev reviewed *As He Saw It*, Elliott Roosevelt's account of his father's views on foreign policy. Throughout the previous year Soviet relations with the west had steadily deteriorated. With Truman present, in March 1946 Winston Churchill had delivered his "iron curtain" speech in Fulton Missouri. Churchill called for a "fraternal association of the English-speaking peoples" to reorder the world and resist Soviet power in Eastern Europe.[70] Citing Elliott Roosevelt as his source, Georgiev claimed that the plan for an "Anglo-American bloc" had always been opposed by the former president. Churchill had been the principal force behind delay of the second front, and now he and Truman were both serving "the magnates of finance capital" in a coordinated program of "reaction and imperialism."[71]

On March 12, 1947, Truman announced America's determination to resist Soviet advances on a global scale. In response to communist threats to Greece and Turkey, he promised American support wherever "armed minorities" or "outside pressures" threatened to impose "totalitarian regimes" upon "free peoples." The Truman Doctrine represented America's declaration of Cold War in a world that Truman said had become divided between "alternative ways of life." The Soviet historian I.M. Lemin responded by accusing Truman of declaring "ideological war" and of attempting to divide the postwar world into hostile "ideological blocs."[72] Accounting for this hardening of American policy, Lemin remarked that Roosevelt's death had given free reign to reactionaries: "Roosevelt foresaw the possibility of a growth of reaction in the USA after the war, including the possibility of a fascist reaction."[73]

Recalling Stalinist interpretations of the 1930s, Lemin found the common denominator of Truman's foreign and domestic policies in the "confining limits of the domestic market,"[74] which were causing the United States to become "the most militaristic country of the modern world."[75] Return of the problem of markets meant that:

The gigantic monopolies, having long ago outgrown the limits of the national market, view the entire world as an arena for expansion. The striving for world supremacy is especially intensified in the period of capitalism's general crisis. . . . The doctrine of American domination of the world is inspired and dictated by the Morgans and Rockefellers, the Chryslers and Fords—the gigantic trusts that regard the entire world as an object for colonial exploitation by the USA.[76]

In an article on "American Expansion, Past and Present," published in June 1947, A. Leont'ev similarly weighed the significance of Roosevelt's death against the economic imperatives of capitalism's general crisis. Leont'ev acknowledged that Roosevelt had stood for "friendly collaboration with the Soviet Union," but he also thought it was time to abandon the illusion that the New Deal had fundamentally altered the nature of imperialism. The Truman Doctrine was a program for "economic subjugation of the countries temporarily weakened by the war . . . with a view to establishing the world dictatorship of the dollar."

[The] alteration of the course of the American ship of state . . . cannot be explained solely by the departure of Roosevelt, although there can be no denying that in him America lost a far-sighted statesman of the first rank. Roosevelt's untimely death was a veritable gift of the gods to the more reactionary and aggressive of the American monopolist elements. . . . But the roots of these changes lie far deeper, and must be looked for in the economic life of the country.[77]

V.A. Cheprakov, an ardent Stalinist, likewise attributed reversal of American policy to the "limited purchasing power" of workers and return of the problem of markets.[78] In August 1945 the Federal Reserve Board's index of industrial production, with 1935-39 as the base, had been 211; by early 1947 it fell to 180.[79] According to Cheprakov, inventories had reached "the highest level in the entire history of the United States."[80] Wartime savings had either been spent or erased by inflation following the removal of price controls, and 70 percent of families no longer had any savings in the banks. Official statistics registered 2.4 million unemployed by the end of 1946, but American trade unions placed the number at 5 million.[81] Cheprakov reported that "Hardly any of the serious bourgeois economists deny the fact that the

USA, and with it the entire capitalist world, faces a new economic crisis."[82]

Quoting Stalin's interview in 1934 with H.G. Wells, Cheprakov reminded Soviet readers that to eliminate economic crises would first require elimination of capitalism.[83] His article was clearly meant to demonstrate that Varga had misinterpreted the capitalist state. Cheprakov emphasized that wartime regulations had been administered by "representatives of the largest trusts," who received 70 percent of government orders and were now buying state-financed plants for a fraction of their original cost to taxpayers.[84] The influence of the financial oligarchy had grown to the point where a "merger" (*sliyanie*) had occurred between the state and the most powerful capitalists. Rather than mediating between classes—as Varga's analysis suggested—the state had in reality undergone complete "subjugation" (*podchinenie*) to the monopolies. Varga had thought the state might become a third party; Cheprakov spoke instead of a "coalescence" (*srashchivanie*) between public and private power.[85] Citing Truman's "loyalty" program, he insisted that the United States was becoming a "police state of the financial oligarchy."[86]

As other writers grew increasingly skeptical of capitalist democracy, in March 1947 Varga published a chapter of a projected new book. He repeated that the East European experience of "democracy of a new type" proved the possibility of the "political supremacy of the toilers" within parliamentary republics.[87] Since socialism was the prevailing historical tendency, he added that "separate elements of the transition to new democracy" could also be seen in "a number of other countries."[88] On May 4, 1947, the Socialist prime minister of France undercut this interpretation by removing Communist ministers from his coalition government. Three days later, a meeting of Soviet economists convened for a critical "discussion" of Varga's *Changes in the Economic Structure of Capitalism as a Result of the Second World War*. The outcome of this meeting cast a pall over Soviet writing for the next decade.

5. The Varga "Discussion" of May 1947

In his opening report, Varga conceded that Roosevelt's death and the Republicans' victory in congressional elections had confounded his forecast of price stability in America. The very fact that monopolies were so anxious to eliminate price controls, however, proved that during the war the state had acted as "an organization of the bourgeois class as a whole," restraining the profit-seeking ambitions of individual capitalists and recognizing working-class needs.[89] The state had been forced "to plan" the war economy, and it was nonsense to claim that market anarchy had continued. "No one," Varga declared, "can convince me otherwise on this issue."[90]

M.N. Smit, one of Varga's associates at the Institute of World Economy and World Politics since the 1920s, was the first to respond. Following the lead given in Cheprakov's article, she charged that Varga's assessment of postwar capitalism failed to recognize "coalescence" of the state with the monopolies.[91] A succession of other critics made the identical claim. Sh.B. Lif objected to Varga's suggestion that the state might assume a "nonclass character": "It seems to me," he argued, "that what is new in the development of the state . . . is that, coalescing more and more with the monopolies, it is being transformed into [their exclusive] instrument. . . ."[92] A.I. Kats protested that Varga had ignored "deepening of the general crisis of capitalism."[93] A.I. Shneerson insisted that "coalescence" meant the state always guarantees monopolies the highest possible profits; for this reason it clearly could not represent nonmonopoly capital or "the interests of the bourgeoisie as a whole." Still less could it be regarded as a "nonclass" institution open to significant working-class influence.[94]

P.K. Figurnov also denied that the state might play a "decisive role"; Varga's reference to capitalist planning only confused issues that had been "perfectly clear" since Lenin's theory of imperialism.[95] Lenin had dismissed capitalist planning as "a fable spread by bourgeois economists."[96] V.V. Reikhardt quoted Stalin's opinion that the state does not act upon the monopolies, rather the monopolies act upon the state.[97] I.N. Dvorkin, a committed Stalinist, was adamant that planning presupposed the end of private property.[98] M.A. Arzhanov thought Varga's economic focus had prevented him from seeing the resurgent threat of political reaction and fascism in America.[99] V.E. Motylev made the same complaint: Varga's confusion arose from failure to take into account the elementary political facts of class struggle. Motylev warned that the entire Institute of World Economy and World Politics was suffering from a "techno-economic" approach that ignored political realities.[100]

After the purges of the 1930s, Soviet economists were perfectly aware of the gravity of these allegations. M.I. Rubinshtein, another of Varga's collaborators at the Institute of World Economy for more than two decades, objected to the intimidating tone of Motylev's remarks and exclaimed that he should not presume to act as "prosecutor" for the state security services.[101] Ya.A. Kronrod agreed that a scientific discussion must not be treated as a trial.[102] S.G. Strumilin, one of the most respected economists of the day, even described *Changes in the Economic Structure of Capitalism* as "a major contribution to Soviet economic science."[103] L.A. Mendel'son, the most prominent authority on the history of business cycles, disagreed with some of Varga's conclusions but also affirmed that the book displayed "vital, creative thought."[104]

I.A. Trakhtenberg, who had worked with Varga on several studies both before and during the war, likewise came to his colleague's defense. State regulation, he attested, could include not only concessions to the workers but even elements of economic planning—although a fully planned capitalist economy was clearly impossible. Like Strumilin and Mendel'son, Trakhtenberg expressed warm praise for Varga's theoretical contributions: "There are works that can be ignored; there are works that stimulate scientific creativity. It is precisely in the latter category of works, that is, those enriching scientific thought, that the book of comrade Varga belongs."[105]

Despite many harsh comments, Varga's supporters managed to preserve decorum in a debate that, in the language of the day, would be classified as critical but "comradely." K.V. Ostrovityanov, who had helped to organize the session, reassured all present that "this is not a trial, and comrade Varga is not a defendant. This is a scientific discussion, which requires neither procurators nor advocates."[106] But in his official summary of the proceedings, Ostrovityanov made it perfectly clear that Varga's errors were political. In particular, Varga had failed to emphasize the class character of the capitalist state and ignored the "struggle of two systems." These shortcomings arose from forgetting the "Stalinist formulation of the problem of the general crisis of capitalism."[107] Although these were serious transgressions, Ostrovityanov delicately referred to them as a "methodological flaw."[108]

Encouraged by support from a handful of colleagues, Varga did not take such criticism seriously. To the claim that he had not given a Stalinist formulation of the general crisis, he replied that his whole book had dealt with nothing but the general crisis.[109] In other words, he ignored the essential point, the demand for a *Stalinist* approach that emphasized the "depression of a special kind" and denied the possibility of capitalist stabilization. On the question of the state, he refused to admit that he was "wrong"[110] and even repeated his belief that all classes, including farmers and workers, could exercise significant political influence within existing capitalist institutions:

> Take England, for example. England is, without doubt, a country of monopolistic capitalism. But can we say today, in 1947, that the working class and the Labour Party have no influence on the politics of England, that the whole of policy is made by the financial oligarchy?[111]

Admitting only minor defects in his work, Varga answered critics with his own ironic riposte. He thanked those who had recited quotations from either Lenin or Stalin in the hope of discrediting his work. Such comparisons, he acknowledged, were "a great honor," but modesty required him to be more restrained in estimating his own abilities. He was, after all, merely a "student" of the party's leaders,[112] and it was inappropriate to compare his accomplishments with those of Lenin or Stalin. The cleverness of this remark demonstrated that he was unaware of the real gravity of the discussion.

The significance of this first organized criticism of Varga could be measured both by the scale of the meeting and by the stature of its "defendant." Varga was the long-established dean of Soviet studies of the west, yet more than twenty speakers participated in the controversial sessions and generated sixty-four pages of closely printed transcript, of which thirty-five thousand copies were distributed as a special supplement to the November 1947 issue of the monthly journal of Varga's institute. The event was obviously staged to alert economists to the need for vigilance and "party-mindedness" as the Cold War intensified. The global struggle between "two systems" did not allow for any third parties—either in the form of the capitalist state or in the person of a Soviet academic who underestimated class struggle.

6. The Marshall Plan and American Imperialism

Stalinist denunciations of Varga in the spring of 1947 accelerated reversion to the conventions of prewar discussions, in which the chronic "problem of markets" had been associated with imperialist aggression and the "general crisis" of the capitalist system. In February 1946—less than a month before Churchill's comments on the "iron curtain"—Stalin had warned Moscow "voters" of capitalism's inherent tendency to provoke new wars in response to systemic crises: "Thus the first crisis of the capitalist system of world economy resulted in the First World War, and the second crisis resulted in the Second World War."[113] The obvious implication was that new economic difficulties could be expected to provoke resurgent militarism.

In an article entitled "Two Crises of the Capitalist System," I.M. Lemin hailed Stalin's remarks as "an enormous new contribution to the treasure house of Marxism-Leninism."[114] Claiming that "the fundamental economic and political causes" of war had not been eliminated, Lemin cited Churchill's reference to the "iron curtain" as evidence that "Imperialist tendencies are being stimulated by the blind hatred of the reactionary elements for the growing forces of democracy in Europe, by their blind hatred for the Soviet Union. . . ." The general crisis, as Stalin indicated, was responsible for "further intensification of the struggle for markets, for militarily and politically secure spheres in which to invest capital."[115]

In June 1947, General George C. Marshall, Truman's secretary of state, announced America's intention to combine military containment of communism with financial support for a European Recovery Program. The *Marshall Plan* was designed to restore international trade between capitalist countries and to stabilize Western Europe politically. Its immediate consequence in the Soviet Union was to intensify Cold War hostilities and further isolate Varga. Varga had questioned the urgency of the problem of markets during postwar reconstruction, suggesting the possibility of stable international relations; his opponents portrayed the Marshall Plan as a brazen program of American imperialism and a second attempt to "Dawesize" Europe.

In the 1920s, Dawes Plan assistance to Germany had been interpreted as a plot to restore German industry in order that reparations might be paid out of revenues earned by exporting manufactured goods to the Soviet Union. "Dawesization," Stalin had argued, was intended both to subordinate Germany to American capital and to prevent Soviet industrialization. Stalin vowed that the Land of Soviets would never become "an agrarian country for the benefit of some other country."[116] Varga had likewise warned in 1925 that the Dawes Plan sought to reduce the Soviet Union to "a German agricultural colony."[117] Identical arguments were deployed after 1947 in response to Marshall's proposed European Recovery Program. American "assistance" was said to be a threat to the national sovereignty of recipient countries and a scheme to prevent industrialization in Soviet-controlled Eastern Europe.[118]

Responding to Soviet pressure, Poland, Yugoslavia, Romania, and Bulgaria all declined to take part in a European conference summoned to draw up a response to Marshall's proposals. Soviet foreign minister

Molotov did attend, but shortly afterward Moscow determined that neither the Soviet Union nor any of its allies would participate in the Marshall Plan. A Soviet English-language weekly, *New Times*, explained that American supervision of aid expenditures was "a condition utterly unacceptable to all those countries and peoples that refuse to trade in their national independence, preferring to . . . build up . . . their own industries rather than . . . [accept] American handouts."[119] Already tied to the Soviet Union through bilateral barter trade, the East European countries entered into more formal arrangements with Moscow first through creation of the Cominform in September 1947 and later by forming the Council of Mutual Economic Assistance (Comecon) in 1949.

Whether or not the Marshall Plan was intended to divide Europe, it certainly accelerated that outcome. Stalin's representative at the inaugural meeting of the Cominform, Andrei Zhdanov, resurrected the theme of a world divided into "two systems" of economy and two opposing camps: "the imperialist and antidemocratic camp on the one side, the anti-imperialist and democratic camp on the other."[120] Zhdanov told East European delegates that the United States, anticipating a new economic crisis, had embarked upon "enslavement of Europe" to satisfy its own need for export markets and spheres of investment.[121] While economic cooperation with the Soviet Union protected the sovereignty and independence of East European countries, the Labour government had reduced Britain to a "vassal power" by accepting American loans,[122] and the "socialist" government of French premier Ramadier had been forced to expel Communist ministers as a condition for receiving American credits.[123]

7. Return to the Varga "Discussion"

By the autumn of 1947, the main themes of Varga's *Changes in the Economic Structure of Capitalism as a Result of the Second World War* were totally at odds with events. In part Varga continued to attribute this fact to the death of Roosevelt:

> Roosevelt, the late president of the USA, understanding very well the interests of the American bourgeoisie, knew how to moderate the class struggle between the bourgeoisie and the proletariat through timely concessions that did not pose a threat to the existing order. After his death, and especially after the

Republican election victory, social reaction in the USA is more and more becoming the prevailing tendency.[124]

By this time, however, Varga also conceded the role of economic factors in America's new imperialist expansionism: " . . . American industry, having increased its capacity by one-third during the war, cannot sell its products in the domestic market. . . . [T]he export of commodities must be sharply increased in order to avoid chronic idleness on the part of more than half of the industrial enterprises and the emergence of a permanent army of 10 million unemployed."[125]

In *The Marshall Plan and the Economies of England and the USA*, Varga repudiated part of his own previous work by claiming that "bourgeois economists" had been proved wrong in their belief that postponed consumer demand would avert an economic crisis.[126] Lifting of wartime price controls meant that from February 1945 to February 1947 the real incomes of American workers had fallen by 30 percent, creating a "latent crisis" that threatened to become a "manifest crash" unless exports could be expanded.[127] The Marshall Plan was a response to these domestic difficulties and an attempt to isolate the Soviet Union: "It is clear," Varga commented, "that the invitation to the Soviet Union [to participate in the Marshall Plan] was merely a maneuver. No one could seriously expect that the USSR—a world power—with its socialist planned economy, could submit to 'regulation' by the USA."[128]

By October 1947, Varga made further concessions to Stalinist detractors: the struggle between "two camps" was said to be a result of the "general crisis" of the capitalist system,[129] and there was no longer any prospect even for a "temporary stabilization."[130] "A small group of the financial oligarchy" was establishing "undivided rule" over the economies of the leading capitalist countries because the prewar problem of markets had now returned in chronic form.[131] Five months after *Changes in the Economic Structure of Capitalism* was first denounced, Varga finally provided a *Stalinist* formulation of the general crisis in terms reminiscent of Rosa Luxemburg:

> the longer capitalism exists, the more incapable it becomes of mastering and fully utilizing the productive forces it creates. . . . This leads to the fact that the growth of capitalist society's production capacity systematically outstrips its consuming power. This is manifested directly in the chronic narrowness of the market for sales.[132]

Varga's attempt to placate his critics only provoked further attacks. In the party journal *Bol'shevik*, I. Gladkov resurrected charges leveled during the earlier discussion. But Gladkov's tone was now a good deal less "comradely" as he linked Varga's work not only with bourgeois ideology but also (implicitly) with Hilferding and Bukharin. Varga, he contended, had abandoned Marxism-Leninism by identifying the war economy with "organized" capitalism and by entertaining the possibility of crisis-free development.[133] These elemental errors arose from ignoring the "coalescence of finance capital with the state"[134] and then led to the mistaken view that the state possessed a "supraclass character."[135] Complaining of a lack of self-criticism on the part of Varga and his associates, Gladkov demanded that the entire Institute of World Economy and World Politics be held accountable for dangerous ideological confusion.[136]

In January 1948, K.V. Ostrovityanov announced dissolution of Varga's Institute of World Economy and its absorption by the more conservative Institute of Economics. He explained this action by pointing out that Varga had yet to repudiate adequately his past work. Promoting the view that there might be a "peaceful transition to socialism" if workers could win "influence" in the capitalist state, Varga was disorienting western communist parties with a "clearly reformist thesis" that would discourage revolutionary class struggle.[137] What Ostrovityanov had seen as a methodological flaw in the "discussion" of May 1947 now turned out to be a grave departure from Marxism-Leninism that had spread throughout the entire Institute.

Casting the net widely to include Varga's most prominent coworkers, Ostrovityanov complained that Eventov's book, *The War Economy of England*, had also failed to give a Stalinist account of the "general crisis." Another work in the same category was M.L. Bokshitsky's *Technical-Economic Changes in the Industry of the USA During the Second World War*. This "non-Marxist" book had assessed American technology in an "objectivist" manner, overlooking the antagonism between labor and capital and expressing servile "admiration" of capitalism. Similar errors had occurred in another work by S.M. Vishnev, *The Industry of the Capitalist Countries During the Second World War*. Neglecting to discuss the "decay" of capitalism during the general crisis, Vishnev had provided "a clear example of an apologetic and objectivist approach."[138]

Reviewing numerous books and articles written by members of Varga's former Institute, Ostrovityanov announced that an entire "system of errors" was involved. These included: ignoring the Leninist-Stalinist theory of imperialism; forgetting the general crisis and the struggle of two systems; allowing descriptive work to replace theory; replacing party-mindedness with a narrow "technico-economic" orientation; adopting a position of "neutrality" in the struggle against bourgeois ideology; approaching bourgeois statistics with an uncritical attitude; and expressing "admiration" for bourgeois science and technology. Such errors had been allowed to multiply because members of Varga's Institute had worked in an atmosphere of "nepotism" and "mutual guarantees" of tolerance for each other's deviations. This "harmful monopoly of a narrow circle of senior workers" must now be broken.[139]

Following dissolution of the Institute of World Economy and World Politics, new criticism of Varga and his associates appeared in several major journals. In March 1948, L.M. Gatovsky wrote in *Bol'shevik* of economists who had become captives of "anti-Marxist bourgeois ideology."[140] In the same month *Voprosy ekonomiki*, the journal of the Institute of Economics, warned that "objectivism," "apologetics," and "groveling" before bourgeois science and technology would not be tolerated.[141]

The most senior official to enter the fray at this juncture was Nikolai A. Voznesensky, chief Soviet planner. In *The War Economy of the Soviet Union*, Voznesensky ridiculed the notion that capitalism was capable either of economic planning or of moderating class conflict: "The bourgeois state of the USA is characterized by a coalescence of the state apparatus, especially its upper levels, with the bosses and agents of the capitalist monopolies and finance capital."[142] As chairman of Gosplan, Voznesensky had his own score to settle. In his mind, the Soviet Union had triumphed over Hitler because he and his comrades at Gosplan had equipped the Red Army for its victorious offensives. Whereas Varga had once predicted Germany's economic collapse, Voznesensky undertook to set the record straight: "The assertion that the collapse of Hitlerite Germany . . . is the result of uninterrupted 'economic exhaustion' . . . as certain economists at one time 'demonstrated,' has nothing in common with reality."[143]

At the end of March 1948, this new campaign of intimidation claimed its first victims. In another discussion, this time at the Institute of Economics, Trakhtenberg repudiated a book he had previously edited on the American war economy and accepted "without any reservation" the charge that he had shared Varga's view concerning the "decisive role" of the bourgeois state.[144] With the exception of Eventov, other contributors to the volume made similar recantations. When Eventov refused to do so, Ostrovityanov charged him with being a "liberal" and a "purveyor of bourgeois ideology."[145] Dissatisfied with the outcome of this meeting, Ostrovityanov relentlessly began preparations for another.

In October 1948 an expanded session of the Academic Council of the Institute of Economics met to review "profound anti-Marxist errors and distortions" in recent publications.[146] On this occasion several more of Varga's colleagues confessed, including L.Ya. Eventov, V.A. Maslennikov (former deputy director of the Institute of World Economy), I.M. Lemin, S.M. Vishnev, and M.L. Bokshitsky. With friends and coworkers abandoning him one after another, Varga stubbornly refused to make a full retraction of *Changes in the Economic Structure of Capitalism*. He admitted that he had made some "errors," particularly in using the term "planning" (*planirovanie*) with reference to the capitalist state,[147] but he still maintained that his analysis of the capitalist war economy had been fundamentally sound:

> It is possible, and it happened during the war, that the state, in the interests of waging war, in the *common* interest of all monopolies, of the entire financial oligarchy, of the whole bourgeoisie, is compelled occasionally to oppose the interests of *separate* monopolies. That is all I wrote. . . . Perhaps I am not right. Should new arguments appear, showing that I am not right, I will openly and honestly admit that I am not right.[148]

Ostrovityanov menacingly replied that "Comrade Varga refuses honestly, like a Bolshevik, to recognize his errors." Turning to Varga he warned: "You must know, from the history of our party, what unfortunate consequences can result from stubborn persistence in one's errors."[149] At the end of March 1949, the Academic Council of the Institute of Economics met again to discuss "the struggle against bourgeois cosmopolitanism in economic science."[150] According to A.I. Pashkov, the rapporteur on this occasion, "cosmopolitans" were not merely theoretical "reformists," a charge frequently directed at Varga in recent months, but also "renegades" who lacked any sense of "love for the Fatherland." "The Soviet people," Pashkov warned, "despise and hate rootless cosmopolitans."[151] In the Stalinist lexicon the term "cosmopolitan" had two meanings: it implied "groveling" before things foreign, but it was also a coded reference to Zionism and to Jews. Varga and many of his colleagues were Jews.

Since the "comradely" discussion of May 1947, Varga's courage had led to one disgrace after another, culminating in the invocation of official antisemitism as the ultimate explanation of his disloyalty. At this point he concluded that it was senseless to resist. In an article entitled "Against Reformism in Works on Imperialism," he admitted that he should have confessed sooner to his "reformist" and "cosmopolitan" errors, which resulted from failure to investigate capitalism's deepening "general crisis." "Reformists" believed that "finding themselves in 'power,' they can turn the bourgeois state into an instrument of the working class and, through peaceful reforms, reach socialism without a revolution."[152] Varga confessed that he had encouraged such illusions by describing the Labour government's nationalization program as "progress in the direction of democracy of a new type."[153] Disavowing any notion of the "supraclass nature of the bourgeois state" or its "decisive role" in the economy,[154] he now accepted "full responsibility" both for his own errors and for a long list of offending publications by other members of the former Institute of World Economy and World Politics.[155]

8. "Fascization" in the New American War Economy

Varga had drawn upon Roosevelt's New Deal in projecting the possibility of postwar stabilization; his enemies replied that Truman's America had become nothing more than a replica of Hitler's Germany. Hitler had come to power during the Great Depression as an agent of finance capital and the biggest monopolies. The analogy between postwar America and Nazi Germany required that Soviet writers now unmask the finance-capitalist magnates who were manipulating the Truman administration from behind the scenes. Ironically, they discovered the evidence they needed in respectable American sources.

In May 1947, V.A. Cheprakov declared that American capitalism was dominated by a narrow coterie of eight finance-capitalist interests: "the family groups (Morgan, Rockefeller, Kuhn-Loeb, Du Pont, and Mellon) and three . . . regional groups (Chicago, Cleveland, and Boston)."[156] Sh.B. Lif pointed out that Gardiner Means, an economist of considerable influence among supporters of the New Deal, had written in 1939 of the eight groups in *The Structure of the American Economy*.[157] A. Leont'ev found similar references in a Senate committee report on "Economic Concentration and World War II."[158] M.I. Rubinshtein quoted another American source, *The Concentration of Economic Power*, written by D. Lynch and published in 1946 by Columbia University Press.[159]

Once these "real" forces behind American capitalism were identified, together with the 250 largest corporations they controlled, the imperialist reaction that occurred after Roosevelt's death required no further explanation. The American state had, indeed, assumed a more active role, but its real objective was to sustain a fascist war-oriented economy even in peacetime conditions. To hardline Soviet economists it was obvious that a fascist economy required the working class to be terrorized in order to curtail consumption and concentrate on armaments expenditures. The result was a torrent of wildly exaggerated literature portraying postwar America in terms of rampant "fascization."

V.I. Lan claimed in 1947 that the Taft-Hartley Act eliminated all of the rights won by American labor over the past decade.[160] By launching a "holy war" against communists and trade unionists, monopolists were trying to restore "the 'good' old times" of the pre-Roosevelt era.[161] The slogan of the financial oligarchy was "a government of business, for business and by business."[162] In an article on "American Reaction and Its Struggle Against Democracy," Y. Minayev wrote that "a general plan for the suppression of democracy was drawn up in American plutocratic circles after the death of President Roosevelt."[163] The Un-American Activities Committee, suppression of organized labor, the purge of Hollywood, and Truman's checks on the "loyalty" of government workers were all justified by the fiction of a "Red menace." I.I. Kuz'minov investigated the business links of Truman's new cabinet and cited claims by Henry Wallace, Roosevelt's former vice-president, to the effect that Wall Street once again ruled the country.[164]

From the autumn of 1947 onward, Soviet journals portrayed an America in which "massive chronic unemployment" and "absolute impoverishment" prevailed while monopolies were being enriched by taxation to finance armaments.[165] A.I. Shapiro referred to Keynesian economics as a "fascist-cannibalistic 'philosophy,'" whose sole purpose was to rationalize "the imperialist practices of monopolistic capital."[166] N. Sergeeva thought support of fascism had become "the height of good taste" in America, where countless "fascist and near-fascist organizations are maintained by the financial oligarchy."[167] M.N. Smit described the consequences of "fascization" for the toilers: these included pellagra, beriberi, scurvy, and other deficiency diseases;[168] "hooligan" attacks on workers and progressives; and a strike movement that by 1949 was assuming "the character of a real civil war."[169]

V.A. Cheprakov wrote of a "military-police state" in which "war hysteria" was used to justify widespread "repression and terror."[170] His description of the United States included police spies terrorizing workers; coal miners who were veritable "slaves";[171] a population of which one-sixth suffered from chronic illnesses while one out of seven city dwellers was starving;[172] use of "Gestapo methods" by Pinkerton detectives and factory police to suppress strikes;[173] and workers who were housed in garrets and eating garbage.[174] By July 1949 Cheprakov was writing of a new economic crisis involving declining output, falling prices on commodity and stock markets, and 6 million unemployed.[175]

The recession that began in the United States in the third quarter of 1948 intensified concerns over the prospect of war. In November 1949 Mikhail Suslov addressed a meeting of the Cominform and warned that British and American ruling circles were actively preparing new hostilities: "Historical experience teaches that the more hopeless is the position of imperialist reaction, the more frantic it becomes, the greater is the danger of its embarking upon military adventures."[176] But Suslov also made the contradictory observation that the Soviet people were convinced of "victory in peaceful competition": "The foreign policy of the Soviet government . . . proceeds from the assumption of the possibility of coexistence of the socialist and capitalist systems and peaceful cooperation between them."[177]

Remarks such as these typified the confusion with which Stalinists now had to deal. Was imperialist war inevitable, as Stalin appeared to suggest when predicting a new systemic crisis, or was peaceful coexistence really a viable policy? The answer seemed to depend partly upon the outcome of the new economic difficulties in America. If the "depression of a special kind" remained in force, war would be a likely consequence. On the other hand, Marx had demonstrated that *cyclical* (as distinct from *systemic*) crises are always followed by normal economic recoveries. In these circumstances, a handful of economists questioned whether the Stalinist theories of "general crisis" and "depression of a special kind" could be reconciled with Marx's *Capital*. From Varga's theory of the state and capitalist planning, attention now turned to Marx's theory of the business cycle and capitalist reproduction.

CHAPTER 3

STALIN'S LEGACY: PEACEFUL COEXISTENCE OR THE INEVITABILITY OF WAR?

Varga's *Changes in the Economic Structure of Capitalism* took the middle ground between conflicting interpretations of *Capital*. Like Luxemburg, Varga believed the chronic problem of markets was a theoretical attribute of "pure capitalism"; like Bukharin, he also thought the state had in practice assumed a regulating role. Functioning as a "third party," the state was said to create markets by borrowing the uninvested savings of capitalists in order to finance either armaments or public works. Stalinists replied that Varga had committed the same error as Bukharin with his theory of stabilization in the 1920s. In both cases the class struggle was minimized and proletarian revolution was relegated to an indefinite future.

Despite Stalinist criticism, however, Varga's book proved to be one of the most influential studies of western economies for the next two decades. Each thaw in domestic politics extended the boundaries of legitimate discussion; each attempt to reassess postwar capitalism contributed to Varga's gradual rehabilitation. By the mid-1960s virtually no Soviet economist denied either the reality of capitalist planning or the role of the state in promoting the general interests of the capitalist class— even, when necessary, at the expense of significant concessions to working-class demands. The strategy of peaceful transition to socialism, enunciated by Khrushchev in the 1950s and later endorsed by all "Eurocommunist" parties, originated with Varga's belief in the ability of the state to play the mediating role of "third party." The direct consequence of Varga's humiliation, however, was a new period of academic repression similar to that of the 1930s. Economists were instructed to be both researchers and fighters in the struggle between "two systems," applauding capitalism's difficulties while minimizing its technological and economic accomplishments. In September 1950 *Pravda* announced that "Every Marxist work on the economics of capitalist countries must be a bill of indictment."[1] The "correct" view held that the state was dominated exclusively by monopoly capital and could never surmount the "depression of a special kind."

Once Stalinists identified postwar capitalism with Hitler's Germany, all that seemed to remain was the inevitability of imperialist wars. The Korean war was taken to substantiate the official view and to disprove Varga's prediction of stabilization. But despite use of administrative measures to suppress dissent, another group of economists arrived at conclusions similar to Varga's by considering the probable consequences of the 1948 recession. If it could be shown that postwar problems were not substantially different from those of earlier periods, the implication would be a normal cyclical recovery and the possibility of averting a new war involving the Soviet Union. The problem with this approach was that it too entailed denial of the "general crisis." For this reason, the efforts of Soviet business-cycle theorists met with the same hostility as Varga's *Changes in the Economic Structure of Capitalism.*

A second alternative to Stalinist orthodoxy was to consider new ways of addressing the supposedly chronic "problem of markets." On the eve of Stalin's death in 1953, several economists began to think of the "socialist camp" as itself a kind of third party with the potential to avert imperialist aggression by cultivating intercapitalist rivalries. Belief that the internal forces of the cycle could no longer sustain expansion inspired hopes that western governments would compete to serve socialist markets. Not until the late 1950s did the officials responsible for organizing Soviet research finally concede that the "problem of markets" had to be reinterpreted in terms of the classical cycle. Until that time, Marx's work was treated with the same suspicion as Varga's.

1. Soviet Business-Cycle Theory

Stalinist aversion to Marxist business-cycle theory had originated in efforts to explain the Great Depression. Whereas the concept of the "general crisis" could be traced to Rosa Luxemburg's *Accumulation of Capital*, Soviet business-cycle theorists were typically influenced by Rudolf Hilferding's *Finance Capital*. Hilferding believed that Marx had demonstrated the ability of capitalism to increase production "without interruption as long as . . . [intersectoral] proportions are maintained.

. . . It does not follow at all, therefore, that a crisis in capitalist production is caused by the underconsumption of the masses. . . ."[2] Hilferding insisted that chronic "underconsumption" could never account for
cyclical crises: it was logically impossible to explain *periodic* phenomena
by referring to an allegedly *chronic* condition.[3]

This argument was developed in the Soviet Union by M.I. Nakhimson
(better known by the pseudonym of Spektator), who in 1928 wrote a
pioneering article on "Marx's Theory of Crises." Although Stalinists
were already associating "rotten stabilization" with the chronic problem
of markets, Spektator recalled that Marx had explained cycles by studying the material basis of market creation and destruction: ". . . Marx
pointed to the fact that capitalism creates its own market insofar as a
growing part of social output goes into the formation of . . . fixed
capital."[4] Market creation resulted from growing investments, market
destruction from a cyclical decline of investments due to a falling rate of
profit. Whereas Luxemburg's theory suggested "permanent crises,"
Spektator thought the real issue was:

> Why do [crises] appear only at certain times? Moreover, why do
> they appear at precisely those moments when the position of the
> working class relatively improves, when wages are rising and
> unemployment is declining during an industrial recovery. . .?[5]

Studying the cycle in terms of the relation between saving and
investment, Spektator anticipated much of what Varga and Keynes had
to say by the mid-1930s: if some capitalists saved more than others were
currently investing, part of the social output would not be sold;[6]
conversely, if investments exceeded savings, higher profit rates would
lead to further investments until rising costs again impinged on profits.
Contrary to the Stalinist belief in "absolute impoverishment" and a
chronic problem of markets, Spektator followed Marx in relating the rate
of profit to a dialectical movement of wages:

> at first [wages] lag behind the rise of the general price level;
> then, when demand for working hands quickly grows, they out-
> strip price increases for finished goods, causing a sharp fall in
> the rate of surplus value. . . .[7]

A number of other writers made minor contributions in this area during
the 1920s, but business-cycle theory faltered when it became linked with

the political struggle between Stalin and Bukharin. Bukharin argued that a wave of investments in new technologies was responsible for stabilization; Stalinists retorted that such investments were impossible in the absence of new noncapitalist markets. On these grounds A. Lyusin dismissed Spektator's work in 1929 as "profoundly non-Marxist."[8] M.N. Smit objected that capitalism was experiencing the "agony of a slow death" that excluded "the possibility of projecting earlier generalizations [of the cycle] into the future."[9] M. Gol'man repudiated cycle theory by quoting Engels' "genius-like formulation" of a "chronic crisis of overproduction."[10]

The most spectacular prewar debate over cycle theory occurred in 1931 following publication of Evgeny Preobrazhensky's *The Decline of Capitalism*.[11] Preobrazhensky thought that Spektator had demonstrated "the exceptionally important role of the process of reproduction of fixed capital . . . for the theory of crises."[12] A former associate of Leon Trotsky, Preobrazhensky dismissed Stalinist theories of chronic underconsumption and argued that "Marx was perfectly correct to consider consumption in capitalist society [to be] a function of production."[13] *Capital's* "laws of proportionality" demonstrated that replacement and expansion of fixed capital "creates an additional market."[14] Lenin had also provided "convincing evidence of how incorrect was Rosa Luxemburg's theory of reproduction."[15]

Preobrazhensky provoked a fury in the early 1930s by considering the possibility of cyclical recovery from the Great Depression: once critical components of industrial equipment began to wear out, he thought a new cycle of investments might result from initial attempts merely to maintain machinery and keep factories operating. Because he concentrated, however, on material conditions affecting the reproduction of fixed capital, the Stalinist reaction to his book focused on "objectivism" and the charge that he ignored the politics of class struggle. E. Gromov complained that *The Decline of Capitalism* committed "a number of serious errors, at the root of which [is] abstraction from class contradictions in the epoch of the general crisis of capitalism and reduction of the problem of the cycle's modification to the conditions of the turnover of fixed capital."[16] According to Gromov, "Marx never, in any place, said that the basic cause of periodic crises could be the turnover and renewal of fixed capital."[17]

E. Gurvich charged that Preobrazhensky had "completely distorted the position of Marx and Lenin in saying that capitalist production creates its own markets."[18] Stalin had shown that the problem of markets, "the main problem of capitalism," had become "monstrously acute."[19] I.N. Dvorkin described Preobrazhensky's work as having a "social-fascist essence"[20] because it followed Hilferding by concentrating upon relations between Marx's two Departments. A. Breitman condemned the book as "a variant of the usual bourgeois theory of disproportionality."[21] Scandalized by "the bourgeois and Menshevik theory of disproportionalities," another critic demanded that all future economic research begin with Stalin's "new additions to the arsenal of Marxist-Leninist science," which were said to be "extraordinary in [their] theoretical profundity, clarity and political accuracy."[22]

The attacks on Spektator and Preobrazhensky in the 1930s should have alerted economists in the postwar period to the incompatibility of Stalinism with classical Marxism. But despite this history of "errors," in 1947 Varga's associate at the Institute of World Economy, I.A. Trakhtenberg, published a new book with the title *Capitalist Reproduction and Economic Crises*. Trakhtenberg agreed with Spektator, Preobrazhensky, and Marx that "the material basis of the cycle" was forced renovation of fixed capital in response to a falling rate of profit.[23] Given the predictability of recovery in investments, he added that "the internal forces of capitalist production create the possibility of overcoming the crisis" without any reliance upon third-party markets.[24] Trakhtenberg also supported this interpretation by reference to Lenin, who had shown "how one must understand the idea of proportionality. . . . [Lenin] demonstrated that the lag of consumption's growth behind production cannot serve as a cause of *systematic*, permanent overproduction. . . ."[25]

Refuting the Luxemburgist assumptions underlying the theory of the "general crisis," Trakhtenberg expressed doubts concerning the Stalinist view of proletarian impoverishment. Paraphrasing Marx's criticism of the underconsumptionist "tautology," he declared that

> Crises must not be explained by workers' underconsumption. . . . A crisis usually breaks out during an economic expansion, when the level of workers' consumption . . . is relatively high. On the other hand . . . . recovery begins in those branches producing means of production. Expansion here causes an increased demand for labor power and a corresponding increase of demand for consumer goods. . . . [E]xpansion of production brings with it growth of personal consumption.[26]

In 1930 Stalin had told the sixteenth party congress that the Great Depression resulted from "the contradiction between the social character of production and the capitalist form of appropriation," which he then elaborated in terms of the chronic problem of markets.[27] Trakhtenberg suggested that what Stalin really had in mind was the contradiction between *social "anarchy"* and *"organized" production in individual trusts*. In other words, he reread Stalin's explanation in terms of Hilferding's account of the inability of trusts to coordinate private plans on a social scale.[28] In the Stalinist view, Hilferding's "reformism" resulted from his theory of organized capitalism. Trakhtenberg made the opposite case: it was really belief in a chronic problem of markets that inspired hopes of class reconciliation. According to Trakhtenberg, social democrats believed "that both workers and capitalists are interested in raising consumption. And if that is the case, then the interests of workers and capitalists are not only not contradictory, but, on the contrary, [must] fundamentally correspond."[29]

Trakhtenberg's attempt to reinterpret Stalin led to glaring inconsistencies. Proposing a return to Marx, he felt compelled to admit that Stalin had developed and deepened Marx's theory in the epoch of imperialism and the general crisis.[30] Although the "depression of a special kind" explicitly ruled out cyclical expansions, he even praised Stalin's comments on the subject as "a new idea, enriching not only the theory of crises but also the theory of the economic cycle as a whole."[31] Despite these rhetorical concessions, however, the anti-Stalinist implications of a Marxist theory of the cycle were plainly visible. Trakhtenberg's deceptions merely compromised the integrity of his own study.

Identical problems reappeared in the work of P.K. Figurnov, who in 1948 published *The Marxist-Leninist Theory of Crises*, followed in 1949 by *Capitalist Reproduction and Economic Crises*. Figurnov began with the same interpretation as Preobrazhensky and Trakhtenberg: by tracing the origins of "proportionality and disproportionality between separate branches of social production,"[32] Marx had shown that it was theoretically possible for all output to be "fully realized within the capitalist economy."[33] "The Marxian [reproduction] schemes illustrate how development of capitalist production creates its own internal market. . . ." Marxism-Leninism taught "that capitalism possesses all the necessary conditions for development on its own internal basis." As for Rosa Luxemburg, Lenin had shown that "the question of the foreign market has absolutely no importance." Lenin believed "that capitalist production, on its own, creates the market."[34]

Contrary to the theory of "depression of a special kind," Figurnov quoted Marx's analogy between the movement of social production and the orbits of the planets.[35] Believing that "Crises and the cyclical development of capitalism will exist as long as the capitalist mode of production,"[36] he encountered the same dilemma as Trakhtenberg. On the one hand, he too reinterpreted Stalin in terms of Hilferding's argument on disproportionality;[37] on the other hand, he cited the Stalinist claim that "absolute impoverishment" of workers resulted from the chronic contradiction between social production and private appropriation.[38] After formally conceding Stalin's view, however, Figurnov immediately added something quite different: Marx had seen limited consumption as the "final"—not the "basic"—cause of crises. Thus Marx gave limited consumption a "subordinate place" compared to the reproduction of fixed capital.[39] Trying to give a faithful interpretation of *Capital* while simultaneously deferring to the official line, Figurnov ended, like Trakhtenberg, in futile self-contradiction.

A third economist to consider the relation between classical Marxist theory and postwar capitalism was L.A. Mendel'son, author of a volume of more than eight hundred pages entitled *Economic Crises and Cycles in the Nineteenth Century*. Like Trakhtenberg and Figurnov, Mendel'son cited Lenin's rejection of the theory of third parties: Lenin had said that "the question of the foreign market has *absolutely nothing to do with the question of realization*."[40] Although Mendel'son began with the same approach as other cycle theorists, in his comments on postwar America he took greater pains to comply with Stalinist orthodoxy.

In traditional cycles, he explained, "recovery" began with renovation of fixed capital and grew into an "expansion" when the peak of output in the previous cycle was surpassed. Although investments were the "material basis" of expansion,[41] Mendel'son thought the postwar situation was unique. American production had peaked as early as 1943, at the height of the war effort, with the result that there were no significant investments after 1945 to expand the market. Since postponed consumer demand had also been erased by inflation, the problem of markets had now caused the American economy to become "feverish," "unstable," and "unhealthy."[42]

Mendel'son's interpretation pointed to a new pattern that he believed was perfectly consistent with Stalinist doctrine. In place of the classical phases of recovery and expansion, he predicted that a series of "intermediate crises" would become the distinguishing feature of the general crisis and renewed "depression of a special kind."[43] Production might increase in the short run, but there was little prospect that it would surpass levels already reached during the war. Investments on a scale "unprecedented in history" would be required first to take up existing slack in heavy industry and then to generate "the material basis for a full-blooded cyclical expansion."[44] Lacking such investments, America would experience chronic underutilization of industrial capacity and "extraordinary intensification of the problem of markets."[45]

Mendel'son avoided the obvious inconsistencies of Trakhtenberg and Figurnov, but Stalinists ultimately saw little to distinguish his work from theirs. All three authors were said to have made the same error as Preobrazhensky by taking investments to be the "material basis" of the cycle and by forgetting the role of politics in the class struggle. In August 1950, F. Polyansky condemned Mendel'son's "distortions" in an article in *Voprosy ekonomiki*, the journal of the Institute of Economics. According to Polyansky, Mendel'son had replaced "class-political" analysis with a "technico-economic description": ". . . L. Mendel'son puts at the center of his book the problem of the reproduction of fixed capital, not the development of the contradiction between the social character of production and the private form of appropriation."[46] Omitting class antagonisms and proletarian impoverishment, Mendel'son had succumbed to the same "objectivism" as Varga and numerous other authors at the former Institute of World Economy and World Politics.

Polyansky's criticism was followed on September 29 by an anonymous article in *Pravda* on "Serious Errors in Books Concerning the History of Economic Crises." The "technico-economic" analysis was said to imply that capitalism was a progressive mode of production. Treating investments as the "material basis" of the cycle, Mendel'son's historical research had portrayed the nineteenth century in terms of successive waves of new technologies despite the problem of markets. According to *Pravda*, this error resulted from using falsified bourgeois statistics and adopting a "liberal" attitude to Hilferding and other apologists of imperialism. It was "no coincidence" that Mendel'son's editor had been Figurnov, who likewise thought that the result of every crisis was a "technological revolution." Both authors had adopted an "abstract-scholastic" method and overlooked the "struggle of two systems."[47]

At the end of October 1950, Mendel'son and Figurnov suffered the same fate as Varga. At a three-day meeting of the Institute of Economics, attended by more than five hundred researchers, teachers, and graduate students, their work was savagely condemned. The rapporteur, V.P. D'yachenko, charged that lack of "party-mindedness" had caused both authors to adopt an "anti-Marxist, anti-Bolshevik method."[48] A.F. Yakovlev described Mendel'son's historical study as "cosmopolitan" because it failed to emphasize the importance of Russia in the nineteenth-century world economy.[49] E.S. Lazutkin denounced "rotten liberalism" and "lack of principle" on the part of economists whose "group interests were placed above the interests of science."[50] V.F. Vasyutin remarked that Mendel'son's "abstract-scholastic" and "technico-economic" work had "completely ignored the problem of markets."[51]

Figurnov's most serious offense turned out to be replacement of the chronic problem of markets with the Marxist theory of cyclical disproportions. B.I. Chudok denounced Figurnov in the same terms used to attack Preobrazhensky in 1931:

> the author asserts that "Marx, in his analysis of capitalist reproduction, began with the need (?!) for certain proportions between the branches of capitalist production." . . . It is clear that all these arguments . . . have nothing in common with the Marxist-Leninist theory of capitalist reproduction and are a falsification of that theory.[52]

V.P. Glushkov made the identical objection:

> In his explanation of the causes of crises, Figurnov, like supporters of "the theory of organized capitalism," speaks only of disproportions between the separate branches of production. Instead of revealing . . . the antagonistic class contradictions of capitalism, he reduces the cause of crises to disproportions of a technico-economic order, to the uneven renewal and expansion of fixed capital.[53]

How Trakhtenberg managed to escape denunciation at this meeting is not clear, but when he protested that the charges made by Chudok and Glushkov might lead to the opposite error of a theory of "under-consumption,"[54] his remark was brushed aside on the grounds that it demonstrated a conciliatory attitude to "reformist errors."[55] Varga was implicated several times in the offenses of Figurnov and Mendel'son, but the principal victim of the affair turned out to be Figurnov, who was dismissed from the Academic Council of the Institute. Chairing the meeting, D'yachenko promised that new cadres would be promoted to the section of the Institute of Economics dealing with imperialism and the general crisis. Like Ostrovityanov in the earlier Varga discussion, D'yachenko specified what the party demanded from economic researchers: "We are obliged to be strictly and consistently guided in our work by the instructions of the great coryphaeus of science, Comrade Stalin."[56]

2. The Stalinist Theory of the "One-Sided" War Economy

It might have been easier to comply with such admonishments had anyone known what the current instructions of the "great coryphaeus" really were. Stalin had said virtually nothing about capitalist crises since the 1930s. This meant that in order to interpret *postwar* capitalism, economists had first to comb his *prewar* statements in search of appropriate quotations. In 1933 Stalin had compared the achievements of the First Five-Year Plan with economic catastrophe in the west:

> The unemployed are refused food because they have no money with which to pay for it; they are refused shelter because they have no money with which to pay rent. How and where do they live? They live on miserable crumbs from the rich man's table; by raking refuse bins, where they find decayed scraps of food; they live in the slums of big cities, and more often in hovels outside the towns, hastily put up by the unemployed out of packing cases and the bark of trees.[57]

Following Stalin's example, M.I. Guttsait asserted in June 1950 that 76 percent of American families were "half-starving." A minimum standard of living required an income of $4,000 a year, while the average industrial wage was $2,500. Guttsait wrote that "The massive use of child labor . . . only confirms the low standard of living of the toilers of the USA, who are not able with their modest wages to feed their families and are compelled to send young children into capitalist hard labor."[58] Impoverishment of American workers was due to the impossibility of substantial new investments during the general crisis. In 1945-47, 72.4 percent of total investments had gone to replacement of equipment rather than to new factories.[59] Industrial construction might sustain a flow of incomes over a period of several years, but expenditures on equipment merely raised labor productivity and displaced workers from their jobs.

In 1939 Stalin had also given his official characterization of an imperialist war economy:

> what does placing the economy of a country on a war footing mean? It means giving industry a one-sided war direction; developing to the utmost the production of goods necessary for war and not for consumption by the population; restricting to the utmost the production and, especially, the sale of articles of general consumption and, consequently, reducing consumption by the population and confronting the country with an economic crisis.[60]

Applying this insight, A.A. Manukyan contended in May 1949 that America was "strengthening all the tendencies toward a war economy and establishing the conditions for an inevitable economic crash of catastrophic proportions."[61] Although the *Wall Street Journal* described 1948 as "a year of slight overemployment,"[62] Manukyan wrote that industries producing consumer durables were working at or near one-half of production capacity.[63] Adding that "falsified bourgeois statistics distort reality," M.N. Smit translated American part-time employment into equivalent unemployment and asserted that by mid-1948 the total had reached 8.5 million.[64] Official American data showed that the index of real wages, with 1939 as the base, was 114.3, but Smit also recalculated these statistics to produce a figure of 79.3.[65]

V.A. Cheprakov spoke of equally dismal conditions, describing America in terms of a "permanent, multimillioned army of the unemployed."[66] The decline of production, beginning in the latter part of 1948, was said to prove that "chronic underutilization of enterprises" stood in the way of any large-scale renovation of fixed capital.[67] Monopolies had responded by raising the share of military expenditures in the state budget from 7 percent before the war to nearly 30 percent in 1948/49. The Marshall Plan was an attempt to export the crisis to Europe, where American goods were smothering domestic industry. Meanwhile, American tariffs prevented European countries from exporting their own goods for dollars, causing "currency chaos" in France and "catastrophic inflation" in Italy. Western Europe was facing a new crisis at a time when 1937 levels of production had scarcely been restored.[68]

In January 1950, A.I. Shneerson attempted a summary of postwar developments from the Stalinist perspective. In an article entitled "Stalin on Crises of the Capitalist System of World Economy," he defined the general crisis as "the period of the crash of capitalism, of wars and revolutions, of maximum intensification of all the contradictions of capitalism."[69] Its main features were division of the world into two systems, chronic underutilization of production capacity, protracted economic crisis, and deformation of the business cycle. Because there was no possibility of any new stabilization—not even a "temporary" or "relative" stabilization[70]—monopolies were instead launching a new "attack on the living standards of the toilers" in order to finance rearmament.[71] "The bourgeoisie is searching for a way out of crises in war, in militarization, in creation of a military-inflationary conjuncture, in the transition to a war economy during peacetime, just as Hitlerite Germany did on the eve of World War II. . . ."[72] The "camp of peace and democracy," Shneerson urged, must make every effort to restrain the "Anglo-American imperialist warmongers."[73]

On June 24-25, 1950, Communist North Korea invaded South Korea. In an article entitled "The Capitalist World Heads for a War Economy," A.A. Manukyan explained the dispatch of American troops to the Korean peninsula as a case of imperialist "aggression" resulting from the general crisis of capitalism. On the eve of the war, industrial output had finally been recovering to the prerecession level. But because further expansion appeared doubtful, American capitalists, according to *U.S. News and World Report*, saw the conflict in Korea as "a made-to-order situation to keep business at a high level." Manukyan quoted Stalin to show that this was impossible: a "one-sided" war economy would only reduce popular consumption and precipitate another economic crisis.[74]

By January 1952, Manukyan wrote that restriction of civilian production was adding "hundreds of thousands to the unemployed army";[75] leather goods, footwear, textiles, automobiles, and housing construction all faced "a regular crisis of *overproduction*."[76] In reality, unemployment stood at 3 percent, personal consumption (including services) grew throughout the war,[77] and a small decline in production of consumer durables from early 1951 to mid-1952 was due mainly to speculative advance buying at the outbreak of the conflict.[78] Manukyan misinterpreted the resulting inventory adjustment by claiming that it confirmed Stalin's view of the "one-sided" war economy. "*The armaments drive in the United States,*" he decided, "*is incapable of producing even the semblance of an economic boom, for the development of a crisis of overproduction in the civilian industries more than counter-balances the growth of military production.*"[79]

V.A. Cheprakov agreed that "Transition to a war economy intensifies the basic contradiction of capitalism—between the social character of production and the capitalist form of appropriating the results of production."[80] Ignoring boom conditions at the outbreak of the war, Cheprakov maintained that increases in military spending could have no stimulative effect because the burden of taxation was falling predominantly on the toilers.[81] Chastened by Varga's experience, even Trakhtenberg held that public spending, financed through taxation, could not possibly increase consumer demand: "The apologists of capitalism begin with the view that a crisis is a result of inadequate demand; but [state] budgetary financing of the capitalists, through taxes taken from the toilers, obviously does not increase but rather decreases the effective demand of the broad mass of the population."[82]

From the outbreak of the Korean war in 1950 until the armistice in 1953, Soviet commentators produced endless propaganda concerning working-class impoverishment and swollen corporate profits. B. Vronsky varied the theme by describing the impact of militarization on political life. Fascization meant that America was "more and more turning into a military-police, terrorist state, into a prison for progressive Americans."[83] "War hysteria" and "human-hating propaganda" accompanied demands from senators that Truman use the atomic bomb in Korea. The FBI and the House Committee on Un-American Activities were functioning as a "Hitlerite Gestapo,"[84] blacklisting progressives and purging American academics; the "Dixiecrats" were organizing "mass murders of negroes" because the descendants of slaves were known for their "love and respect for the Soviet Union";[85] Congress was proposing "concentration camps" for Communists should Truman declare a state of emergency.[86] As for American workers, labor intensification was destroying "their nervous systems" and making them unfit for work before they reached forty years of age: "the majority of families of workers and poor farmers are compelled to live in slums, in hovels, in garrets and cellars. About 20% of American housing consists of slums in which 48 million people live. Many sleep in old trucks, in abandoned rail cars or barns."[87]

A rare attempt at more serious analysis came from A.I. Bechin. Like Bukharin in his study of "expanded negative reproduction" in the war economies of 1914-18, Bechin argued that a "military-inflationary" conjuncture involved capital consumption and could not lead to sustained growth. He attempted to explain the Stalinist position by referring to Marx's analysis of the two Departments of capitalist reproduction:

Industry in the first Department . . . . devours a mass of machines, materials and human labor not for multiplying the material riches of society, but for destroying people and the wealth they create. A war economy fulfills the role of destroying and eliminating productive forces on a scale even greater than an economic crisis.[88]

Bechin quoted predictions by American authors to the effect that war would cause production of household appliances to fall by 25 percent and automobiles by 50 percent.[89] But his endeavor to elevate descriptions of America from a polemical to a more theoretical level only pointed to new inconsistencies. How could Stalin's description of the "one-sided" war economy, which deliberately sacrificed consumer goods to armaments, possibly be consistent with Stalin's other pronouncements concerning the chronic problem of markets? How could there be overproduction of consumer goods if those same goods were not being produced? Bechin decided that when Stalin spoke of a "one-sided" economy, what he must have had in mind was *disproportionality*. He proposed to reformulate the Stalinist position this way:

As a result of the intensifying problem of realization, dispro-portions grow in the economy. Production for war does not at all eliminate the problem of markets, as academician Varga mistakenly asserted. . . . Realization, in the conditions of a war economy, destroys the entire process of reproduction insofar as it destroys the normal exchange between the subdivisions of social production. And this predetermines the inevitability of a profound and destructive crisis precisely as the consequence of one-sided development of an economy that is switched to a war operation.[90]

Such comments only emphasized the dead end to which Soviet accounts were leading. A crisis of disproportionality, caused by depletion of fixed capital, presupposed lack of reserve production capacity with which to offset shortages in particular branches of industry. Yet Soviet writers had for years maintained the very opposite: the general crisis was attributed to *chronically idle* capacity, representing an insurmountable obstacle to new investments. How could a country with chronically idle fixed capital be a replica of Nazi Germany, whose distinguishing feature was capital consumption? The further these arguments were pursued, the more absurd they became.[91]

The silliness reached its height when I.I. Kuz'minov decided that the real inspiration for the American war economy came from none other than John Maynard Keynes. During the 1930s, Keynes had been concerned to reactivate idle fixed capital through state borrowing and expenditure of private savings. Since Keynes had said that the object of state expenditures was of secondary importance—even pyramid building or wars might serve the purpose of stimulating recovery—Kuz'minov thought militarization was a consequence of the "reactionary and militaristic essence of his 'theory.'" "What," he asked "does the program of Keynes represent? . . . it is a program of state 'regulation' of economic life in the interests of the monopolies, a program of war and reaction, a program of state-monopoly capitalism."[92]

3. The Problem of Markets and Socialist Trade

Once business-cycle theory was again suppressed through political and administrative sanctions, a vicious circle ensued in which increasingly frequent predictions of another major war amplified the already grotesque portrayals of fascization in America. Underlying every issue was the alleged chronic problem of markets. It was only a matter of time, therefore, until the war danger came to be linked with the question of how the Soviet Union's own policies might be related to the general crisis of capitalism. If the capitalists really depended upon exports, several writers concluded that restoration of East-West trade might be an effective formula for peaceful coexistence. As in the case of other debates, this one too drew upon interwar precedents.

On the eve of the New Economic Policy, Lenin had been confident that the way to avoid renewed foreign intervention was to open Soviet markets to foreign trade and capital investment. In this way, he promised in December 1920, "we shall most certainly attract the sympathy . . . of sensible capitalists . . . regardless of the fact that in their eyes we are 'those terrible Bolshevik terrorists.'"[93] To support his proposal Lenin cited Keynes, whose *Economic Consequences of the Peace* had warned that Europe's postwar reconstruction depended upon Russian materials. Keynes told European statesmen that "we are blockading not so much Russia as ourselves."[94] In 1922 Lenin sent Soviet representatives to the Genoa Conference, where they unsuccessfully offered Soviet resources in exchange for a loan with which to import goods from the west.

After Lenin's death, Leon Trotsky called for new efforts in the mid-1920s to lease Soviet resources to foreign investors in order to expand trade and accelerate industrial growth. Stalin opposed reintegration into the world economy for the same reason that he condemned the Dawes Plan: "socialism in one country" required the USSR to become "a self-sufficient economic unit" free of prerevolutionary Russia's dependence upon the capitalist encirclement.[95] The Great Depression and fears of a new war eventually caused Stalin to reconsider. In 1930 he prophetically told the sixteenth party congress that

> every time the contradictions of capitalism become acute the bourgeoisie turns its gaze toward the USSR, wondering whether it would not be possible to solve this or that contradiction . . . or all the contradictions together, at the expense of the USSR, of that Land of Soviets, that citadel of revolution, which, by its very existence, is revolutionizing the working class and the colonies. . . .[96]

When the League of Nations convened a World Economic Conference in 1933, Stalin sent Maksim Litvinov to London on a mission similar to the one Lenin had assigned Soviet delegates to Genoa more than a decade earlier. "My government," Litvinov told the conference, "has no desire to cut itself off from the rest of the world by economic barriers, or to withdraw into its own economic shell." Although the Soviet foreign minister insisted that his country was perfectly capable of industrializing with its own resources, he also produced a shopping list of mammoth proportions. Given suitable credit arrangements, the USSR would purchase $1 billion worth of goods from capitalist countries whose economies were said to be collapsing for want of markets.[97]

When the United States established diplomatic relations with the USSR later in 1933, Stalin was certain that Roosevelt's primary interest lay in exports. He told a correspondent from the *New York Times* that "What Litvinov said at the London Economic Conference still holds good. We are the biggest market in the world and are ready to order and pay for a large quantity of goods. But we need favorable credit terms. . . . Other states [e.g. Nazi Germany] have stopped payment, but the USSR has not and will not do so."[98] While nothing came of this initiative, during World War II the Soviet government had reason to think that the Americans would become more accommodating.

In 1943 the U.S. Department of Commerce published *The United States in the World Economy* and predicted that within months of the war's end up to 8 million workers would be unemployed.[99] The economist Paul Samuelson wrote that America might experience "the greatest period of unemployment and industrial dislocation which any economy has ever faced."[100] In the same year Averell Harriman, American ambassador to Moscow, told the Russians that trade would be in the interest of the United States and would play an important role in promoting American "full employment during the period of transition from war-time to peace-time economy."[101] Also in 1943 Donald M. Nelson, chairman of the War Production Board, spoke with Stalin of America's "surplus" production capacity and promised that "We can find a way to do business together."[102] Eric Johnston, president of the U.S. Chamber of Commerce, traveled to Russia in 1944 to discuss postwar trade prospects, and Harry Dexter White told Treasury Secretary Henry Morgenthau that Soviet markets could "make an important contribution to the maintenance of full employment during our transition to a peace economy."[103]

In January 1945 Soviet foreign minister Molotov acted upon these signals and requested $6 billion in credits. Convinced that America needed export markets at least as much as the USSR needed American goods, the Soviet government misjudged Washington's commitment to multilateral trade and lost the opportunity to create working economic ties. American plans for the postwar world emphasized the need for new international institutions in order to stabilize currencies, alleviate temporary imbalances of payments, and avoid the kind of protectionism and competitive devaluations that had destroyed world trade in the 1930s. The United States hoped to liberalize the world economy through measures that the Soviet Union regarded as a threat to central planning.

Four months prior to the Bretton Woods Conference of March 1944, Varga explained the Soviet refusal to surrender any degree of economic independence to the proposed World Bank and International Monetary Fund. Writing in an American business newspaper, *The Commercial and Financial Chronicle*, he noted that participants in the IMF would be required to begin dismantling tariffs, quotas, and other trade restrictions. Such demands were completely unacceptable: "the possibility of any sort of proposals affecting the Soviet Union coming from any future outside organization, whether an international bank or [currency] stabilization fund, is out of the question."[104] It was obvious that the Soviet planned economy could not be reconciled with free international movement of goods and that the Soviet ruble needed no ties with the IMF.

When the United States provided Britain with loans totaling $4.4 billion at the end of 1945, Britain was expected to begin dismantling imperial preferential tariffs and to allow members of the sterling bloc to convert their assets into other currencies. K. Velikanov thought these conditions fully justified Soviet intransigence: "dollar diplomacy" was reducing Britain to the humiliating role of "junior partner" of American imperialism.[105] Varga cited L.S. Amery, a prominent Tory, who argued that the loans and participation in the Bretton Woods institutions contradicted British domestic and overseas interests.[106] Although Stalin sent a representative to the first conference of the IMF in the spring of 1946, the Soviet government declined to join the new institution. Shortly afterward, discussions of an American loan to the Soviet Union were postponed indefinitely.

When representatives of twenty-three countries met in Geneva in the spring of 1947 to negotiate a new framework for international trade —resulting in the General Agreement on Tariffs and Trade (GATT) in October—the USSR again stood aloof. Varga announced that the Soviet government had absolutely no interest in the American project for "international free trade" or the "'open door' principle": "The Soviet Union is not taking part in the Geneva talks . . . because the problems discussed there do not directly concern it in view of its government monopoly of foreign trade, which is one of the immutable elements of its economic system."[107] When the question of Soviet participation in the Marshall Plan arose in 1947, Varga cautioned Molotov that to open Soviet markets to the United States was not advisable: the result might be to postpone an American crisis and slow the decay of capitalism. Molotov wrote on the margin of Varga's letter: "Very important —circulate to all members of the Politburo."[108]

Soviet attitudes toward trade with America reflected deep ambivalence. On the one hand, Stalinists eagerly anticipated an American economic collapse; on the other hand, they repeatedly warned that the consequence might be a U.S.-led attempt to secure new markets and materials through aggression against the "socialist camp." Stalin himself frequently addressed the possibility of war with the United States. In September 1946 he told a *Sunday Times* correspondent that such predictions were capitalist propaganda designed to support an increase of military budgets in order to prevent "rapid growth of unemployment."[109] Three months later he told Elliott Roosevelt that the threat of war was "unrealistic" and that the USSR was still interested in American credits.[110]

In 1948 Roosevelt's former vice-president, Henry Wallace, ran for the Progressive Party in the hope of defeating Truman. Stalin enthusiastically declared that Wallace's program would promote a new era of international cooperation: "despite differences of economic systems and ideology, . . . coexistence . . . and peaceful regulation of differences between the USSR and the USA is not only possible, but absolutely necessary in the interests of world peace."[111] When the Berlin crisis erupted in 1948, Stalin was less optimistic: "The policy of the present leaders of the USA and England is one of aggression and of unleashing a new war."[112] Early in 1951, however, Stalin still hoped that the Korean conflict might be contained: there was no inevitability of a new world war—"at least at the present time."[113]

4. The Peace-Through-Trade Offensive of 1952

Starting from the question of whether peaceful coexistence was a real possibility, early in 1952 two new trends emerged in Soviet thought concerning international economic relations. One group of writers argued that access to socialist markets would alleviate capitalist contradictions and reduce the likelihood of war; another replied that the world relation of forces had shifted in favor of socialism—with the implication that the Soviet Union had no business rescuing imperialists from their own rivalries and internal contradictions. Both views were based upon evidence in the Western press of disagreements between prominent capitalists and their governments concerning trade with the Soviet bloc.

   The United States had linked Marshall Plan aid to restrictions on West European exports of strategic goods to socialist countries. In 1951 the chairman of the British Board of Trade expressed the resentment of European allies: "America has not and does not need to have any significant trade with the Soviet Union. It means little or nothing to her to discontinue the importation of furs, caviar and crab. With us things are quite different. We obtain from the Soviet bloc essential foods and raw materials—and we believe that in these trade exchanges we get as good as we give, economically and strategically."[114] The *Economist* of London protested that Washington's insistence on trade restrictions implied that "America's allies are disloyal or that they are incapable of deciding for themselves what is the balance of gain and loss in their exchanges with the Communist countries—in short, that they are either fools or rascals."[115]

A CIA memorandum complained in the autumn of 1950 that "The reluctance of Western European governments to restrict exports of security items to the Soviet orbit . . . stems in part from their concern with maintaining and developing export markets in areas capable of supplying in return 'dollar-saving' food and raw materials. The importance of 'East-West' trade in contributing to the solution of Western Europe's balance of payments problem has been taken as axiomatic."[116] The influential *Christian Science Monitor* similarly wrote that "The United States' European allies are all suffering economically from the postwar blockade of East-West trade. Their dependence on American economic aid is primarily a result of this blockade. . . . [W]ere European manufactured products again to flow Eastward in return for Eastern raw material, it is probable that Western Europe could swiftly regain its independence from American economic aid."[117]

Hoping to cultivate these tensions, the Soviet Union announced that an international trade conference would be held in Moscow in April 1952. As expected, the initiative provoked a positive response in several European countries. N. Osipenko listed numerous officials who supported the proposal. Gunnar Myrdal, executive secretary of the UN Economic Commission for Europe, complained of unnatural restrictions of East-West trade.[118] The Paris newspaper *Figaro* wrote that West European countries were "interested in the maintenance of trade with the East, since if it is completely disrupted the European countries will be more dependent than ever on the dollar area."[119] Harold Wilson, a minister in Britain's former Labour government, declared that "we should resume our freedom to develop our trade with Eastern Europe and other parts of the world which can send us the goods we need and will take the goods we can sell."[120] Anthony Eden, foreign secretary in the new Conservative government, took the same view: "Britain needs the materials she is getting from the Soviet Union, especially timber and coarse grains. . . . It is not a wise principle to cut off trade between East and West."[121]

In light of these responses, an anonymous article in the journal *Voprosy ekonomiki* hinted that doctrinal traditions dating from the quarrel over "socialism in one country" during the 1920s should be reconsidered. Stalin had been the author of this doctrine, opposing Trotsky's view that the economy of the USSR must be reintegrated into the world division of labor. Without mentioning Trotsky, the article in *Voprosy ekonomiki* repeated the arguments he had made almost three decades earlier: it was an "abnormal situation" for world trade to move "in two parallel . . . world markets" isolated from each other, for "internationalization" of production and exchange objectively resulted from the "historically formed international division of labor."[122] The author contended that only fascist countries strive for "a closed-in, autarkic national economy"[123] whereas Stalin favored "loyal, peace-loving relations with all countries."[124]

The same article insisted that history demonstrated real trade potential in Soviet-American relations. For a brief period at the beginning of the First Five-Year Plan, the Soviet Union and the United States had been important partners. In particular, American heavy industry had benefited from exports to the USSR:

> During the world economic crisis, in 1930, the Soviet Union was the only one of 38 countries that not only did not reduce, but even increased its trade with the United States of America. At that time the Soviet Union occupied second place, and in 1931 first place, in American exports of industrial equipment. In 1931 the USA shipped to the Soviet Union 74% of its total exports of foundry equipment, 70% of crushing equipment, 68% of forging equipment, 67% of agricultural machinery, 65% of lathes, etc. Millions of American workers were at that time guaranteed work thanks to Soviet orders.[125]

In the early months of 1952 several economists endorsed the idea that restoration of East-West trade would create a material basis for peaceful coexistence. Ya. Kotkovsky pointed out that even in 1946 the Soviet Union had taken up to 25 percent of all American exports of metalworking equipment.[126] A. Smirnov wrote that "The Soviet Union, the Chinese People's Republic and the European countries of people's democracy represent an enormous potential market for sales of the goods of all countries. . . ."[127] P. Yefanov maintained that the working class of both Western Europe and the United States had "a vital interest in the successful outcome of the International Economic Conference."[128] E.S. Shershnev referred to Lenin's view that "sensible representatives of the bourgeoisie" would also recognize that a planned economy represented an important export market that was "not subject to crisis fluctuations."[129] On the day before the conference assembled, Stalin gave it his personal blessing:

The peaceful coexistence of capitalism and communism is quite possible provided there is a mutual desire to cooperate, readiness to carry out agreed commitments, and observance of the principle of equality and non-interference in the internal affairs of other states.[130]

The conference opened in Moscow's House of Trade Unions on April 3, 1952, with nearly five hundred representatives from more than forty countries. In preparation the Soviet government had appointed M.V. Nesterov as president of a USSR Chamber of Commerce. In a speech resembling Litvinov's performance at the London conference in 1933, Nesterov announced that the Soviet Union was willing to treble its trade with capitalist countries within three years and to provide employment for up to 2 million foreign workers.[131] Soviet plans were already in place for trade expansion with Britain, France, Italy, the Netherlands, Belgium, Sweden, Norway, Denmark, Switzerland, West Germany, the United States, Latin America, Japan, Southeast Asia, and the Near and Middle East. Nesterov's shopping list included both consumer goods and industrial equipment, in return for which the Soviet Union proposed to export grain, materials, coal, oil products, and its own industrial goods.

While a few contracts were signed in Moscow by firms from Britain and France, the main importance of the conference was political. Neither the Soviet Union nor any of its allies had hard currency with which to purchase a significant volume of imports, but they did hope that barter exchanges might weaken trade restrictions and Washington's ties with Western Europe.[132] To sustain the momentum of the conference, a Committee for the Promotion of International Trade was formed. Twenty-nine representatives were elected to the committee, including Joan Robinson from England and Oskar Lange from Poland, two economists who commanded international respect.[133] Immediately following the departure of foreign delegates, however, Soviet conservatives undertook to sabotage the proposed opening to the west on the grounds that capitalists would benefit more than the USSR.

5. The Second Stage of Capitalism's General Crisis

The first conservative response came in an article by G.V. Kozlov, entitled "The General Crisis of Capitalism and Its Intensification at the Current Stage." Kozlov returned to traditional Stalinist themes by emphasizing division of the world into two opposing systems and by analyzing the general crisis in terms of three periods: the "first round of wars and revolutions" lasting until 1923; the period of rotten stabilization in the 1920s; and a third period, distinguished by the "depression of a special kind" and continuing until World War II.[134] As a result of the Second World War, however, an entirely new, "second stage of the general crisis" was said to have begun. The "decisive factor" of the second stage was departure of more than 550 million people in Eastern Europe and China from the world capitalist system. Kozlov argued that this dramatic contraction of markets signaled "a sharp change in the relation of forces between the two systems."[135]

With regard to trade, Kozlov quoted Stalin (in 1921!) saying that "normal" economic cooperation presupposed "international proletarian revolution."[136] In other words, normal trade could only be conducted within the Council of Mutual Economic Assistance (Comecon) formed by the socialist countries in 1949. Kozlov acknowledged that socialist countries were interested in "economic cooperation with other countries," but he also asserted that the imperialists feared peaceful competition "and for this reason they set their hopes on military adventures."[137] Consolidation of "two parallel world markets" was the inevitable consequence of capitalism's rottenness and decay,[138] which in turn led to "fascization" and proved that "imperialism inevitably gives rise to wars."[139] Kozlov vowed that new wars would bring the imperialists "nothing but catastrophe."[140]

Kozlov's article appeared in the April issue of *Voprosy ekonomiki*. The May issue carried an unsigned article taking exactly the opposite view and praising the Moscow conference as "an important step on the way to expanding international trade." The anonymous author pointed out that Stalin, on the eve of the conference, had confirmed the possibility of peaceful coexistence, and this was interpreted to mean that trade might make a significant contribution to demobilization of capitalist war economies. Not only would the capitalists secure the markets they needed, but in addition "The resources, acquired through reduction of military appropriations, could be used to satisfy the essential needs of the toilers—for construction of housing, hospitals and schools."[141] Who was responsible for this article remains unclear, but it is worth noting that Varga's *Changes in the Economic Structure of Capitalism* had also proposed alleviation of the problem of markets by substituting public works for armaments.

The very same issue of *Voprosy ekonomiki* also included another opposing article from A. Alekseev on "The Strengthening of the

Parasitism and Decay of Contemporary Capitalism." Quoting data on capitalist military spending, Alekseev repeated Kozlov's reference to a new stage of the general crisis and insisted that "reduction of purchasing power on the part of the broad popular masses" threatened the economies of America, Britain, France, and other imperialist countries with "an economic crash."[142] If the capitalist world was on the verge of collapse, Alekseev believed that the Soviet Union had no interest in delaying it.

In May 1952 the party journal *Bol'shevik* published a further article on the same topic by V.A. Cheprakov. Like Kozlov and Alekseev, he too stressed formation of the socialist "world market" and "division of the world into two systems."[143] "Further narrowing of the sphere of capitalism's domination," he wrote, "has significantly complicated the problem of external markets."[144] While Cheprakov thought it possible that the west would pursue trade with the "camp of socialism,"[145] he also recalled Stalin's warning in 1930 that capitalists always hope to resolve their internal contradictions at the expense of the USSR. After World War II, Stalin had repeated his warning: "In his speech at the election meeting . . . in Moscow on 9 February, 1946, comrade Stalin gave a genius-like analysis of the causes of two world wars and demonstrated the inevitability of wars under imperialism. . . ."[146] Cheprakov added that were the imperialists to persist in their aggressive course, it would "cost them much more dearly than the first and second world wars."[147]

When the nineteenth party congress met in October 1952, these issues remained unresolved. With Stalin in physical decline, G.M. Malenkov, a prominent member of the politburo, delivered the main report. He began by remarking that "The disintegration of the single world market is the most important economic result of the Second World War. . . ."[148] But Malenkov took care to emphasize that it was the imperialists—not the Soviet Union—who bore total responsibility both for postwar divisions and for the economic consequences. American unemployment resulted from the fact that the ruling circles deprived their own industry of markets in the USSR, China, and Eastern Europe. In the case of Western Europe, it was again the Americans who cut these countries off from their traditional trading partners. The American "blockade" not only damaged capitalist interests directly; it was also the main reason for the "strengthening of a new world socialist market. Thus the imperialists dealt a serious blow to their own exports and even reinforced the contradictions between the production capacity of their industry and the possibilities of selling their products."

On the issue of a new war, Malenkov found his own quotation from Stalin. In 1939 Stalin had told the eighteenth party congress that "We stand for peace and the strengthening of business-like relations with all countries . . . so long as they do not try to violate the interests of our country." This quotation was selected with obvious care, for the Molotov-Ribbentrop pact had followed Stalin's address, committing the Soviet Union to supply Hitler while Germany prepared for war against Britain and France. Malenkov pointed out that today the imperialists might again split among themselves over export markets. Peaceful coexistence and economic cooperation were real possibilities—if not with all capitalist countries, then at least with some:

> While the American-British militant circles affirm that only the arms race can keep industry running in the capitalist countries, in reality there is another perspective—that of the development and expansion of trade relations between all countries, regardless of differences between their social systems, which could keep the industry of the industrially developed countries running for many years. . . .

In his closing remarks Malenkov made his own preference clear in a notable departure from the prevailing view of two parallel world markets: the alternative to war was "restoration of a *single international market* and other similar measures in the spirit of strengthening the peace."[149] This appears to have been the first time since Stalin's struggle with Trotsky when a leading Soviet figure spoke of the world market as an integral whole. It also suggests that it was Malenkov who had encouraged economists to support trade with the west despite conservative opposition. This possibility seems all the more plausible in view of Malenkov's efforts to expand international ties after Stalin's death in the spring of 1953.

Stalin's own final thoughts came in *Economic Problems of Socialism in the USSR*, published at the time of the nineteenth congress. In a section devoted to "Disintegration of the Single World Market and Deepening of the Crisis of the World Capitalist System," Stalin granted that while a new war (as Malenkov said) may not involve the Soviet Union, "the inevitability of wars between capitalist countries remains in force."[150] Britain, France, and other Marshall Plan recipients would be "compelled in the end to break from the embrace of the USA" in order to protect their own industries and their colonial empires.[151] German imperialism had recovered from the First World War and imposition of the Dawes Plan; the British and French would likewise throw off the economic subordination resulting from the Marshall Plan. The historical cycle of imperialist struggles indicated that "To eliminate the inevitability of war, it is necessary to abolish imperialism."[152]

On the question of relations between the socialist and capitalist countries, Stalin wrote in terms of broad historical perspectives. The single "all-embracing world market" had ended when China and the European people's democracies joined with the Soviet Union to create "a united and powerful socialist camp, confronting the camp of capitalism."[153] Formation of "two parallel world markets"—as distinct from the "single international market" mentioned by Malenkov—meant that the problem of markets would grow in intensity. Luxemburg had predicted that imperialism would collapse when all colonial third-party markets had been seized; Stalin was equally certain that capitalism's geographical contraction must result in "further deepening of the general crisis of the world capitalist system."[154] "Relative stability of markets" was impossible because

> the sphere of exploitation of the world's resources by the major capitalist countries (the USA, England, France) will not expand, but contract; . . . their opportunities for sale in the world market will deteriorate, and . . . their industries will be operating more and more below capacity. That, in fact, is what is meant by the deepening of the general crisis of the world capitalist system in connection with the break-up of the world market.[155]

Economic Problems was Stalin's legacy to Soviet economists. When he died on March 5, 1953, he left behind a community of researchers whose thinking was frozen in analogies inherited from the 1930s. The capitalist countries were entering one of the longest periods of economic growth in history; the Stalinist view held that they were languishing in a chronic depression of a special kind. Working-class living standards would soon surpass anything imaginable in the 1930s; Stalinists predicted absolute impoverishment and unemployment for tens of millions. Capitalist countries were incorporating welfare-state measures into the fabric of modern life; Stalinist doctrine claimed that control of the state by monopolies and their reactionary political agents inevitably produced a one-sided war economy.

Only when Malenkov became leader of the Soviet government and Stalin's apparent successor did it gradually become possible for economists to resume their work without fear of political reprisals. When Malenkov proposed his own "New Deal" for the Soviet Union, his supporters realized that to change domestic priorities would require access to western resources through trade. Malenkov's attempt to improve living standards in the Soviet Union ultimately contributed to Khrushchev's redefinition of foreign policy in terms of peaceful coexistence and peaceful transition to socialism. Within three years of Stalin's departure, the most controversial propositions in Varga's *Changes in the Economic Structure of Capitalism* were embraced by Khrushchev as official party doctrine.

CHAPTER 4

MALENKOV'S "NEW DEAL" AND THE "GENERAL CRISIS" OF STALINISM

In *The Eighteenth Brumaire of Louis Bonaparte*, Marx made the famous comment that "Men make their own history, but they do not make it just as they please. . . . The tradition of all the dead generations weighs like a nightmare on the brain of the living."[1] For half a decade after Stalin's death, the nightmare of Varga's ordeal in the late 1940s weighed upon the minds of his colleagues. Under Malenkov and Khrushchev the Communist Party scrutinized economists less closely than in Stalin's time, but it was not until 1958 that the traditions of classical Marxist theory could be freely cited in reappraising the relation between business cycles and capitalism's "general crisis."

Stalinism foreclosed such debate by compressing postwar capitalism into rigid ideological categories contrived in the 1930s. Stalin's world consisted of polar opposites: in international relations, there were "two camps" and two parallel world markets; in the capitalist countries, there were monopolists and the exploited masses; in terms of economic systems, there were one-sided fascist war economies and socialist planned economies; in social science research, there were "correct" views and "errors." As a result of controversies with Varga and his associates at the Institute of World Economy and World Politics, the Stalinist system of thought ended in self-closure; differences of opinion were suppressed, and "facts" had to be determined according to authoritative truths of which Stalin alone was the final arbiter. *Economic Problems of Socialism in the USSR* became the definitive statement of Stalinist orthodoxy.

Immediately after his death, however, Stalin's successors in the party and government leadership realized that modern capitalism involved none of the certainties of official doctrine. The story of Soviet debates after

1953 became one of dismantling Stalinist dichotomies to take into account a plurality of political and economic forces in the capitalist countries. Varga had argued that Roosevelt made use of ruling-class divisions to undertake third-party mediation of class conflict. By the mid-1950s the implications of a divided ruling class became the leitmotif of reformist thought and undermined the Stalinist contention that monopoly capital inevitably subjugated the state. Varga's thesis concerning peaceful transition to socialism encouraged Khrushchev's decision that the monopolies' hold on the state apparatus might be challenged by a multi-class coalition committed to democratic reform.

Varga had stressed internal contradictions of the capitalist class as the condition for Roosevelt's autonomy; other economists had argued that the Soviet Union might itself play the role of third party on an international scale, opening markets in order to divide capitalist countries and keep the Soviet Union out of war. When Malenkov became head of government in 1953, he hoped that Soviet domestic disproportions, resulting from the heavy industrial priorities of Stalinist planning, might be remedied through better access to the world market. Soviet projects for trade expansion assumed that capitalist economies depended upon socialist markets and that enlightened capitalists would prefer trade to war. The belief that capitalist prosperity required socialist markets did not give way to more realistic appraisals until the "depression of a special kind" was discredited in the 1950s by sustained growth in all western countries. By the middle of the decade it also became obvious that military spending could increase aggregate demand and support a cyclical expansion of domestic markets. The "general crisis" of Stalinist thought came when the theories of "depression of a special kind" and "absolute" proletarian impoverishment were officially abandoned under Khrushchev.

1. Stalin's Economic "Laws" and Malenkov's "New Deal"

In *Economic Problems of Socialism in the USSR*, Stalin spoke of political economy as if it were a physical science: "the laws of economic development" were "objective laws, reflecting processes . . . that take place independently of the will of people."[2] But Stalin also maintained that "people can discover laws, get to know them and master them, learn to apply them with full understanding, utilize them in the interests of society, and thus subjugate them, secure mastery over them."[3] The meaning of this paradox was that economic laws operated independently of the will of Soviet workers; they were discovered, mastered and applied by planners, party leaders, and ultimately by Stalin himself.

Stalin argued that socialist economic laws resulted in "balanced, proportionate development"; those of capitalism produced a "one-sided" war economy. He compared the two systems as follows:

> the basic economic law of modern capitalism might be formulated roughly in this way: the securing of the *maximum capitalist profit through the exploitation, ruin and impoverishment of the majority of the population of the given country*, through the enslavement and systematic robbery of the peoples of other countries, especially backward countries, and lastly, through *wars and militarization* of the national economy. . . .[4]

> the basic law of socialism might be formulated roughly in this way: the securing of the maximum satisfaction of the continuously growing material and cultural requirements of the whole of society through the uninterrupted expansion and perfection of socialist production on the basis of higher technologies.[5]

In reality, Stalinist planning served militarization in the identical manner attributed to capitalism. G.M. Malenkov made this point in a speech to the Supreme Soviet in August 1953. He complained that heavy industry's share of total output had risen from 34 percent in 1924/25 to no less than 70 percent in 1953. In view of this striking one-sidedness, Malenkov decided that Stalin's own law of "balanced, proportionate development" made increased production of consumer goods the country's most immediate and "urgent task." Malenkov's priorities included the same kind of policies as Varga had expected in postwar America: improvement of social services, expansion of industries producing traditional consumer goods, and even partial conversion of heavy industry to manufacture such consumer durables as televisions, motorcycles, and refrigerators. Noting "the desire of business circles in a number of countries to remove discriminatory measures of every description," Malenkov associated domestic reform with a commitment to pursue trade "with even greater persistence."[6]

Malenkov's program came to be known as the *Novyi Kurs,* normally translated in the west as the "New Course." But his real intention was to introduce a Soviet version of the *New Deal*, which in Russian was also known as the *Novyi Kurs*. Malenkov proposed to do for the USSR what

Varga claimed Roosevelt had done for America in the 1930s; that is, to shore up the existing order by making timely concessions to popular needs. Theoretical justification for a Soviet New Deal came in a *Pravda* article by Ts. Stepanyan, who admitted that even in socialism "there is a contradiction between production and consumption." Under capitalism this contradiction involved "relative and absolute impoverishment of the proletariat"; in the case of socialism it took the form of a disparity "between the needs of the whole people, which grow without limit, and the level of development . . . in the production of material and cultural goods."[7]

Malenkov introduced his New Deal in the middle of the Fifth Five-Year Plan, embracing the years 1950-55. With domestic resources already committed, it was imperative that his change of priorities be accompanied by growing East-West trade. When the new American president, Dwight D. Eisenhower, declared in April 1953 that no dispute, "great or small, is insoluble," *Pravda* replied that the Soviet Union welcomed "development of international cooperation" regardless of differences between social systems.[8] *Pravda* attributed Eisenhower's realism to the fact that Britain and other allies of the United States were no longer willing to see their trade with the "democratic camp dictated from Washington." Malenkov also quoted Eisenhower's remarks and personally stated that "there are no disputes or outstanding issues today that cannot be settled peacefully by mutual agreement."[9]

Economists who supported Malenkov's program were predictably anxious to deny the inevitability of war. In *Economic Problems,* Stalin had declared that while the USSR might avoid entanglement in inter-imperialist struggles, "To eliminate the inevitability of war, it is necessary to abolish imperialism."[10] In May 1953, A. Nikonov saw quite a different prospect. Anticipating "serious improvement of the international situation,"[11] Nikonov denied that the USSR had any interest in "export of revolution" and condemned the "criminal goals" of those who were spreading "malicious fabrications of the inevitability of war." Echoing Malenkov, he assured capitalist groups who were interested in mutually advantageous trade that the Soviet Union favored relaxation of the Cold War through reestablishing "a single world market."[12]

Following the armistice in Korea in July 1953, Yu. Pavlov similarly dismissed the "fatal inevitability" of war as western propaganda intended to tighten the blockade of socialist countries and to impose West European unity "under the aegis of the United States."[13] According to

Pavlov, many West European capitalists were already recognizing that their real interest lay in trade with the "democratic countries." The Marshall Plan had sought to deprive European countries of their sovereignty, but the end of the Korean conflict created opportunities to restore an independent foreign policy and to correct imbalances with the dollar area by substituting trade with the Soviet Union and Eastern Europe.

To Malenkov's supporters it seemed that Western Europe and the socialist countries were natural economic partners. War-induced disproportions in Europe and plan-induced disproportions in the Soviet Union might be simultaneously redressed through Soviet supply of materials in exchange for equipment and manufactured goods. A comprehensive study of international trade, edited by I.S. Potapov, G.S. Roginsky, and Yu.N. Kapelinsky, referred to Lenin's view that capitalist countries needed trade not, as Luxemburg argued, because of a chronic problem of markets, but in order to rectify domestic disproportions. Contrary to Luxemburg's theory, which predicted an "automatic crash of capitalism," the authors thought Lenin's approach explained why European capitalists were anxious to supply socialist markets while the United States wanted to preserve Cold War trade restrictions.[14]

In April 1953, the UN Economic Commission for Europe organized an experts' conference on East-West European trade in Geneva, followed by a meeting of the International Chamber of Commerce in Vienna. M.V. Nesterov indicated that these discussions revealed "a profound difference of attitude between the United States and . . . Western Europe."[15] In February 1954, Nesterov reported that the Federation of British Industries wanted to expand trade with the Soviet Union and China and that a delegation of British manufacturers was currently in Moscow for that purpose. At a reception for the British representatives, USSR Minister of Foreign Trade Anastas I. Mikoyan expressed Soviet willingness to make purchases worth more than 400 million pounds sterling.[16] The delegation left Moscow with orders for fishing vessels, textile and food-industry equipment, diesel power plants, and electric substations.[17]

Nesterov expected that similar pressures would continue to grow in all of the leading capitalist countries. He referred to an article in *Les Echos*, a journal of French manufacturers, calling for business delegations to search out markets in the Soviet Union, China, and Eastern Europe. He also assured Soviet readers that the Eisenhower administration faced growing demands from American capitalists to increase contacts with the socialist countries. Warren Lee Pierson, chairman of the United States Council of the International Chamber of Commerce, was quoted saying:

> international trade is . . . the broad highway to peace. . . . I would like to see a re-examination of our East-West trade policy. . . . Re-establishment of traditional markets, or even development of new ones . . . will . . . do more than embargoes to head off a shooting war.[18]

Nesterov thought that Pierson's statement reflected "a quite understandable desire of certain American business circles to . . . [recognize] the bankruptcy of the . . . policy of trade discrimination and blockade."[19] In August 1954 his faith in "more sober-minded representatives of the business world" seemed to be justified. The United States acceded to European proposals for a significant reduction in the number of goods on western embargo lists.[20] According to Philip J. Funigiello, an American historian of trade during the Cold War, the Eisenhower administration made these concessions in order to preserve harmony within NATO and to prevent a total collapse of export controls.[21] The *New York Times* commented at the time that the European countries "desperately need the business to keep their economies going."[22]

During his tenure as premier, Malenkov made modest trade gains and did enjoy some success in playing European interests against the United States. Growth of trade was far too limited, however, to support a fundamental reorientation of the Soviet domestic economy. The total value of Soviet trade by 1955 was twice that of 1950, yet nearly 80 percent was still with socialist countries.[23] By 1956 the share of total trade with industrial capitalist countries was only 16.8 percent (having risen from 14.5 percent in 1953).[24] Unable to break out of the five-year plan, Malenkov failed to deliver a significant increase of consumer goods and became vulnerable to allegations that he underestimated the Stalinist economic law requiring priority for investments in heavy industry.

At a plenary meeting of the Central Committee in January 1955, Khrushchev solicited military support in his power struggle with Malenkov by insisting that continued expansion of heavy industry was the "main task" and that it was an intolerable, "anti-Leninist," and "rightist deviation" to urge the primacy of the light and food sectors. Quoting Stalin, Khrushchev warned that Malenkov's neglect of heavy industry would reduce the USSR to "an appendage of the world capitalist economic system" and pose the risk of another invasion.[25] In February,

Malenkov was replaced as premier by N.A. Bulganin. In March, K.V. Ostrovityanov—Varga's nemesis in 1947-48—condemned "vulgarizing interpretations of the basic economic law of socialism."[26] Quoting both Lenin and Stalin, Ostrovityanov declared that in order to raise material and cultural living standards, it was necessary first to continue concentrating on domestic production of new machinery and technologies.

Khrushchev skillfully exploited Malenkov's departures from orthodoxy, but his attack on the so-called "rightist deviation" proved to be more rhetorical than real. Certainly he had no intention of relenting in the attempt to expand trade. Until the capitalists became more accommodating, he proposed ambitious measures to coordinate the plans of socialist countries through Comecon. Specialization within this organization was to create a socialist division of labor and free a portion of domestic resources in order gradually to fulfill Malenkov's commitments to light industry and agriculture.[27] In the meantime, Khrushchev eagerly promoted economic relations with Western Europe. By 1960 trade with developed capitalist countries was more than double what it had been in the mid-1950s,[28] having grown at an average rate of more than 16 percent per year.[29]

In February 1956, the twentieth party congress passed a resolution enthusiastically supporting Khrushchev's program. The "course of improving relations, strengthening confidence and developing cooperation with all countries" was described as "absolutely correct."[30] In April, Khrushchev and Bulganin made a highly publicized trip to Britain and urged rapid expansion of sales to the USSR. Suffering from chronic balance of payments difficulties, Britain had frequently evaded western controls. Khrushchev promised that lucrative orders for industrial equipment were waiting to be placed.[31] Of seventy-seven types of equipment that he offered to purchase, forty-two were either banned, restricted, or of questionable availability to socialist countries.[32] Anastas Mikoyan, involved in one capacity or another with Soviet trade since the 1920s, endorsed efforts to break the embargo and agreed with Khrushchev that "The time is gone when the Soviet land of socialism existed in isolation." Regarding commerce as the material foundation of stable international relations, Mikoyan insisted that peaceful coexistence was "unthinkable without trade" and a "rational division of labor between peoples."[33]

Reporting on Khrushchev's trip to Britain, Nesterov repeatedly denied claims in the western press to the effect that the Soviet planning system and state monopoly of foreign trade entailed a commitment to self-sufficiency. Were it not for western restrictions, the USSR would purchase up to 6 or 7 percent of total British exports.[34] Z.V. Sviridova reminded businessmen of the advantages provided by a "stable market" in socialist planned economies: "The doors of this market are open to commodities from the capitalist countries, and some of these countries have already had the opportunity to see for themselves that peaceful coexistence and economic cooperation . . . are profitable for both sides."[35]

Although Khrushchev condemned Malenkov on the grounds that his "New Deal" violated Stalinist planning priorities, he also dismayed the twentieth party congress with his famous "secret speech," which portrayed Stalin as a megalomaniacal killer who had committed mass atrocities against the party and the Soviet people.[36] Following his denunciation of Stalin's crimes, Khrushchev denied any intention to "export" revolution, appealed for a "united front" with social democrats to prevent war, and even endorsed Varga's projection of peaceful transition to socialism:

> it is possible to defeat the reactionary anti-popular forces, to win a stable majority in parliament, and to convert it from an organ of bourgeois democracy into an instrument of genuine popular will. In that case, this traditional institution of many highly developed capitalist countries can become an organ of genuine democracy, democracy for the toilers.[37]

In 1947 Varga had been forced to censure "reformists"—himself included—for thinking that "they can turn the bourgeois state into an instrument of the working class and, through peaceful reforms, reach socialism without a revolution."[38] After the twentieth party congress the top Soviet leadership became reformist in exactly the sense of Varga's self-criticism. Khrushchev allowed that "in countries where capitalism is still strong and has a huge military and police apparatus at its disposal, the reactionary forces will, of course, inevitably offer serious resistance." On the other hand, he also assured the congress that "The winning of a stable parliamentary majority . . . could create for the working class of a number of capitalist . . . countries the conditions needed to secure fundamental social changes."[39] Anastas Mikoyan took the same view: the USSR had no interest in exporting "bloody civil war" to the capitalist countries because, in modern conditions, it was possible for the working class to organize for elections and come to power "using the existing parliamentary institutions."[40]

Khrushchev understood the folly of attempting to improve relations with western governments while simultaneously urging their overthrow by foreign communist parties. From the Stalinist perspective, however, his ideas were preposterous. In *Economic Problems*, Stalin had claimed that not even "coalescence" adequately described the relation between the state and the monopolies; the correct formulation was "*subjugation* of the state machine to the monopolies."[41] Stalin attributed one function to the state: to terrorize workers in order to extract taxes with which to finance the armaments industry and guarantee "maximum capitalist profit." Khrushchev's policy implied the opposite; that is, the possibility of redirecting government spending—even before full socialist planning—for the purpose of increasing employment and working-class incomes.

2. Monopolies and the State

In order to make sense of Khrushchev's new views, economists had to reassess both the political power of monopoly capital and Keynesian theories of fiscal policy. The problem was to relate peaceful transition to the two opposing views of the state inherited from the 1930s. Since progressive reforms were clearly impossible in a fascist war economy, it had to follow that a reform-minded coalition could execute the kind of "left maneuver" that Varga had seen in the New Deal. Since the Moscow trade conference of 1952, it had become commonplace in Soviet literature to emphasize the opportunities created by capitalist rivalries over socialist markets. If a real possibility existed for domestic reforms in the capitalist countries, the implication appeared to be that the capitalist class must also be divided over internal policies of taxation and social expenditure.

One of the first hints of a revision of Soviet thinking on internal politics in the west came in a new book by Varga entitled *Basic Questions of the Economics and Politics of Imperialism (After the Second World War)*. The title reflected Varga's response to criticisms that his previous work had been characterized by a technical-economic approach and had omitted the politics of class struggle. The new work was also a product of the troubled times during which it was written. A first draft was completed in 1948-51; it then had to be revised in 1952-53 to take account of Stalin's *Economic Problems*; and a final version was published in August 1953.

To correct his earlier errors, Varga devoted twelve chapters to a Stalinist account of the "depression of a special kind," subjugation of the state by the monopolies, and similarities between postwar America and Nazi Germany. Writing his conclusions after Stalin's death, however, he contradicted the main body of his own text by pointing to differences within the ruling class over domestic as well as foreign economic policy. The key passage reads as follows:

> The most reactionary, militant section of the industrial magnates of the USA wants a new world war. By contrast, the bourgeoisie producing commodities for peaceful consumption suffers from narrowness of the market due to extraordinary military expenditures; they are interested in the liquidation of war hysteria, in concluding a peace in Korea, and in peaceful regulation of all questions in dispute between the two camps. . . .[42]

In 1947 Varga had claimed that his analysis of class relations was perfectly consistent with Lenin's *Imperialism*. Lenin had thought that the capitalist class included both monopolists and unorganized capitalists, or small businessmen whose interests could not be the same as those of banks, trusts, and cartels. Lenin criticized Bukharin's "pure imperialism" on the grounds that it was "an incorrect generalisation of everything that was said of the syndicates, cartels, trusts and finance capitalism, when finance capitalism was depicted as though it had none of the foundations of the old capitalism under it."[43] Almost immediately after Stalin's death, a number of economists began to think that the theory of state "subjugation" to monopoly capital sounded more like "pure imperialism" than the analysis found in Lenin's writings.

Reviewing Varga's book in May 1954, A.G. Mileikovsky hailed it as a constructive departure from (Stalinist) "abstract schemes" and "an important landmark not only in the scientific creativity of its author, but also in the work of the Institute of Economics of the USSR Academy of Sciences."[44] Mileikovsky's only reservation was that Varga had not sufficiently emphasized the political consequences of economic tensions within the ruling class. In particular, Varga should have elaborated the possibilities for social reform through isolating the most reactionary monopolists from other elements of their own class. Mileikovsky made this point in terms almost identical to Varga's explanation of the New Deal in the 1930s:

The intensification of the basic contradiction of capitalism leads not only to growth of class contradictions between the bourgeoisie and the proletariat, but also to greater rivalry between separate groups of the bourgeoisie. . . . [T]he monopolies . . . deprive the nonmonopoly bourgeoisie of the opportunity to acquire an average profit. . . . For precisely this reason it is possible, in the struggle against the financial oligarchy . . . to create a broad popular coalition, which, in addition to the toilers and the petty bourgeoisie, *might also temporarily include certain groups of the nonmonopoly bourgeoisie.*[45]

In the same month as Mileikovsky's review appeared, Valentin S. Zorin, a specialist on American politics, took a similar approach in the journal *Kommunist*. Although he paid lip service to Stalinism by speaking of a "concrete and immediate" threat of fascism, Zorin placed his real emphasis on conflict between various monopoly groups as each strove to have its own representatives in control of state offices. While the most powerful monopolists—the Morgans, Rockefellers, Du Ponts, Mellons, and Kuhn-Loeb—continued to be based on Wall Street, younger rivals were now said to be emerging in the northwestern and southwestern states. Zorin claimed that the "most reactionary, chauvinistic and imperialistic elements of American finance capital" were behind McCarthyism, "the American variant of fascism," but he also noted that the Democratic Party still included "a so-called liberal wing," which represented more moderate capitalist elements and was inclined to make concessions to workers and farmers.[46] Preparing for the 1954 elections, the American Communist Party had drawn the appropriate conclusions by adopting a new political strategy, which Zorin summarized this way:

The draft program says that it is necessary to create a new political majority, which could both change the composition of government and compel the newly elected congress to adopt a new direction in foreign and domestic affairs. . . . It would be a government and congress created by a broad alliance of classes: the working class, the poor and middle farmers, the urban intermediate strata, nonmonopoly groups of capitalists and the less reactionary circles of big capital. . . . it would be a broad coalition of class forces with the goal of blocking extreme reaction (McCarthyism) and averting . . . a direct threat of war.[47]

In January 1955, *Kommunist* gave William Z. Foster the opportunity to speak directly on behalf of American Communists. Like Zorin, Foster traced "ultrareactionary and fascist tendencies" to Wall Street but denied that the Eisenhower administration was fascist "as such."[48] Given a "lack of unity on the part of monopoly capital in the attempt to establish a comprehensive fascist system," Foster maintained that the threat of reaction could be averted through an alliance of "the working class, toiling farmers, negroes, the intelligentsia and broad strata of small entrepreneurs." By imposing political curbs on the monopolies, it would be possible—as Varga had claimed in 1946-47—to curtail the military budget, expand public works, improve social security programs, reduce taxes for low-income groups, and provide credits to small farmers.[49]

Writing in the journal *Mezhdunarodnaya zhizn'* (International Affairs), Yu.A. Shvedkov reported that midwestern capitalists were demanding tax reductions and a "cheap" foreign policy because their primary interest lay in domestic markets:[50] "The position in the camp of the financial oligarchy of the USA . . . is characterized by a deepening of internal contradictions, intensive rivalry between various groups, discord and a genuine civil war between them."[51] S.M. Men'shikov affirmed that "There is only one, extremely small, section of the population in the capitalist countries for whom the armament drive means prosperity—the bosses of the war monopolies."[52] V.G. Solodovnikov referred to contradictions "between big capital, which acquires fabulous profits from the arms race, and medium and small capitalists, who produce civilian goods and are forced to surrender part of their surplus value to the monopolies in the form of taxes. . . . This is . . . why the small and medium bourgeoisie in all the capitalist countries, and even certain circles of the big bourgeoisie, are now beginning all the more decisively to oppose military hysteria. . . ."[53]

Even some Soviet conservatives attached new importance to ruling-class disunity. In an article entitled "The Bourgeois State—An Instrument for the Enrichment of Monopolies," I.I. Kuz'minov described an acute struggle "between separate groups of the ruling classes, between separate cliques of monopolists." Although he approvingly cited Stalin's law of "maximum capitalist profit," Kuz'minov explained it by repeating Mileikovsky's view that monopolies expropriated "part of the profits of small and medium firms, which often do not receive even the average profit and go under."[54] V.P. Glushkov took the same view: arms expenditures allowed monopolies to seize "a part of the surplus value received by their . . . . competitors, [which means] robbing and ruining the small and medium bourgeoisie . . . and leads to intensification of contradictions within the exploiting classes."[55]

3. Monopoly Profit and Proletarian Impoverishment

The argument that monopoly profits resulted from expropriating part of the surplus value created in small enterprises had a lineage reaching back to Marx's *Capital*. Marx had written that a monopoly price transfers "a portion of the profit of the other commodity producers to the commodities having the monopoly price."[56] As V. Sushchenko noted in August 1954, Lenin had also said that monopolies exact "tribute" from small capitalists.[57] The problem was that Lenin borrowed this insight from Rudolf Hilferding. In *Finance Capital*, Hilferding described cartel profit as "nothing but a participation in, or appropriation of, the profit of other branches of industry":

> There is one rate [of profit] for the large cartelized industries and another for the spheres of small-scale industry which have become dependent upon them; and the capitalists in the cartelized industries rob the latter of part of their surplus value. . . .[58]

Hilferding's theory of intercapitalist transfers provided an economic explanation for tensions within the capitalist class, but it also ran afoul of Stalin's law of "maximum capitalist profit," which emphasized "the exploitation, ruin, and impoverishment of *the majority of the population*."[59] From the viewpoint of Stalinist writers, reformist interpretations focused upon the capitalists' rivalry to divide surplus value while glossing over the fact that *all surplus value* originated in the exploitation of labor. S.L. Vygodsky typified Stalinist thinking when he dismissed Hilferding's comments as a diversion from the politics of revolutionary class struggle. Praising Stalin's "precious contribution to Marxist-Leninist political economy," Vygodsky wrote that

> Bourgeois economists, and following them, right-wing socialists, avoid in every way possible the fact of intensified exploitation of the toilers. . . . They reduce monopoly capitalism to monopoly prices, which they see . . . resulting from redistribution of profit between cartelized and noncartelized branches. Following

Hilferding, they assert that monopoly prices inflict nothing on the toilers; they are simply a matter of arithmetic—the gain of one group of capitalists is the loss of another group.[60]

Vygodsky's attack on Hilferding implied that economists who saw a prospect for peaceful transition were betraying the revolution by ignoring intensification of labor and proletarian impoverishment during capitalism's "general crisis."[61] In the 1930s Varga had initially thought the Nazis could suppress wages and *redistribute* social income to the benefit of monopolies but not *increase* it. Not until the eve of World War II did Varga conclude that state spending on armaments and public works could increase both employment and the total social product. During the early 1950s this issue reappeared as Stalinists insisted that growth was impossible in the west and that any increase of monopoly profits could only result from further reduction of popular living standards. Until Khrushchev's adoption of Varga's position in 1956, conservative articles on mass impoverishment discounted the possibility of substituting reforms for revolutionary class struggle.

In *Capital*, Marx had defined "intensification" of labor in terms of "increased expenditure of labour in a given time," or the extraction of more effort (and more surplus value) from workers for the same wage.[62] If wages were assumed to be at or near subsistence to begin with, intensification would mean that they would no longer provide for reproduction of labor power. Vygodsky made exactly this argument: in modern capitalism, intensification had reached the point where it destroyed the workers' health and even physical ability to work. "Maximum capitalist profit" depended upon starvation wages, which in turn required "fascization of the state apparatus."[63] Destruction of democratic freedoms made emancipation impossible without first replacing the capitalist state with the dictatorship of the proletariat.

In April 1953, V. Vladimirov published an article on "Impoverishment of the Toilers in the Capitalist Countries" and quoted Lenin (in 1912) saying that workers are *relatively* impoverished when their class share of social income declines; the individual worker is "impoverished *absolutely* when he has less to eat, suffers from undernourishment and huddles in a cellar or garret."[64] Vladimirov pointed out that W.W. Heller—then at University of California and later chairman of John F. Kennedy's Council of Economic Advisers—calculated that an income of $4,512 was needed to support a family of four, whereas Federal Reserve Board data showed that 79 percent of families were below this minimum and up to 10 million earned less than $2,000 a year.[65]

M.N. Smit, author of countless Stalinist tracts on the misery of western workers, calculated that average Americans spent 63 percent of their working hours producing surplus value and tax revenues to support "a handful of monopolistic exploiters, warmongers and their parasitic servants" in the state apparatus, the army, and police.[66] The result was a dramatic increase of illnesses and premature deaths.[67] Although U.S. sources indicated that real after-tax earnings of industrial workers in 1954 were 46 percent higher than in 1939,[68] Smit contended that they remained below prewar levels: in America, the figure (for 1954) was said to be 85 percent;[69] in France (for 1955), 33 percent;[70] in Britain (for 1955), 84 percent.[71] Citing American psychiatrists, Smit reported that five million people were suffering from nervous disorders due to maximum capitalist profit and "merciless intensification" of labor.[72]

M.G. Guttsait similarly explained chronic unemployment by arguing that labor intensification had become the only means of increasing monopoly profits in the second stage of the general crisis. Chronically idle production capacity blocked investments in new fixed capital; and given the narrowness of the existing market, intensification inevitably caused fewer workers to be employed.[73] Guttsait estimated that each percentage increase of intensification threw four to five hundred thousand Americans out of their jobs,[74] causing "deformation of the cycle"[75] and an absolute decline of employment from levels reached during the war. "Massive chronic unemployment" was the cause of "a rising death rate, an increase of illnesses, particularly psychological illnesses, suicides, prostitution, etc."[76]

Labor *intensification* was one issue cited by conservatives to explain Stalin's law of maximum capitalist profit; another was use of new technologies to increase exploitation through higher labor *productivity*. Whereas intensification extracted more effort from the worker in any given period of time, Marx had spoken of technological change making it possible to create more output with the same expenditure of labor power.[77] Higher productivity would displace some workers from their jobs, but Marx expected total employment to grow with continuing capital accumulation.[78] Stalinists denied this possibility on the grounds that Marx's prediction no longer applied in one-sided war economies with a chronic problem of markets.

I.I. Kuz'minov wrote that more than 15 million Americans were either unemployed or working part-time due to rationalization, automation, and labor intensification.[79] Although new technologies required investment in some sectors, the effects were more than offset by loss of jobs elsewhere due to inadequate consumer demand.[80] Ya. Segal recited a sweeping list of new technologies, including advances in electro-chemistry, electro-metallurgy, the first computers, plastics, synthetic rubber, synthetic fibers, and insecticides, but he too thought nothing fundamental had altered: traditional industries, producing basic commodities such as food products, textiles, and leather goods, were not significantly above their 1948 levels of output because of mass unemployment.[81] Attributing technological change to accelerated depreciation allowances in war-related production, V. Antonov similarly argued that capitalism created chronic unemployment at the same time as taxpayers were compelled to subsidize monopoly profits.[82]

4. The Capitalist State and Market Creation

So long as they assumed that an *increase* of total national income, including both wages and profits, could not be stimulated by Keynesian fiscal expenditures, conservatives claimed that "maximum capitalist profit" aggravated class contradictions and made revolution inevitable. Until the mid-1950s, no Soviet writer questioned the conclusions reached in the Varga discussion of 1946-47: the existing state was a political instrument used by monopolies. On these grounds, Stalinists denied any significant changes in capitalism since the imperialist war economies of the 1930s. In 1953, E.Ya. Bregel' summarized the prevailing view of Keynesianism in *Taxes, Loans and Inflation in the Service of Imperialism:* monopolies "subjugated" the state to ensure their own enrichment.[83] Stalin had told H.G. Wells in 1934 that "The capitalist state does not deal much with [the] economy in the strict sense of the word, the latter is not in the hands of the state. On the contrary, the state is in the hands of [the] capitalist economy."[84]

Criticizing Alvin H. Hansen, an American Keynesian, for proposing to regulate the cycle through fiscal policy, Bregel' insisted that state expenditures could do nothing to reduce unemployment: they represented "*redistribution* of national income [to monopoly capital], not an *increase* of the total national income and of effective demand."[85] Although social democrats thought that state spending could moderate class conflict and facilitate "peaceful transition from capitalism to socialism,"[86] they were subscribing to Keynes' "psychological" explanation of the cycle and forgetting Marx's "real *economic* law of working-class impoverishment."[87] According to Bregel', western socialists took "subjugation of the bourgeois state to the capitalist monopolies and its use in the interest of guaranteeing maximum profit" and systematically misrepresented it as "state 'regulation' of the capitalist economy."[88]

In *State-Monopoly Capitalism*, I.I. Kuz'minov similarly denied that state policy could cause the slightest improvement in the position of workers, for Stalin had also told Wells that capitalists would never agree to give up the reserve army of the unemployed.[89] "For the working class," Kuz'minov argued, " . . . state regulation means a reduction of real wages due to the increase of taxes."[90] Keynesian economics was "an ideology of imperialist reaction and war."[91] Cold War experience proved that "under capitalism state investments are directed above all to construction of military enterprises, military bases and other installations of a military character; that is, to the arms race and preparation for new wars, which impose new deprivations upon the toilers."[92]

I.G. Blyumin, an authority on western economic theory, was only slightly less dogmatic. In *An Outline of Contemporary Bourgeois Political Economy in the USA*, he recognized that demand might temporarily increase with construction of new factories in the armaments industry.[93] Once this phase ended, however, a crisis must ensue because continuing taxation would reduce civilian consumption. "This is the 'Achilles heel' of bourgeois 'anticrisis' programs. 'Anticrisis' measures help to increase exploitation of workers, . . . but they are not able to prevent crises."[94] Blyumin followed Stalinist conventions by refusing to take seriously Keynesian claims concerning the "multiplier" effect of public expenditures.

In *The General Theory of Employment, Interest and Money*, Keynes had demonstrated that any increment of investment or government spending, given unused resources, will have a final impact far greater than the initial sum involved. When an industry expands production, it hires more workers, who spend part of their income and save the remainder. The income that they spend becomes income for others, who then spend part of their income, until eventually the original increase of spending is absorbed by equivalent saving.[95] If each income recipient saved 20 percent, the total income stream (leaving aside taxation) would grow five times over. If the increase of total incomes were large enough to reactivate capacity in some branches of industry, a spontaneous acceleration of investments might also occur, causing a self-generating cyclical expansion. Stalinists did not understand the multiplier process because the theory of "one-sided" war economies emphasized monopoly profits while ignoring the effect of military spending on wages and civilian consumption.

One of the first Soviet economists to take state regulation of aggregate demand more seriously was A.A. Manukyan, who in January 1955 repeated the conclusion Varga had reached on the eve of the Second World War: "Given unused production capacity, unused resources of material and labor power, the arms race creates the possibility for a certain increase of industrial production, a certain recovery in industry. The arms race can lead to a temporary expansion of markets."[96] In September 1955, A.I. Bechin agreed that the effects of state expenditure could not be determined *a priori* but depended upon changing circumstances. Bechin thought "life" had demonstrated that the "depression of a special kind" would not provide the pattern for all cycles in the epoch of capitalism's general crisis:[97]

> Given an excess of production capacity [and] . . . significant unemployment . . . conversion of a large part of industry to military production can, to a certain degree, either accelerate the transition from depression to a military-inflationary conjuncture [as in the 1930s] . . . or temporarily delay the onset of a crisis, . . . as occurred in the USA in the postwar years. . . .[98]

Bechin's article coincided with a decisive intervention by the USSR Academy of Sciences. In September the Academy lent its support to reformists by rebuking the Institute of Economics, headed by V.P. D'yachenko, for disregarding "the Leninist heritage in Marxist economic theory."[99] Lenin had rejected the theory of a chronic problem of markets; by calling for a return to Leninist traditions, the Academy intended that economists should forget Stalin's *Economic Problems*. Criticizing Stalinists, particularly M.N. Smit, for exaggerating proletarian impoverishment, the Academy specified several areas in which current research was inadequate:

> the Institute [of Economics] has not worked out such important problems as the specific characteristics of the capitalist cycle in the second stage of the general crisis . . . , chronic mass unemployment and the real wages of workers in the capitalist countries, or the sources of maximum profit. . . . The theoretical level of most works . . . concerning questions of contemporary capitalism is low.[100]

To remedy these shortcomings, the Academy resolved to create a new Institute of World Economy and International Relations (known by the acronym IMEMO) as a successor to Varga's former Institute of World Economy and World Politics. Varga's age may have been a factor in preventing him from becoming director of the new institute, which began operations in August 1956, but it was obvious by this time that he had been fully rehabilitated. In 1954 he had celebrated his seventy-fifth birthday at a joint meeting of the Institute of Economics and the Academy's Department of Economics, Philosophy, and Law. On that occasion, V.P. D'yachenko had praised his "truly encyclopedic knowledge" and exemplary role as "a genuine scholar-revolutionary."[101] Immediately after the Academy criticized D'yachenko's institute, Varga had further cause for satisfaction. In January 1956, V.A. Cheprakov, who had led the attack on reformism in 1947-48, conceded all of the views for which Varga had been reprimanded.

On the question of monopoly subjugation of the state, Cheprakov admitted the "simple and well-known truth" that the bourgeoisie rules through political parties, which depend on votes from the toilers and therefore must make concessions.[102] Repeating Varga's position almost word for word, Cheprakov added that "from time to time the capitalist state infringes upon the interests of particular groups of the bourgeoisie and even those of individual monopolies. What is involved in such instances is, in fact, a defense of the interests of monopoly capital as a whole."[103] To the extent that "middle strata" of the bourgeoisie were victims of state redistribution of surplus value, Cheprakov also acknowledged that divisions within the ruling class could facilitate the workers' struggle for wage increases and "general-democratic" reforms.[104]

5. Reinterpreting the "General Crisis"

The effects of the Academy's decisions in September 1955 were apparent not only in Varga's enhanced status, but also in important changes in the literature on economic theory. In December 1955, E.Ya. Bregel' went further than any other writer thus far in recognizing the expansionary potential of fiscal policy—even when used for purposes of militarization. Only two years earlier, Bregel's *Taxes, Loans, and Inflation* had adhered strictly to Stalinist positions. In an article published by *Voprosy ekonomiki*, he now claimed that German arms output had increased no less than fifty times over from 1933 to 1943,[105] proving that simplified analyses of war economies exaggerated the inevitability of capital consumption.

As for personal consumption, Bregel' argued that its "absolute curtailment"[106] would not occur until reserves of production capacity were
used up, which would typically require military spending to account for
10-15 percent of total national income.[107] Until that threshold was
crossed, there was no obvious reason military spending could not serve
as an effective countercyclical measure. Bregel' explained the effect of
heavy industrial expansion on other branches of the economy in terms of
the relation between Marx's two Departments:

> What is of essential importance here is *the chain connection*
> between different branches of capitalist production. The rapidly
> expanding armaments industry creates increased demand for
> materials, fuel, machinery, etc. . . . Expansion of production in
> the war industry and related branches presupposes an increase of
> the number of workers they employ, who then increase their
> demand for means of consumption. Thus growth of military
> production . . . grows over into a general increase of production
> and demand.[108]

Following the twentieth party congress in February 1956, reappraisal
of Keynesian theory turned into direct criticism of Stalin. In October,
G.S. Roginsky quoted Khrushchev's remark to the effect that arms
expenditures had obviously helped to increase capitalist production since
World War II. Roginsky summarized the debate over militarization and
"one-sided" war economies in terms of three propositions: 1) military
orders could indirectly increase production in other branches; 2) the
principal cause of the expansion was new investments in response to state
contracts; and 3) militarization provided only a temporary stimulus,
ultimately resulting in disproportions.[109] Of these three propositions,
Roginsky argued that the third had been least adequately explained. It
happened that the originator of the third proposition was Stalin himself,
who in 1939 had described one-sidedness as follows:

> what does placing the economy of a country on a war footing
> mean? It means giving industry a one-sided war direction,
> developing to the utmost the production of goods necessary for
> war and not for consumption by the population; restricting to the
> utmost the production and, especially, the sale of articles of
> general consumption—and consequently, reducing consumption
> by the population and confronting the country with an economic
> crisis.[110]

Roginsky pointed out that Stalin had committed an obvious self-contradiction: "In this statement, everything is clear and correct except the conclusion. It is completely unclear . . . how curtailment of production of consumer goods . . . can lead to a crisis of *over-production*."[111] Some authors had tried to salvage Stalin's argument in "naturalist" terms, emphasizing that military production withdrew resources from the real process of reproduction, but this strategy accomplished nothing: if the material basis of reproduction narrowed, there would still be a *drop* in production—not a crisis of overproduction. Furthermore, it was clear that some countries could afford to increase military production while simultaneously investing in other branches of the economy. How then could militarization cause a crisis? The only answer Roginsky could suggest was that at some point workers would refuse to pay more in taxation: "The time of reaching this turning point . . . is determined by the conditions of the class struggle. . . ."[112]

R.Kh. Khafizov was even more contentious in arguing that a significant portion of the tax revenues needed to support the military must in fact come not from the toilers at all but from capitalists. Marx's analysis of "pure capitalism" had assumed that all expenditures originated with the capitalist class, and Stalinists had routinely maintained that labor intensification accelerated proletarian impoverishment. If workers could not save any part of their income after satisfying their most urgent physical needs, how could they possibly bear a substantial burden of taxation?[113] The obvious answer was that the capitalists themselves must be financing most of the military budget. What better proof could there be that militarization created a market and provided protection against cyclical crises? Khafizov concluded that

> when the government . . . places orders for military and other industrial production, this leads to an increase of aggregate effective demand. Consequently, the bourgeois state can, within certain limits, artificially extend the limits of the market, accumulating in the budget and putting back into circulation redundant capital that is idle due to lack of opportunities for profit.[114]

Once the state was acknowledged to play a role in creating employment and markets, the Stalinist theory of absolute proletarian impoverishment also became untenable. Responsibility for revising the official view on this issue fell to A.A. Arzumanyan, a protege of Anastas Mikoyan and first director of the new Institute of World Economy and International Relations (IMEMO). In July 1956, Arzumanyan criticized Soviet writers for too often treating western workers as if they were "some kind of inert mass," incapable of organizing the struggle for wage gains and economic improvements: "certain economists, ignoring the facts, assert that 'the working class receives less from year to year.' This is a 'leftist' phrase that contradicts the Marxist theory of wages. If real wages fell from year to year in all countries and throughout the entire period of capitalist development, they would be completely detached from the value of labor power. . . ."[115] Marx had shown that wages depend upon the subsistence-determined cost of reproducing labor power; but Marx also regarded subsistence as including socially determined, not merely physical, needs. Marx included in the subsistence wage both "natural wants" and those associated with the prevailing "habits and degree of comfort."[116] Arzumanyan decided, despite Stalinist views to the contrary, that real wages had risen in the capitalist countries because the value of labor power (its culturally modified cost of reproduction) had risen even more quickly.

As a measure of labor power's true value, Arzumanyan also referred to the Heller budget for the typical American family. Since average wages were only 70 percent of Heller's budget (in 1954), the IMEMO director hoped to retain the form of the Stalinist view even if the substance must be sacrificed. Real wages, he admitted, were obviously rising, but the fact that they lagged behind the minimal acceptable level continued to signify "absolute impoverishment."[117] This attempt to preserve dignity at the expense of truth proved to be too clever. When Arzumanyan's article was republished by the French Communist Party, a socialist journal protested that Soviet officials were still ignorant of capitalist reality. Arzumanyan replied that real wages in France had yet to regain the 1938 level. In any case, recent gains were merely a consequence of trade union victories during a temporary cyclical expansion:

> It is no coincidence that it is precisely in the years 1955-1956 that bourgeois economists have strengthened their attack on the Marxist theory of the impoverishment of the working class. Always in the phase of cyclical expansion, when the working class succeeds in achieving a certain wage increase, these gentlemen come out of their shells like snails and begin an

outcry about "a fundamental improvement in the position of the working class." The same is true of *Revue Socialiste*.[118]

Attempting to modify the Stalinist theory of impoverishment while simultaneously mounting a rearguard defense, Arzumanyan helped to open the central questions to which the entire debate over Stalin's *Economic Problems* ultimately led. If the state was admitted to be capable of promoting economic growth, what were the implications for Marx's theory of the capitalist cycle? If a cyclical expansion was under way, as Arzumanyan indicated, would it end in a classical crisis, or might Keynesian policies usher in a new era of stabilization? Arzumanyan hesitated to answer. In October 1957 he quoted Lenin to argue that capitalism could never experience chronic stagnation. On the other hand, he also rejected any possibility of "partial, relative stabilization." The state could not overcome the general crisis because it remained "subjugated" by the monopolies and was not a "decisive force."[119]

6. The End of the "Depression of a Special Kind"

While the director of IMEMO wavered between facts and Stalinist slogans, Khrushchev grew impatient. Demanding less attention to abstract schemes and more to the lessons of "life," he complained that he was tired of hearing from "parrots, who learn certain phrases by rote and then repeat them. This kind of 'theoretical work' is not worth half a kopek."[120] By 1957 conservative economists were in disarray and the conceptual impediments to a full-scale review of postwar capitalism were crumbling. Just five years after Stalin's *Economic Problems*, the time had come to attempt a new synthesis of theory and historical interpretation. Since the main cause of European growth after World War II had been reconstruction, the most difficult challenge was to explain why there was no evidence of "depression of a special kind" in the United States.

In February 1957, A.A. Manukyan concluded that Varga had been right in 1946: postwar growth had initially been spurred by the need to satisfy demand for consumer goods. Because equipment in the consumer goods industries had been neglected since the 1930s, there had also been a high rate of spontaneous capital investment. Activity had slowed during the crisis of 1948, but then it resumed in 1950 with a "military-inflationary recovery" due to the Korean war. Although military spending continued at a high level in subsequent years, consumer credit and rising wages had been mainly responsible for expanding the market through rapidly increasing sales of household durables.[121]

Stalinists thought that impoverishment caused crises of overproduction and that technological change added to chronic unemployment through labor displacement. Manukyan turned this argument in reverse: monopolies had been "compelled, to one extent or another, to satisfy the workers' demand for an increase in wages."[122] From this perspective, it seemed that new technologies were less an indicator of labor intensification than an objective result of the need to raise productivity in order to prevent a falling rate of profit. Marx had shown that every classical cycle began with fixed-capital investments and ended with a crisis of disproportionality. Manukyan believed the American economy had followed the same pattern. Postwar investments had first supported economic growth, but continuing additions to fixed capital were now leading to disproportionate expansion in heavy industry. By 1957 industrial activity was based "more than ever before on demand in Department I." America had created "such an excess of production capacity" in heavy industry that it was becoming "the precondition for a particularly deep and prolonged crisis."[123]

A.I. Bechin, deputy director of IMEMO, likewise thought that "convulsive expansion of production of means of production"[124] was finally causing capacity to outpace demand. Like Varga in the late 1930s, Bechin attached particular importance to a changed structure of investment. In earlier periods of capitalist development, infrastructural expenditures on railways, port facilities, canals, and public utilities had created enormous capital requirements and supported a market for heavy industry over prolonged intervals of time. By contrast, the Americans were currently renovating existing factories with new technologies and creating an entirely different market of much shorter duration: "A large part of the output of branches producing means of production consists now of machinery and other equipment, which goes [directly] to branches producing finished commodities," particularly consumer goods.[125] This reasoning led Bechin to the same conclusion as Manukyan: "the enormous growth of production capacity and the significant increase of labor productivity, resulting from the accumulation of capital, have created preconditions for a profound economic crisis of overproduction."[126]

Varga made the same prediction in a second edition of *Basic Questions of the Economics and Politics of Imperialism*, published in 1957. Observing that the years 1951-55 had involved a more rapid growth of production than at any other time in history, Varga scoffed at Stalin's claim that capitalism's geographical contraction entailed a chronic problem of markets: "This assertion is mistaken. . . . [I]ndustrial production in the capitalist world during the postwar period has grown by 80% . . . [W]hat has occurred in this period is not a narrowing, but an expansion of the market."[127]

A high rate of capital accumulation during the 1950s had raised both employment and wages, clearly demonstrating that there had also been no absolute impoverishment: "Is it possible," Varga asked, ". . . for real wages to grow under capitalism? Of course it is temporarily possible, given favorable conditions for the struggle of the working class."[128] With investments now slowing, however, due to excessive capacity in heavy industry, Varga also expected that unspent savings would re-create the problem of markets in the form of another cyclical crisis. He agreed with Manukyan and Bechin that America would soon experience "a general crisis of overproduction."[129]

In the autumn of 1957 the IMEMO journal, *World Economy and International Relations*, published a lead article interpreting events since Stalin's death. The most important conclusion was that the "depression of a special kind" no longer had any relevance to postwar capitalism:

> the assertion that the phase of expansion drops out of the cycle in the period of the general crisis is untrue . . . because the world capitalist economy is now passing through this phase. . . . [E]ver since the 1930s, the depression of a special kind has not been repeated. One must not extend this formula concerning deformation of the cycle over the entire period of the general crisis of capitalism.[130]

On the question of working-class living standards, IMEMO demanded new research to overcome "the vulgar representation of the absolute impoverishment of the proletariat."[131] Although it was still not clear exactly what role the state played, there was no denying that its importance had increased "to a remarkable degree." Soviet economists were correct to deny "bourgeois and revisionist theories of the . . . state's 'decisive role,'" but they were also cautioned not to follow Stalin in "denying any role whatever to the capitalist state in the economy. Such a simplified and schematic approach to this important question hinders understanding of real processes."[132]

IMEMO further emphasized that "One must not underestimate the important influence of . . . [militarization] on the process of reproduction"—although it would be "an error to explain expansion of production in the capitalist countries exclusively by the action of this factor."[133] As for who ultimately paid for militarization, the capitalist state obviously redistributed income from the toilers to the monopolies.[134] On the other hand, a large portion of the capitalists' surplus value also went to maintain war industries because "military-parasitic consumption" contributed to "a certain expansion of the market."[135] All of these findings demonstrated that economists must refocus their inquiry on

> the reproduction of fixed capital, which creates the material basis of the periodicity of economic crises. . . . Without a study of the character, scale and peculiarities of the reproduction of fixed capital, of the condition of the capitalist market and effective demand, it is impossible to give a true picture . . . of the contradiction between the level of production and the level of consumption . . . [I]n recent years our economists have not paid the necessary attention to research into the dynamic of fixed capital.[136]

Intended to put an end to the struggle over Stalin's *Economic Problems*, IMEMO's directives had no such result. After Khrushchev's condemnation of terror at the twentieth party congress, a change of official views no longer guaranteed that dissenters would be intimidated. By the late 1950s the weakness of party controls over economic research was apparent. Varga's "reformism" had been denounced by Stalinists only to resurface under Malenkov and Khrushchev through the debate over foreign trade and monopoly profits. Business-cycle theory had been suppressed under Stalin, yet IMEMO was now urging exactly the kind of investigation for which Figurnov and Mendel'son had been punished only seven years earlier.

When the American economy lapsed into another recession shortly after IMEMO's conclusions appeared, the need for closer study of cyclical disturbances became all the more pressing. By 1958 no economist could seriously argue that the crash of capitalism was at hand. As it turned out, however, there was still no agreement as to whether Marx's cycle continued to operate. Marx had explained cycles by reference to objective laws. Stalin had also claimed that "the laws of economic development

. . . are objective laws, reflecting processes . . . that take place independently of the will of people."[137] When the American government appeared to respond effectively to the 1958 recession, Soviet writers confronted a new set of problems. For the first time since the 1930s they had to reexamine the relation between spontaneous forces and discretionary policies in state-monopoly capitalism.

CHAPTER 5

REINTERPRETING POSTWAR AMERICA: A NORMAL CYCLE OR A "ONE-SIDED" WAR ECONOMY?

On the eve of World War II, Varga had written that "government expenditures . . . for armaments and public works influence and modify the cyclical development of reproduction, which is based upon the internal laws of capitalist society."[1] In the autumn of 1957, IMEMO directed economists to reexamine the relation between state policy and spontaneous cyclical forces, beginning with "the reproduction of fixed capital, which creates the material basis of the periodicity of economic crises." Khrushchev wanted less dogma and more attention to the lessons of "life." To study life, however, presupposed a framework of theory in order to determine which events of recent history were truly significant.

The American recession of 1957-58 posed the question of whether a normal cycle was again operating or whether—as Stalinists had claimed since the 1930s—it had been deformed by the general crisis. Having denied any positive effects of public expenditures, conservatives responded to IMEMO's challenge by continuing to emphasize the negative consequences of militarization. The unifying theme of conservative arguments, despite IMEMO's decision to the contrary, remained the likelihood of return to the "depression of a special kind." Although Varga dismissed that possibility, his own view was not clear: initially he thought the cycle had been lengthened; in 1959 he decided it had been restored in classical form; by 1961 he associated cyclical deformation with a tendency toward shortened depressions, an argument that appeared to suggest cycles might eventually occur *with no depressions at all*. With issues of this importance at stake, debates from 1957 to 1961 yielded no lasting consensus.

The fact that a cycle of one kind or another had been restored, however, indicated to Khrushchev that capitalism had become far more stable than Stalinists anticipated. Two consequences followed: there was no alternative to peaceful coexistence, and the general crisis had to be redefined. Khrushchev attributed a new, third stage of the general crisis not to capitalism's impending collapse, but rather to a change in the global relation of forces resulting from Soviet successes (real and anticipated) in peaceful economic competition. A new seven-year plan, covering the years 1959-65, projected that by 1965 per-capita output in Soviet agriculture would exceed that of the United States; within another five years, the same was to occur in industry.[2]

To promote trade with the west as a means of realizing his domestic objectives, Khrushchev called upon Communists and social democrats to find a "common language" and join forces in order to restrain militarists and fight for peaceful coexistence.[3] His proposal for an antimonopoly front assumed the possibility of extracting concessions in both foreign and domestic policy. Khrushchev thought working-class parties, rather than attempting to overthrow the state, must participate more actively in existing institutions. As a result, attempts to reconceptualize the cycle went hand in hand with a new emphasis upon "democratic" nationalization as a transitional stage between capitalism and socialism.

1. Postwar Capitalism: The Economic Cycle and its Determinants

Since their clash with Varga in 1947-48, Stalinists had argued that sustained growth was impossible in postwar capitalism because chronically idle capacity stood in the way of investments. American statistics revealed the opposite to be true. From 1950 to 1960, the real net value of industrial plant and equipment increased by more than 32 percent.[4] In *The U.S. Economy in the 1950's*, Harold G. Vatter described America as having an "abundant economy" that was capable of eliminating poverty "in the foreseeable future."[5] According to Vatter, postwar experience demonstrated that "the scourge of cyclical mass unemployment could be dispelled by sufficient public spending of almost any kind."[6]

Despite Vatter's enthusiasm, other economists thought America's performance was mixed. The paradox of the 1950s lay in a combination of long-term growth with frequent short-term interruptions. In a study of *Growth and Stability of the Postwar Economy*, Bert G. Hickman described cycles occurring every three to four years between 1945 and 1958: the first from late 1945 to 1949; a second beginning with the

Korean inflation and lasting until the contraction of 1953-54; and a third from late 1954 to the recession of 1957-58. Although Hickman expected that "brief but severe contractions" might continue, he also wrote that "it is extremely unlikely that the United States will again experience a prolonged and severe contraction like that of the early 1930's."[7]

Alvin H. Hansen, one of the foremost American Keynesians, took much the same view: cycles had become more frequent, but they were also more moderate and there had been "no truly *major* cycle in the postwar period."[8] In *The Postwar American Economy: Performance and Problems* (1964), Hansen described three minor cycles and part of a fourth in the period from 1945 to 1964. In his chronology—which differed from Hickman's—the first cycle lasted from late 1948 to mid-1953; the second, from mid-1953 to mid-1957; the third, from mid-1957 to the spring of 1960. A fourth began in the spring of 1960 and was yet to be completed in 1964.[9]

Although recessions were approximately equal in length, Hansen expressed uneasiness over the fact that each recovery was shorter than its predecessor. The first lasted forty-five months; the second, thirty-five months; the third, only twenty-five months. Compared to the "long and buoyant recoveries" of earlier years, the 1958 recession, despite lasting only a few months, turned out to be the most severe since the 1930s. The index of industrial production fell by 14 percent, and unemployment rose to 7.5 percent.[10] At the peak of the third cycle in the spring of 1960, unemployment remained at 5 percent, suggesting a trend toward what Hansen called "semistagnation."[11]

At the same time as the pattern of cycles changed, the overall rate of growth slowed. From 1948 to 1956 the industrial index climbed by 55 percent; from 1956 to 1962 the increase was only 13 percent.[12] Like Manukyan, Bechin, and Varga, Hansen underscored the importance of spontaneous factors as the principal source of growth in both periods. Gross private investments increased from 1948 to 1956 by an average of 3.1 percent annually. When this rate fell to only 0.4 percent in 1956-63,[13] the weakness of private expenditures was not offset by long-term government policies. The American government did not attempt systematically to regulate aggregate demand until the Kennedy administration embraced a Keynesian fiscal program in 1963. Hansen attributed a 30 percent increase of per-capita private consumption from 1948 to 1962 less to deliberate policies than to the "built-in stabilizers" of the postwar economic system:

In the recession phase, tax receipts fall off, while expenditures, such as unemployment compensation, relief, etc., rise. In the recovery phase, revenues rise rapidly, indeed more rapidly than GNP, owing partly to the progressivity of the individual income tax and especially to the sharp cyclical fluctuations in corporate profits. A cushion is thus placed under a recession and restraint is imposed on the upward movement. The economy is more or less stabilized.[14]

If American experience contradicted Soviet expectations concerning the frequency of cycles, that of Western Europe raised different issues. Here the pattern was in many ways the opposite of what had occurred in the United States. Apart from brief declines of output in separate countries, Andrea Boltho found no cycle or serious recession in Western Europe as a whole until the mid-1970s.[15] Reconstruction and expansion were supported by high levels of private investment and consumption, buoyant export markets, and extensive social security systems, which, as in America, provided "a considerable degree of automatic counter-cyclical stabilization."[16] According to Boltho, it was not so much the practice of Keynesian policies that sustained growth and prevented cycles as the confidence resulting from knowledge that such tools were available:

> The development of Keynes's ideas had shown that full employ-
> ment was not impossible in a capitalist economy. . . . Business
> may well have thought that, in the event of a downturn, govern-
> ment would and could step in. . . . Influenced by this considera-
> tion, . . . [business] invested, kept up the growth of aggregate
> demand, and made government intervention unnecessary.[17]

Philip Armstrong, Andrew Glyn, and John Harrison attributed business confidence in postwar Europe to other factors, including expulsion of Communists from coalition governments in Italy and France in the spring of 1947, splits between Communists and social democrats in the trade union movement, and the encouragement capitalists received from the Marshall Plan in their effort to restore "financial and social discipline." Once working-class unrest was curtailed, currency and wage stabilization facilitated a high rate of capital accumulation; this, according to Armstrong and his coauthors, was "the period's outstanding contribution towards the foundations of the great boom of the fifties and sixties."[18]

In *Modern Capitalism,* Andrew Shonfield referred to two minor recessions in postwar Europe: one in 1951-52, following the Korean war boom; another in 1957-58, caused by "a series of deliberate measures of restraint."[19] But Shonfield expressed the same optimism as most western economists when he proclaimed that major crises could be avoided: "there is no reason to suppose that the patterns of the past, which have been ingeniously unravelled by the historians of trade cycles, will reassert themselves in the future." All that modern capitalism required in order to avoid traditional cycles was the "political will and skill" to adapt modern institutions for effective macroeconomic management.[20]

A fundamental difference between Keynesians and Marxists concerned the importance of investor and consumer *confidence*. Keynes thought much economic behavior depends on "spontaneous optimism":[21] "a mere change in expectation is capable of producing an oscillation of the same kind . . . as a cyclical movement."[22] In the Keynesian analysis, governments had a responsibility to support expectations of steady growth. Attributing America's halting performance to a "recession psychology," or investor nervousness resulting from the unusual frequency of recessions, Shonfield called for a more powerful public sector: "Once businessmen become convinced that they can safely ignore the risk of a serious recession during the productive life of . . . capital in which they are thinking of investing, the whole tempo of an economy is likely to change."[23]

Marx saw a totally different kind of causality. For him it was not psychology that determined investments but the struggle to survive competition and crises. Marx emphasized objective imperatives inherent in the accumulation and reproduction of fixed capital: recovery from a crisis was driven by demand for new equipment in order to reduce costs in response to falling prices and profits. Department I reacted to increased demand by overhauling existing plants and constructing new ones. By the time this additional capacity was fully in operation, however, the original wave of investment would be receding. The reserve army of the unemployed would be drawn back into production, leading to higher wages and again threatening the rate of profit.

Marx thought speculation might continue temporarily to fuel growth in both Departments, but once credits were no longer readily available to finance inventories—or "disguised overproduction"—another crisis was inevitable. Capitalists would be unable to transform commodities into money with which to purchase the equipment, materials, and labor power needed to continue operations. "Then," Marx wrote, "a crisis breaks out. It becomes visible not in the direct decrease of consumer demand, the demand for individual consumption, but [rather] in . . . the reproductive process of capital."[24] Assuming the average life of fixed capital to be ten years, Marx saw each cycle objectively determining the next:

> One may assume that in the essential branches of modern industry this life cycle [of fixed capital] now averages ten years. . . . True, periods in which capital is invested differ greatly and far from coincide in time. But a crisis always forms the starting point of large new investments. Therefore, from the point of view of society as a whole . . . [these investments form] a new material basis for the next turnover cycle.[25]

2. The Postwar Cycle and the "One-Sided" War Economy

One of the few Soviet authors who saw the recession of 1957-58 conforming perfectly with Marx's description was V.A. Maslennikov. He denied that the contractions of 1948-49 and 1953-54 had been genuinely cyclical on the grounds that each had been followed by a speedy recovery: "What kind of strange cycle is it," he asked, "that embraces a three-year period . . . with no postcrisis phase of depression?"[26] Measuring cycles in terms of the *world capitalist economy*, whose links had not been restored until the early 1950s, Maslennikov thought the first postwar cycle began in 1950-51, was driven by fixed-capital renovation, and lasted eight to nine years, well within Marx's range of expectations. Since the material basis of the classical cycle remained intact, Maslennikov rejected "all 'theories' to the effect that capitalism is in such a state of decay that one can no longer speak of technological progress in the second stage of the general crisis."[27]

Maslennikov avoided the issue of shorter and more frequent cycles by concentrating on the international economy rather than domestic fluctuations. Other writers were more concerned with how Marx's analysis might be reconciled with the uneven course of events in America. In various places Marx had suggested that the pattern might gradually change. In Volume II of *Capital* he related the possibility of shorter cycles to technological advances, which tended to accelerate the "moral depreciation" of capital (or the rate of obsolescence), leading to replacement of means of production "long before they expire physically."[28] In a revision to the French-language edition of *Capital*, he wrote that "Up to now the cycle usually lasted ten to eleven years. But we have no reason to believe that this is a constant figure. On the contrary, the laws of capitalism we have described give us reason to believe that this is a changing figure and that it will gradually decrease."[29] In Volume I, Marx referred to "a decennial cycle (*interrupted by smaller oscillations*)";[30] elsewhere in the same volume he wrote of "irregular oscillations" following each other "more and more quickly" as accumulation advanced.[31] Engels also spoke of interruptions of the normal cycle, calling them "intermediate crises."[32]

A.A. Manukyan decided that a classical cycle continued to operate in the United States, but it was now being punctuated by Marx's "irregular oscillations" and Engels' "intermediate crises." Manukyan thought the postwar cycle began in 1947-48, paused during the intermediate crisis of 1953-54, and then continued until 1957-58.[33] Since intermediate crises were too brief to eliminate all contradictions, in the spring of 1958 Manukyan expected "a longer and deeper crisis than any since the war."[34] A.I. Bechin also wrote of a crisis in essentially "classical forms."[35] Whereas Manukyan dated the postwar cycle from 1947-48, however, Bechin thought it began as early as 1945, making the contraction of 1948 another "intermediate" crisis.[36]

The question of when the postwar cycle began turned out to have important consequences in terms of controversies over state regulation in "one-sided" war economies. Varga had argued that state orders eliminated the cycle during the war by providing a virtually unlimited third-party market. After 1945 he had seen postponed consumer demand sustaining a high level of activity, with a normal cycle resuming only in 1947-48. If it could be shown instead that the war itself precipitated an *immediate* postwar crisis, then it might also be argued that the state had not been able, despite unprecedented wartime expenditures, even temporarily to alleviate the problem of markets. During 1958 the effects of the Varga controversy spilled over into discussions of the cycle when Soviet conservatives insisted that the American economy had been permanently distorted by weak consumer demand and excessive capacity in heavy industry.

S.L. Vygodsky thought Varga's assessments of America had been mistaken ever since World War II. He argued that the first postwar crisis began as early as 1943, when wartime production peaked. The acute phase of the crisis came in 1946 because postponed consumer demand proved to be a fiction. Had such demand really existed, it would have been satisfied at once by production capacity created during the war. Varga had explained a brief drop in output after 1945 in terms of technical dislocations resulting from conversion to civilian operations.

Vygodsky countered that militarization had created permanent structural disproportions, including a chronic "excess of means of production" and a chronic shortage of consuming power on the part of impoverished workers: "that was the basis of the economic crisis of overproduction in 1943-1946."[37]

In Vygodsky's account, militarization had continued throughout the 1950s with the result that by 1958 heavy industrial capacity dramatically exceeded normal requirements. Whereas a "classical" crisis implied a predictable recovery and expansion, he expected the recession of 1957-58 to match or even exceed the catastrophe of 1929-33. From September 1929 to February 1930, industrial production had fallen by 11.4 percent; the comparable figure for the same months of 1957-58 was 10.3 percent.[38] Vygodsky did not explicitly refer to the "depression of a special kind"; it was enough to point out that industrial output peaked in 1957 at a level only 12.6 percent above that of 1943. By May 1958 this modest gain had already been erased, throwing the economy back by fifteen years.[39] The frequency of postwar crises demonstrated that it was impossible to apply a "classical"[40] interpretation of the cycle to a permanently mobilized "semi-war economy."[41]

Professor I.I. Kuz'minov, another leading conservative, shared Vygodsky's contention that permanent militarization had structurally distorted the American economy, making "a 'pure,' classical, 'normal' cycle" impossible.[42] Varga had regarded war as the interruption of a normal cycle; Kuz'minov replied that wars had become a *normal feature* of capitalism's general crisis. In Europe, the Second World War had substituted for the phase of crisis; in America, it had played the part of an expansion. Kuz'minov claimed that the resulting lack of synchrony explained why "intermediate crises" in America had not developed into a *world* crisis of overproduction until 1958, when European and American cycles appeared to be converging.[43] Expecting crises in Europe and America to reinforce each other, he too saw no prospect for a rapid recovery after 1958.

A.I. Kats, an eccentric exponent of capitalism's "automatic crash," sided with Vygodsky and Kuz'minov; normal cycles were impossible because the United States had never overcome the disproportions of a one-sided war economy. Kats held that fixed-capital investments, from 1948 to 1957, had been propelled almost exclusively by military orders, causing "a rapid and one-sided development of the machine-building branches. . . . As a result, there appeared by 1957 such an excess of production capacity that it exceeded the overaccumulation of fixed capital that existed on the eve of the profound economic crisis of 1929-1933."[44] Kats pointed out that in 1929 13 percent of American steel capacity had been idle; by 1957 the figure was 20 percent. For automobiles the corresponding figures were 15 percent and 30 percent.[45]

Kats believed that modern capitalism was permanently incapable of utilizing the available means of production. Sales of consumer durables had been financed mainly by credit because there had been an "absolute decline" of workers' real incomes from 1944 to 1956.[46] By the time of the 1957-58 recession, payments on consumer and mortgage loans accounted for 17 percent of total net personal incomes, indicating that there was little possibility of continuing to expand credit.[47] On the contrary, the 1958 crisis might well cause the entire edifice of consumer loans to collapse if the unemployed failed to meet existing obligations. Nor was it possible for the American government to undertake Keynesian countercrisis measures: tax receipts were falling, and inflation would only further reduce real wages, prolonging both the crisis and the ensuing depression.[48]

Kats was convinced that "had it not been for the artificial military factor, the crisis of 1949 would have assumed a protracted character and, in all probability, would have repeated a deformed industrial cycle analogous to that of the 1930s."[49] By September 1958 he too saw a real prospect of the depression of the 1930s being repeated: "The renewal of fixed capital is now occurring on such a reduced scale that, in contrast to previous cycles, it can no longer serve as the material basis for a cyclical phase of expansion."[50] With the internal forces of the traditional cycle unable to relieve the "problem of markets,"[51] the American financial oligarchy faced a choice between "suicide" and salvation through trade with the socialist world market.[52]

L.A. Mendel'son had been one of the first to refer to "intermediate crises" when describing a "feverish," "unstable," and "unhealthy" situation in the late 1940s. A decade later his view had not changed: high levels of military spending had resulted in chronic disproportions, periodically erupting in what he now called "economic crises of a special kind" and "military-inflationary crises." Mendel'son used these terms to emphasize that the effects of militarization were neither random nor accidental but represented a fundamental change in the pattern of capitalist reproduction:

> [Military-inflationary] crises are subject to laws . . .; they are inevitable in cycles that include periods of war. . . . [T]hey can

also arise in cycles that, although they may not include periods of war, do include far-reaching militarization of the economy or the effects of a previous war.[53]

World War II had caused some countries to have an inflationary crisis of *underproduction* (Western Europe) while others had an inflationary crisis of *overproduction* (the United States). But Mendel'son considered these to be two aspects of one phenomenon: "the general crisis and disruption of the capitalist system of world economy."[54] Because Khrushchev insisted that wars were no longer fatally inevitable, Mendel'son did not say that they had become a *necessary* feature of the cycle; he did claim, though, that "military-inflationary crises" would necessarily recur so long as capitalist economies were committed to the arms race. Instability in America confirmed that there could be no return to Marx's cycles in "pure form."[55]

In the late 1940s, P.K. Figurnov (together with Mendel'son) had been a victim of Stalinist reprisals for attempting to revive business-cycle theory. Figurnov now also subscribed to the view that *Capital* had been overtaken by events. Although he was skeptical of allusions to a new "depression of a special kind,"[56] he disputed Varga's contention that war expenditures might eliminate crises. The war, he claimed, had created "profound disproportions" and mass impoverishment;[57] the crisis of 1945-46 had resulted from "general overproduction of [both] capital and commodities."[58] In the frequent interruptions of growth since 1945, Figurnov saw signs of further "deepening of the general crisis": "Under the influence of militarization," he wrote, " . . . disproportions became more acute, especially the disproportion between production and consumption. . . ."[59]

3. The "Crisis" of 1957-58

In June 1958, Varga answered these references to the "one-sided" war economy. The importance of his article, "Problems of the Postwar Industrial Cycle and the New Crisis of Overproduction," could be seen in the fact that it was published simultaneously in two leading journals: *Kommunist*, the theoretical organ of the Communist Party, and *Mirovaya ekonomika i mezhdunarodnye otnosheniya* (World Economy and International Relations), the journal of IMEMO. Varga began by associating unnamed "comrades" with Stalinism. Failure to distinguish between a true war economy and the period since 1945 was "dogmatic" and betrayed "what Lenin called the living spirit of Marxism: a concrete analysis of concrete conditions."[60]

Since conservatives were now speaking of chronic disproportions rather than directly quoting Stalin, Varga rhetorically charged that they had adopted a "bourgeois and revisionist" theory originating in Say's law of markets; that is, the contention that all goods could be sold if only they were produced in correct proportions. Varga allowed that disproportions might explain "a partial crisis in separate branches of industry,"[61] but he was determined that an explanation of the cycle as a whole had to begin with aggregate demand and supply. As in 1946, he insisted that state expenditures in a war economy rendered the problem of markets inoperative:

> The Second World War, like every great war, interrupted the normal course of the cycle. Involving an enormous, extraordinary demand for war materials at a time when production for civilian purposes was curtailed, it created an effective demand that exceeded the supply of commodities for several years. In such circumstances . . . a crisis of overproduction is simply impossible.[62]

Varga thought output had declined in 1945-46 because industry had to convert from military to peacetime production. Once this process was completed, the first postwar crisis came in 1947 and the second did not begin until ten or eleven years later. This periodicity was determined by the reproduction of fixed capital, the "material basis" of Marx's cycle.[63] As far as military expenditures were concerned, Varga insisted that even in peacetime they might have beneficial effects in supporting aggregate demand:

> If a country has unused reserves of production capacity, materials and labor power due to an insufficiency of effective demand . . . then military orders lead to increased output, expand the market, and contribute to *lengthening the phases of recovery, expansion (and overexpansion), that is, the length of the cycle.* . . . If a country has no unused reserves of production capacity, then military production does not lead to expansion of the volume of production as a whole, but instead occurs at the expense of civilian production.[64]

Rather than causing structural disproportions in the United States, Varga thought military spending had dampened "intermediate crises" and prolonged the cycle. The very length of the expansion also suggested, however, that the crisis of 1958 would be unusually severe. Because Congress had assigned only an inconsequential sum to public works, there would be no important countercyclical effect. American "corporate interests" were even opposing Eisenhower's modest proposal to extend the duration of unemployment benefits. Big business thought labor was becoming "too arrogant" with only 2.5 million unemployed, and capitalists wanted "to use the crisis to undermine, or at least weaken, the American labour movement."[65] Varga concluded that "although the crisis in the USA will not be as deep or protracted as that of 1929-1933, it will be deeper and longer than previous . . . [intermediate crises] and is the beginning of a world crisis of overproduction."[66]

At a meeting of IMEMO called to discuss Varga's findings, numerous participants thought he had conceded too much to conservative predictions of imminent catastrophe. Ya.A. Kronrod denied that a long expansion necessarily pointed to a severe contraction. Financial and stock markets remained stable, and Kronrod could detect no signs of crisis phenomena in Western Europe.[67] I.M. Lemin suspected that technological progress would continue to result in new investments and that Varga had underestimated the role of state-monopoly anticrisis measures.[68] N.V. Orlov, director of research for the USSR Ministry of Foreign Trade, saw no reason to think that output would continue to fall in America or that investments would slow throughout Europe. Even if some European countries did encounter difficulties, Orlov doubted that there would be a world crisis of overproduction.[69] V.D. Kazakevich flatly rejected comparisons of 1958 with 1929-33; thus far American industrial output had fallen by 13 percent, whereas in 1929-33 the figure had been 54 percent.[70]

A survey of Soviet and foreign economists in June 1958 added to the confusion. Viktor Agartz, of West Germany, expected decisive state action to moderate the crisis.[71] Sam Aaronovitch, a "progressive" British economist, took the opposing view and suggested that conditions in both America and Europe would further deteriorate.[72] Victor Perlo, an American "progressive," predicted that the crisis would worsen.[73] Fernand Baudhuin, of the Louvain Catholic University in Belgium, said "it will be only of limited length and severity."[74] A.A. Manukyan foresaw "deepening of the economic crisis."[75] Joan Robinson, a left-Keynesian at Cambridge University, criticized American government inaction. She added, however: "I would like to warn my Marxist friends against wishful thinking. Remedial action will be taken in the end. This is not going to be the great final crisis of capitalism."[76]

By January 1959, Varga found himself agreeing with Joan Robinson. Contrary to his own prediction of an unusually severe downturn, the American economy had already passed through the worst phase in the spring of 1958 and had now moved from crisis to depression, indicating that recovery and expansion would follow. Varga associated the unexpectedly rapid improvement with a "sharp increase in government spending on armaments, roads, etc., which led to a budget deficit of $12,000-15,000 million in the 1958/59 fiscal year and . . . moderated the impact of the overproduction crisis."[77] Although much of this deficit was in fact due to automatic stabilizers—falling taxation revenues and unplanned increases of expenditures—Varga credited the American government with decisive anticrisis measures.

By the summer of 1959 numerous Soviet writers began to think that state action had turned out to be far more effective than originally anticipated. S.A. Dalin attributed the unusual brevity of the crisis to both "the internal, spontaneous forces of capitalism" and the fact that government spending had compensated for a temporary fall of consumption and private investment.[78] In the 1930s Dalin had written the most comprehensive Soviet study of the New Deal. He now thought Eisenhower was applying New Deal logic for Cold War purposes. Publicly financed construction expenditures under Eisenhower had turned out to be even higher than under Roosevelt, thereby shortening the crisis and artificially accelerating a recovery. Dalin commented that

> In light of these facts, it strikes one as very strange that the Republican Eisenhower should declare that he is an opponent of the Democrat Roosevelt's "New Deal". The real difference . . . is that under Roosevelt, in 1933-1938, Congress prevented the government from undertaking military construction projects, whereas the policy of "cold war", waged by Eisenhower's government, is accompanied by expansion of state military construction.[79]

In August 1959, A.A. Manukyan also wrote that "a sharp rise in war contracts"[80] had caused "a considerable increase in output."[81] Manukyan thought the latest crisis had again been "intermediate," as in 1953-54, and had been followed by "return to an uninterrupted boom phase." Precisely because the crisis was so brief, however, he cautioned that it had failed to clear the way for a normal expansion: "a [genuine] cyclical crisis tends to iron out . . . the contradictions produced in the preceding period. . . . An intermediate crisis . . . is no more than a temporary respite."[82] Manukyan noted that *U.S. News and World Report* was already warning of "trouble to follow" by late 1960.[83]

Whatever the cause of the recovery, many analysts concluded that the system of state-monopoly capitalism had clearly demonstrated a capacity to broaden internal markets. Even I.I. Kuz'minov conceded that militarization should not be given too one-sided an interpretation. Drawing upon reserves of chronically idle productive forces, the ruling class had used arms expenditures with a stimulating effect: "Experience shows that militarization of the economy can, in certain circumstances, . . . promote . . . greater use of enterprise capacity and reduce unemployment."[84] In October 1959, L.A. Mendel'son told a conference in Berlin that Stalin had been mistaken: "Denial of the possibility of expansion of the capitalist market is also denial of the possibility of capitalist expanded reproduction."[85] A.A. Arzumanyan thought the market had seen a "relative narrowing" compared to growth of the productive forces, but "It would, of course, be incorrect to deny the absolute increase in the absorptive capacity of the capitalist market that has occurred in the postwar period."[86]

Having begun with a quarrel over one-sided war economies, interpretations of the recession of 1957-58 ended in limited agreement that recovery had in fact been supported by arms purchases and military construction. No Soviet writer believed, however, that militarization could provide a permanent solution. Kuz'minov still argued that the basic tendency of the general crisis was toward "absolute" working-class impoverishment and chronic unemployment;[87] Mendel'son thought that industrial reequipping, in place of new construction, would continue to limit job creation;[88] and A.A. Manukyan emphasized that recovery had left 3 million workers permanently displaced "as a result of technological changes, automation, the closing of old plants, and concentration of production. The net result: industry has regained its maximum production level with a considerably smaller number of workers."[89]

By encouraging measures to raise labor productivity, the recession appeared to have made the American economy even more dependent upon militarization in order to compensate for reduced personal incomes. Varga agreed that new technology required "fewer workers per unit of output. This will, of course, mean a smaller volume of capital investment. . . . All American economists believe that it will take several years for investments to regain the pre-crisis volume. In other words, . . . the American working class will be faced with a long period of chronic mass unemployment."[90] D. Kostyukhin wrote that "The absolute number of industrial workers is steadily declining: last year the manufacturing industries were turning out 5 per cent more than in 1957 with 5 per cent . . . [fewer] workers, and 60 per cent more than 12 years ago with a much smaller labour force." By April 1960 Kostyukhin warned that there were already new "recession clouds . . . on the horizon."[91]

While it temporarily calmed the dispute over one-sided war economies, the American recovery also had the effect of creating new apprehension in the Soviet Union. If arms expenditures had been the government's response to this crisis, what should be expected the next time production declined? If higher labor productivity meant lower levels of industrial employment, did it not follow that even more military spending would be needed in the next crisis? If the Americans were going to rely on militarization to deal with every cyclical fluctuation, what were the implications for the Cold War? Many writers saw a direct connection between economic instability in the late 1950s and a global increase of Cold War tensions.

4. Capitalist Crises and Socialist Markets

However much they quarreled over his economic insight, neither economists nor Soviet political leaders had forgotten Stalin's warning that "every time the contradictions of capitalism become acute the bourgeoisie turns its gaze toward the USSR." Since Lenin's response to the Genoa Conference in 1922 and Stalin's dispatch of Litvinov to the London economic conference in 1933, it had been axiomatic in Soviet thought that capitalists react to crises with imperialist adventures and that socialist markets might avert the risk of war. Khrushchev returned to this theme in 1958 when he urged that both the United States and the Soviet Union would benefit if trade were substituted for the arms race as an anticyclical instrument.

In May the IMEMO journal published an interview in which the Soviet leader told the editor of an American newspaper, *The Journal of Commerce*, that "The Soviet Union, the People's Republic of China and other socialist countries could absorb a large volume of commodities produced in America. In that way the slump, which is currently taking place in American industry, could be liquidated on a healthy basis."[92]

Underlining the connection between trade and peaceful coexistence, Anastas Mikoyan also criticized Stalinists for continuing to speak of two world markets while forgetting the dialectical unity between them:

> These comrade economists apparently overlook the fact that there is a unity of opposites. . . . To deny this is to be misled, to commit a serious error, to begin with a dogmatic interpretation and to close one's eyes to the fact that there exists a significant commodity turnover between these markets as well as other forms of economic ties. If one looks into the matter further, one sees that such comments essentially contradict the Leninist principle of coexistence of two systems.[93]

On June 2, 1958, Khrushchev wrote to Eisenhower proposing trade expansion and recalling the words of Cordell Hull, Roosevelt's secretary of state, that "commerce and association may be the antidote for war."[94] Anxious to restructure his domestic economy, Khrushchev reaffirmed that the Soviet government was interested in importing consumer goods; machinery for the paper, woodworking, textile, leather, food-processing, and other industries; refrigeration and air-conditioning equipment; gas pipelines, chemical, and pharmaceutical products; and even complete systems of equipment for factories to manufacture synthetic materials, all of which might amount to several billions of dollars in coming years—provided the U.S. government made long-term credits available.[95]

Khrushchev did not get his credits, but in August 1958 the western embargo lists were again slashed. The president of the British Board of Trade echoed sentiments in Moscow when he declared that "the free world should not hesitate to increase its trade with the Communists, for it is through trade and growing rich together that we have the best chance of making them prefer a quiet life."[96] The Eisenhower administration, in contrast, made a political decision not to encourage American firms to do business with communist countries. A State Department memorandum remarked that "The major considerations in our response [to Khrushchev] are political. The economic consequences of an affirmative reply would be relatively small."[97]

In September 1959, Khrushchev visited Eisenhower in Camp David on a mission that at least one historian, Louis J. Halle, speculates was genuinely intended to promote settlement of the Cold War.[98] Commenting on Khrushchev's trip, the Soviet journal *New Times* wrote: "the very fact that the talks are taking place has created a political climate that brings the world much closer to international detente than at any time since the war."[99] Before he would propose to Congress any further easing of American trade restrictions, however, Eisenhower wanted a settlement of lend-lease debts. Since the "delay" of the second front, Russians had believed for a decade and a half that they repaid lend-lease obligations many times over with their own appalling war casualties.[100]

I.S. Glagolev and Yu.N. Kapelinsky thought Khrushchev's initiative failed for altogether different reasons: one hundred of the largest American corporations were receiving more than two-thirds of military orders, worth up to $15 billion per year, and were intent on perpetuating international tensions. General Dynamics, Boeing, General Electric, and other monopolies had "their people" in the State Department and were "much more interested in the arms race than those strata of the bourgeoisie who are connected with production of commodities for civilian consumption in the domestic market."[101] The monopolies were warning Eisenhower that if military spending were cut there would be another economic crisis. Glagolev and Kapelinsky estimated that if 15-20 percent of the military budget were spent instead on housing, the result would be five hundred thousand new homes per year and employment for eight to nine hundred thousand workers.[102]

Soviet observers were convinced that American foreign policy reflected the country's domestic problems. Following the launch of Sputnik in 1957, the United States accelerated its own missile-building program. In the summer and autumn of 1958, the Seventh Fleet escorted Chinese Nationalist troops and supplies to the islands of Quemoy and Matsu in response to shelling by the mainland Chinese. On Quemoy the Marines installed howitzers capable of firing atomic shells. In July 1958 Eisenhower sent troops to Lebanon to stabilize the Middle East and protect western access to oil. In February 1960 the Soviet Union agreed to supply Castro's Cuba with oil, machinery, and technicians in exchange for sugar and a strategic foothold off the American coast. In May the Soviet Union brought down an American spy plane over Soviet territory, ending any prospect for a successful summit meeting scheduled for the same month. By August 1960 plans were under way in the United States to train an anti-Castro army to invade Cuba early in 1961.

Throughout this period of military buildup, Soviet analysts repeatedly advised their leaders that ultimately the Americans would seek to stabilize their own economy by helping Khrushchev with his seven-year plan of industrial modernization. Associating the Middle East crisis with

American domestic recession, I.I. Kuz'minov was one of many who urged that trade be recognized as "another way of easing the crisis":

> The advantages of this way are obvious. It does not require an increase of military expenditures and taxes on the population but, on the contrary, creates the possibility of reducing them and increasing the purchasing power of the masses. . . . It does not require diversion of resources into nonproductive consumption in the military branches but, on the contrary, creates the possibility of directing these resources into the production of goods to satisfy civilian needs.[103]

Kuz'minov was convinced that "far-sighted representatives" of American business must favor coexistence. There was only one conceivable explanation for Washington's refusal to cooperate: the most reactionary monopolists continued to orchestrate policy behind the scenes. I. Mikuson held American oil companies responsible for conflicts in the Middle East and referred to reports from the Rockefeller brothers calling for "a new world order." Henry Kissinger, director of special studies for the Rockefeller Brothers Fund, had proposed that in the age of nuclear stalemate America gear up to fight "limited wars," whereas Democratic senators such as Morse, Fulbright, Mansfield, Humphrey, and Kennedy reflected mass pressures when they criticized the adventurist policies of the State Department.[104]

S.M. Men'shikov predicted in October 1958 that if liberal Democrats strengthened their representation through impending congressional elections, there would be "fresh hope of a return to the New Deal."[105] Following "the biggest Democratic landslide since the days of Roosevelt,"[106] Men'shikov told Soviet readers that "millions of Americans want an end to the present balancing on the brink of war and attacks on labour. What they want is a return to the Roosevelt policies. . . ."[107] When Democratic majorities in both the Senate and the House failed to produce more conciliatory policies, Men'shikov explained that Nelson Rockefeller and Vice-President Richard Nixon, both potential Republican candidates to succeed Eisenhower, were the most influential spokesmen of big business interests who opposed trade and peaceful coexistence.[108]

When John F. Kennedy won the Democratic nomination in July 1960, Men'shikov wrote that Kennedy was "chiefly known for his ability to be on good terms [with both] the reactionary and liberal forces of his party."[109] "The racialist element and the big oil interests"[110] had persuaded Kennedy to take Lyndon B. Johnson as his running mate, however, with the consequence that Kennedy talked of peace at the same time that he promised to increase military spending by $3 billion a year.[111] Richard Nixon, the Republican candidate, was "known for his direct ties with the big California banking interests" and preferred an increase of $3.5 billion.[112] Describing Nixon as "an unprincipled careerist who owes his political advancement to McCarthy hysteria and anti-Communist repression,"[113] Men'shikov worried that neither presidential contender would encourage trade and coexistence.

By the autumn of 1960, Soviet writers claimed to detect a familiar reflex action on the part of American imperialists. Kuz'minov linked the intensifying arms race with yet another industrial recession, which had broken out the previous April. The issue of military spending was dominating American politics because big capital would contemplate no other form of economic stimulus. Kuz'minov expressed a common Soviet conviction when he wrote that

> Any hitch in production and trade, all the more so an economic crisis, aggravates the contradictions of capitalism and increases the aggressiveness of the imperialist powers. This was the case in the past and is the case this year as well. The growing economic difficulties and shrinking production have brought on a new fit of militarist fever and further heightened the aggressiveness of U.S. imperialist elements. Hence the increase of military appropriations and the extolling of economic militarization as a panacea against crises and "recessions".[114]

5. A New Crisis in America

The new recession in America began in the spring of 1960, only two years after the previous one, and immediately reopened the debate over just how to account for such extraordinary fluctuations. Varga had been confident as late as August 1959 that Marx's classical cycle had been restored: "the cyclical movement inherent in the capitalist mode of production will . . . resume its normal course, accompanied, as the experience of a century shows, roughly every six to eight years by a world economic crisis."[115] More conservative thinkers replied that Varga had once again misjudged American prospects. According to A.A. Arzumanyan, arms production had contributed only a modest counter-cyclical stimulus because, instead of new construction, it merely involved more output from existing factories in an economy that was already militarized.[116]

Arguing that the recession of 1960-61 confirmed his appraisal of the one-sided war economy, A.I. Kats applied a similar argument to the entire American industrial sector. New technologies were displacing living labor and causing such rapid productivity gains as to prevent *either military expenditures or private investments* from contributing to an overall increase of employment. Each additional unit of output required a smaller investment, thereby weakening the material basis upon which classical cycles depended and proving that fixed-capital expenditures could never generate a normal expansion:

> An important factor in the intensification of contradictions . . . is the enormous progress of science and technology, which has led to a society-wide increase of output per unit of fixed capital. As a result . . ., *the problem of markets has become extraordinarily acute. . . .* [A] decline of investments in fixed capital per unit of output leads to rapid growth of idle production capacity. . . . The result is that there accumulates such a volume of potential production capacity that a sharp increase of military production . . . causes, even at the outset, only a limited wave of capital investments and, in the final analysis, has only a modest effect on the conjuncture.[117]

As technological change added to chronic unemployment, low real wages meant that any increase of production in Department II must lead to overaccumulation of inventories and a new crisis of general overproduction. Kats warned that "the comparatively rapid surmounting of the economic crisis of 1957-1958 by no means changed the prospect of marking time over a long period or a weak development of capitalist production in the USA, accompanied by new and frequent outbreaks of crisis."[118] In April 1961, Kats said publicly what more discreet conservatives kept to themselves: "It is perfectly obvious that what is coming is a kind of industrial cycle that, whatever its fluctuations, will not yield any significant growth of industrial production. That will be a kind of variant of the depression of a special kind."[119]

Varga thought this was an absurd conclusion. He conceded that it was not possible to speak of "stability"[120] at a time when Canada and the United States were again in the stage of crisis; he also admitted that, contrary to his own expectation, American cycles were indeed becoming significantly shorter.[121] Although he believed that the "material basis" of the cycle continued to be replacement and expansion of fixed capital, which in turn expanded the market,[122] he was obviously anxious to explain why the United States was having a cycle every four years or less. He offered several suggestions: technological change, as Marx had predicted, involved earlier replacement of equipment and shorter cycles of investment; state-monopoly measures facilitated such investment by allowing tax deductions for accelerated depreciation; and more investments than ever before were taking the form of reequipping existing factories rather than new construction—65 percent of the total in 1960 (according to *Business Week*).[123]

Because reequipping factories increased output more quickly, Varga agreed with conservatives that earlier appearance of redundant capacity was the main factor reducing the cycle's length. On the matter of which *phase* was being shortened, however, his conclusion turned out to be the opposite of the one proposed by Kats. In the conservative interpretation, the phase of *expansion* was being cut short by chronic unemployment and insufficient consumer demand; Kats' reference to the "depression of a special kind" implied that no cyclical expansion was possible at all. Varga protested that not only was there no "depression of a special kind," but even the normal phase of depression was becoming less evident:

> The question arises as to which of the phases of the cycle is being shortened. If one takes as an example what has been happening in the USA in the postwar period, then it is clear that *above all the phase of depression is being shortened*. And this is quite understandable. If the capitalists are able, using depreciation funds, to undertake [more frequent and rapid] renewal and expansion of fixed capital, then the phase of depression, that is, the period when production marks time on approximately the same level, must become less prolonged.[124]

In April the journal *World Economy and International Relations* published a summary of another meeting at IMEMO to discuss Varga's latest conclusions. Although S.A. Dalin agreed that the cycle had been abbreviated, he disputed Varga's projection of a shortened depression: "it is absolutely clear that given such an enormous underutilization of enterprises, the postcrisis phase of depression . . . will be much more prolonged than in previous postwar cycles."[125] Ya.A. Kronrod denied that cycles were becoming shorter: "an analysis of the rate of amortization still indicates that the turnover of fixed capital takes, on average, 8-10 years. This is an objective fact."[126] A.A. Manukyan found Varga's argument incomprehensible: even allowing for an abbreviated depression, how could one possibly take the *two-year period* from 1958 to 1960 to be an entire cycle?[127] L.A. Mendel'son answered Manukyan by claiming that the recession of 1960-61 was merely another in a series of "crises of a special kind" caused by continuous militarization.[128]

By far the most original response came from Stanislav M. Men'shikov, who supported Varga in principle but thought he was wrong to assume that every cycle must include all four classical phases: crisis, depression, recovery, and expansion. If one insisted on finding all phases, it was impossible to regard the period since 1958 as a complete cycle. Varga had already recognized, however, that the depression phase was the one being shortened. Men'shikov thought depressions might be disappearing altogether:

> In the period of the general crisis of capitalism the cycle is deformed and there is no strict sequence of phases. . . . In the 1930s we witnessed a cycle consisting of three, not four phases. . . . Theoretically it is not impossible to have a cycle consisting only of two phases: crisis and recovery. . . . E.S. Varga himself writes that "the phase of depression is being shortened". . . . Why not go further and say that in such a cycle there might be no depression whatsoever?[129]

Not only were depressions becoming immeasurably brief, but there was also no certainty that they would any longer be transmitted from one country to another. Noting that American instability had left Western Europe virtually untouched, Men'shikov pointed to several new, non-cyclical factors that worked against a global crisis of the kind experienced in the 1930s: trade with socialist markets had lessened the vulnerability of some capitalist countries; working-class struggles had broadened domestic markets through wage increases; state purchases often accounted for 10-25 percent of the final product and 30-45 percent of all investments; and a new scientific-technical revolution required continuous renovation of fixed capital even during crisis periods.[130]

While conservatives emphasized the labor-displacing effects of new technologies, Men'shikov saw another possibility. What appeared to be emerging was a new pattern of market creation. In previous decades capitalism had grown mainly through *"extensive* expansion of production,"* either opening new markets in other countries or building more factories. This process now seemed to be giving way to *"intensive* expansion,"* or steady productivity increases through replacement of obsolescent equipment. With a sufficiently rapid pace of technological change, Men'shikov saw no reason why employment should not continue to grow in order to supply firms with new means of production. Continuous reequipping would minimize crises and depressions in Department I.

Moreover, even if new equipment did displace workers from some industries, they were now finding alternative employment in the growing service sector, suggesting that crises would also be moderated in Department II. The earnings of service workers were less sensitive to cyclical influences and were "only to a small extent associated with the economic situation."[131] Dismissing Kats' "primitive" conception of "an 'automatic crash' of the capitalist system,"[132] Men'shikov cited other "reserves" that might alleviate the alleged chronic problem of markets:

> Especially important would be an increase of state spending on *civilian* construction, in particular by using resources that would be freed as a result of curtailing military appropriations. . . . It is a fact that in the wealthiest country of the capitalist world the authorities "cannot afford" resources for the liquidation of slums, construction of schools, provision of medical services to the masses, subsidization of scientific research, etc. An increase of expenditures on social needs would have not only a direct effect, keeping construction orders at a high level, but also an important indirect effect, increasing that portion of their incomes that people cannot presently spend on ordinary commodities because of inadequate social services. In that way, every additional dollar of state spending on civilian needs would cause a multiple growth of demand for products from Departments I and II.[133]

In Keynesian terms, Men'shikov was saying that public money, wisely spent, could increase workers' discretionary income, raise the social propensity to consume, quicken investments, and promote higher and more stable levels of employment. Representing a younger generation of economists, who had played no part in Stalinist attacks on Varga, Men'shikov saw no reason why the capitalist state could not become an important and perhaps even what Varga had called a "decisive factor." By the mid-1960s Men'shikov would take the lead in developing a new interpretation of capitalist "regulation" and countercyclical "planning." In 1961, however, economists were no closer to a consensus than they had been in 1957. In the resulting stalemate, IMEMO supported Varga and instructed exponents of the one-sided war economy to overcome "remnants of dogmatism and vulgarization." Predictions of an "automatic collapse" were said to make serious economic analysis impossible, while references to "an uninterrupted decline of real wages" only embarrassed foreign communists.[134]

6. The "Third Stage" and Parliamentary Transition to Socialism

As economists wrestled with the American cycle, Khrushchev had more practical concerns. In his mind, at least two things were clear: the "depression of a special kind" was over, and recessions in the United States were proving to be both limited and localized. With capitalism showing no signs of collapse, Khrushchev judged that Communists had to find new ways to transform it from within. In *Changes in the Economic Structure of Capitalism*, Varga had predicted that "The question of the greater or lesser participation in management of the state will be the main content of the political struggle between the two basic classes of capitalist society: the bourgeoisie and the proletariat."[135] Khrushchev's political strategy began with the identical premise.

Khrushchev linked the prospective victory of a left-wing electoral coalition with his claim that the world socialist system was becoming "the decisive factor." With the Americans facing one recession after another, in November 1960 delegates from eighty-one parties met in Moscow to proclaim a new, third stage of the general crisis at the same time as the Soviet Union entered its own new stage of "full-scale construction of a communist society."[136] Given this change in the world relation of forces, the delegates decided that the example of the Soviet Union and other socialist countries would inspire progressives everywhere to join forces, demand peaceful reforms, and oppose the militarist ambitions of a handful of monopolists.

A communique, issued by the eighty-one parties, urged formation of "a broad mass movement for the use of funds and resources, to be released through disarmament, for the needs of civilian production, housing, health, public education, social security, scientific research, etc."[137] Communists were to cooperate with social democrats, "their class brothers," in order to isolate reactionaries through "nationalisation of the key branches of economy and democratisation of their management."[138] A new program of the Soviet party, adopted in October 1961, anticipated situations "in which it will be preferable for the bourgeoisie, as Marx and Lenin foresaw, to agree to the basic means of production being purchased . . . and for the proletariat to 'pay off' the bourgeoisie."[139]

In the late 1940s Varga and his colleagues at the Institute of World Economy had been vilified for speaking of the British Labour government's nationalization program as "progress in the direction of democracy of a new type." By 1961 democratic nationalization—with compensation—became an integral part of the program of peaceful transition. In *Finance Capital* Rudolf Hilferding had claimed that nationalization of six Berlin banks would place effective control of industry in the hands of a socialist government. In 1960 Otto Kuusinen, one of Khrushchev's chief ideologists, quoted Lenin's view that state-monopoly capitalism is "the material preparation for socialism." According to Kuusinen, "the simple act of nationalising the property of the monopolies in the highly developed capitalist countries turns from 60 to 70 percent of social production into national property."[140] Kuusinen used exactly Varga's words when he associated peaceful transition with "*democracy of a new type*, . . . democracy which would uphold the interests of the people."[141]

In May 1960, A.A. Arzumanyan also rejected the Stalinist slogan of the state's inevitable "subjugation" to the monopolies. As director of IMEMO, he indicated that the political superstructure should be regarded as "dialectically" related to monopoly capital, implying both cooperation and opposition.[142] The monopolistic bourgeoisie were said to derive economic benefit from nationalization, but they also opposed it as an incursion upon the sacred principles of private property.[143] Taking nationalized industry to be the material basis for peaceful transition, Arzumanyan claimed that popular pressures to expand the state's role would intensify "the division of society into [two] opposing forces: the people and the monopolies."[144] All classes of society, including small capitalists, shared a common interest in curbing militarists and reactionaries.

In terms of European politics, these changes pointed to efforts to form coalition governments with social democrats as in the period up to 1947. In the United States, a comparable short-term objective would be resumption of the New Deal. When John F. Kennedy took office as president in January 1961, the United States had been in recession since the spring of 1960. The Soviet journal *New Times* expressed hope that Kennedy would pick up where Roosevelt left off: "Mr. Kennedy . . . declared he would follow the policy of Franklin D. Roosevelt. This won him valuable support, for Roosevelt and the policies he stood for enjoy wide popularity, and many Americans . . . hope that the Democrats . . . will revive the Roosevelt tradition. . . ."[145] On behalf of the Soviet government, Khrushchev told Kennedy: "We hope that during your stay in office relations between our countries will take the path they followed in the days of Franklin Roosevelt."[146]

According to S. Bol'shakov, Kennedy's victory resulted from "the protest of the industrial proletariat against the economic policy of the [Eisenhower] government of 'big business.'"[147] Kennedy had been supported by trade unions, the urban poor, and American negroes, elements of the same coalition that elected Roosevelt in the 1930s. There was no doubt that "awakening voters' memories of the policy of Franklin Roosevelt, the Democratic party promoted the victory of its candidate."[148] Arthur Schlesinger, Harvard professor and a key Kennedy adviser, had proposed repeal of corporate tax exemptions in order to eliminate the gap between private wealth and the penury of public services. Kennedy had also promised to use state regulation in order to achieve an annual growth rate of 5 percent. Bol'shakov understood such statements to mean that "in order to save capitalism, it must be reformed, even partly at the expense of the capitalists themselves. The identical goal was the basis of Roosevelt's New Deal."[149]

Bol'shakov also advised Soviet readers, however, that in his book *Strategy for Peace*, Kennedy had emphasized his commitment to American military strength. Besides calling for increased production of Polaris and Minuteman missiles, he had promised to prepare the country for "so-called 'local wars.'"[150] Kennedy's contradictory proposals were said to reflect the opposing political and economic forces of American society. Since the official Soviet view held that neither war nor state subjugation by the monopolies was any longer inevitable, Bol'shakov wished Kennedy well in overcoming Cold War "brinkmanship" and the "hostility to reforms" prevalent in the "monopolistic circles that stood behind Nixon."[151]

CHAPTER 6

"NEW FRONTIERS" OF STATE-MONOPOLY CAPITALISM

The unresolved conflict over American cycles left several irreconcilable themes in Soviet literature by the beginning of the 1960s. Conservatives remained convinced that monopolies subjugated the state; reformists emphasized that the ruling class was divided and susceptible to pressures from below. Conservatives held that state support of monopolies was a permanent feature of the one-sided American war economy; Varga, Men'shikov, and others thought that civilian expenditures might offset cyclical disturbances to the benefit of workers. When John F. Kennedy assumed the presidency in January 1961, liberal-minded authors hoped that his slogan of New Frontiers pointed to reforms similar to Roosevelt's New Deal. This prospect implied that Kennedy, like Roosevelt, might exercise a degree of *political autonomy* in relation to monopoly capital.

Stalinists dismissed such ideas as naive illusions. According to Stalin, the law of "maximum capitalist profit" operated "independently of the will of people" and made state spending on armaments objectively necessary. In October 1961, Khrushchev gave the twenty-second party congress a mixed message that reformists and Stalinists could both quote. On the one hand, Khrushchev acknowledged that state intervention clearly had "a certain effect, inducing some growth of production and renewal of basic capital"; on the other hand, he also declared that "state-monopoly capitalism does not cancel—nor can it cancel—the objective economic laws of capitalism." The state was not "a supra-class force that . . . safeguards . . . the interests of both labor and capital to an equal degree." Until an antimonopoly coalition took power, state-monopoly capitalism would continue to entail "fusion of the monopoly forces and the forces of the state into a single mechanism."[1]

Adding to the difficulty of resolving these issues was the fact that both conservatives and reformists could also invoke long-established traditions. Marxism emphasized determination of politics by economic laws, but at the same time Engels anticipated growing interaction between the political "superstructure" and the economic "base." Engels had expected trusts and cartels to "outgrow the laws of the capitalist mode of commodity exchange," causing the state eventually to regulate the economy in the new role of "collective capitalist." Marx attached less significance to the state, but he too wrote that centralization and concentration of capital "establishes a monopoly in certain spheres and thereby requires state interference."[2]

During the first half of the 1960s, novel forms of state-monopoly capitalism lent unexpected credibility to reformism. The European Economic Community (EEC) appeared to demonstrate the possibility of interstate cooperation in planning market expansion. At the same time, Kennedy recruited a Council of Economic Advisers who called for a Keynesian revolution to avert stagnation. When Varga and others praised Kennedy's initiatives, their opponents countered that the results would be inconsequential. Stalin had said in 1934 that Roosevelt could not single-handedly reform capitalism. Three decades later his ideological heirs said the same of Kennedy.

As empirical evidence began to favor reformist interpretations, conservatives turned from the "depression of a special kind" to more technical arguments. In 1961, the first year of Kennedy's presidency, S.L. Vygodsky published *Essays on the Theory of Modern Capitalism*. In 1964, one year after Kennedy's assassination, G.A. Kozlov published *The Action of the Law of Value in Conditions of Modern Capitalism*. Both authors held that Stalin's law of "maximum capitalist profit" precluded state autonomy and, in an economy characterized by chronic disproportions, replaced Marx's law of value.

1. S.L. Vygodsky: Monopoly Prices and Chronic Disproportionality

Marx thought the law of value tended to restructure industrial proportions through the spontaneous mechanism of cyclical price changes. In a letter of July 11, 1868, he compared this process to a law of nature: its form of operation might alter, but at all stages of capitalism the law of value would remain objectively necessary.[3] For Marx, the *value* of a commodity was measured by "the labour time socially necessary for its production."[4] Since *prices* were subject to numerous short-run influences, Marx wrote that "price . . . constantly stands above or below the value of the commodity, and the value of the commodity itself exists in this up-and-down movement of commodity prices."[5] Labor content, in other words, determined value as a norm around which "market prices" fluctuated.

In a developed capitalist economy, price included not only the cost of labor and materials but also an important element of fixed-capital depreciation. Because technical conditions varied between industries and firms, the organic composition of capital would also be different; some branches would use more fixed capital relative to labor, others less. But if they all produced in the same competitive market, the law of value indicated that they must all tend to earn the same rate of profit. Marx called the theoretical price that would yield the average rate of profit in each endeavor the "price of production." If capital could not earn the average rate of profit in one industry, it would move elsewhere. Every cyclical crisis disturbed profit rates, causing technological change and restructuring. These "constant divergences" in profit rates would tend to be minimized "the more mobile the capital" and "the more quickly labour power can be transferred from one sphere to another."[6]

Stalinists discounted the significance of capital mobility during the general crisis. In their view, chronic disproportions originated with military procurement in World War II and continued throughout the 1950s. In 1952, S.L. Vygodsky had praised the law of "maximum capitalist profit" as the most "precious contribution" of Stalin's *Economic Problems*.[7] In *Essays on the Theory of Modern Capitalism,* he explained the "gigantic superprofits"[8] of American monopolies in terms of barriers to the free movement of capital. Protected against new entrants, monopolies imposed artificially high prices for means of production, slowed expansion of the consumer goods sector, and created chronic imbalance between the two Departments. "Proportional distribution of production" was said to be impossible once monopoly prices interfered with the tendency Marx had seen toward an average rate of profit.[9]

In *Finance Capital*, Hilferding had spoken of "one rate [of profit] for the large cartelized industries and another for the spheres of small-scale industry which have become dependent upon them; . . . capitalists in the cartelized industries rob the latter of a part of their surplus value."[10] Despite his previous association of the theory of intercapitalist transfers with reformism,[11] Vygodsky now agreed that monopoly prices exacted "tribute from all the other branches of industry and from agriculture."[12] He interpreted this to mean that the law of value had ceased to function in the economy as a whole and had been limited to relations between monopolies. While they artificially suppressed profit rates in the small-business sector, in dealings with each other the dominant firms demanded price concessions and thus preserved a tendency toward "a certain equalization of monopolistically high profits."[13]

Although he now appropriated Hilferding's theory, Vygodsky still emphasized that intercapitalist transfers must not obscure the origin of all surplus value in unpaid labor. In his calculation, U.S. output per worker had increased by 78.9 percent from 1939 to 1959; but only one-third of labor intensification had been compensated by higher real wages,[14] confirming that proletarian living standards had been driven far below the level even of physical subsistence.[15] Continuing to see unprecedented exploitation as the "decisive factor," Vygodsky estimated that the overall rate of surplus value had risen from 203.3 percent in 1939 to no less than 289.3 percent in 1959: after all costs of production were met, the surplus appropriated by capitalists was supposedly three times the total sum of wages.[16] The resulting chronic excess of industrial capacity had caused the number of productive workers to fall by 1.6 million from 1953 to 1960.[17]

Whereas Varga tried to reconcile American recessions with Marx's classical cycle, Vygodsky thought such efforts were contrived and pointless:[18] in the absence of *price flexibility*, spontaneous restructuring had become impossible. During each crisis of the 1950s iron and steel output had fallen, yet prices either rose or remained unchanged.[19] The steel industry exemplified a universal phenomenon: instead of reducing prices in response to falling demand, monopolies cut production and employment. As a result, Vygodsky made the absurd claim that the average rate of capacity utilization in American industry from 1953 to 1960 had been merely 56 percent—even lower than in the years 1933-40.[20]

Since Lenin had written that there could be no "pure" monopoly capitalism, excluding *all* competition, Vygodsky decided that monopolistic production had created its own unique contradiction: competition required each firm to install new technology and expand production capacity, but at the same time artificial restriction of output had become a new "law" of production.[21] In a "one-sided militarized economy,"[22] the state suppressed consumer demand by taxing wages to finance armaments.[23] Monopolies required this "guaranteed demand" because they could not otherwise alleviate the chronic problem of markets. Vygodsky contrasted classical capitalism with its modern form as follows:

> In the conditions of free competitive capitalism, the process of equalization [of supply with demand] occurred through . . . a reduction in the total sum of commodity prices to the level of effective demand. . . . In this way . . . conditions were created for the ensuing expansion. . . . In conditions of monopoly capitalism, and especially in its general crisis . . . . [monopoly] prices generally remain at the high, precrisis level. The contraction of production turns out to be all the more intensive, the greater is the disparity between production capacity and effective demand.[24]

The contradiction between high prices and the purchasing power of impoverished workers suggested that the U.S. government increased military expenditures not as an autonomous initiator of policy but in response to distortion of market laws. Because the "semiwar economy"[25] required continuous expenditure on armaments, it seemed equally apparent that the new recovery, which began in July 1961, would quickly be cut short by inadequate demand. Idle capacity meant that renovation of fixed capital would at best play a modest role; a weak industrial upturn would give way to another crisis, followed by renewed militarization.[26] Quoting Khrushchev to support this Stalinist argument, Vygodsky recited a familiar refrain: "State-monopoly capitalism means a fusion of the forces of the capitalist monopolies with the forces of the state into a single mechanism. . . ."[27]

2. G.A. Kozlov: Monopolies and the Law of Value

In *The Action of the Law of Value in Conditions of Modern Capitalism*, G.A. Kozlov ostensibly paid more heed to Marx. He wrote that the law of value—even in the distorted form of monopoly pricing—continued to be "an objectively necessary regulator"[28] and "the only possible regulator of the national economy."[29] The lower limit of monopoly profit was determined by the social average rate; the upper limit could not be specified because it included surplus value resulting from labor intensification, absolute and relative mass impoverishment,[30] transfers from small capitalists, and colonial exploitation.[31]

Marx had explained the tendency toward equalization of profit rates in terms of capital mobility. Although Vygodsky argued that this condition no longer applied, Kozlov thought capital continued to be mobile insofar as modern industry created new technologies and new branches of production. The eight financial groups who dominated the American economy, "including the Mellons, Du Ponts, Rockefellers, and Morgans,"[32] were able to move rapidly into expanding branches by drawing upon "strategic reserves" of liquid capital.[33] According to Kozlov, Kennedy increased these reserves by allowing a tax credit for new investments and more generous deductions for depreciation of existing fixed capital. With these qualifications, Kozlov arrived at the same conclusion as Vygodsky: the law of value remained in operation—but only in distorted form. Profits of small capitalists were held down by monopoly prices, and equalization of profit rates was confined to large firms in the form of "a tendency toward . . . a monopolistically modified price of production."[34]

Kozlov also agreed with Vygodsky that a normal cycle was impossible. In his view, reproduction of fixed capital no longer served as a predictable "material basis." Availability of enormous depreciation accounts, resulting from the high organic composition of capital in modern industry, had caused the scheduling of monopoly investments to become indeterminate. Tax credits and accelerated depreciation allowances provided funds that could be reinvested before existing equipment was due for physical replacement; on the other hand, because existing equipment was partly paid for with the aid of the state budget, it also functioned like "a free force of nature" and might not be replaced at all, despite technological obsolescence, until it ceased to operate. "In other words, the turnover of fixed capital is completely deformed."[35]

In the classical cycle, declining profits imposed fixed-capital renovation in order to reduce production costs. Kozlov followed Vygodsky by pointing out that monopoly prices tended to rise regardless of economic conditions. During the crisis of 1945-46, American steel prices had risen while production and sales fell.[36] The next crisis, in 1947-49, saw productivity in iron and steel grow by 25 percent, but lower production costs were again accompanied by higher prices.[37] In 1954 iron and steel production dropped by 21-22 percent, yet wholesale prices rose by a further 1.5 percent.[38] In 1957-58 steel output contracted by 25 percent, but in this case too some price increases occurred.[39] With monopoly prices in heavy industry deforming the entire economy, the state was forced to intervene. Militarization was an inevitable consequence of chronic disproportions. As Kozlov wrote,

> High prices on equipment impede the renovation of fixed capital. . . . Then [the monopolies] begin to look for salvation in artificial measures, in support from the state. Monopolistically

> inflated prices require artificially forced demand . . . . primarily
> through increased purchases of armaments.[40]

Bourgeois ideologists and Kennedy's economic advisers hoped that the
state, by managing aggregate demand, could function as "savior of
society" and "regulator of the economy."[41] Kozlov insisted that such
efforts only intensified contradictions. State subsidies, either directly in
the form of militarization or indirectly through tax concessions, supported the very monopolistic practices that caused crises to become more
frequent and irregular. The fundamental contradiction of state-monopoly
capitalism was that monopoly prices *reduced popular consumption* at the
same time as anticrisis measures required *increased demand* at the
expense of taxpayers. Monopolies subjugated the state because their
profits could not be secured "without state intervention." "This," Kozlov
declared, "is the essence of all theories of state regulation."[42]

3. The First Year of the Kennedy Administration

By the early 1960s leading American economists—for altogether different
reasons—had come to a similar conclusion: the greater frequency of
recessions in the 1950s called for deliberate government measures to
stimulate investments and consumer demand. Walter W. Heller, chairman of the Council of Economic Advisers, wrote of the Kennedy years
in terms of "completion of the Keynesian revolution."[43] Critical of *ad
hoc* management by the Eisenhower administration, Heller thought it was
obvious that "the economy cannot regulate itself. We now take for
granted that the government must step in to provide the essential stability
at high levels of growth and employment that the market mechanism, left
alone, cannot deliver."[44]

Many Americans considered that growth could best be promoted by
investing in public services and human capital. In *The Affluent Society*,
John Kenneth Galbraith criticized "conventional wisdom" for exalting
private investments at the expense of social services and education.[45]
Alvin Hansen worried that having satisfied much of the demand for
consumer durables, America faced a secular decline of investment outlets
unless stimulus were provided by expenditures on public services and
social infrastructure, which in turn would generate higher private
investments.[46] When the Democratic election platform promised to
increase government spending on health, education, and housing, more

liberal Soviet economists anticipated that the result might be an important contribution to social purchasing power.

S.M. Men'shikov and V.M. Shamberg wrote that "The state could moderate [contradictions] somewhat if it took decisive measures to raise the purchasing power of the broad masses and to expand nonmilitary social consumption" through devoting resources to schools, slum clearance, and peaceful scientific research.[47] In *The Economic Policy of the Kennedy Administration* (edited by Men'shikov), Shamberg noted that Kennedy was influenced by Galbraith's economics and by Roosevelt's social reforms: "In the struggle for votes, Kennedy linked faster rates of economic growth with increased social expenditures and an extension of public works, which were extremely popular among the broad masses since the first term of F.D. Roosevelt." However, Shamberg added that monopolies had their own interpretation of Kennedy's promises; to them, accelerated growth meant "an increase of military expenditures, higher profits, and reinforcement of the domestic and international positions of American imperialism."[48]

Shamberg was concerned that Kennedy's Task Force on the Economy, organized during the election campaign and headed by Paul Samuelson, preferred military to social programs.[49] Seymour E. Harris, a member of the task force, acknowledged that its report in January 1961 was not yet strongly Keynesian and that, "On public expenditures, the verdict was to go slowly."[50] Troubled by rising defense spending, federal budget deficits, and a deteriorating balance of payments, the report's authors also emphasized the need for a cautious monetary and interest-rate policy. Following this advice, early in his presidency Kennedy began to sacrifice promised social programs in order to finance Polaris submarines and the conventional armed forces.

Although Eisenhower had warned in his farewell address against the influence of the "military-industrial complex"—which he said was "felt in every city, every state house, every office of the federal government"—Kennedy secured a 15 percent increase of the military budget in 1961.[51] Higher military spending coincided with further deterioration of relations with the Soviet Union. In April 1961, American-supported Cuban exiles failed in their invasion of the Bay of Pigs. In June, Kennedy met with Khrushchev in Vienna and was told that the Berlin crisis must be settled on Russian terms within six months. In July, Kennedy called for a 25 percent increase of U.S. military strength. August brought the Berlin Wall, followed by explosion of a fifty-eight megaton Soviet nuclear device in November. During this same period,

U.S. military advisers were becoming more active in Laos, and America was taking the first fateful steps toward war in Vietnam.

With Kennedy less than a year into his presidency, Soviet commentators were convinced that he had already abandoned the progressive traditions of Roosevelt and succumbed to pressures from imperialist reactionaries. In October 1961, L.A. Leont'ev attributed the record peacetime military budget to the fact that major branches of industry were using only 69 percent of capacity. Because America was losing both the economic competition and the "struggle of ideas"[52] with communism, the imaginary "Soviet threat" was again being invoked to generate "war hysteria" and to rationalize militarization.[53] A.A. Arzumanyan said that Kennedy and the arms manufacturers, despite the Democrats' campaign promises of enlightened social policy, had no real interest in raising the incomes of workers and farmers and would therefore fail to alleviate the "problem of the market."[54] V.I. Lan remarked that "in the struggle between supporters of a more flexible policy and militant reactionaries, the advantage thus far has remained with the latter."[55]

4. Kennedy's Clash with U.S. Steel

In the spring of 1962, Kennedy stunned both Soviet onlookers and American businessmen by forcing steel manufacturers to rescind what he considered to be another inflationary price increase. Warning the industry that its pricing policies over the previous decade had caused unemployment and damage to the balance of payments,[56] the president had appealed to both the labor union and the industry to reach a moderate wage settlement. Immediately after the collective agreement was signed, however, U.S. Steel and other major producers simultaneously raised prices by $6 a ton. At a press conference in April 1962, Kennedy furiously denounced the price increase as "unjustifiable and irresponsible":

> In this serious hour in our Nation's history, when we are confronted with grave crises in Berlin and Southeast Asia, when we are devoting our energies to economic recovery and stability, when we are asking reservists to leave their homes and families for months on end and servicemen to risk their lives . . . and asking Union members to hold down their wage requests, . . . the American people will find it hard, as I do, to accept a

situation in which a tiny handful of steel executives, whose pursuit of private power and profit exceeds their sense of public responsibility, can show such utter contempt for the interests of 185 million Americans.[57]

Kennedy's tirade against the steel industry provided exactly the evidence needed to support a case for *state autonomy*. Varga saw in the president's response total vindication of views he had expressed before and after World War II. Like Roosevelt in the 1930s, Kennedy had isolated the "tiny handful" of steel magnates in a skillful maneuver to take advantage of intermonopoly contradictions. When the price increases were canceled, Varga wrote that "The chief reason why the President was successful was the *lack of unity among the monopolists, even among the steel barons.*"[58] The automobile monopolies, engineering industries, railway companies, and others had opposed the increase, and ". . . Kennedy expressed the general dissatisfaction and indignation of all steel consumers at the absolutely unwarranted rise in the price of steel."[59] Although Kennedy's action did not imply any "supraclass character of the state," Varga was not in the least surprised to see the president protecting the common interests of the ruling class at the expense of particular monopolies.[60]

At a conference held by IMEMO in May 1962, S.A. Dalin reacted to Kennedy's attack on the steel industry by demanding an end to "dogmatic" conceptions of state-monopoly capitalism. Stalin's formula of the state's "subjugation" (*podchinenie*) had to be replaced by Lenin's reference to "coalescence" (*srashchivanie*), in which the state at times acts in the interest of particular monopolies, while at other times it "acts in the interests of the bourgeoisie as a class, . . . [subordinating] the private interests of the monopolies . . . to general class interests."[61] Stanislav Men'shikov likewise believed that Kennedy had defended "the interests of his class" because private wealth gave him "relative autonomy" and placed him, like Roosevelt, "above" the immediate concerns of the monopolistic bourgeoisie: "Such a political course could not help but lead to a contradiction with the interests of separate monopoly groups, whose activity Kennedy wanted to restrict in the interests of the entire ruling class. Hence the . . . clashes with the world of 'big business'. . . . The monopoly press nicknamed [Kennedy] 'the president opposed to businessmen.'"[62]

Kennedy won the first round against the steel industry, but not long afterward doubts emerged as to the final outcome. On May 28, 1962, the

New York stock exchange suffered what Varga called "the biggest slump since the memorable Black Friday of the autumn of 1929." Varga speculated that "the *time* for the slump was chosen by the monopoly interests who cannot forgive Kennedy for preventing a steel price rise." The battle between the president and the steel companies concerned a cardinal question: "*have the monopolies exclusive rights in setting prices, or must they accept government intervention?*" Kennedy's action discredited Stalinist claims of state subjugation, but Varga also thought that "the monopolies opposed to the President wanted to teach him an object lesson." They had therefore "instructed their banks to start a selling spree, while the press frightened the small investor with predictions that the president's price-restraint policy would cut into dividends."[63]

Varga's interpretation seemed to be confirmed by the president's own supporters. Seymour E. Harris later wrote of the attitude of businessmen in a tone of bitter irony:

> In the spring of 1962, the stock market suffered a serious decline. Looking for a scapegoat, the business community blamed the President. Had he not reduced the prospects of business profits and threatened the free enterprise system through his interference with the steel industry? Had he not, during and after the campaign, threatened the stability of the system through the acceptance of large public spending deficits? Was not the unfavorable balance of payments a symptom of irresponsible fiscal and monetary policies . . .?[64]

Harris also noted, however, that during 1963 the stock market recovered and Kennedy's relations with big business "greatly improved." Two reasons for the change were a 7 percent investment tax credit and more generous provisions for fixed-capital depreciation.[65] In 1962 alone, the combined effect of these measures was a $2.5 billion reduction of corporate taxes. McGraw-Hill estimated the result to be a $1 billion per year increase in investments.[66] When social programs were at issue, Congress expressed alarm at budget deficits; when Kennedy surrendered such programs in order to win tax cuts, the Keynesian revolution began in America. Walter Heller described replacement of Eisenhower's reactive policies by a deliberate commitment to growth as a triumph of the "new economics" over "the old mythology" of balanced budgets.[67]

5. The Keynesian "Revolution" in America

During the election campaign, Kennedy had warned that American leadership in the Cold War required a strong economy with a 5 percent annual rate of growth. Soviet economists interpreted his conversion to Keynesianism as both a response to the challenge of socialism and a belated compromise with big business. The steel industry had defended price increases on the grounds that they were needed to finance modernization. By introducing investment tax credits and more generous depreciation allowances, Kennedy hoped to encourage technological renovation, improve productivity, and raise the level of employment.

Soviet critics believed this was precisely the wrong strategy. Vygodsky contended that tax credits and accelerated depreciation allowances could do nothing to encourage investments in an economy afflicted by chronic disproportionality: large corporations already possessed far more in depreciation accounts than they were willing to spend. In 1961 the total depreciation fund of American industry was 69 percent larger than in 1953; at the same time, manufacture of capital goods had grown by only 7 percent. According to Vygodsky, these data proved there was no basis "for the doctrine that faster depreciation speeds up the rate of industrial growth." Because depreciation charges were included as costs in the selling price of commodities, he predicted that Kennedy's concessions would only raise prices and further reduce mass purchasing power.[68] "What better proof is there," he asked, "that state-monopoly capitalism and militarism . . . have a negative effect on the economy?"[69]

Numerous other writers agreed that Kennedy could do little to solve the chronic problem of markets. A.A. Arzumanyan wrote that "An expansion of the domestic market could only be linked with an increase of personal consumption";[70] even if tax reductions did result in new investments, further automation would add to "chronic mass unemployment."[71] A.I. Kats pointed out that because of higher productivity and limited markets, industrial employment by 1960 was 2.1 percent lower than in 1943.[72] Citing Heller's own estimate that over five years new technology would displace up to 10 million additional workers, N. Ivanov predicted that productivity gains in industry would drive even more workers into the nonproductive service sector and thus slow real growth.[73] G. Naidenov concurred that Kennedy's measures to promote "corporate savings" by reducing taxes would merely aggravate the "problem of the market."[74]

Kennedy's advisers were aware of the need for more decisive action. They concluded that in order to close the "performance gap" between actual and potential rates of growth, both personal and corporate income taxes must be reduced. Seymour Harris believed that excessively high taxation contributed to idle capacity and was costing the country from $30-50 billion a year in lost production.[75] Walter Heller claimed that existing tax rates were so high that they choked off recoveries long before full employment could be approached. Heller estimated that the "full employment surplus" of 1960—the budget surplus that would have been generated with 4 percent unemployment at existing rates of taxation—was $13 billion. This "oppressive economic drag" had been a major force pulling the country into the recession of 1960-61.[76]

In January 1963, Kennedy proposed a tax reduction that would take effect by stages over a three-year period. In his economic report to Congress, he complained that "too many workers remain without jobs; too many machines continue idle; too much output goes unrealized."[77] In April he told a press conference that over an eighteen-month period the tax measure "would put $10 billion directly . . . into the hands of our people, which under the multiplier, will mean $30 billion, and I think can make a very important difference in reducing our unemployment."[78] Although the tax legislation was not passed until after his death, the effects of earlier policies were becoming apparent. In terms of constant prices, GNP grew by 6 percent in 1962,[79] investments rose by 8.2 percent,[80] and industrial production expanded in the first nine months of 1963 by 4.7 percent.[81] Observing that real GNP rose by an average of 5.5 percent per year from the first quarter of 1961 through to early 1964, Seymour Harris described economic performance in the Kennedy years as "amazing for peacetime."[82]

Soviet conservatives remained unimpressed. I.I. Kuz'minov translated the president's report to Congress into Stalinist language: Kennedy had admitted the existence of "chronic mass unemployment, chronic under-employment of capacity and slow . . . growth rates."[83] Kuz'minov attributed Kennedy's frantic measures to fear of another recession before the 1964 election. Writing in the journal *New Times,* A. Kashkarov argued in April 1963 that unemployment had not significantly fallen and that the tax measures would benefit mainly corporations and the rich. Kashkarov predicted that America would soon face "economic stagnation similar to the Great Depression."[84] Because three-quarters of increased government spending was going to military and related programs, V.S. Zorin linked Kennedy's policies to political pressures. Henry Kissinger and other "grey eminences," acting as spokesmen for "America's most aggressive imperialist forces," continued to promote monopoly capital's program of militarization, "limited war," and "flexible response."[85]

6. Cold War and the Balance of Payments

Despite differences over Kennedy's domestic policies, all Soviet writers agreed that his increases of peacetime military spending were responsible for serious deterioration in the balance of payments and would ultimately restrict America's capacity to project military power. From 1945 to the end of 1962 the United States had provided more than $91 billion in economic and military aid to governments opposed to the spread of communism.[86] It seemed that the ability to continue these commitments was now being circumscribed by concerns for long-run stability of the dollar. Sergei Dalin reported that in the decade before Kennedy's election, the cumulative balance of payments deficit exceeded $21 billion, more than $11 billion of which occurred in the last three Eisenhower years. From 1961 to 1963, the cumulative deficit grew by another $7.4 billion.[87]

So long as the postwar "dollar shortage" prevailed, European governments had willingly accumulated claims on the United States in order to acquire the reserves needed to restore convertibility of their own currencies and to ensure sufficient liquidity to accommodate growth of international trade. With recovery of Western Europe, however, the American balance of payments suffered from increased competition with European goods both in world markets and even within the United States itself. Khrushchev referred to the payments deficit when he told the twenty-second party congress that "American capitalism has passed its prime and is declining." The American financial oligarchy, in the words of the Soviet leader, no longer possessed "the strength or the means to implement its claims to the role of savior of capitalism."[88]

In 1945 the United States had held gold reserves of $24.6 billion, or 69.4 percent of the monetary gold of all capitalist countries. By November 1960 that figure had fallen to $18.1 billion, compared to $14.4 billion in net short-term obligations to other countries.[89] Seeing the dollar as the symbol of American imperialism, from 1960 onward the Soviet press gleefully predicted its erosion and eventual collapse as the dominant world currency. Varga quoted the London *Times*, which warned that a "flight from the dollar" would spread throughout Europe if central bank holdings became excessive and Europeans decided to convert their dollar deposits into gold.[90] Robert Triffin, an American specialist on the international currency system, encouraged Soviet hopes for a dollar crisis when he wrote that "a wind of panic swept over Washington officialdom" as early as October 1959 because of instability in the London gold market.[91] Kennedy told Congress that

> This loss of gold . . . concerns the whole free world. For we are the principal banker of the free world, and any potential weakness in our dollar spells trouble, not only for us but also for our friends and allies who rely on the dollar to finance a substantial portion of their trade.[92]

Varga thought the Americans, like the British a decade earlier, were discovering that they could no longer afford the Cold War. Although the trade balance remained in surplus and capital exports tended to be offset by foreign investment income, the United States was spending up to $8 billion a year on foreign aid and support of overseas armed forces.[93] Varga explained that "*The underlying cause of the present unfavourable balance of payments position, the depletion of gold reserves and the dollar crisis, should be sought in the huge expenditures necessitated by the cold war and America's claim to world domination.*"[94]

Kennedy attempted to improve the balance of payments in several ways. European allies were pressed to assume more of the foreign aid burden, to prepay some of their previous debts, and to increase weapons purchases from the United States. Some U.S. bases in Europe were shut down; foreign aid was increasingly tied to purchases from U.S. firms; and subsidies to foreign governments were partly replaced by loans.[95] Kennedy was also the first president since Roosevelt to consider liberalization of trade with the Soviet Union and Eastern Europe. A change of policy had been urged during the election campaign by a task force headed by George W. Ball, who reasoned that because western restrictions had "all but broken down," the new administration should reconsider "the potential advantages of expanded East-West trade."[96] John Kenneth Galbraith wrote that "We may . . . have more to [gain] . . . from Soviet trade than we lose from denying them some machine which, with a little delay, they can get from the Swedes or the Czechs."[97]

During 1960 and the first half of 1961, Western Europe sold close to $1 billion worth of strategic goods and equipment to the Soviet Union;[98] American sales of nonstrategic goods in 1961 amounted to only $42.6 million.[99] Although federal government departments worked throughout the Kennedy years to reconstruct economic relations with the Soviet bloc, their efforts were frustrated by Cold War conflicts.[100] The balance of payments deficit also continued to grow by approximately \$3 billion per year. In May 1963, U.S. short-term liabilities reached \$22.3 billion, while gold reserves had declined to \$15.8 billion. Since most of the short-term liabilities were owed to members of the European Economic Community, Soviet analysts ultimately associated America's decline with the EEC's emergence as a "third force" in world affairs.[101]

7. The European Community and American "Decline"

When six West European countries—Italy, France, the Federal Republic of Germany, Holland, Belgium, and Luxembourg—formed the Common Market in January 1958, Soviet economists were at first slow to recognize its significance. The first serious discussion of the EEC occurred at an IMEMO conference in the summer of 1959. Most participants minimized the potential for market expansion and predicted the EEC's disintegration once the relation of forces changed between member countries. Varga dismissed the Common Market as a romantic attempt to restore the free competition of pre-1914 capitalism.[102] Others saw it as nothing more than an American-sponsored scheme to coordinate the NATO blockade of socialist countries, erect a collective defense against national liberation movements in the colonies, and resist demands from workers for progressive reforms.

The tone of the IMEMO conference was almost uniformly negative. P. Suslin and V. Vetlanin referred to dominance of the EEC by West Germany, which longed for return of Hitler's "New Order."[103] I. Blishchenko spoke of "unified Europe" as the minimum program of monopoly capital, which hoped eventually to create an imperialist "world government."[104] G.P. Chernikov condemned the EEC as an "anti-national" conspiracy by the "cosmopolitan" bourgeoisie to harmonize wages at the levels of southern Italy.[105] D. Kostyukhin thought the Rockefeller Foundation had promoted unification in order to expand opportunities for subsidiaries of U.S. monopolies in the African possessions of France and Belgium.[106] Of a total of two dozen contributors to the conference only one, A.V. Kirsanov, denied that the EEC was doomed to failure and recognized that it would promote technological modernization and extend the scale of production.[107]

Of leading Soviet economists, the one who most seriously misjudged the EEC turned out to be Varga, who insisted that integration of developed capitalist economies could only have "insignificant" effects.[108] Some monopolies might expand their production capacity, but at the same time smaller enterprises, previously protected by tariffs, would face bankruptcy. If monopolies invested in new technologies, they would initiate a brief market expansion in Department I; but industrial modernization would also eventually curtail demand for labor and narrow the market for Department II. The final result would be overall market contraction, "the diametrical opposite of what is predicted by the apologists of the 'Common Market.'"[109]

Like Luxemburg in *The Accumulation of Capital*, Varga held that joining together the markets of industrialized capitalist countries could not possibly extend total market capacity. In theory, the union of a developed country with a *precapitalist* one might produce a "one-time" market expansion, but this process would end as soon as self-sufficient commodity producers in the less developed country were replaced by capitalists employing hired labor. As for the African countries associated with the EEC, they were not significant even in this connection. Their total population was only 30 million, compared to 170 million in the EEC proper. If growth of domestic capitalism in these countries were to expand their existing market as much as three times over, the total market of the EEC would still grow by no more than 5-6 percent.[110]

At another conference in Moscow from August 27 to September 3, 1962, the question of market creation in the EEC again became a focus of contention. Although trade between member states was increasing far more rapidly than industrial output, Varga persisted in his view that temporary expansion would soon lead to "a crisis of overproduction and to a contraction of the market. . . . Therefore, one can hardly expect any permanent or even prolonged increase of production in the integrated countries."[111] A.G. Mileikovsky responded that "Comrade Varga's hypotheses are certainly interesting, but one cannot agree that the adding up of national markets yields merely their arithmetical sum, producing no new quality and causing no expansion of the market."[112]

IMEMO's theses indicated that Varga had lost this debate before the conference met. In the official interpretation, the new "Europe of the trusts" represented a higher stage in the development of state-monopoly capitalism.[113] Before the war, trusts and cartels had reached international agreements on a sectoral basis; now they were using the state apparatus of member countries and the European Council of Ministers to extend the market by excluding foreign monopolies and eliminating small domestic competitors. By seizing undivided control of Europe's internal markets, the monopolies were also coordinating efforts to confront America in the global economy. The EEC was designed to create "a West European imperialist 'power centre' equal or close to the United States in manpower and material resources, industrial output and volume of foreign trade."[114]

According to IMEMO, regional trading blocs—or "cartel associations of a new type"—were the monopolies' response to capital-intensive technologies of mass production that objectively required "internationalization of economic life" and "a huge expansion of markets" in pursuit of superprofits.[115] Noting that West European industrial growth rates already surpassed those in America, the theses forecast that domestic market creation would soon allow EEC monopolies to challenge U.S. hegemony:

> the Treaty of Rome . . . has stimulated increased investment, accelerated the modernization of industry, and entailed a certain economic and organizational reconstruction of the monopolies. The lowering of [internal] customs barriers has stimulated a change-over to production on a larger scale. The Common Market is not simply an arithmetical sum of the national markets of the member countries. . . . [E]conomic "integration" can give an impulse to increasing the volume of production and of home and foreign trade.[116]

IMEMO was less certain, though, of how the emerging "third force" would affect interimperialist rivalries and the Cold War. The alliance of "Adenauer's clerical-militarist dictatorship" with "the authoritarian regime of General de Gaulle" suggested a new economic foundation for the aggressive NATO alliance.[117] Yet at the same time, Britain and her partners in EFTA—the seven-member European Free Trade Association formed in 1959 in response to the EEC—now constituted a separate bloc, indicating a growing threat to imperialist unity. With American encouragement, Britain was attempting to negotiate entry into the EEC, but a successful conclusion to these discussions appeared doubtful as Britain was not likely to surrender preferential trade with her Commonwealth partners.

The fact that the United States encouraged Britain to apply for EEC membership raised additional questions. By supporting British entry, perhaps the Americans were trying to win new markets for themselves in the former British colonies; possibly they hoped to absorb both Britain and the Common Market in a broader economic bloc of "Atlantic" proportions. American monopolies had protected their immediate interests by setting up subsidiaries within the EEC tariff wall; but these capital exports, in turn, weakened the American balance of payments, while goods manufactured with lower labor costs in Europe aggravated the problem by competing in international markets with American-produced goods. Although Kennedy's Trade Expansion Act of 1962 contemplated mutual tariff reductions between the U.S. and the EEC, the full effects of the legislation required British entry. In the meantime, IMEMO was satisfied that "The growth of West-European competition is further worsening the US balance of payments and intensifying the 'currency war' between the imperialist powers."[118]

8. The EEC and the USSR

With regard to the Soviet Union's role in the world economy, the EEC appeared to pose both an opportunity and a threat. A real "third force" might be persuaded to eliminate East-West trade restrictions and isolate the Americans in their futile effort to retard the triumphs of socialism. On the other hand, IMEMO voiced concern that the EEC also represented

> an expression of the class solidarity of the imperialists, who, notwithstanding their mutual hostility, seek to unite, trying to reinforce the positions of capitalism with the aid of international state-monopoly alliances. . . . The financial oligarchy is trying to find in "integration" a kind of "answer" to the growing might of socialism, which is becoming the decisive factor in mankind's development. . . .[119]

Soviet anxiety over the EEC evoked memories of earlier debates concerning relations between the USSR and the capitalist encirclement. In *Economic Problems,* Stalin had claimed that formation of "two world markets" and "two opposite camps" signified "further deepening of the general crisis of the world capitalist system."[120] Leon Trotsky had condemned Stalinism in the 1920s on the grounds that the doctrine of two camps implied a "state-economic unit that is closed in upon itself,"[121] pursuing autarky at the expense of benefits from trade. Assessing the implications of the EEC, many Soviet economists feared an historic role reversal: Soviet Russia needed trade to speed modernization through Khrushchev's seven-year plan, but now the imperialists—who were supposed to be afflicted by the chronic problem of markets—seemed to be creating their own new markets within "closed-in" economic blocs.

In an article on "Essential Questions of the International Division of Labor," P. Chernyshev and L. Lobanov worried that formation of the EEC was a serious threat to Soviet trade prospects. In exactly the language used by Trotsky, they wrote that

> The modern epoch . . . is characterized not only by development of a progressive tendency toward economic drawing together of peoples, toward overcoming national seclusion and limitation, but also, unfortunately, by strengthening of a dangerous tendency toward economic estrangement, toward creation of mutually hostile, closed-in trade and economic groupings. . . .[122]

Quoting Mikoyan's view that trade could reduce costs and economize on capital investments, Chernyshev and Lobanov again denied that the USSR or its East European allies had any interest in slowing their own development by "closing themselves in within autarkic limits."[123]

The prospect of being excluded from normal relations with the new Europe created both alarm and hostility in Moscow. P. Suslin wrote in August 1962 that the EEC was a "holy alliance" of imperialist powers, symbolizing the class solidarity of monopolists in pursuit of "an openly reactionary dictatorship" within a "closed-in economic bloc."[124] V.A. Cheprakov condemned "cosmopolitanization"[125] of capital and formation of a "closed-in aggressive economic and military bloc" at the expense of trade relations with other countries.[126] E. Menzhinsky complained that internationalization of production was assuming a "one-sided" deformed character, in which "free trade" within the EEC really meant "artificial isolation" from the socialist bloc and disorganization of world trade as a whole.[127] Protesting discrimination against Soviet oil exports, A. Frumkin blamed "closed-in" economic blocs for the fact that socialist countries accounted for 37 percent of world industrial production but only 13 percent of total exports.[128] A.M. Rumyantsev resurrected Malenkov's theme: two world markets and two world systems could not be separated by a "Chinese wall"; together they constituted a single "global market."[129]

Since the mid-1950s, Moscow had prevailed upon the UN Economic Commission for Europe to work for reciprocal tariff reductions between east and west.[130] In May 1962, UNESCO recommended a global conference to promote nondiscriminatory trade. On December 8, 1962, the UN General Assembly resolved to hold the conference on trade and development by early 1964. In anticipation, M.V. Nesterov commented that "discrimination is manifest, first, in the organization and activity of the Common Market and similar economic blocs, second, in monopoly price fixing."[131] Pending the UN conference, Khrushchev decided to apply in Eastern Europe the lessons learned from EEC monopolies.

Khrushchev had told the twenty-second party congress that "we should not scorn useful foreign experience and should critically adopt all [that is] technically and organizationally valuable . . . in the West, including . . . greater returns from capital investments."[132] In June 1962 Comecon adopted "Basic Principles of the International Socialist Division of Labor" and called for "rational distribution of the productive forces throughout the world socialist system."[133] According to Michael Kaser, "Khrushchev drew from the evolution of the supranational EEC . . . the lesson that Comecon should itself establish 'a unified planning organ, empowered to compile common plans and to decide organizational matters'."[134] The USSR hoped to coordinate national plans up to 1980 and to have East Europeans share in financing investments.

I. Ivanov explained the new Soviet proposals by commenting that the East European countries had mistakenly adopted the Stalinist model of planning, each striving for industrial "universalization," or self-sufficient miniature replicas of socialism in one country. Ivanov expected Khrushchev's call for "concentration of capital" to result in bloc-wide specialization, longer production runs, and lower costs.[135] Playing to domestic nationalism, however, the maverick regime of Gheorghiu-Dej in Romania objected that the Soviet project sounded curiously similar to bourgeois cosmopolitanism.

Nicolae Ceausescu, a secretary of the Romanian party and later Gheorgiu-Dej's Stalinist successor, cited Lenin in arguing that every communist country required its own heavy and machine-building industries.[136] While Russians condemned the EEC as a threat to national sovereignty, Romania reminded Khrushchev that socialist "super-state or extra-state bodies would turn sovereignty into a notion without any content."[137] Khrushchev's attempt to emulate the EEC contributed to fissures within Comecon that later encouraged the American policy of bridge-building, or selective use of trade to weaken Moscow's hold over the satellite countries.

9. State-Monopoly Planning and Antimonopoly Coalitions

The Soviet response to the EEC threatened the nominal independence of
East European countries at the same time as Soviet leaders were urging
West European Communists to expend every effort in defense of national
sovereignty against the cosmopolitan plans of monopolies. There was
little difference between current advice to foreign Communists and that
given by Stalin at the nineteenth party congress in 1952. Stalin had
warned that the bourgeoisie was selling out to the Americans in exchange
for Marshall Plan aid:

> In the past, the bourgeoisie considered itself head of the nation,
> it defended the rights and independence of the nation, placing
> them "above all else". Now nothing remains of the "national
> principle". Now the bourgeoisie is selling the rights and
> independence of the nation for dollars. The banner of national
> independence and sovereignty has been thrown overboard. There
> is no doubt that the duty of raising this banner falls to you, the
> representatives of communist and democratic parties, and you
> must carry it forward if you wish to be patriots of your country,
> if you wish to become the leading force of the nation.[138]

The new program of the Soviet Communist Party, adopted in 1961,
proclaimed that by uniting democratic forces, western Communists, even
before the victory of socialism, could "bring about implementation of a
national programme for peace, national independence, democratic rights,
and a certain improvement of the living conditions of the people."[139]
With Khrushchev claiming that electoral politics could achieve peaceful
transition to socialism, many writers concluded by the early 1960s that
politics must be more important than economics. If Kennedy could face
down American monopolies, while West European governments took
steps toward resolving the problem of markets, it was understandable that
doubts should arise concerning the objectivity of economic laws.

A.M. Rumyantsev, chief editor of *World Marxist Review*, told the
conference on the EEC in 1962 that "In our days the masses are
coming to realise more and more that their present and their future
depend directly on politics, on who wields governmental power."[140]
Contrary to Vygodsky and Kozlov, who explained state-monopoly capitalism in terms of the economic base determining the political superstructure, E. Menzhinsky also argued that international class solidarity

of EEC imperialists demonstrated "the growing primacy of politics over economics."[141] A.G. Mileikovsky declared that "It is impossible to assess correctly the nature of contemporary state-monopoly alliances unless . . . we begin with the primacy of politics over economics, understanding politics as the concentrated expression of economic processes."[142]

If politics had the capacity to shape economics, important implications must result for the organization of class struggle. Western Communists were now told that they must elevate the day-to-day economic struggle of trade unions to the political level. When the state legislates wage controls—or, in the case of the Kennedy administration, recommends voluntary guideposts—strikes against employers must grow over into political strikes against state power. T.T. Timofeev wrote that "Under state-monopoly capitalism the proletariat, struggling for its economic and social rights, inevitably enters into a more and more acute clash not merely with separate monopolies, but also with the entire bureaucratic machine of the bourgeois state, which defends the interests of the monopolies."[143] V.A. Cheprakov affirmed that the state, functioning as a "combined monopoly capitalist" in nationalized industries, made political strikes inevitable by exploiting workers in order to subsidize the production costs of private monopolies.[144]

Referring to strikes in the French public sector, A.A. Arzumanyan called for a "national front" of workers' and middle-class parties to transform the wage struggle into a mass political movement.[145] Since the state had become a "combined capitalist," the struggle over state-monopoly regulation must become political in order to raise living standards at the expense of monopoly profits.[146] With EEC monopolies creating a common labor market in order to reduce wages, *supranational state-monopoly regulation* must be challenged by popular demands for *democratic nationalization* of monopoly capital and workers' control of nationalized industries.[147]

The idea of a transitional program of democratic nationalization and workers' control began with a crucial assumption that contradicted the whole of Stalinist doctrine: that is, that capitalist economies were capable of being *programmed at the nation-state level*. Since Varga's humiliation in the late 1940s, no Soviet economist had disputed the orthodox view that only a socialist economy, with complete state ownership of the means of production, could be genuinely planned. By the early 1960s, however, new forms of state-monopoly capitalism led to recognition that between the anarchy of the classical market and full socialist planning there might be several intermediate stages. For the first time since

Stalin's death, practical experience in Europe and America compelled serious reconsideration of the planning potential of the modern state.

Attracted to a study of Western growth theories by Kennedy's use of fiscal policy, L.B. Al'ter maintained that capitalist countries had adopted far-reaching interventionism because it was their only hope of sustaining economic competition with socialism.[148] Since it was impossible to dispute the reality of state "regulation," the only remaining issue was whose interests it would serve. Like Rudolf Hilferding, Al'ter thought a program of "democratic regulation" could employ existing institutions to control market anarchy and raise the purchasing power of the toilers. Small capitalists would support such an endeavor, for the results would be an expanding market, mitigation of cyclical crises, increased opportunities for investment, and more rapid growth.[149]

In a scholarly article on "The Theory and Practice of Capitalist Regulation," Al'ter took the view that all capitalist states had created institutions that could either be taken over directly or adapted to progressive ends. In France, the Planning Office (*Commissariat du Plan*) had been operating since 1946; in Britain, the Conservative government of Macmillan had created the National Economic Development Council in 1961; in the United States, the Joint Economic Committee of Congress, the Budget Bureau, and various departments of the administration could likewise be coordinated for social reform. The problem in capitalist countries was not the inability of governments to promote and shape economic growth, but rather the determination of monopolies to subordinate public institutions to their own narrow purposes.

Believing that government intervention had become an objective necessity, Al'ter recommended that it be scrutinized in terms of three distinct concepts: "regulation," or use of Keynesian monetary and fiscal policy for countercyclical purposes; "economic prognostication" (or forecasting), intended to facilitate coordination between government branches in fulfillment of expected growth potential; and "planning" (*planirovanie*), or the integration of regulation with forecasting for purposes of controlling growth through direct government measures.[150] Surveying the experience of several countries and publications by economists such as Paul Samuelson, Alvin Hansen, and John Kenneth Galbraith, Al'ter concluded that all three types of state intervention had "a certain degree of reality." Serious analysis of modern capitalism required that Soviet economists:

> decisively reject dogmatic notions that exclude all possibility of regulation in a capitalist economy, ignoring new conditions of

development and the corresponding forms of class and general-democratic struggle. In our day, the objective foundations for a democratic alternative to capitalist regulation have greatly expanded.[151]

A.G. Mileikovsky, chief of IMEMO's section on general problems of imperialism, was equally convinced that state-monopoly regulation had become an "organic component of the production relations of modern capitalism." Soviet economists would have recognized such obvious facts long ago had it not been for the "personality cult" of Stalin and his "fossilized dogmas" dating from the conversation in 1934 with H.G. Wells. Stalin's insistence that the state could not influence the economy had paralyzed creative research; and since Stalin's day economists had remained fearful of being charged, like Varga, with adopting a reformist conception of the state's "above-class role."[152]

Whereas Vygodsky and Kozlov began with the law of maximum capitalist profit to explain the state's complicity in creating one-sided war economies, Mileikovsky argued the opposite case: modification of the law of value actually required the state to play an increasing role not only in determining the requirements of proportionality, but also in planning *continuous restructuring* in response to technological advances. It was true that in premonopoly capitalism, capital had moved more freely from one branch to another. However, once monopolies impaired interbranch mobility and interfered with equalization of profit rates, it was the state that inherited responsibility for subsidizing declining branches, such as energy or transportation in England, while simultaneously financing research and investment in emerging industries. The fact that some countries adopted the form of "mixed property," or joint public-private ventures, did not prove that monopolies subjugated the state; on the contrary, it demonstrated that the financial oligarchy feared that the state, if left to act independently, would confirm the ease of organizing production without relying upon capitalist monopolies.[153]

10. John F. Kennedy and "Relative Autonomy"

The market-creating activities of the EEC and Kennedy's clash with big business diverted Soviet thought from Stalinist traditions toward a new awareness of capitalist resilience. In the case of America, A.I. Bechin believed that Kennedy's fiscal policies had finally settled the issue of whether public spending impeded or accelerated growth. Kennedy had refuted Stalinism in practice by improving utilization of industrial capacity, expediting capital accumulation, increasing employment, raising real wages, and facilitating greater production of nonmilitary goods.[154] In an article on "Peculiarities of Reproduction in the USA," Bechin interpreted fiscal policy in the same manner as Varga and Keynes in the 1930s:

> the budget deficits are covered by borrowing. The cash proceeds are used not only to purchase commodities, but also to pay wages and salaries. The corresponding sums create a secondary demand when state employees spend their income, and the same applies to workers and employees of enterprises involved in producing military technology or in military and other construction. . . . Expenditure of enormous sums by the state . . . has become an integral part of the process of reproduction.[155]

Because Kennedy spent on armaments rather than public services, however, many economists also continued to see sinister forces at work. Yu. Yudin explained that Roosevelt had acquired "freedom to maneuver" by promoting new finance-capitalist groups in Texas, California, and elsewhere in order to counter the influence of the Rockefellers, Morgans, Mellons, Du Ponts, and Fords, who were based on Wall Street. Kennedy, in contrast, had come to power at a time when the outlying financial groups were divided and Wall Street, the Rockefeller group in particular, had consolidated its hold on government as a result of the Cold War.[156]

In June 1963, however, Kennedy called for a review of the Cold War; in August, a limited nuclear test-ban agreement was reached with Khrushchev; in September, the agreement was ratified by the Senate; and in October, the United States undertook to sell large quantities of wheat to the Soviet Union. According to Theodore C. Sorenson, Kennedy "welcomed the opportunity to demonstrate to the Soviet leaders that the improved climate of agreement could serve the interests of both nations . . . and hoped that more trade in nonstrategic goods would follow."[157]

How were these manifestations of Kennedy's independence to be explained? V.S. Zorin thought Kennedy was steering a perilous course between rival monopoly groups. Even when he persuaded Wall Street to make concessions, "the war concerns of the 'young' monopoly combines," especially "the California, Texas and Chicago-Cleveland big business groups," regarded him as a threat to their investments in the aerospace and electronics industries.[158]

On November 22, 1963, Kennedy was assassinated in Dallas. The Soviet press portrayed him as the victim of a "military junta" backed by the Central Intelligence Agency, the Air Force, and defense contractors, who were launching "a titanic power struggle" and a challenge to constitutional government through the candidacy of Barry M. Goldwater.[159] *New Times* argued that "The straw which broke the junta's patience was the partial nuclear test-ban treaty. . . . [A]s far as the junta was concerned, [Kennedy] was a living corpse."[160] Boris Izakov exclaimed that "Kennedy signed the Moscow Treaty with his blood." Eisenhower had warned of the threat posed by the "military-industrial complex," and now the "lunatic fringe" of American reaction had slain the president in the Texas citadel of finance capital.[161]

Reviewing the Kennedy years, Stanislav Men'shikov detected significant parallels between Kennedy and Roosevelt. Personal wealth had enabled the late president, like Roosevelt, to pursue "relative autonomy" and "independence" in an effort to serve the entire ruling class: "In short, the government of Kennedy conducted a bourgeois-reformist line in the interest of expanding and perfecting the system of state-monopoly capitalism. In the circumstances of the USA, this met with disapproval and opposition from an important part of the monopoly bourgeoisie."[162] Varga was prepared to go further. He concluded that state-monopoly capitalism, whether in America or in Europe, involved a dialectical relationship in which both the state and the monopolies "to a certain degree preserved their autonomy."[163]

By the time of Kennedy's death in 1963 and Khrushchev's own retirement in the following year, Soviet writers were beginning to contemplate new possibilities for state-monopoly capitalism. Khrushchev had helped to initiate this process by calling for abandonment of abstract schemes. After his departure, the intellectual forces that he had set loose developed in directions few would have thought possible. Forgetting the law of maximum capitalist profit and the "one-sided" war economy, for the next several years economists concentrated on the successes of capitalist planning and even the possibility that socialism might benefit from imitating western experience. Until the world currency crisis at the close of the decade, Stalinist underestimation of capitalism gave way to exaggerated misjudgment of its accomplishments.

CHAPTER 7

MONOPOLY PLANNING AND "SCIENTIFIC-TECHNICAL REVOLUTION"

Since the 1930s, Soviet views of capitalism had been distorted by belief that a chronic problem of markets caused idle industrial capacity and mass unemployment. Vygodsky and Kozlov reformulated the Stalinist position by attributing permanent disproportionality to deformation of Marx's law of value. Stalin had written in *Economic Problems* that the law of maximum capitalist profit entailed "wars and militarization of the national economy" together with "exploitation, ruin and impoverishment of the majority of the population." While Khrushchev held that electoral transition to socialism was possible, even in the 1960s Vygodsky and Kozlov still saw little to distinguish American capitalism from the Nazi war economy. In both cases, workers were said to be impoverished to support monopolies and an arms race.

When the United States and the European Community adopted new forms of state-monopoly planning, other economists explained a tendency toward (what Bukharin had called) *organized capitalism* by focusing upon institutional changes. If modern institutions regulated market expansion, two implications were possible. First, the threat of war might further recede, allowing the Soviet government to direct more attention to the needs of its own citizens; but second, continuing prosperity in the west might also diminish the likelihood of socialist transition in Europe. With steady economic growth, the "toiling masses" of capitalism might be co-opted into supporting the *status quo*.

By the mid-1960s, Soviet economists had finally to come to terms with the Keynesian state and capitalist planning. Many compensated for previous skepticism by assigning to the political superstructure greater importance than at any time since Varga's *Changes in the Economic Structure of Capitalism as a Result of the Second World War*. State-monopoly capitalism's ability to moderate the cycle was understood to result from partial resolution of two key problems: the unevenness of investments, and the resulting instability of employment. By mid-decade, cyclical fluctuations appeared to have been tamed through planning and forecasting, both made possible by what Soviet journals called a scientific-technical revolution.

Marx had expected cyclical crises to enforce industrial centralization and concentration; a diminishing number of "the magnates of capital" would preside over objective "socialisation of labour," which would ultimately undermine private property.[1] Engels had linked this process, however, with a parallel tendency to adjust production to demand and thus to minimize industrial fluctuations: "When we pass from joint-stock companies to trusts, which assume control over and monopolise whole branches of industry, it is not only [small-scale] private production that ceases, but also planlessness."[2] Hilferding followed Engels by relating comprehensive planning to a hypothetical universal cartel: the full potential of organized capitalism would be realized when a social-democratic government coordinated separate trusts through partial nationalization, beginning with the largest banks.[3]

Because planning presupposed accounting and control, Marxists traditionally regarded banking and finance capital as precursors of socialism. Marx had commented that "The banking system possesses . . . the form of universal book-keeping and distribution of means of production on a social scale, but solely the form."[4] Lenin added that socialism would take over the banking system *"ready-made"* in order to ensure "country-wide *book-keeping*, country-wide *accounting* of the production and distribution of goods."[5] With socialism, "the whole of society" would function like "a single office and a single factory."[6] In *Imperialism, The Highest Stage of Capitalism*, Lenin thought capital had already achieved forms of organization pointing beyond private property:

> When a big enterprise assumes gigantic proportions, and, on the basis of an exact computation of mass data, organises according to plan the supply of . . . raw materials . . . for tens of millions of people; when the raw materials are transported in a systematic and organised manner to the most suitable place of production . . .; when a single centre directs all the consecutive stages of work . . .; when . . . products are distributed according to a

single plan among tens and hundreds of millions of consumers
. . . —then it becomes evident that we have [objective] socialisation of production. . . .[7]

Self-financing made corporations less dependent on banks than at the
time of Hilferding's *Finance Capital* or Lenin's *Imperialism*, but the
Keynesian revolution also demonstrated that the modern state served the
capitalist class by regulating demand on the basis of national income
accounting. If Keynesianism could prevent cyclical instability, many
economists concluded that monopolies would be able to perfect planning
techniques in anticipation of continuous growth. Giant firms were less
vulnerable than small enterprises, and new technologies were making it
possible to produce for a "known" market. Through computerization,
capitalism seemed to be replacing market anarchy with the prior exercise
of economic reason. For decades Soviet writers had denied the possibility
of capitalist planning; during the 1960s many went to the other extreme
and began to doubt the necessity for spontaneous crises in a new era of
state-monopoly capitalism.

1. V. A. Cheprakov on State-Monopoly Capitalism

The change in thinking began with the role of the state and was apparent
in a book entitled *State-Monopoly Capitalism*, published in 1964 by V.A.
Cheprakov. Immediately after World War II, Cheprakov had led the
vendetta against Varga. Describing the relation between the state and the
monopolies, he had used the terms "*sliyanie,*" "*srashchivanie,*" and
"*podchinenie*"[8]—merger, coalescence, and subjugation—to argue that
America was a "police state of the financial oligarchy."[9] By 1964 he
took a different view: the first two terms still applied, but he repudiated
"*podchinenie*" because it expressed Stalin's claim that "The capitalist
state does not deal much with the economy in the strict sense of the word
. . . ."[10] Cheprakov now conceded that "*sliyanie*" must be understood
exactly in Varga's sense: it could not imply "mechanical subjugation,"
for "separate monopoly organizations struggle among themselves for
influence in the state apparatus, [and] the interests of this apparatus clash
with the interests of separate monopolies."[11]
Cheprakov's disavowal of his previous ideas resulted from rereading
Engels, who had expected that the capital requirements of modern
industry would eventually cause "the official representative of capitalist
society—the state— . . . to undertake the direction of production."[12]
"Why," Engels asked, "do we fight for the dictatorship of the proletariat

if political power is economically impotent? Force (that is, state power), is also an economic power!"[13] Speaking of its role as a *"collective capitalist,"*[14] Engels had characterized the state as an "independent power" with its own "particular interests." Rather than being merely a "political superstructure," it exercised "inherent relative independence"[15] and interacted continuously with the economic base.[16]

Cheprakov repeated what Engels had written: the state exercised "relative independence" in order to promote "the interests of monopoly capital as a whole."[17] It not only functioned as an "aggregate capitalist,"[18] regulating demand and redistributing incomes, but also pursued its "own interests"[19] when making "concessions" to the working class.[20] Engels had written in *Anti-Duhring* that the scale of modern industry would reduce small capitalists to "the clipping of coupons and gambling on the Stock Exchange."[21] If the majority of capitalists were already marginalized, Cheprakov thought they would support a return to "Roosevelt's program"[22] and "general-democratic, antimonopoly" reforms.[23]

The irony of Cheprakov's about-face was compounded in 1968, when he was assigned to write the introduction to a posthumous English-language edition of Varga's own final book, *Essays on Problems of the Political Economy of Capitalism*, which first appeared in 1964. Praising his former adversary as an "outstanding Marxist economist," committed to defending the "living soul" of Marxism,[24] Cheprakov quibbled over just one issue: because the capitalist class was divided, the state still could not serve the bourgeoisie as a whole, as distinct from monopoly capital. Were it not for such divisions, of which Varga had written many times, there would be no grounds for expecting small capitalists to participate in the "antimonopoly coalition."[25]

2. Varga: The State, Monopolies, and Economic "Laws"

Since Varga had been around this circle on countless occasions, he was content to say that both the state and the monopolies enjoyed "a certain autonomy."[26] A dialectical relation between economics and politics explained the capacity of state-monopoly capitalism to develop in the direction *either* of Roosevelt's New Deal *or* of Hitler's Germany.[27] But Varga was concerned by 1964 that this indeterminacy pointed to more fundamental issues concerning the relation between politics and economic laws. Although Marx had treated economic laws as objective, he had also consistently qualified such references by speaking of *objective tendencies*. Concerning the law of the falling rate of profit, he wrote that "There must be some counteracting influences at work, which cross and annul the effect of the general law, and which give it merely the effect of a tendency. . . ."[28]

Capital presupposed an understanding of laws as tendencies: an (unqualified) law of the falling rate of profit would imply irreversible decline; a law (acting as a tendency) allowed for short-term profit rates to rise and fall within the cycle. If reproduction were governed by absolute laws, there could not even be an economic cycle, only uninterrupted movement toward the final systemic "crash." Such expectations accorded with Stalinist doctrine, but they also led to gross duplicity. Varga held Stalin personally responsible for crippling Soviet scholarship by failing to distinguish between economic laws and physical laws of nature: natural laws could be observed in "pure form" through scientific experiment; economic laws operated "in a constantly changing environment. . . [P]olitical economy is, therefore, an historical science."[29]

Marx referred to growth of the industrial reserve army and proletarian impoverishment as "*the absolute general law of capitalist accumulation.*" In the next sentence he added that even this law "is modified in its working by many circumstances."[30] Varga thought the most fraudulent of all Stalinist laws concerned absolute impoverishment. Excoriating "dogmatists" such as I.I. Kuz'minov and A.I. Kats, who still asserted that real wages had fallen throughout the twentieth century, he insisted that living standards were jointly determined by the political struggle and the economic cycle.[31]

> The worst fault in the work of our dogmatists is that they *separate economics from politics*. We consider their view on the uninterrupted and . . . absolute impoverishment of the working class to be not only untrue but also *politically harmful*. How can communists organize the working class to defend its interests in the strike struggle if they themselves assert that the continuous absolute impoverishment of workers is inevitable?[32]

Varga had been condemned after the war for allegedly subordinating politics and "party-mindedness" to a "techno-economic" methodology. He settled accounts in 1964 by charging that conservatives ignored state autonomy and falsified statistics. Since 1945 there had occurred "a significant growth of real wages, not absolute impoverishment—this is perfectly obvious."[33] Whereas Vygodsky and Kozlov attributed monopoly profits to labor intensification, Varga cited American data to show that monopolies paid higher wages than small capitalists.[34] With more fixed capital exposed to paralysis through a strike, large corporations had more to lose and were therefore more responsive to working-class demands.[35]

If real wages were rising, it was also clear that Hilferding had been correct on the issue of intercapitalist transfers: small capitalists were the chief victims of monopoly pricing, disproving Stalinist explanations of the law of "maximum capitalist profit" in terms of workers' impoverishment. "As a result of the relation of prices established by the monopolies," Varga wrote, ". . . small commodity producers are forced to hand over a part of their incomes."[36] Workers *created* surplus value; who *appropriated* it was a matter for the owners of capital:

> in a pure capitalist society, monopoly superprofits can arise only as a result of the uneven distribution of the aggregate surplus value or the aggregate profit—a distribution that does not correspond to the amount of capital [each capitalist has] invested. There can be no other source of monopoly superprofits. Insofar as monopolies make a profit above the average rate, non-monopoly enterprises receive a lower profit than they would receive according to the volume of their capital.[37]

In real capitalism, the issue was more complex because the state validated monopoly pricing through monetary policy. When small firms incurred high costs through purchases from monopolies, they tried to pass on part of those costs to consumers.[38] Since the sum of prices exceeded the sum of values, or what Marx had called prices of production, the consequence was a Keynesian policy of regulated inflation.[39] Given monopoly pricing, the state had to adjust macroeconomic policy to guarantee sufficient demand. In his final judgment of the so-called "problem of markets," Varga declared that "J.V. Stalin was wrong in predicting an absolute narrowing of the capitalist market. No such narrowing has occurred, nor will it occur, except during periodic crises of overproduction."[40]

Varga died in the autumn of 1964 at the age of eighty-four years. An obituary in *Voprosy ekonomiki* praised his "enormous scientific-organizational work" and his monumental list of publications, including seventy-five books and pamphlets and more than five hundred articles. He was credited with "truly encyclopedic knowledge and the indomitable creative spirit of a scholar." The obituary also made clear what Varga's colleagues thought of his conflicts with Stalinists: "The works of E.S. Varga are characterized throughout by profound party-mindedness and implacable aversion to all manifestations of dogmatism and revisionism, to the vulgarization . . . imposed upon science in the years of [Stalin's] cult of personality."[41]

3. The State as Economic "Subject"

Varga's book helped to remove any remaining obstacles to a fundamental revision of Soviet views of the state. Beginning in 1964, numerous publications gave unprecedented attention to the relative autonomy of political institutions. Even Bukharin was indirectly rehabilitated. He had written in 1920 that state-capitalist trusts converted "the capitalist 'national economy' . . . *from an irrational system into a rational organization,* from an economy without a subject into an economic subject."[42] Reviewing Cheprakov's *State-Monopoly Capitalism,* V.A. Maslennikov complained that despite concessions to Varga, Cheprakov had not yet sufficiently emphasized the state's role as "*an important subject* of state-monopoly capitalism. . . . Academician E. Varga was right. . . . Besides monopolies, Varga mentioned the parliamentary system, the working class and other classes and strata of the population as being among the factors affecting the policy of the capitalist state."[43]

At an international Marxist conference on the theme of "Finance Capital Today," S.M. Men'shikov criticized Stalin and pointed out that Varga had also been correct in the postwar debate over the British Labour government: "The capitalist countries do not always have governments consisting of representatives of the monopolies. The Labour government in Britain was a case in point. . . . [I]t would be incorrect to say that the Labour government was subordinated to the monopolies."[44] I.M. Lemin similarly denied that the American state was a "humble agent of business"; Kennedy's "New Frontiers" had illustrated the possibility of a more flexible approach to peace and disarmament. According to Lemin, the Marxist classics had anticipated a dramatic increase of state responsibilities:

> The founders of Marxism-Leninism warned against underestimating the role of the state. They always emphasized that . . . government is not merely a shop clerk but also a shareholder; that is, a participant in the ruling-class system; . . . one must not underestimate its relative independence . . . and its invariable

> tendency to change from servant into master; . . . occasionally
> it even acts against the ruling class, defending their common
> interests even though they may not be fully aware of those
> interests. . . .[45]

In June 1965, A.G. Mileikovsky, V.M. Shundeev, and R.M. Entov
published an article in *Kommunist* dealing with "Imaginary and Real
Changes in Modern Capitalism." They argued that in conditions of the
scientific-technical revolution, involving automation, cybernetic control
systems, and countless new products in chemistry, electronics, and pre-
cision instruments, state coordination had become "a necessary condition
of the reproduction of capital." The American government defined
research priorities and absorbed up to two-thirds of costs in order to
promote "capitalist rationalization" and to improve the country's position
in world markets. The state exercised "relative economic independence"
by assuming "broad powers to resolve general economic tasks."[46]

By the mid-1960s, the issue of the state was clearly settled in Varga's
favor. L.A. Leont'ev maintained that Varga's treatment of economic
laws had likewise been vindicated. If laws were tendencies, there were
no objective grounds for "*a priori* judgments." Leont'ev saw capitalism
being influenced not only by its own tendencies but also by the need for
"maneuvering" in the class struggle and the global competition with
socialism. Since maneuvering entailed class concessions, there could be
no law of proletarian impoverishment such as "vulgarizers" contended.[47] "Planning," "programming," and "regulation" demonstrated that
the "anarchy of production" might be contained.[48] Marx had said that
"social reason asserts itself only *post festum*."[49] Leont'ev argued, on the
contrary, that new technologies modified market processes by allowing
for deliberate foresight:

> With the help of modern electronic computing technologies . . .
> [the capitalists] undertake calculations and forecasts, on the basis
> of which they determine an investment policy over rather long
> periods. State-monopoly measures for regulating the economy
> . . . are also based on definite calculations and forecasts.
> Without taking these factors into account, it would hardly be
> possible to explain the specific features of the concrete process
> of reproduction in modern capitalism, especially the tempos of
> this reproduction.[50]

In an article on "The Methodology of 'Capital' and Certain Questions in the Study of Capitalism," Ya.A. Pevzner decided in November 1966 that of all Marx's laws only one could be said to operate in every circumstance, namely, the law of surplus value and profit.[51] Even this law presupposed "the *economic necessity* of state intervention" and could not be abstracted from politics.[52] At a conference in 1967 to mark the fiftieth anniversary of Lenin's *Imperialism*, Mileikovsky referred both to the state's "independence" and to its role as "*mediator* in the class struggle."[53] Not since 1947 had a Soviet economist cast the state so explicitly in the role of political third party.

IMEMO's theses for the conference affirmed that "The state regulates the rate of accumulation and influences the tempo of renovation and expansion of fixed capital, the change of proportions between branches, and the territorial location of production."[54] Ya.A. Pevzner told participants that research over the past decade had put an end to "simplified" views of the state's subjugation by recognizing "active influence of the bourgeois state on the reproduction process."[55] F.G. Rudenko objected to claims that the capitalist economy developed in strict accordance with laws: he suggested that the public sector be thought of as a cybernetic "subsystem," interacting with and regulating "the basic subsystem of private enterprise."[56] E.L. Khmel'nitskaya agreed that it was futile to deny systemic "programming."[57] When Belgian and Italian delegates referred to state-monopoly capitalism as an entirely "new stage" of development, V.A. Cheprakov had to defend Lenin's *Imperialism, the Highest Stage of Capitalism,* against the implication that it was out of date.[58]

Varga had initiated these changes, and following his death in 1964 his work was repeatedly acclaimed. On November 19, 1969, members of the economics department of the Soviet Academy of Sciences and representatives from eight research institutes observed what would have been Varga's ninetieth birthday. Virtually all the official luminaries of Soviet political economy attended, including G.A. Arbatov (Director of the new Institute of the USA), O.T. Bogomolov (Director of the Institute for the Economy of the World Socialist System), L.M. Gatovsky (Director of the Institute of Economics), and T.T. Timofeev (Director of the Institute for the International Workers' Movement). Ivan M. Maisky, former ambassador to Britain, sent a letter praising Varga's work during World War II. A.M. Rumyantsev, Vice-President of the Academy of Sciences, announced that Varga's collected works would be republished. N.N. Inozemtsev, Director of IMEMO after Arzumanyan's death in 1965, praised Varga for combining astute economic analysis with careful study of politics. According to Inozemtsev, one of Varga's greatest contributions had been to insist on the "relative independence" of the state.[59]

4. S.M. Men'shikov on the "Material Basis" of Reproduction

The new consensus concerning the state settled one issue at the cost of seriously complicating another. If the state programmed and regulated the economy, to what extent was reproduction any longer determined by what Marx had called its "material basis"? The primacy of politics appeared to suggest not only that depressions would no longer occur, as Varga had expected, but also that the entire cycle might be replaced by steady growth. In 1961, S.M. Men'shikov had referred to a new form of cycle resulting from "intensive" growth, technological change, and expansion of services, which might stabilize both heavy and light industry. At a conference on business cycles in November 1965, Men'shikov elaborated this hypothesis into a new theory of reproduction.

Men'shikov believed that the world cycle, allowing for variations between countries due to individual "programming," continued to involve a crisis every eight to twelve years.[60] He cautioned, however, against expecting either a "'normal', 'classical' scheme" or "deformation" in the Stalinist sense.[61] Lenin had said that socialism would coordinate enterprises as if they were a single factory; Men'shikov pointed out that monopolistic "concerns," or conglomerates with operations in several industries, were already using computers to achieve the accounting and control Lenin had expected of socialist planning. In 1955, 450 computers were operating in the United States. By 1963 the number was 15,000, rising to 27,000 two years later.[62] Monopolies were able to track current demand; they also combined short-term plans for production, sales, and investment with projections of five years or more. Men'shikov claimed that

> All of this has had an essential influence upon the conditions of reproduction. Monopolistic enterprises increasingly work for a more or less known market. Monopolies have become more able to make strategic adjustments of production in anticipation of a reduction in demand. The extent of commodity overproduction . . . has diminished. . . . Crises have not ended, but they have become less serious and less prolonged, for less time is now required to curtail relatively smaller commodity "surpluses".[63]

In the early history of capitalism, employers discovered the rate of profit only after commodities entered the market. Relations between buyers and sellers were spontaneously mediated by prices. Modern corporations, in contrast, defined terms of purchase and sale through long-term contracts.[64] "Disguised overproduction" was minimized through better inventory control,[65] while state expenditures and "built-in automatic stabilizers" simultaneously regulated aggregate demand.[66] As market spontaneity yielded to rational calculation, only one conclusion was possible: the periodic overproduction analyzed by Marx could no longer be the principal cause for renovation of fixed capital.

Marx had concentrated on *unevenness* of investment; each wave of accumulation was followed by a crisis. Men'shikov thought this pattern had been irreversibly altered: the scientific-technical revolution required *continuous* replacement of equipment in order to avoid obsolescence. American corporations provided for "moral wear" of assets through high rates of depreciation, which ensured both self-financing and the possibility of planning investments with no regard to brief recessions. The consequence was a modified cycle in which recoveries were more rapid and expansions were lengthened.

"Planning of accelerated moral wear"[67] tended to eliminate uneven growth on the part of individual monopolies; the economy as a whole became more stable when new products and new branches of manufacturing offset secular decline in older industries.[68] Technological innovations also amplified changes in the structure of fixed capital, a phenomenon which Varga had first detected in the 1930s. Stalinists associated reequipping of factories with chronically redundant capacity that prevented industrial construction; Men'shikov saw that the real cause was more efficient use of capital. New technologies made equipment a more "active" (or frequently replaced) component of fixed capital, allowing for increased production without parallel investments in "passive" elements such as buildings. In America, the physical volume of industrial construction exceeded that of 1929 only in 1946, 1956, and 1957.[69]

Men'shikov decided that steadily rising productivity was reducing the significance of fixed capital as the material basis of cycles.[70] As capital expenditures declined per unit of output, however, a new "supplementary material basis" was also emerging.[71] Higher living standards entailed mass production of consumer durables on a scale beyond anything previously experienced. To the extent that a cyclical movement still occurred, *it had more to do with consumption than with investments*:

> The role played by consumer durables . . . is comparable to the [traditional] role of fixed capital in production. Such commodities lose their value through wear, but they continue to function perfectly well until the time when partial repairs become inadequate and they must be replaced. . . . Thus . . . it is possible and inevitable . . . that there will be spontaneous waves of mass renovation. . . .[72]

Furniture, appliances, and automobiles were the "active" assets in household "basic funds"; housing was the "passive" element. To illustrate the importance of the household replacement cycle, Men'shikov quoted American statistics. Excluding services and state purchases, active household assets accounted in 1958-62 for 16.8 percent of GNP, compared to only 9.5 percent for active assets in production; private housing construction represented 7.3 percent of GNP, business construction only 6.8 percent. Not only did current demand for household assets exceed that for fixed capital, but the total basic funds of urban households also amounted to $601.6 billion, compared to only $395.8 billion worth of buildings and equipment owned by nonfinancial corporations in industry, transportation, commerce, and communications.[73]

Household basic funds had obviously become the most important material basis of reproduction. The salient question now concerned consumer demand. How could monopolies produce for a "known market" unless they also knew what consumers would be likely to spend? Men'shikov answered that wage determination had itself become an aspect of capitalist planning. Just as monopolies planned production on the basis of long-term contracts, so collective bargaining involved scheduling wage increases over a period of several years—*even during recessions*. "As a result, hourly wage rates in [American] manufacturing . . . grew during the crisis of 1948-1949 by 4%, in 1953-1954 by 2.5%, in 1957-1958 by 3%, and in 1960-1961 by 3%."[74] "The reality of the postwar period is that, for the first time in the history of capitalism, there has been an almost continuous and uninterrupted rise in hourly rates of pay. . . ."[75] In the United States, Britain, France, West Germany, Italy, and Japan, money wages had grown more rapidly than the cost of living during the entire period since 1948.[76]

Rising real incomes accounted for the unprecedented importance of consumer durables. Moreover, a unique feature of the household replacement cycle was its tendency to offset fluctuations of fixed-capital investments and thus to contribute a further element of stabilization.

Falling investments caused lower interest rates; lower interest rates encouraged more spending on housing and consumer goods. In the longer term, monopolies ensured a high level of consumer demand in the same way as they minimized unevenness of fixed-capital replacements; new technologies produced an uninterrupted flow of new models and types of goods, guaranteeing both the obsolescence of "active" household assets and continuous re-creation of demand.[77]

5. Men'shikov and Preobrazhensky on Fixed-Capital Reserves

Men'shikov's interpretation could be partly supported by reference to *Capital*. Marx had written that "competition compels the replacement of the old instruments of labour by new ones before the expiration of their natural life, especially when decisive changes occur." The difference was that Marx had said, "Such premature renewals of factory equipment on a rather large social scale are mainly enforced by *catastrophes or crises*."[78] Marx saw part of the existing equipment ceasing to function when its owners went bankrupt; another part was purchased at bankruptcy prices by stronger capitalists who were endeavoring to reduce costs.

The next question raised by Men'shikov was the following: What happens, in the new circumstances of state-monopoly capitalism, to technologically obsolescent but still useful fixed capital? Since monopolies rarely went bankrupt, he concluded that they would neither scrap their assets nor dispose of them through the market. Instead, they would retain the older equipment as a "reserve" of production capacity to be brought back into operation as the market expanded.[79] At this point the new theory of reproduction became politically contentious. Although Men'shikov made no mention of the fact, he was adopting ideas first expressed by Preobrazhensky in his book *The Decline of Capitalism*, which had been published and condemned in 1931.

Preobrazhensky had claimed that large firms, when renovating existing capital, also planned a *reserve capacity* in expectation of future demand that would otherwise invite competition. The result was to add a new phase to the cycle. Reserve building occurred at the peak of an expansion, when existing facilities were fully employed. The expansion was thereby prolonged, but a unique impediment was also created to recovery from the eventual crisis. Fixed-capital investments traditionally occurred *after* a crisis; if monopolies now added to capacity *before* the crisis, there were serious doubts as to how investments and growth might resume.

Preobrazhensky predicted "a gradual loss of the mechanism of recovery" and a tendency toward secular stagnation. Comparing the Great Depression to a "thrombosis" of the productive forces, he expected "a general social crisis of the entire historic system of capitalism."[80]

Stalinists professed to be horrified by the "law of increasing reserves,"[81] which they interpreted to be a claim on behalf of planning. In light of this history, Men'shikov was not about to explain his own view by quoting a Trotskyist who had been shot as a counter-revolutionary. Nevertheless, his intellectual debt was evident as he repeated Preobrazhensky's argument point by point:

> New industrial capacity is created for a more or less long period of time, during which demand fluctuations are inevitable. For this reason, a reserve of capacity must always be planned in case of a sudden increase of demand. Moreover, every monopoly, when building a new enterprise and installing new equipment, counts not only on preserving its place in the market, but also on replacing its competitors. . . . Thus planned capacity, as a rule, is always greater than is really necessary. . . .[82]

Once Men'shikov embraced Preobrazhensky's ideas, he immediately faced the problem of explaining why reserves had not prevented recoveries. On the one hand, he intended to demonstrate that cycles were of diminishing significance; on the other hand, Preobrazhensky's argument had been tailored to explain the greatest depression in history. Men'shikov recognized the obvious dilemma:

> If monopolies want to keep prices at a high level in a period of crisis, they must curtail production. . . . An important part of the capacity, installed at the final stage of the expansion, is in this case not amortized. Thus, while old capacity [which is already amortized] can be eliminated in a crisis relatively easily, the new will weigh all the longer upon the following cycle, delaying the start of a cyclical expansion. . . .[83]

The solution to this puzzle, according to Men'shikov, involved a difference of historical context: in 1931 it had been impossible to foresee that state policy would create a new market. The answer to the threat of stagnation turned out to be the same one given by Varga in the late 1930s; the state had become the third party. By the time of the 1960 recession, an estimated $100 billion of American industrial equipment was technologically outdated but still physically useful and incompletely amortized. Men'shikov pointed out that Kennedy's "measures to encourage accelerated depreciation and to reduce taxes on profits helped . . . expansion to become a reality in 1964-1965."[84] Overaccumulation of reserves had been avoided when the American government assisted in writing off older means of production by forgoing corporate taxation. Kennedy's turn to Keynesianism had confirmed that state autonomy made it possible to reconcile reserve building with a high and stable rate of growth.

6. S.A. Dalin: Monopoly Reserves and the "General Crisis"

Men'shikov led the way in revising the theory of reproduction; S.A. Dalin finished the task by transforming the theory of capitalist reserves into a criticism of Stalinist planning. Dalin referred to the same technology as Men'shikov in accounting for the state's "relative independence":[85]

> Electronic calculating and decision-making machines have created the possibility of tracking an enormous number of indicators and, in particular, of conducting very complex calculations in a fantastically short time and publishing the results with such speed as to permit the state and the monopolies to use the rapidly acquired economic statistics to influence the conjuncture. . . . [T]his represents a qualitatively new possibility of assessing the limits of the market . . . not only within individual branches of the economy, but even on the national and international scale.[86]

Because monopolies produced for a "known market,"[87] Dalin agreed with Men'shikov that "the mechanism of [automatic] recovery . . . has been destroyed."[88] Reducing output in a recession, monopolies maintained high prices on capital goods to protect their reserves. However, they also created the "political threat" of mass unemployment and thereby compelled the state to restore demand "in the interests of the whole bourgeois class."[89] Criticizing I.I. Kuz'minov for claiming that monopoly prices prevented recoveries,[90] Dalin objected that state planning bodies "do not limit themselves merely to Platonic wishes and empty prognoses. They actively influence, above all, the process of capital accumulation, credit, and to a certain extent the sphere of consumption."[91]

Dalin reported that in England the state was responsible for more than 42 percent of gross capital investments, in France for 30 percent, in Italy for 29 percent. Even in America the state purchased up to 20 percent of all goods and services.[92] From 1959 to 1964, the American government had also been responsible for 30 percent of construction.[93] Dalin thought recoveries occurred because "planned state action upon the private capitalist economy" supplemented and regulated market forces.[94] Planning by the state and the monopolies illustrated the tendency Marx had foreseen toward objective socialization within capitalist forms.

If capitalist planning already anticipated socialism, Dalin thought industrial reserves must also be an attribute of a centrally planned economy. Marx had predicted that socialism would plan reserves in order to offset unforeseeable disproportions. Scientifically controlled inventories, or "*continuous* relative overproduction," would replace the *spontaneous* overproduction that caused capitalist crises.[95] Stalinists referred to capitalism's chronically idle production capacity when justifying their own overly ambitious planning practices. Whereas capitalism appeared to be incapable of using the productive forces at its disposal, the targets of the five-year plans were so excessive as to deprive Soviet industry of the flexibility needed to respond to unplanned shortages caused by breakdowns in the system of state supply. Dalin suggested that planners should learn from the West: the alleged "chronic underutilization of capacity," far from confirming the general crisis, really demonstrated that reserves "are necessary *in every society* in order to prevent crises arising from unevenness in the movement of fixed capital."[96]

7. "Chronic Unemployment" and the Growth of Services

While Men'shikov and Dalin acknowledged capitalist achievements, Stalinists were just as persistent in arguing that the scientific-technical revolution intensified the "general crisis." Marx had written that if technology raised productivity to the point where fewer workers were required, the result must be proletarian revolution.[97] Yu.M. Ivanov held that monopolistic planning could only aggravate mass unemployment: reserves meant that idle capacity continued to be "the normal condition of a capitalist economy."[98] Deliberately restricting operations, monopolies were causing loss of a greater percentage of potential output than in the crisis years 1929-33.[99] Ivanov argued that "lack of correspondence between production and consumption . . . now permanently excludes from the production process a growing volume of the productive forces of society. . . ."[100]

Conservatives thought Men'shikov's theory of planned capitalism overlooked technological unemployment. Even Dalin noted that from 1953 to 1964 American production grew in volume by 44 percent, while the number of industrial workers and supervisory personnel marginally declined.[101] Since the labor force was about to expand rapidly due to postwar births, I.N. Dvorkin predicted that 36 million Americans would be unemployed by 1975: "In the conditions of capitalism, with its limited purchasing power on the part of the masses, continuous spread of automation poses the threat of a catastrophic growth of unemployment."[102] N.D. Gauzner thought it more likely that by 1975 up to 62 percent of American workers would be engaged in "nonproduction" activities:[103] 58 percent of employment, as early as 1961, had been in the nonproduction branches—commerce, finance, services, and government—with only 42 percent of workers "productively" employed in manufacturing, mining, construction, transportation, utilities, and agriculture.[104]

Men'shikov discounted technological unemployment on the grounds that industrial workers were being displaced into the rapidly growing service sector. But if services were nonproductive, as Soviet theory traditionally claimed, how was it possible for the American economy to continue expanding with a majority of the work force making no contribution to national income? Men'shikov saw that the question entailed its own obvious answer: American experience proved that the conventional view of nonproduction activities was mistaken. Employment in services and marketing had become just as important as state-monopoly planning in explaining capitalist efficiency:

> the nonproduction sphere is now an important purchaser and consumer of the products of both Departments of social production. Thus, the very existence of the nonproduction sphere allows the production sphere to turn out significantly more output than it could itself absorb, and absolute growth of the nonproduction sphere is one of the essential causes of the growth of production in recent decades.[105]

Men'shikov attributed expansion of nonproduction activities to the fact that they accelerated the turnover of industrial capital, broadened the market, and permitted productive workers to turn out a larger volume of material goods. A.A. Manukyan added that public services, by supporting "relative expansion of the consuming power of society," were also the precondition for a higher standard of living: "The expansion of the consuming base of society . . . is connected, in particular, with the growing importance of the nonproduction sphere. . . ."[106]

By the 1960s, western economists were revising the meaning of "capital" itself in terms of expenditures on health services, education and other investments in human resources. Americans such as Edward Denison, Theodore W. Schultz, and Simon Kuznets, saw *human capital* as a key factor of growth and innovation.[107] In *The Affluent Society,* John Kenneth Galbraith remarked that "Investment in human beings is, *prima facie*, as important as investment in material capital. . . . What is more important, the *improvement* in capital—technological advance—is now almost wholly dependent on investment in education, training, and scientific opportunity for individuals."[108]

Two decades after Malenkov's call for a Soviet New Deal, reappraisal of capitalist services now led to renewed questioning of domestic priorities. If investments in human capital were as essential as Galbraith maintained, many Soviet authors worried that Gosplan's fixation upon heavy industry would impede socialism's ability to compete in the global scientific-technical revolution. L.B. Al'ter, himself a Gosplan researcher, described improved services in health care and education as an objective response to "new conditions for the reproduction of labor power."[109] A.G. Mileikovsky similarly referred to growth of the service sector as an "objectively progressive process."[110] A.I. Bechin argued that Soviet conservatives, who "underestimated" services, were "absolutely mistaken":

> the civilian branches of the nonproduction sphere create *special use values of a nonmaterial character*, which satisfy extremely necessary personal needs of the population and the society as a whole. The satisfaction of popular needs for education, health care, for the organization of vacations and leisure, for general cultural and esthetic development, and for services that create more free time for the toilers—for example, in the form of well organized retail trade, municipal services, transportation and so on—all these ways of satisfying needs are an indispensable condition for social development, including both the growth of material production and the well-being of the population.[111]

8. Are Services Productive?

Differences of opinion concerning the productivity of services reflected ambiguity originating with Marx, who had associated such labor with servants and tradespeople hired by the idle rich. In *Theories of Surplus Value*, Marx wrote that these kinds of activities "will not increase (material) wealth by a single farthing."[112] Marx was influenced by Adam Smith, who defined productive labor as that which "realizes itself in some . . . vendible commodity, which lasts for some time. . . . It is, as it were, a certain quantity of labour stocked and stored up to be employed, if necessary, upon some other occasion."[113] Because Smith's definition excluded services that were direct extensions of material production—for example, transporting material to factories or commodities to market—Marx thought it was too restrictive.[114] His own definition treated all labor as productive that "produces surplus value for the capitalist, and thus works for the self-expansion of capital."[115]

Stalinists uncritically applied the identical criterion to socialist society: labor was productive only when it promoted accumulation. G.A. Kozlov and S.P. Pervushin reproduced the official view in an economic dictionary that they coedited: most service workers were said not to create "value," for all value was measured by "the social labor *embodied and materialized* in a commodity."[116] Bechin's "special use values of a nonmaterial character" could not fit this definition. Although personal and public services clearly had both use value and exchange value (or a price), Kozlov insisted that incomes spent to hire service workers must originate in material production. A service was sold for a "profit" only because the capitalist who employed the service worker acquired a share of surplus value created elsewhere.[117] In themselves, most services were said to contribute nothing to the social product and were not even recorded in Soviet national income statistics.

Defending this practice, A. Koryagin argued that neither health care, education, nor any other service not directly connected with material production could possibly create "value."[118] A. Konovalov quoted Marx saying that health services were part of the "*faux frais* [false or incidental costs] of production."[119] D. Pravdin underlined the substantive issue when he claimed that "scientific political economy" must distinguish between material and nonmaterial production in order to establish correct proportions between branches of the economy:[120] "the leading role belongs to material production. Material conditions . . . determine the effectiveness of social labor. . . ."[121] Pravdin implied that expansion of the Soviet service sector must await a developed communist society.

Soviet reformers cited western experience to argue the opposite case. E. Gromov held that "The limited material conception of the productive character of labor results in a very primitive notion of the real economic potential of society."[122] Gromov saw the role of any branch of the economy being determined by the entire system: wholesale and retail trade must be productive because they ensured efficient distribution;[123] financial services and state administration were necessary for efficient organization;[124] science, education, and health care created values "of a special kind" needed for reproduction of labor power and accumulation of knowledge.[125] In any society with a high level of industrialization, services were "one of the basic and most dynamic parts of the national economic complex."[126]

The question of services provoked a war of quotations because Marx himself had thought the definition of productive labor was *socially determined*. Marx specified that "Productive labour, *in its meaning for capitalist production*, is wage labour which . . . produces surplus value for the capitalist."[127] He added, however, that this definition was "*not derived from the material characteristics of labour . . . but from the social relations of production. . . .* An actor, for example, or even a clown, according to this definition, is a productive labourer if he works in the service of a capitalist" and generates a revenue in excess of his wages.[128]

Marx did not limit productive labor to material production even in capitalist society; still less did he expect that socialism, with entirely different relations of production, would subscribe to the narrow view taken by Stalinists.[129] In the notebooks that preceded *Capital*, Marx wrote of living labor ultimately being replaced by advanced systems of machinery representing embodied thought, or "the power of knowledge, objectified."[130] Once technology depended more upon "general scientific labour"[131] than the physical energy needed to build and operate a machine, "real wealth"—in communist society—would take the form of "*disposable time* outside that needed in direct production."[132] Social knowledge would emerge as the most important "*direct force of production*";[133] the worker would become a "watchman and regulator" of automated systems;[134] and labor time would cease to be the measure of value. In a society beyond scarcity, the purpose of production would not be material goods at all but rather human self-development. Free time would make possible a shift of investments into a higher form of fixed capital, "this fixed capital being man himself."[135]

S.M. Zagladina drew upon this part of Marx's writing when she declared that the scientific-technical revolution made "organized intellect" at least as important as fixed capital.[136] P. Oldak also maintained that knowledge is embodied in material commodities in the same way as labor power.[137] N.D. Gauzner argued that the labor of researchers and teachers must be productive: "To the extent that the labor of a teacher raises the qualifications of labor power, it creates value."[138] Noting that Marx had expected technology to free workers from material production, Gauzner pointed out that this was already occurring in the west. Computerization meant that "Machines are increasingly being used for the control of machines."[139] Ya.A. Pevzner thought it was absurd for Soviet statistics to exclude services from the national income.[140] Academician N.N. Inozemtsev, the director of IMEMO, confirmed that Marxists could not ignore "objective" patterns of development: improvements in commerce, education, and other services were needed to raise the overall efficiency of all modern economies.[141]

9. The "New Middle Class" and the New Left

Challenging the Stalinist priority of heavy industry, the new theory concerning the labor of service workers also had important implications for projecting class struggle in the west. If service workers were in fact productive, then they also created surplus value for capitalist employers. By definition, therefore, they remained exploited proletarians—regardless of their apparent "middle-class" status. Revision of Soviet thinking on these issues was as much a response to western theories of a vanishing proletariat as a summons to expand services in the USSR. By recognizing the productivity of service workers, Soviet reformers were simultaneously attempting to refute claims by western sociologists to the effect that Marxism had become antiquated with the scientific-technical revolution and the impending disappearance of a traditional working class.

Daniel Bell helped to popularize this argument when he wrote in 1961 that "the end of ideology" signified the end of class politics; communism had failed in America because it never sank roots among those it promised to save. The party's support had been limited "to the dispossessed intelligentsia of the depression generation and to the 'engineers of the future' who were attracted by [its] elitist appeal."[142] In "a politico-technological world," however, Bell claimed that property had "lost its force as a determinant of power, and sometimes, even, of wealth. In almost all modern societies, technical skill becomes more important than inheritance as a determination of occupation, and political power takes precedence over economics. What then is the meaning of class?"[143]

In an article on "Structural Changes in the Working Class of the USA," N.D. Gauzner took up Bell's challenge by replying that in spite of technical qualifications, all who sold labor power to capitalists were objectively proletarians. The percentage of "workers" in the gainfully employed American population had risen from 79.6 in 1950 to 83.7 in 1960.[144] Although the number of "employees"—those hired for a salary rather than a wage—had grown seven times more rapidly, Gauzner saw no evidence of a "new middle class." Average employee earnings were below those of skilled workers; and even the most highly skilled teachers, researchers, and technical personnel were exploited precisely because their services were productive and did create surplus value.[145] While monopolies tried to separate this "proletariat of mental labor" from the rest of the working class, Gauzner insisted that "unconsciously proletarian strata" were destined to participate in the antimonopoly struggle.[146]

E. Gromov similarly repudiated Bell's prediction that capitalists and workers would both be replaced in "postindustrial society" by practitioners of "intellectual technology."[147] Gromov claimed that American sociologists were being carried away by "sensational myths" of "deproletarianization"; the theory of the vanishing working class was "a fairy tale of the apologists of monopolistic business."[148] A. Mel'nikov took the same view: employees in commercial and office jobs were converging with factory workers in terms of living standards and conditions of employment. C. Wright Mills distinguished these "white collar" workers from the traditional proletariat, but Mel'nikov estimated that of 23 million white collar workers in the United States, 18 million were objectively members of the proletariat.[149]

Other Soviet writers were just as forthright, however, in expressing their misgivings. Reviewing the theory of "deproletarianization" in the work of Jacques Ellul, John Kenneth Galbraith, Raymond Aron, and Herbert Marcuse, S.A. Dalin admitted that owning shares in capitalist enterprises imposed "ideological" burdens on the consciousness of engineers, teachers, and doctors.[150] Dalin hoped the scientific-technical revolution would result in "the proletarianization of the intelligentsia and the intellectualization of the proletariat,"[151] but he also worried that mental workers might adopt a petty-bourgeois or even a bourgeois consciousness.[152] E.P. Pletnev agreed that class consciousness might be impaired when higher living standards enabled both technicians and even trade unionists to invest in the stock market and acquire a personal interest in the fate of capital.[153] Although he estimated the objective proletariat to comprise 78 percent of the American population, S.N. Nadel' admitted that "there is no direct and simple link between social structure, interests, and the behavior of people."[154]

Representing the conservative wing of Soviet opinion, V.A. Cheprakov was particularly annoyed by Herbert Marcuse, neo-Marxist philosopher of the New Left, who argued that both the working class and the old left, especially the Communist parties, had been "integrated into the existing regime."[155] Marcuse saw the only remaining force for social change in the substratum of "pariahs and outsiders": ghetto residents, intellectuals, and radical students, who alone were capable of rebuilding society from the bottom up.[156] Cheprakov admitted that such people might participate in a "rebellion" against state-monopoly capitalism, but they certainly could not replace it with a coherently organized new society. They were, as Marcuse said, "forces of negation"[157] and "redundant people."[158] Cheprakov thought such *déclassé* elements were suited, at most, for manipulation by "adventurist elements" committed to "mindless activism."[159]

Whereas Marcuse regarded the political and technological apparatuses of modern society as instruments of domination, Cheprakov answered that the same apparatuses must be captured for socialist reconstruction, a task for which only disciplined communists were suited. By emphasizing party organization and electoral politics, Cheprakov in fact lent support to Marcuse's argument. Following Khrushchev's prompting, western communists were doing their utmost in the 1960s to participate in capitalist institutions by modeling themselves after social democrats. The problem was that party generals had yet to organize a victorious army of proletarian voters. Moreover, with living standards rising and no indication of a spontaneous cyclical crisis, the prospect of doing so was beginning to seem remote.

10. Disproportion Between Capital and Exploitable Labor Power

The most reassuring response to these concerns over class consciousness came when Stanislav Men'shikov related political struggle to his theory of capitalist planning. Men'shikov had initiated much of the current doubt by denying the likelihood of traditional cycles. Precisely because modern capitalism was now planned, however, Men'shikov also suspected that an alternative form of reducing wages would have to be created by design: eventually the state would be compelled to *manufacture crises* in order to ensure profitability. Marx had associated crises with a "disproportion between capital and exploitable labour power," or the need to restore profit rates when they were jeopardized by full employment. Given the new conditions of reproduction, Men'shikov decided that the political superstructure, hitherto the guarantor of private property and capitalist production relations, must now serve the paradoxical purpose of inciting class militancy by imposing unemployment on skilled and unskilled workers alike.

Men'shikov found the prototype of a new form of "deflationary crisis" in Italy. A regular expansion had approached its end in 1962, but a recession had been postponed by monopolistic reserve building, causing average industrial earnings to rise by 8.2 percent in 1962 and by a further 10.7 percent in 1963.[160] Having just renovated fixed capital, employers were neither able nor willing to reduce wage costs by incorporating new technology. Instead, they raised prices. When the center-left government nationalized electricity supply, a wave of illegal capital exports ensued, reaching as much as $1.5 billion in 1963.[161] Capital flight endangered the lira, which had to be saved from devaluation through foreign borrowing. Late in 1963 monetary policy was tightened, followed by fiscal restraint in 1964.

This reversal of government policy caused "mass" dismissal of Italian workers, which Men'shikov argued was deliberately intended to relieve wage pressures: "the apparatus of planning, created in order to secure high rates of economic growth, is turning into a mechanism with which the bourgeoisie consciously causes crises and recessions."[162] No sooner had state-monopoly techniques brought classical crises under control than those same techniques had to be used in reverse to precipitate an "artificial blood-letting:"[163]

> state-monopoly programs of economic growth inevitably turn into their opposite. Moderation of the depth and scale of crises of overproduction has weakened the spontaneous mechanism inherent in capitalism for reducing wages. . . . But now the monopolies use state-monopoly regulation for the same purpose. The anti-working class intent of regulation is manifested in deliberate measures aimed at artificial "fabrication" of crises and recessions, at slowing the rate of growth, at artificially creating

and increasing unemployment, at curtailing the strike struggle, putting pressure on the incomes of the toilers, etc.[164]

Variants of the Italian example could be found in several countries where high levels of employment provoked state action to rein in wage demands. The French government attempted to negotiate a voluntary "incomes policy" in 1964. When negotiations failed, wage restraint was imposed in the public sector. From 1961 onward both Conservative and Labour governments in Britain pursued one incomes policy after another, climaxing in a six-month freeze in 1966 and deliberate deflation to protect the exchange rate. The German Bundesbank tightened monetary policy in 1965; when the Social Democrats entered government a year later as coalition partners, they persuaded unions to sign long-term contracts with ceilings on increases. Similar measures were adopted at various times in Holland, Austria, Belgium, Denmark, Sweden, Norway, and even the United States (in the form of Kennedy's wage guidelines).

Although proponents of anti-inflation measures promised to stabilize income distribution by relating wages to gains in productivity, incomes policies were generally regarded by organized labor as being designed to benefit capital. After declining in the early 1960s, from 1966 to 1969 European profit rates rose. This temporary success was accompanied, however, by an explosion of mass strikes from 1968 to 1970. Germany and Holland experienced unofficial strikes in 1969; Italy endured the "Hot Autumn" of the same year; the incomes policy of Harold Wilson's Labour government collapsed during Britain's "winter of discontent" in 1969-70; and despite the highest level of unemployment since 1960, 10 million French workers took part in a general strike in May-June 1968.[165]

In an article on "'Incomes Policy' and the Working Class," F.E. Burdzhalov applauded the general strike in France as proof of the need to replace antilabor regulations with "democratic programming."[166] A.I. Pokrovsky thought all countries with a large public sector would sooner or later experience strikes aimed "directly against the regime of state-monopoly capitalism."[167] A.G. Mileikovsky wrote that efforts to "de-proletarianise and de-ideologise" the working class had failed because educated workers were better prepared to organize against exploitation.[168] N.N. Inozemtsev expected economic crises to give way to "acute social-political crises"[169] in which "subjective factors" would be decisive.[170] N.D. Gauzner and R. Matveev proclaimed that struggle against the state, as "collective capitalist,"[171] must lead to what French

Communists—using Varga's terminology—were calling "democracy of a new type."[172]

Social unrest in the late 1960s helped to sustain hopes that state-monopoly capitalism would remain politically unstable despite its new economic tools. But after urging peaceful electoral transition for more than a decade, neither Soviet nor French Communists were prepared for a genuinely revolutionary situation in Paris in May 1968. Determined that their own leadership was imperative for scientific planning, party leaders disastrously isolated themselves from student radicals, whom they contemptuously described as "adventurists" playing at "rebellion." The party first discouraged workers from supporting the student-led uprising and then attempted to avoid street battles through parliamentary elections. Gaullists regrouped and won the elections at the end of June. The *Economist* described the events in Paris as *"a revolution set alight by students* [and] *snuffed out by communists"*:

> A modern revolution requires the coincidence of a revolutionary situation and a party or organization ready to seize power. As France comes virtually to a halt, the situation might look revolutionary. But the party which has always claimed the revolutionary role now shows no signs of fulfilling it. The Communists have climbed on the bandwagon, but only to put the brakes on. . . . [T]hey are using a revolutionary weapon—general and unlimited strikes—in order to achieve a parliamentary aim, the formation of a popular front government.[173]

The French fiasco was the ultimate test of the strategy Khrushchev had initiated in 1956. While Soviet writers tried to convince themselves that intellectuals and the new proletariat of mental labor continued to be a revolutionary force, the French party ended up betraying the very constituency it should have been courting. Commenting upon this depressing spectacle, E.L. Khmel'nitskaya gave the only possible response; defeat was temporary, and objective forces would ultimately prevail. In October 1969, Khmel'nitskaya claimed that "petty-bourgeois insurrectionism and immature ultraleft sallies" would inevitably be replaced by true revolutionary struggle when frustrated young people joined "the camp of genuine fighters for a better life, headed by . . . the Marxist-Leninist parties."[174]

Notwithstanding this show of fortitude, the combined effect of political disaster in France and new theories of capitalist planning was to reinforce

Soviet introspection. While party leaders continued to speak of the new stage of Communist construction, economists recognized that the outcome of global competition was becoming problematic. Above all, they worried that the USSR was falling behind in the race to improve planning and to incorporate new technologies. Once organized capitalism demonstrated its economic potential in the 1960s, reformers grew increasingly concerned over how Soviet performance might be accelerated. Reassessments of capitalism were accompanied throughout the decade by attempts to apply the lessons of state-monopoly planning to domestic reorganization and restructuring (*perestroika*). The result was both to revive the concerns of Malenkov's New Deal and also to anticipate the failures of Mikhail Gorbachev two decades later.

CHAPTER 8

STATE-MONOPOLY PLANNING AND ECONOMIC RESTRUCTURING (CAPITALIST PERESTROIKA)

A little more than a decade after Stalin's death, Soviet economists had discovered a new potential for stabilization in the west. References to one-sided war economies were replaced by studies of corporate planning and economic restructuring made possible by computers and the scientific-technical revolution. With high employment raising real wages, it obviously made no sense to speak any longer of inadequate consumer demand. The theory of the chronic problem of markets had originated with Rosa Luxemburg and been embraced by Stalinists since the 1930s. In the 1960s the tradition of Luxemburgism gave way to a renewed influence of Marxist institutionalism deriving from Rudolf Hilferding and Lenin.

In *The USA: Postwar State-Monopoly Capitalism*, S.A. Dalin called for rejection of Luxemburg's theory and categorically denied that military spending was necessary for realization of surplus value. From 80 to 90 percent of all values represented costs of production in the form of fixed capital, materials, and labor power. If military procurement were responsible for realizing the remaining 10-20 percent, no expanded reproduction would occur. Arms and military supplies served neither as means of production nor as means of consumption, yet it was obvious that modern capitalism was expanding output at a pace that Soviet authors had previously thought to be impossible.[1]

In a collective work entitled *Marx's "Capital" and Problems of Contemporary Capitalism*, A.G. Mileikovsky likewise criticized Rosa Luxemburg's *Accumulation of Capital* as the source of Stalinist doctrine concerning war economies and militarization. Luxemburg's "incorrect interpretation" of Marx had been "resurrected . . . in the economic literature after the Second World War . . . [encouraging] the view that conditions in the world market would deteriorate for the leading capitalist countries."[2] As Mileikovsky pointed out, however, Lenin had "demonstrated the abstract possibility of expansion of the capitalist market . . . and exposed petty-bourgeois illusions of the automatic crash of capitalism."[3] Mileikovsky blamed Luxemburg's approach for distortion of Marxism by bourgeois ideologists and Stalinist "vulgarizers" alike. Among the vulgarizers he included Maoists, who had lost confidence in the western proletariat. Instead of waiting for peaceful transition, Maoists proposed to destabilize capitalism through national-liberation struggles in the third world. The Maoist strategy resulted from Stalin's forecast, in *Economic Problems*, that geographical contraction of the capitalist system would intensify the problem of markets and make economic growth impossible. Mileikovsky noted that despite loss of colonies since 1945, the capitalist countries had used new technologies to develop domestic markets "in depth" at the same time as imperialism contracted "in breadth."[4]

In the introduction to the same volume in which Mileikovsky condemned Luxemburg, N.A. Tsagolov turned to Hilferding's theme that partial plans could not yield comprehensive proportionality. Acknowledging that the state had become an independent "subject of *economic policy*," Tsagolov denied that it could be "subject of *the economy*"[5] as a whole so long as each monopoly did its own planning with no knowledge of the intentions of other firms. Although "planned organization of production within the enterprise" was a necessary attribute of all large-scale industry, Tsagolov maintained that lack of coordination meant disproportions must continue:

> The planning (*planomernost'*) of individual branches *does not* add up to planning of the *entire* social production. Planning on a social scale can never emerge as a sum of planning in separate branches. . . . The goal of planned management within the limits of [a single] branch . . . contradicts planning on the scale of the entire society.[6]

Vygodsky and Kozlov had explained the problem of markets by reference to chronic disproportionality, monopoly pricing, and the arms race. Tsagolov thought that chronic disproportionality must give way to relative shortages in some sectors, surpluses in others. Yet when modern capitalism was interpreted in these terms, it quickly became evident to other writers that structural disproportions were far less serious in the west than in the Soviet Union. Economic programming suggested that state-monopoly capitalism was capable of continuous restructuring and development of new industries at a time when Soviet planners were impeding modernization by perpetuating Stalin's commitment to heavy industry.

Opponents of Stalinism concluded that the real one-sided war economy was not to be found in the west at all but rather in the USSR. Closer approximation to the capitalist model appeared to be necessary in order to improve efficiency in the global competition between two systems. Although Soviet authors rejected the *theory* that capitalism and socialism were converging—an argument associated in the United States with John Kenneth Galbraith and W.W. Rostow—many also encouraged convergence *in practice*. Once Stalinist priorities were seriously questioned, criticism of the west gave way to self-criticism regarding the strategy, techniques, and institutions of socialist planning. If capitalists had succeeded in planning a market economy, reformers thought it should be equally possible to incorporate market elements into socialism.

The idea of convergence resulted from empirical studies that disregarded established orthodoxies. In America, Galbraith scorned the textbook theory of markets on the grounds that all industrial economies were essentially planned. Soviet writers found the historical record to be equally incompatible with claims made on behalf of Stalinism. The difference between the two cases was that capitalists ignored economic textbooks and went about the business of making profit; Soviet bureaucrats, in contrast, recited Stalin's law of "balanced, proportionate development" in order to rationalize their inability either to justify the structure of the Soviet economy or to explain what the "correct" proportions of planning really were.

From the mid-1960s there was mounting concern in Soviet economic literature that the Cold War competition was going badly. Official pronouncements trumpeted achievements at the same time as researchers demonstrated the technological lag of Soviet industry. In highly visible endeavors such as missiles and space exploration, the Soviet Union continued to impress the west. In research institutes such as IMEMO, however, the worry prevailed that the Soviet economy might be too weak to sustain these efforts, let alone approach western standards of public services and mass consumption. Until the international currency crises of the late 1960s and early 1970s, the tone of Soviet literature became increasingly apprehensive.

1. Stalinist Planning and the Priority of Department I

In the western theory of market behavior, intersectoral proportions are spontaneously determined by continuous marginal adjustments on the part of individual firms, none of which is large enough to alter the total outcome. The model of perfect competition depicts each firm choosing a combination of factors of production—capital and labor, for example —that minimizes production costs for a projected level of output. Firms behave efficiently when they combine factors so that the marginal rate of technical substitution—the ratio at which physical units of capital and labor can be substituted for each other—is equal to the ratio of factor prices. Each firm is then expected to produce to the point where the cost of its last unit of output just equals the prevailing market price for the finished commodity. Assuming no monopolies, the model posits a determinate equilibrium for each possible combination of prices for factors and finished goods.

No Soviet economist could take this description seriously. In the first place, it was obvious that a few hundred large corporations dominated the American economy and planned investments for years in advance rather than reacting to day-to-day price changes.[7] Secondly, Marx's theory of value indicated that labor was the sole "factor" creating value and surplus value; capital was merely the embodied product of workers, and capitalists had no legitimate claim upon social income. Finally, because Marx thought centralization and concentration would eventually impair capital mobility, he also emphasized the opposite of a theory of incremental adjustments: capital was "held fast by its fixed constituent part" over a period of several years, causing each wave of investments to become "a new material basis for the next turnover cycle."[8] Proportionality ultimately had to be to be reconstructed through crises.

Marxists learned from *Capital* that flexible prices, even when they did operate in premonopoly capitalism, were an irrational basis for allocational decisions: prices signaled *short-run changes*, yet they were supposed to guide *long-run commitments*. Short-run price increases encouraged disproportionate accumulation in some branches; short-run declines imposed premature destruction of existing capital through bankruptcies. The obvious consequence was that the market "law of value" could not serve as regulator of a planned economy. Because Marx gave no theory of his own concerning resource allocation through socialist planning, however, it fell to Stalin to explain how priorities were established.

In *Economic Problems,* Stalin wrote that the law of value applied only to commodities whose circulation involved transfer of property rights.[9] Since the planned economy was to function like a single factory, *commodities* were replaced by *products,* whose movement within state industry entailed no change of ownership. Similarly, because workers nominally owned the means of production, they no longer sold labor power as a commodity to capitalists. The law of value determined neither the distribution of labor nor the allocation of means of production.[10] If "balanced, proportionate development" were sacrificed to the whims of consumers, Stalin declared, "we should have to cease giving primacy to the production of means of production in favor of the production of articles of consumption. . . . The effect would be to destroy the possibility of continuous expansion of our national economy. . . ."[11]

The law of the primacy of Department I was not Stalin's invention; it originated with Lenin's exposition of Marx's law of the rising organic composition of capital. If new technologies were assumed always to use more capital relative to labor, Lenin thought that heavy industry must always have priority over light. In his article "On the So-called Market Question," Lenin held that priority of Department I—and within that Department, of industries producing means of production for producer goods rather than for consumer goods—was a necessary condition both for capital accumulation and for creating a market to absorb the output of Department II. Given this condition, capitalists had no need of "third-party" markets.[12]

Alec Nove has written that in historical terms Lenin's view of proportionality was understandable. During the early stages of industrialization, investments did concentrate in capital-intensive heavy industries.[13] Economists date the beginning of a change in this pattern from the 1920s. From the outset, however, there was a theoretical problem with Lenin's interpretation. Marx spoke of the organic composition of capital in two ways: technical composition referred to the ratio between "the *mass* of the means of production employed . . . and the *mass* of labour necessary for their employment"; value composition involved the "*value* of the means of production and . . . the sum total of *wages.*"[14]

Expecting mass and value normally to change in "strict correlation," Marx used the term "organic composition" as an expression of "the value composition of capital, insofar as it is determined by its technical composition and mirrors the changes of the latter."[15] But Marx also recognized that increased productivity in Department I could reduce costs for materials and equipment, in which case the value of means of production would grow more slowly than the volume. The value of the total means of production might even decline as volume increased.[16] The permanent priority that Lenin assigned to Department I neglected this qualification.

Lenin's view gave no practical guidance if technological change were to alter the relative costs of different types of fixed capital or if fixed capital generally were to become less expensive to produce. In these circumstances, planners could not possibly determine the degree of priority to be attached to Department I. Should output of the *mass* of means of production continue indefinitely to be maximized? Or should concern with mass give way to concern for *cost effectiveness* in satisfying social needs? In the latter event, how could effectiveness be assessed? Efficient allocation of resources presupposed specification of a socially preferred product mix and choice of the most efficient technology. With no market prices to reflect either social needs or costs, planners adhered to established priorities and became resistant to technological change. The law of the priority of heavy industry served as an ideological rationalization for the immutability of existing proportions.

Centralized planning was intended to avoid the cyclical disproportions of capitalism; in fact, the planned economy created its own chronic disproportion between Departments I and II. The meaning of Stalin's law of "balanced, proportionate development," as Malenkov saw at the time of his New Deal, was really nothing more than a matter for political judgment. In 1955, Khrushchev defended heavy industry by attacking Malenkov's proposal to increase production of consumer goods and services. Yet by the end of 1957, Khrushchev was himself claiming that "without detriment to the further development of heavy industry and machine-building, we can develop light industry at a considerably higher speed."[17]

After condemning Stalinist terror, Khrushchev realized that economic incentives would have to be improved in order to raise labor productivity. In May 1961 he declared that: "Now we consider our heavy industry as built. So we are not going to give it priority. Light industry and heavy industry will develop at the same pace."[18] The Party Program of 1961 proposed to meet the needs of both heavy industry and consumers through "intensive development." To match western accomplishments, the Soviet Union would rely upon computers, automation, new fuels, electronics, and synthetic materials associated with modern chemistry.[19] In his official report of October 1961 to the twenty-second congress, Khrushchev promised that more efficient use of resources would allow "considerably closer correlation between the rates of growth in the production of means of production and the production of articles of consumption." Heavy industry would retain priority—provided it also contributed "increasing quantities of cultural and household goods."[20]

The overthrow of Khrushchev in 1964 has been attributed to several causes, including his test-ban treaty with Kennedy, his effort to downgrade the military sector and ferrous metallurgy in favor of the chemical industry, and his determination that the "main task" of planners must become the expanded output of consumer goods.[21] Attempting to impose these priorities, Khrushchev was supported by economists who cited American experience to demonstrate that the proportions inherited from Stalin were no more objectively necessary than Luxemburg's chronic problem of markets.

2. Efficiency and Proportionality: The USA and the USSR

An important measure of efficiency in western economic analysis is the relation between capital and output. When output grows more quickly than capital stock, the capital-output ratio declines. In his study of business cycles in America, Bert G. Hickman showed that the capital-output ratio had been declining since the 1920s. In the private sector, the decline of the aggregate ratio was 22 percent between 1923-29 and 1947-59.[22] During the same period, the ratio of manufacturers' inventories to finished goods, or what Marx called the costs of "circulating" capital, also fell by approximately 25 percent.[23] Hickman associated more efficient use of capital with new industries, improved organization, and increased expenditures on equipment rather than construction.[24]

Since America was relying less on production in Department I for each additional unit of final output, Soviet writers began their own calculations of what was happening. In September 1961, M. Golansky separated American manufacturing from the rest of the private sector and estimated that the capital-output ratio had fallen by an even larger figure of 35 percent from 1929 to 1959.[25] Throughout the nineteenth century the volume and value of fixed capital had grown simultaneously, but since 1919 the trend had been reversed: increased productivity enabled industry to use less of both fixed capital and materials relative to labor. Golansky explained the change by recalling the distinction that Marx had made between the technical and the value composition of capital:

> Marx wrote [that] "In isolated cases the mass of the elements of constant capital [plant, equipment, fuel and materials] may even increase, while its value remains the same, or falls." But where-

as a change of the mass and value in opposite directions . . .
used to be an exception, now it has become the rule.[26]

Following Golansky's article, several other economists turned to the
same issue. A.A. Arzumanyan calculated the fall of the capital-output
ratio in American manufacturing to be as much as 40 percent since
1929.[27] A.I. Bechin compared a 340 percent increase in output per man
hour with his own estimate of a 31 percent decline of the capital-output
ratio from 1900 to 1957.[28] For the period 1909-49, I. Ivanov attributed
13 percent of the increase in output per man hour to the volume of
investment and 87 percent to technological improvements.[29] S. Kheinman cited even more disturbing figures: not only was the capital-output
ratio declining, but in 1962 the United States also produced 59 percent
more industrial output than the USSR with 35 percent fewer workers.[30]

In an article on economic competition between the two systems, Ya.
Kotkovsky pointed out that while the total volume of industrial
investments in the Soviet Union was higher than in America, the Soviet
capital-output ratio was rising because too large a portion of resources
was being devoted to expanding the conventional raw material base, fuel
supplies, and metallurgy. Kotkovsky claimed that by reducing expenditures of labor and materials, improving the availability of services,
investing more heavily in scientific research, and shortening construction
periods, industrial production could be increased by up to 50 percent.[31]
To realize this potential, however, the planning system would have to
devolve more initiative to plant-level decision makers and pay more
attention to consumer goods and labor incentives.[32] Although total
Soviet industrial production in 1967 lagged behind that of the United
States by eleven to thirteen years, Kotkovsky thought the gap could be
narrowed to seven years by 1970.[33]

In *The Stages of Economic Growth* (subtitled *A Non-Communist
Manifesto*), W.W. Rostow produced a much less favorable comparison.
Describing "a remarkable parallel" between industrialization in America
and the Soviet Union, Rostow noted that both countries began with
railways, coal, iron, and heavy engineering—capital-intensive industries—which are normally followed by chemicals, electricity, and modern
machine tools, ultimately permitting higher per-capita consumption in a
mature industrial economy. Reproducing a graph borrowed from Warren
G. Nutter, however, Rostow emphasized a striking difference in terms
of stages of development: Soviet Russia lagged behind the United States

by "about thirty-five years in the level of industrial output and . . . about a half-century in *per-capita* output in industry."[34]

Rostow depicted the Soviet economy as a backward version of the American; eventually the two would converge at the mature stage of high mass consumption, but in the meantime Soviet progress would become slower and more difficult. In the 1920s planners had adopted prototypes of western technology and incurred virtually no cost for research and development; an increasing part of income must now go to depreciating existing plant, while future technological change would become more costly and incremental.[35] Soviet leaders boasted of catching up with and surpassing the capitalist countries; Rostow expected America's lead to continue for decades. Soviet statistics lent support to his prediction. From 1951 to 1963 the industrial growth rate actually fell in the Soviet Union from 16.4 percent per year to 6.7 percent. Western sources estimate that the rate of change in capital productivity fell during the same period from 0.0 percent to minus 6.3 percent.[36]

Recalling how studies of western technology had been condemned under Stalin for "bourgeois objectivism," A.G. Mileikovsky insisted in 1963 that more realistic comparisons were essential in order to improve socialist planning and organization.[37] Western experience demonstrated the need for systematic restructuring of Soviet economic proportions, including industrialization of agriculture; concentration of investment in "active" rather than "passive" assets; development of new fuels; substitution of aluminum, plastic, and concrete for steel; and, above all, commitment of more resources to chemicals and synthetic materials. In America, 60 percent of the chemical and pharmaceutical products sold in 1959 had not even been produced in 1955, illustrating the urgency of developing what Mileikovsky called "the most dynamic of modern branches."[38]

In July 1964, L.B. Al'ter (deputy director of a Gosplan research institute) also criticized comparisons of the Soviet and American economies for focusing on steel and other early industrial commodities. He too argued that improvement of living standards would require changes in the industrial branch structure, closer attention to the "tempos, proportions and development prospects of the most progressive branches," and more comparative study of "the effectiveness of capital investments."[39] I.M. Osadchaya, a leading specialist on Keynesian and neo-Keynesian theory, wrote that measurements of labor productivity alone were not adequate for judging efficiency; closer attention must be paid to the yield from capital as measured by the capital-output ratio.[40]

When Khrushchev was removed from office in October 1964, his successors—Leonid I. Brezhnev as party leader and Aleksei N. Kosygin as head of government—determined that heavy industry would continue to grow more rapidly than light, although the two rates would gradually be brought closer together. S.L. Vygodsky thought the change of leadership created an opportunity to reiterate traditional views. In October 1965 he protested that other writers were exaggerating American achievements: changes in the capital-output ratio were misleading if cyclical fluctuations were not taken into account. In the 1930s, for example, the ratio fell mainly because American investments collapsed even more precipitously than current production;[41] a decline from 1956 to 1962 similarly coincided with poor growth and weak investment.[42] When the American economy recovered after 1962, investments in fixed capital grew at a yearly average of 10.4 percent while output increased only at the rate of 6.1 percent.[43]

Although Vygodsky recognized that long-term improvements in the use of capital resulted from better technology, he did not think this trend disproved the law of the priority of Department I. As evidence he compared the American economy in the 1950s with the more rapidly expanding economies of Western Europe. In the latter countries the share of means of production in total industrial output grew by more than 8 percent from 1953 to 1963, proving that a high rate of capital accumulation depended mainly upon heavy industrial expansion. Vygodsky concluded that "The law of the priority of growth in heavy industry continues to operate, even though growth of the share of means of production has slowed somewhat [in the United States] over the past decade."[44]

3. S.M. Nikitin: The Convergence of Departments I and II

In 1965, S.M. Nikitin published a book-length inquiry into these issues with the title *Structural Changes in the Capitalist Economy*. Nikitin attributed Soviet inefficiency to systemic disproportions resulting from Stalin's law of "balanced, proportionate development." In the introduction to Nikitin's book, A.G. Mileikovsky underscored its domestic implications by commenting that critical study of the relation between Departments I and II was "important not only for a deeper understanding of the laws of capitalism, but also for resolving certain problems of socialist reproduction."[45] Mileikovsky summarized Nikitin's theme this way:

> The facts demonstrate that proportions between Departments I and II are flexible. Relations between the two Departments, between accumulation and consumption, depend on concrete-historical conditions, in particular on the degree of industrialization, the level of development of the productive forces and of technological progress, the productivity of labor, the lifetime of basic assets, the yield on investments, etc.[46]

Nikitin began his study with long-term trends in the United States, where the data appeared to support Vygodsky's contention that rapid growth must always be associated with priority for heavy industry. Since 1899 the rate of expansion in heavy industry had exceeded that in light industry with the exception of only two periods: the depression decade of 1929-37 and the years of recurring recessions from 1953 to the early 1960s.[47] Because heavy industry produced both investment goods and some consumer goods, Soviet statistics divided industry as a whole into Group A (means of production) and Group B (consumer goods). Radios, televisions, refrigerators, automobiles, and other consumer durables were produced in heavy industry, but they belonged in the Group B category as consumer goods. When American industry was subdivided in the same manner, it became even more apparent that Group A had lagged behind B during the decade of relatively slow growth from the end of the Korean war until 1963. Since American industrial production had nevertheless increased during these years by 35.9 percent, one conclusion was obvious: *expanded reproduction did not require continuous priority for means of production.*[48]

Turning from America to West Germany and Japan, where the rate of accumulation was much higher, Nikitin found that Group A had grown more quickly than B during the 1950s because these countries were undergoing "Americanization" and restructuring (*perestroika*) in order to compete in world markets.[49] Yet even in these circumstances the gap between A and B "was on the whole insignificant, and in certain periods or specific years the growth of Group B exceeded Group A."[50] Taking the period 1950-62 as a whole, the difference in Japan was 0.3 percent in favor of Group A; in West Germany the comparable figure was 2.5 percent.[51] These countries demonstrated that the highest growth rates in the capitalist world could be achieved with production of investment goods and consumer goods increasing at approximately the same rate. Nikitin expected that the long-run trend would be toward equal rates:

> at the current level of development of the productive forces a fall of the capital-output ratio . . . is the prevailing tendency. For all [the leading capitalist countries] a decline or stabilization of the industrial capital-output ratio is typical. . . .[52]

In the Soviet Union, production of investment goods had increased more rapidly than consumer goods in every year since Malenkov's New Deal. Moreover, the gap was widening during the early 1960s. Notwithstanding Khrushchev's objections, from 1960-61 to 1963-64 Group A grew at an average rate of 9.75 percent, Group B at 5.75 percent.[53] Even more important was the fact that the Soviet Union had hardly begun the industrial restructuring process that accounted for high rates of accumulation in Japan and West Germany; in other words, Group A was growing more quickly because inefficient and backward industries were absorbing an inordinate volume of resources. Nikitin thought this comparison proved that

> in the socialist countries the orientation in planning for the future . . . must not be the concept of the faster growth of production of means of production in itself, but rather the concept of faster growth of the progressive branches of production, those branches whose development will make it possible, in the shortest time, to solve the problem of significantly raising the level of efficiency of the entire economy.[54]

The capitalist countries could give more attention to consumer goods because new and more efficient industries in Group A were supplying the necessary means of production at lower cost. The Soviet Union was devoting a greater share of resources to investment goods merely to compensate for wasteful use of capital. Because the capitalists had shown that all inputs could be reduced per unit of final output, Nikitin believed that they had disproved "the most important argument of those who support the eternal need for a more rapid growth in production of means of production."[55] The "objective necessity" of continuous priority for Department I (Group A industry plus the fuel and materials sectors) did not exist.[56] The Stalinist pattern must be replaced by "a maximum drawing together of growth rates in the two Departments."[57]

204 ECONOMIC RESTRUCTURING

Just as Alec Nove explained Lenin's interpretation of Marx by referring to the capital-intensive early stages of industrial development, so Nikitin arrived at the same judgment of Soviet planning:

> the period of early industrial development is characterized by . . . priority of the growth of production of means of production. . . . With creation of a developed industry, the processes that determine the relation between the two Departments of social production begin to act differently. . . . [B]ecause of a number of factors—the greater efficiency of new technology, the rising share of equipment in all capital investments, the accelerated modernization of equipment, faster construction, etc.—there occurs a fall of the capital-output ratio in production.[58]

If the share of fixed capital and material expenditures in the social product were reduced, personal living standards could be raised through higher wages, better social services, and more investments in training and skills. Nikitin thought that John Kenneth Galbraith had demonstrated the vital role of services in an affluent society.[59] In *Theories of Surplus Value,* Marx had also commented that "A country is . . . richer the smaller its productive population is [relative] to the total product . . . just as for the individual capitalist: the fewer labourers he needs to produce the same surplus, so much the better for him."[60] Nikitin paraphrased Marx to underline the importance of services: "The more developed a country's economy, the greater is the portion of national wealth intended for nonproduction consumption. It becomes especially important in socialist society, whose goal is maximum satisfaction of the needs of man."[61]

4. The Capitalist State and Planned Proportionality

Nikitin documented the need and the potential to improve Soviet growth rates and labor incentives. Emphasizing the progressive consequences of western restructuring, particularly developments in petrochemicals, electronics, fuels, and engineering, he also indicated that the capitalist countries had dealt more successfully with changes of proportionality than Soviet planners. How they had done so was another question. It was obvious to all Soviet economists that the price system and the theory of competitive markets could not explain the scientific-technical revolution. Monopolies and the state were the real economic actors, but the question remained as to how industrial restructuring had actually been co-ordinated.

In Soviet thinking, monopolies were usually credited with industrial planning, the state with regulating aggregate demand in order to solve the supposed problem of markets. By the mid-1960s, however, it was widely believed in all capitalist countries that governments must play a part in guiding private activities in pursuit of public priorities. Galbraith claimed that the "imperatives of technology" required continuous collaboration between government and business in order to minimize the risks accompanying modern investments. The sheer volume of resources at stake "put the problems of planning beyond the reach of the industrial firm. Technological compulsions . . . require the firm to seek the help and protection of the state."[62] Since capitalist and socialist countries faced identical risks in developing new products and new industries, Galbraith discounted "images of ideology" and foresaw "a broad convergence" between industrial systems as they all engaged in increasingly similar forms of planning.[63]

In Galbraith's analysis, dominant American firms avoided price competition in much the same way as the state managed prices in the USSR. Industrial planning was impossible when production costs and rates of return on capital were unpredictable: "The modern large corporation and the modern apparatus of socialist planning are variant accommodations to the same need."[64] Capital accumulation by the socialist state was also analogous to corporate financing of investments through retained earnings. Both measures guaranteed predictable access to the resources needed for planning.[65] Effective planning depended upon both size and autonomy, and neither western corporations nor state-owned enterprises could be "subordinate and subject to uncontrolled markets."[66] Wage expenditures had to be controlled in the same way as the cost of capital and materials. "At full employment," Galbraith wrote, "there is no mechanism for holding prices and wages stable. This stabilization too is a function of the state."[67] Trade unions were therefore becoming part of the planning system, and "no sharp line" any longer separated business from government: "Each organization is . . . an extension of the other."[68]

While Galbraith was describing America during the years of Keynesian growth policies, many western economists looked to France as the most important innovator in democratic planning and a model for other countries. Andrew Shonfield referred to French "indicative planning" as "the most characteristic expression of the new capitalism."[69] Although

France had a large nationalized sector, the novelty of the French system lay in use of joint public-private enterprises, contractual relations, and financial incentives to encourage voluntary plan compliance. Shonfield wrote in *Modern Capitalism* that

> The planners developed an intricate network of commitments on the part of private firms—to invest in certain objects, to take their business to a certain region of the country, to adopt specific techniques of production, and so on—all in return for favours from the state. These favours have generally taken the form of tax reliefs or cheap loans. . . . [T]he enterprises directly owned by the state, either wholly or in part, fulfil the role of pace-setters of the system.[70]

In *Economic Programming in the Countries of Western Europe*, a group of Soviet economists, headed by A.I. Pokrovsky, compared French planning to various forms of government control in England, Italy, West Germany, Belgium, and Holland. Pokrovsky acknowledged that the capitalist state now assumed responsibilities far beyond what Soviet writers had previously thought possible. Planning embraced science policy, manpower and skills development, industrial modernization, regional policy, promotion of new industries, and ultimately restructuring of the entire national economy.[71] Pokrovsky explained state-monopoly planning by pointing to the same technological imperatives as Galbraith: "On the scale of individual monopolies, the rapid development of science and technology required a transition to the long-term planning of production; on the scale of an entire capitalist economy, adjustment to the requirements of the scientific-technical revolution created the need for long-term state programming."[72]

Beginning with the Monnet plan for 1947-52 (later extended to 1953), France exemplified the ability of the capitalist state to guide modernization. Concentrating on the core industries needed for postwar reconstruction, the first plan contained investment and production goals for electricity, coal, steel, cement, transportation, and agricultural machinery. The Hirsch plan for 1954-57 was more ambitious and affected virtually all sectors of the economy, representing what Pokrovsky called the first attempt "to program the basic proportions of the French economy as a whole." Industrial investments exceeded expectations by 10 percent, production grew by 45 percent, GNP by 29 percent. Although conjunctural circumstances favored the plan,

Pokrovsky wrote that "There is no doubt that the plan's measures, and state investments in particular, promoted the intensity of the expansion."[73]

The Rueff plan (1958-61) projected a 27 percent increase in GNP (30 percent in industry and 20 percent in agriculture). Industry fell short of its target by only 2-3 percent, while capital investments grew by 29 percent.[74] The fourth plan (1962-65) involved changes in industrial organization to meet the challenge of the Common Market. Although the economy was slowed in 1963-65 by anti-inflation policies, Pokrovsky thought the results were still impressive: "The fourth plan promoted rationalization of France's industrial structure, particularly in the area of energy: at the same time as expenditures were cut in the coal industry, capital investments were increased in the gas and electrical energy branches. In transportation, the center of . . . construction moved from railways to highways. . . ."[75]

The fifth plan (1966-70) encouraged further industrial mergers; one or two large firms were to dominate each field in order to compete on a world scale with American multinational corporations. Priority was attached to electronics, synthetic chemistry, the nuclear industry, electricity, oil, and gas.[76] Services were to represent 21 percent of final demand by 1970, with the nonproduction sphere as a whole accounting for up to 40 percent.[77] This plan had to be modified following the social crisis of 1968, but its overall objectives confirmed the priorities that Soviet economists wanted to see incorporated in the USSR's own five-year plans.

Like Andrew Shonfield, Soviet writers thought the most striking characteristic of indicative planning was use of financial levers to secure voluntary compliance. Pokrovsky remarked that "Cases of direct administrative action by the state upon private enterprises and monopolies are extremely rare. The program is obligatory mainly for state enterprises and institutions. As for private production, the state uses the system of taxes, credits and prices . . . [to encourage] fulfillment of plan recommendations."[78] Criticizing Stalin's "extraordinarily centralized administrative-directive planning," A.G. Mileikovsky was equally impressed by the combination of plan and market techniques:

V.I. Lenin . . . called upon us to study the experience of the developed capitalist countries in order more effectively to organize management of the national economy. . . . But many of Lenin's instructions were later forgotten. . . . [N]ot enough attention was paid to the analysis of *economic levers*. . . . Only after being freed of . . . [Stalinist] dogmas did Soviet economic science begin to pay more attention to study of objectively progressive changes in the economic structure of the developed capitalist countries.[79]

In *New Phenomena in the Accumulation of Capital in the Imperialist Countries*, Mileikovsky saw western governments performing all of the strategic functions ideally associated with Soviet planning. But having no direct responsibility for microeconomic decisions, capitalist planners could focus all the more effectively on restructuring macroeconomic proportions:

> What is new in the role of the state is that it takes upon itself . . . the function of "capitalist rationalization" of the entire national economy. . . . It works to change proportions between the production and nonproduction spheres, between the Departments of material production, between separate branches; it reconstructs and restores weak links of the economy and organizes and finances fundamental scientific research, which reaches beyond the interests of individual firms but is also a necessary condition for stimulating technological progress.[80]

The state encouraged technological change not as a taskmaster but rather as "an associate of private capital."[81] Capitalist *"perestroika"*[82] did not depend on public ownership so much as on the share of government spending in the gross national product. Public enterprise was limited in West Germany to railways, electricity, and communications, yet the state accounted in 1961 for more than 40 percent of gross capital investments; in Japan, where public enterprise played an equally modest role, the state was just as actively engaged in creating the infrastructure needed to improve national economic efficiency.[83] Modern capitalism worked *through* the market mechanism to coordinate private investments with public policy; it also *bypassed* the market in order to satisfy "collective, public needs" for utilities, recreational facilities, health care, and education.[84] Soviet planners sacrificed services for the sake of steel; Mileikovsky suggested that they look to Europe and America for evidence of "the objectively progressive tendencies that have caused the growing role of the nonproduction sphere":[85]

The scientific and technological revolution has substantially expanded the part played by the state in the training of manpower. As a result, there has been a notable growth in the basic non-production assets . . . [used for] education, . . . medical care and urban improvement. These "human investments" are recognized today in all the developed capitalist countries as a cardinal prerequisite for heightening their competitive capacity on the external markets.[86]

In the 1950s state-monopoly planning had provoked derision in the Soviet Union on the grounds that its sole purpose was to transfer income from toilers to the monopolies. Mileikovsky thought the new forms of planning confirmed Varga's thesis of a more flexible relation between private and public power: "the strategic interests of the whole monopoly bourgeoisie" required the state to exercise "relative independence" because technological restructuring of proportions involved sacrificing particular firms and industries in order to promote new ones.[87] Every monopoly continued to do its own planning, and the state could never provide "a master plan" by which all monopolies would abide.[88] Nevertheless, it was clear that the state, deploying incentives in a third-party capacity, had answered Hilferding's challenge by reintegrating "the various branches of the economy into *a single whole*."[89]

5. Property and Planning

The principal Soviet objection to organized capitalism had always been that the state could not plan what it did not own. Stalin told H.G. Wells in 1934 that "Without getting rid of the capitalists, without abolishing the principle of private property in the means of production, it is impossible to create planned economy."[90] In 1968, N.A. Tsagolov still believed that private property prevented state-monopoly capitalism from functioning as a "planned unity": *nationalized* industries could be planned, but all other state activities were superstructural in character and could be ignored by monopolies in the pursuit of "superprofits." State-monopoly capitalism was neither a new stage nor could it entail planning on a society-wide scale: "This would be in contradiction with the nature of monopolies and capitalist appropriation." Tsagolov dismissed "so-called theories of convergence" as merely another form of apology for capitalist exploitation and private property.[91]

A long history of American institutional economics suggested that Tsagolov's argument overlooked crucial changes in the meaning and significance of property. As early as the 1920s, Thorstein Veblen had depicted the wealthy as a "leisure class" while treating engineers and the technical intelligentsia as the real driving forces of modern industry.[92] In *The Modern Corporation and Private Property* (1934), Adolf A. Berle and Gardiner C. Means showed that in most corporations ownership and control were effectively separated by the time of the Great Depression.[93] Differentiating between the "active" property of traditional entrepreneurs and the "passive" property of modern shareholders, Berle and Means argued that neither the claims of ownership nor those of management could be allowed to stand against the paramount interests of the community.[94]

The economist who most persuasively described the abstraction of modern property and evaporation of its material "substance" was Joseph Schumpeter. In *Capitalism, Socialism and Democracy* (1942), Schumpeter claimed that shareholding property had become a mere title, or "dematerialized, defunctionalized and absentee ownership."[95] As a consequence, there was no longer a real bourgeoisie to resist socialist transition: "The perfectly bureaucratized giant industrial unit not only ousts the small and medium-sized firm and 'expropriates' its owners, but in the end it also ousts . . . the bourgeoisie as a class. . . ."[96] Schumpeter thought the great entrepreneurs of the past had been replaced by managers with "the psychology of the salaried employee working in a bureaucratic organization." Whether or not managers were also shareholders, they could never possess the same will to fight as real capitalists, "who knew ownership and its responsibilities in the fullblooded sense. . . . Thus the modern corporation, although the product of the capitalist process, socializes the bourgeois mind; it relentlessly narrows the scope of capitalist motivation; not only that, it will eventually kill its roots."[97]

Despite capitalism's success in promoting mass consumption, Schumpeter did not believe the system could survive. Modern technologies were beyond individual entrepreneurs and had become the business of "teams of trained specialists."[98] Galbraith took the same view: capitalists were losing both function and power in the social process because capital was no longer the most difficult factor to obtain or replace. In technological society the decisive factor was "organized intelligence,"[99] or the technical, planning, and other specialized staff constituting the "technostructure."[100] According to Galbraith, "what the entrepreneur created passed inexorably beyond the scope of his authority." Modern corporations depended upon the "specialized information" available only to experts.[101]

In *The Limits of American Capitalism*, Robert L. Heilbroner likewise saw the power of business being limited by government administrators, organized labor, and a new elite of academics and professionals. In terms similar to Soviet descriptions of the scientific-technical revolution, Heilbroner spoke of conflict between the nineteenth-century theory of self-regulating markets and the twentieth-century ambitions of science:

> What is certain is . . . the profound incompatibility between the new idea of the active use of science within society and the ideal of capitalism as a social system. . . . Before the activist policy of science . . . . [t]he "self-regulating" economy . . . stands condemned. . . . [C]apitalism is weighed in the scale of science and found wanting, not alone as a system but as a philosophy.[102]

Western theories of capitalism's managerial transformation lent plausibility to the concept of convergence. If capitalist property was merely form without substance, how did it differ from socialist property, which formally belonged to workers but in fact was controlled by planners and party officials? Moreover, if capitalist firms could be indirectly guided by state incentives, while at the same time day-to-day decisions were left to branch managers, why should socialist property stand in the way of an equally efficient combination of plan and market? Ritual demanded that theories of convergence be refuted; hope of reforming the Soviet system required recognition of capitalism's organizational and administrative achievements.

6. Managerialism and Objective Socialization

One of the first responses to the "false theory of convergence" came in 1963. S. Khavina followed Stalin by emphasizing irreconcilable differences of class relations, property, and economic laws. The idea of a "hybrid" industrial society was a fantasy because capitalism was organized by the law of value and surplus value. Socialism's surplus product could not take the form of surplus value; nor, for that reason, could socialism include exploitation. Because labor was no longer a commodity, only "non-antagonistic" differences could exist between socialist citizens due to income variations based on personal skills. In the United States, by contrast, the top 10 percent of property-owning families still received 27 percent of pretax income while the bottom 10 percent received 1 percent.[103] Even if property no longer entailed direct participation in management, it certainly constituted the foundation for wealth, privilege, and power.

V.A. Cheprakov argued that Galbraith's "social liberalism" neglected to point out that "the managers, the representatives of the financial oligarchy, the leaders of government and the top ranks of the military are all part of the . . . state-monopoly oligarchy."[104] S.L. Vygodsky also attacked Galbraith for failing to understand monopoly pricing. Had he been aware of Stalin's law of maximum monopoly profit, Galbraith would have understood that modern corporations were still profit maximizers and that disproportions and militarization were inevitable due to the limited effective demand of the masses.[105] K. Kozlova accepted Galbraith's claim that monopolies occasionally charged less than the maximum price in the interest of winning market share; but this was nothing more than a tactical maneuver to increase total profits in the long run.[106] Galbraith misinterpreted monopoly behavior because *The New Industrial State* substituted "technico-economic imperatives" for social-economic analysis of the class struggle over surplus value.[107]

In *Millionaires and Managers,* S.M. Men'shikov traced the evolution of property from individual ownership through joint-stock companies to the emergence of the *"finance capitalist in pure form* . . . a parasite, a tycoon-rentier who 'clips coupons.'" But Men'shikov did not think that finance capital had been displaced so easily as Galbraith and Schumpeter suggested: "if everything boiled down to this, the class of money-capitalists would long ago have turned into a sort of 'House of Lords' shorn of real power."[108] In reality most finance capitalists hired managers to oversee individual firms in order personally to coordinate vast empires of banking and industry. As examples, Men'shikov gave the customary list of Morgans, Rockefellers, and regional groups of American capital.

In *Actual Economic Problems of Modern Capitalism,* edited by Vygodsky, Sh. Shorkin admitted that Galbraith had made "a certain step forward" by connecting social relations with changes in the forces of production.[109] But Galbraith fetishized technology when he suggested that relocation of power from property owners to technical specialists might reconcile the conflicting interests of society as a whole. As for the state, Galbraith said nothing more than Varga after World War II, when he foresaw that its importance would steadily increase.[110] There was a difference, however, between capitalist regulation or even indicative planning on the one hand, and Soviet "directive" planning on the other. Galbraith did not see that "The spontaneity characteristic of a capitalist economy results from the nature of private property."[111] He failed to go beyond bourgeois forms of thought because his technological interpretation of state-monopoly capitalism made no provision for class struggle leading to socialism.

S.A. Dalin found both strengths and weaknesses in the writings of Galbraith and other American institutionalists. He agreed that "separation of capital as property from capital as function, or the dispersion of shares, has gone so far that modern monopolies have been transformed into a collective capitalist";[112] but he also insisted that dispersion of *shares* could not be equated with genuine dispersion of *property*. In the case of America, three thousand people in the "top crust of the financial oligarchy" continued to exploit the engineers, economists, and financial experts who directly managed industry. In 1965 only 10 percent of Americans owned shares, and 76 percent of all shares were in the hands of 1 percent of the population.[113] As major shareholders, top corporate managers belonged to the exploiting class, whereas the specialists of the technostructure were "hired employees" destined to move "closer to the working class."[114]

While Dalin rejected Galbraith's contention that "the two 'formally' different industrial systems are actually similar,"[115] he nevertheless believed that *The New Industrial State* convincingly demonstrated the "superfluousness" of the capitalist class.[116] It was precisely the separation of ownership from daily operation of the firm that Marx had in mind when he predicted "the abolition of capital as private property within the framework of capitalist production."[117] Marx wrote that "In stock companies the function is divorced from capital ownership. . . . This . . . ultimate development of capitalist production is a necessary transitional phase towards the reconversion of capital into the property of . . . associated producers, as outright social property."[118] Engels also commented that "conversion of the great organisations of production and communication into joint-stock companies and state property shows that . . . the bourgeoisie can be dispensed with."[119]

Dalin thought Galbraith's theory of the technostructure confirmed the predictions of Marx and Engels: the owners of capital had degenerated into "pure rentiers,"[120] clearing the way for socialism by removing themselves from real production activity. Like Schumpeter, he saw no similarity between the entrepreneurial pioneers of early capitalism and their modern successors:

> The capitalist of the turn of the century would have been aghast at the idea of the state intervening in production, fixing prices, regulating wages and instituting a system of contracts with trade unions. But all this is reality today. And tomorrow's reality will be the guidance of socialized production directly by society and not by a handful of finance tycoons.[121]

7. The Practice of Convergence

However critical they were of Galbraith's theory of convergence, Soviet economists took it seriously enough to reply in several books and most of the leading journals. Apart from the contentious issue of property, there were similarities between the two systems too obvious not to be seen: both were engaged in planning; both had systemic inequalities of power and income; and both were dominated by a privileged elite—the capitalists in the west, the party and planners in socialism—who contributed little or nothing to the direct production process. The outstanding difference appeared to be that the capitalist oligarchy collected its dividends and respected the functional prerogatives of the technostructure whereas Soviet bureaucrats did not. If finance capitalists were really redundant, as Dalin claimed, the concept of convergence must inevitably raise questions concerning the contribution of Soviet officials to real economic management.

Studying the empires of finance capital, Soviet analysts hinted at and often made explicit comparisons with the performance of their own industrial ministries. Through contracts for parts and materials, capitalist monopolies were said to subordinate small enterprises to planning, thus extending the division of labor and further curtailing market anarchy; Soviet ministries claimed to plan, but the enterprises within their jurisdiction were frequently driven toward autarky because central controls failed to guarantee deliveries. Instead of contracting with specialized suppliers, every large Soviet plant did much of its own engineering, produced its own spare parts, and repaired its own equipment. Because production targets were invariably too ambitious, firms hoarded whatever resources came their way and intensified supply breakdowns. Inventories of circulating capital amounted to 70-80 percent of the total social product compared to 35 percent in America.[122]

Both macroeconomic disproportionality and microeconomic inefficiency resulted from overcentralization and inadequate incentives for management and shop-floor workers. With labor productivity at roughly half the American level, and investments in material production more than half again as large, by 1973 the Soviet Union produced 105 percent of the American output of iron, 95 percent of steel, and 140 percent of cement. These figures compared with 13 percent for automobiles, 44 percent for electrical energy, 39 percent for radios, and 42 percent for televisions.[123] Studying the two systems, economists realized that the Soviet Union must use labor, equipment, and materials more efficiently, which in turn required development of new industries, introduction of more advanced technologies, and reform of planning and management.

Marx had attributed the wastefulness of capitalism to cyclical crises and bankruptcies. To create new means of production, capitalism had first to destroy part of the existing industrial capacity. But Marx was equally emphatic in linking *technological progress* with competition and the threat of financial failure. Soviet enterprises, no matter how inefficient, faced neither competition nor bankruptcy. Thus planners resisted scrapping either factories or equipment so long as they contributed to current production. Fixed capital remained in operation twice as long as in America, and depreciation funds were dissipated on repairs rather than replacements.

Additions to capacity usually took the form of new construction, but construction was rarely completed on schedule due to material shortages, causing large amounts of capital to be immobilized over long periods of time. As Nikitin pointed out, the Americans did the opposite: up to 70 percent of industrial investments were concentrated on modernizing existing plants.[124] Studies of capitalist planning demonstrated that Soviet central authorities were too involved in details to respond to the need for systematic restructuring of national economic proportions. Meanwhile, overcentralization created exactly the same spontaneous disorganization normally attributed to capitalist markets.

In the real world of capitalism, as N.I. Mnogolet and E.S. Khesin pointed out, rather than exercising "petty tutelage" western conglomerates made central administrators responsible for strategic decisions and left operational responsibilities to lower-level management.[125] In a study of monopoly organization, Mnogolet and Men'shikov claimed that computerization allowed "a flexible combination of decentralization of operational-economic activities with centralization of coordination and control."[126] V.A. Kirov thought computers had merely imparted a new degree of efficiency to long-established capitalist practice:

> Even before the Second World War, the growing scale of production . . . led to decentralization of management. . . . Within monopoly associations there arose divisional branches. The day-to-day leadership of production activity in such divisions came from managers. The administrators of the associations as a whole looked after "high policy" in the area of profits, long-term production plans, and the volume and direction of investments.[127]

In 1968 the weekly *Ekonomicheskaya gazeta* and The Institute of World Economy and International Relations published a three-part survey of programming, national economic restructuring, and corporate planning "based on the methods of economic cybernetics." The authors emphasized that "day-to-day economic management . . . is entrusted to hired employees—the managers."[128] General Motors, the Philips electronics concern, and Mitsubishi were cited as examples of how vertical organization could be effectively combined with lower-level managerial autonomy.[129] IMEMO made these comparisons with the intention of supporting Premier Aleksei Kosygin's attempt to incorporate into the Soviet economy at least some of the principles at work in the west.

Under Kosygin's supervision, from 1967 to 1971 consumer goods were given marginal priority over heavy industry.[130] Kosygin also hoped to convert industry by 1968 to a new system of targets and incentives that would extend the limits of managerial discretion. In order to improve product quality, sales were to replace gross output as the main criterion for judging enterprise performance; interest was to be charged on capital in order to encourage enterprise directors to use it more effectively; enterprise profits and bank loans were to finance some decentralized investment activity; enterprises were to enter into and be responsible for fulfillment of their own contractual obligations; and planning was to be modernized through more extensive use of computers and mathematical programming. As in the case of western corporations, individual enterprises were to be grouped together in "production associations" that would function as mediating links between local decision makers and central officials.

These reforms did produce greater managerial spontaneity, although not of the kind intended. Managers distributed larger bonuses to themselves while neglecting labor productivity and quality improvements. In the absence of a wholesale market for equipment and materials, decentralized investments proved virtually impossible, and defects in the system of centralized supply continued to impede effective use of plant capacity.[131] Each "incorrect" decision by a wayward manager provoked central retribution, with the consequence that instead of entering its "intensive" phase in 1970, this first attempt at Soviet *perestroika* was reversed. Kosygin's production associations did not emerge until 1973, and by that time supervisory power had already been reconcentrated in Moscow bureaucracies.

IMEMO economists promoted the practice of convergence while polemicizing with Galbraith on matters of theory. The lasting result of Kosygin's initiatives was the reverse: to permit convergence in theory while abandoning it in practice. In 1970 Evsei G. Liberman, an original advocate of the reforms, explained their significance by renouncing Stalinist doctrine concerning the law of value. According to Liberman, effective socialist planning required a combination of plan and market much as Galbraith had described in America: the importance that Kosygin intended for economic levers "confirmed the essential role of commodity-monetary relations in the system of planned economic management."[132] Liberman maintained that neither the plan nor the law of value could be the sole regulator of a socialist economy, for "Regulatory functions are exerted by all laws together, in their unity, rather than by each law in isolation from the others."[133]

Liberman described interaction of plan and market laws as "the essence of . . . the cybernetic principle of socialist economic management."[134] He hoped, like Nikitin, that partial adoption of western organization would increase the supply of consumer goods and services through more efficient use of resources: "society should spend less and less material resources, including fixed capital, per unit of output, since during the period of developed industrial production there is simultaneously an increase in labor productivity and a decrease in the capital-output ratio."[135] Liberman argued that Stalin's commitment to heavy industry and extraordinary rates of capital accumulation was ultimately self-defeating: "any encroachment on consumption threatens a reduction in the growth of labor productivity, i.e., in . . . [capital] accumulation."[136]

The collapse of Kosygin's reform project occurred partly because of bureaucratic inertia: any significant decentralization would have made Soviet officials as visibly redundant as finance capitalists were said to be in the west. On the other hand, so long as the Soviet system promoted spontaneous disorganization, planners could rationalize their own role in terms of the need to correct the errors of lower-level managers. A more fundamental flaw was failure to provide any form of market prices to facilitate decentralization and competition. The problem in the late 1960s was the same as during the First Five-Year Plan: Marxist economic theory rejected the "anarchy" of the price system without discovering an effective substitute.

Galbraith's theory of convergence appeared to minimize this dilemma by suggesting that capitalist firms also administered prices. *The New Industrial State* portrayed large corporations as risk averters who competed in product innovation but shared a "common interest in secure and certain prices."[137] When critics objected that at least half of American GNP originated with the service sector and competitive small businesses, in *Economics and the Public Purpose* Galbraith acknowledged the coexistence of planned and market sectors.[138] A more comprehensive account of modern capitalism would also include the world market and its implications for planning within nation-states.

By the late 1960s western optimism concerning capitalist planning was beginning to be replaced by new concerns for stability of the world economic order. Hilferding had argued that the plans of individual firms could not add up to a coherent whole. Collapse of the international monetary system appeared to support this contention in a much larger context. Attempts to plan national economies were ultimately frustrated by lack of a supranational institution capable of organizing interstate relations. After conceding the ability of the capitalist state to plan within its own borders, Soviet economists now recognized that capitalism's inherent contradictions were being projected all the more forcefully into the world economy. As in the historical development from Marx's *Capital* to early twentieth-century theories of imperialism, Soviet writers turned in the late 1960s from nation-state planning to global crises of the capitalist system.

CHAPTER 9

NATIONAL PLANS AND THE INTERNATIONAL MONETARY CRISIS

Influenced by Galbraith's theory of convergence, during the latter half of the 1960s Soviet economic literature swung from Stalinist denial to exaggerated praise of the capitalist state and its role in modernization and restructuring. This reversal was partly a reaction to the former theory of one-sided war economies, partly an attempt to invoke western institutions as a model for reforming the Soviet Union's own economy. At the same time as the theory of state-monopoly planning was being positively reevaluated, however, a wave of currency crises interrupted economic growth in several western countries and undermined the international monetary system designed in 1944 at Bretton Woods.

The extent of the monetary crisis first became evident in Britain's devaluation of sterling in 1967. By August 1971, President Nixon also had to stem a run on U.S. gold reserves through temporarily suspending dollar convertibility. In December 1971, the parities of all major currencies were realigned in an attempt to preserve the system of fixed exchange rates. Abandonment of the Bretton Woods system in 1973 resulted from the inability of national governments to coordinate domestic policies on a multilateral basis and thus prevent serious imbalances in international payments. When "uneven development" appeared to disorganize capitalism on a world scale, Soviet analysts began to anticipate new opportunities to reconstruct ties between the "two camps." The crisis of the international monetary system became the prelude to detente agreements between Richard Nixon and Leonid Brezhnev.

1. The Nation-State and the World Economy

Until the late 1960s, Soviet literature paid little heed to the international system as a whole. Most studies focused on individual countries, particularly the United States, as the center of world imperialism, and

219

France, as the innovator in indicative planning. In methodological terms, this narrow focus was a departure from earlier Marxist traditions, which treated the world economy as the final determinant of all its parts. Although Marx's model of reproduction abstracted from foreign trade to discern the laws of "pure capitalism," his historical writing portrayed a movement from localized self-sufficiency toward universal exchange. In his chapter on the "Historical Tendency of Capitalist Accumulation," Marx summarized the first volume of *Capital* with these comments:

> One capitalist always kills many. Hand in hand with this centralisation, or this expropriation of many capitalists by few, develop . . . the conscious technical application of science, . . . the economising of all means of production . . ., socialised labour, the entanglement of all peoples in the net of the world market, and with this, the international character of the capitalistic regime.[1]

In *The Communist Manifesto,* Marx and Engels credited the bourgeoisie with the historically progressive mission of imparting "a cosmopolitan character to production and consumption:"

> All old-established national industries . . . . are dislodged by new industries . . . whose products are consumed . . . in every quarter of the globe. . . . In place of the old local and national seclusion and self-sufficiency, we have intercourse in every direction, universal inter-dependence of nations.[2]

The *Manifesto* compared the capitalist class to a sorcerer "who is no longer able to control the powers of the nether world . . . he has called up by his spells."[3] "The need of a constantly expanding market for its products chases the bourgeoisie over the whole surface of the globe. It must nestle everywhere, settle everywhere, establish connexions everywhere."[4] The resulting world economy also implied a world cycle in which interdependence would link all countries in "more extensive and more destructive crises."[5]

The importance that Marx attached to capitalism's universalizing role was apparent in his plan to write a *Critique of Political Economy* that would ultimately include six volumes: *Capital; Landed Property; Wage Labor; The State; International Trade;* and *The World Market.*[6] The three volumes of *Capital* represented only part of the work planned for the first book of the *Critique*. Although the world market was to be considered in the last of the volumes Marx planned to write, he also emphasized that in conceptual terms it was the necessary "point of departure." The simpler economic categories were devoid of historical meaning without presupposing "an already given, concrete, living whole."[7] The world capitalist market gave determinate content to the concepts of labor, division of labor, needs, exchange value, states, and international trade.

Subsequent theories of imperialism continued Marx's plan for the *Critique of Political Economy*. Luxemburg, Lenin, Bukharin, and Trotsky all considered the relation of national economies to the world capitalist system. Luxemburg claimed that when third-party markets were exhausted, further capital accumulation would be impossible. Lenin, on the other hand, thought "the limits of the . . . market . . . are set by the specialisation of social labour. But this specialisation, by its very nature, is as infinite as technical developments."[8] In *Imperialism, The Highest Stage of Capitalism*, Lenin wrote of a "world market"[9] in which national economies had already become "links in the chain of world finance capital."[10]

Bukharin differed from Lenin and most other Marxists by beginning his analysis of imperialism with internally organized national economies opposing one another in a context of world-market anarchy. Within separate countries, Bukharin wrote, "The individual production branches are in various ways knit together into one collective body, organized on a large scale. Finance capital seizes the entire country in an iron grip. 'National economy' turns into one gigantic combined trust whose partners are the financial groups and the state. Such formations we call state-capitalist trusts."[11] Since imperialists controlled imports and exports, Bukharin expected trade wars and cyclical crises of the world system to be replaced by military confrontations over territorial spheres in which to appropriate surplus value.[12]

Trotsky rejected Bukharin's theory of internally organized capitalism on the grounds that modern technology had expanded the scale of production and outgrown the nation-state. Because the requirements of industrial proportionality had become global in scale, one of the consequences of socialist revolution would be a planned international division of labor. In an article on "The Nation and the Economy," Trotsky wrote in 1915 that "The productive forces have finally become cramped within the limits of the state. . . . The place of the shut-in national state must inevitably be taken by a broad democratic federation of the leading states, with the abolition of all tariff divisions."[13]

> A democratic unification of Europe, the creation of a European United States, is the only political form in which the proletariat can resolve the implacable contradiction between the contemporary productive forces and the limitations of nation-state organization.[14]

Whereas Trotsky believed that all of Europe had matured for revolution, Lenin expected the chain of imperialism to break first at its weakest links. In reply to Trotsky, Lenin wrote that "Uneven economic and political development is an absolute law of capitalism. Hence the victory of socialism is possible first in several or even in one capitalist country alone."[15] Lenin worried that by setting revolutionary objectives too high, Trotsky's call for a United States of Europe might divert attention from immediate opportunities for the proletariat to seize power in individual countries. Although this quarrel concerned slogans and tactics rather than Marx's priority of the world economy, the views expressed by Trotsky were proscribed after his defeat in the mid-1920s.

Stalin frequently quoted Lenin's criticism of Trotsky to rationalize his own canon of Socialism in One Country, which evolved into the imagery of two "camps" in the 1920s and two opposing "systems" after World War II. Trotsky answered that historically formed patterns of trade and interdependence made industrial self-sufficiency impossible for either a socialist or a capitalist country:

> The world division of labor and the exchange which derives from it is not disrupted by the fact that a socialist system prevails in one country while a capitalist one prevails in the others. . . . The fact that the workers and peasants in our country wield state power . . . in no way upsets the world division of labor, which results [not from ideology but] from differences in natural circumstances and national history.[16]

2. Internationalization of the Post-1945 Economy

Following the struggles of the 1920s, Malenkov was the first Soviet leader to question the theory of two systems and "two parallel world markets" by associating his New Deal with "restoration of a single international market." It was not until emergence of the European

Economic Community, however, that economists returned directly to the issues raised by Trotsky and Lenin concerning the United States of Europe. Formation of the EEC required an analysis of nation-states in relation to the expanding scale of capitalist trade and production. When industry was seen to be internationalized, new questions were bound to arise concerning the effectiveness of national planning.

The EEC transcended national economies, but in their place monopolies appeared to create a closed economic bloc, restricting trade with socialist countries and limiting American competition through a common tariff wall. By the early 1960s, Soviet authors were criticizing the EEC in the same terms used by Trotsky four decades earlier: the productive forces of modern industry, their development accelerated through the scientific-technical revolution, required markets broader than any state could provide. In 1962, IMEMO published "'Integration' of Monopoly Capital—Some New Developments" and commented that "The growth of the productive forces has engendered a trend in the direction of inter-linking national economies, of breaking down national insularity."[17]

Having been a witness to the Trotsky-Stalin confrontation, E.L. Khmel'nitskaya was aware of the connection between the EEC and Trotsky's call for a United States of Europe. Editing a book on *Economic Problems of the Common Market*, she wrote in 1962 that "capitalism has become cramped within the limits of nation-states. . . . Hence the internationalization of economic relations and the internationalization of capital."[18] In an article on "Little Europe—Conflicts and Compromises," Khmel'nitskaya praised Lenin but repeated the views of Trotsky: internationalization had been "significantly reinforced as a result of the fact that the contemporary level of the productive forces is increasingly going beyond the narrow limits of bourgeois states."[19] Capitalist integration reflected an objective need for "large-scale serial production, which is possible only through far-reaching specialization and cooperation."[20]

In 1964, V.I Stepanov published *The Economic Foundations of Peaceful Coexistence*. A specialist in trade theory, Stepanov explained the origins of the EEC in terms meant to encourage more active Soviet participation in the international division of labor:

> growth of the productive forces, an increase in the optimal scale of modern enterprises, and the automation and standardization of production—all objectively move various countries toward economic rapprochement (*sblizhenie*) and unification (*ob'edinenie*), particularly . . . the highly industrialized countries of Western

Europe. The concentration and centralization of capital, which goes beyond the limits of separate states, expresses the internationalization of modern forces of production and represents the material basis of monopolistic integration.[21]

The Stalinist theory of a chronic problem of markets had treated imperialists as rivals in a permanent struggle to redivide colonial possessions. Since all industrial countries produced the same or similar goods, they were assumed to have little to sell each other. Trotsky had argued that although capitalist countries develop at uneven tempos, they also experience economic and cultural "leveling" (*nivelirovka*), in which similarity of production patterns and industrial structures expands trade opportunities.[22] By 1970, A.A. Manukyan referred to the same process of "leveling" to account for an "essential expansion of the general limits of the international market" even after most colonies had acquired formal independence.[23]

From 1945 to 1969 the volume of world trade, excluding that of socialist countries, grew by 3.7 times. Three-quarters of the increase, including 70 percent of equipment exports, represented sales by one industrial country to another.[24] In 1965-66, West Germany exported 44.8 percent of the machinery it produced and imported 18.5 percent of its own requirements; in France, the figures were 24.5 percent and 21 percent.[25] Reflecting upon this pattern, Manukyan wrote that "Development of narrow . . . specialization between the enterprises of different countries explains the enormous scale of mutual trade in similar and often identical commodities."[26] Capitalists specialized in order to lengthen production runs and minimize per-unit costs. With Soviet traditions of semi-autarky in mind, Manukyan pointed out that it was

> incomparably more advantageous to produce a few types of standardized items on a mass scale (and cheaply!), looking to sell them in the broadest possible market, than to produce a more diverse (and expensive!) output in small quantities aimed at a limited [national] market.[27]

3. The IMF and the Bretton Woods System

Once Soviet analysts recognized that the prosperity of industrial countries depended far more upon mutual trade than upon exports to third-party markets in former colonies, they turned to the financial processes that mediate the international exchange of commodities. Although Marx believed that international trade required gold to function as "universal money,"[28] he looked to world crises as the key factor in restructuring proportionality. Other nineteenth-century economists explained correction of payments imbalances through changes in relative price levels. If one country imported more than it exported, eventually its currency would tend to depreciate and it would be required to export gold in payment for goods. Gold exports would reduce the domestic money supply, curtail demand, lower prices, and thereby promote increased sales in foreign markets; conversely, a country importing gold would eventually experience price increases, making its goods less attractive to foreign buyers.

Although economists portrayed the gold standard as an automatic regulator of the world economy, the system was modified after World War I. To increase total reserves, governments began to hold key currencies that were convertible into gold rather than just gold itself. This economizing in the use of gold was intended to ease the need for radical adjustments of prices and employment except in cases of protracted imbalance. But because the gold-exchange standard retained fixed exchange rates, the violent trade contraction of the early 1930s forced one country after another to undergo deflation in the hope of promoting exports. When general deflation caused general unemployment, governments turned to other measures that disorganized world trade still further: exchange controls were instituted; currencies were devalued or even detached from gold in order to permit domestic reflation; multiple exchange rates were established for dealings with different countries; tariffs were raised to discourage imports; or trade was simply administered through quotas, barter agreements, licenses, and prohibitions.

After World War II, governments hoped to avoid the deflation-inducing consequences of fixed exchange rates while at the same time restoring the orderly relation between currencies associated historically with the gold standard. The International Monetary Fund, conceived in 1944 and operating by 1947, required members to subscribe a quota partly in gold or U.S. dollars and partly in their own currency. From these pooled resources, each country would be able to borrow and thus gain time in which to adjust domestic policies in order to deal with either a payments deficit or a persistent surplus. In the event of a "fundamental disequilibrium," a currency's par value could be altered with the Fund's approval. Otherwise central banks were to limit fluctuations within a range of 1 percent on either side of parity, expressed in terms of the gold value of the dollar set by the Roosevelt administration in 1935.

The postwar monetary system assumed that by managing domestic demand, governments would avoid frequent parity changes. If any single country were to grow more rapidly than others, excessive demand would raise prices, attract imports, and reduce exports. But so long as the major trading countries grew at approximately similar rates and combined full-employment policies with relative price stability, none would attract a volume of imports that could not, in principle, be paid for through exports to other expanding markets. The system implied not only what Soviet economists called state-monopoly regulation, but also a degree of *collective coordination* on the part of the leading industrial countries.

The problem was that the IMF possessed no authority either to decide or even significantly to influence the policies of sovereign states. At most it could attach progressively more stringent conditions to loans, and this would occur only after countries had depleted their reserves and exercised preliminary drawing rights on IMF resources. If the Fund's ability to enforce discipline was limited, so too was its capacity to lend. In 1944, Keynes had proposed a system of international credit creation that would have increased reserves in the form of "bancor," a new international accounting unit. This suggestion was too ambitious for Washington at a time when the United States would have had to satisfy practically the full volume of newly created postwar demand.

Rejection of Keynes' proposal meant that new international liquidity would in future have to come from three possible sources: gold production, which was discouraged by the fact that the dollar price of gold had not changed since 1935; an increase of IMF quotas, which did occur in 1959, 1965, and 1970; or increased availability of dollars and sterling, the two currencies commonly held in reserve by other countries.[29] Until the mid-1960s governments showed no hesitation in accumulating the supply of dollars that entered the world economy through U.S. foreign investments, overseas military spending, and the payments deficit; as the volume of trade grew, each country needed larger reserves with which to protect its domestic economy against temporary external imbalances. As dollars became more abundant, however, speculators also began to suspect their eventual devaluation.

If corporations, money-market traders, and central banks began converting their dollars to gold, the United States would have to choose between losing its own reserves, curtailing domestic growth in order to reduce prices relative to those in other countries, or else raising the price of gold. A gold price rise would increase U.S. reserves, but it would not resolve the American balance of payments deficit. Because all par values were pegged to the gold content of the dollar—or indirectly to the dollar via the pound sterling—the relation between other currencies and the dollar would not alter. On its own, dollar devaluation would mean a simultaneous and equal devaluation of all other currencies. Here the dilemma of the Bretton Woods system became evident: created in order to avoid a deflationary repetition of the 1930s, three decades later the system appeared to require deflation in America, which in turn might disorganize world trade and even precipitate a global crisis.

Andrei V. Anikin, one of the most knowledgeable Soviet specialists on international finance, defined the principal themes of Soviet responses to the crisis of world currencies by pointing to at least four essential flaws in postwar arrangements. First, there was no body capable of ensuring that countries would keep price levels in line with one another; "collective state-monopoly regulation" lacked a real executive with power to override national sovereignties.[30] Second, smooth balance of payments adjustments had become even more problematic than between the wars, for monopolies would curtail production before lowering prices.[31] Third, any persistent effort to slow domestic growth would have the political consequence of exacerbating class conflict. Finally, the only obvious alternative to deflation—currency devaluation—promised exactly the same results: the burden of higher import prices and lower real incomes would fall mainly on "the working class and other strata of the toilers." Anikin noted that "devaluation normally intensifies social contradictions . . . and this is one of the most important reasons why governments usually turn to it only in extreme circumstances."[32]

4. Multinationals and Eurodollars

Even if governments were to brave the political implications of deflation or devaluation, there was no guarantee that such policies would succeed. By the 1960s many western economists were concerned that planning on the part of multinational corporations was seriously weakening state policy. Some authors compared multinational firms to the monopolies of sixteenth-century mercantilism, enriching metropolitan countries at the expense of the third-world periphery; others saw them as a vehicle for technology transfers and industrial enlightenment. But most agreed that the internationalization of capital undermined national policies. In *The International Economy Since 1945*, W.M. Scammell wrote of the 1960s:

> Perhaps the greatest power switch of the period was that in which the economic power of the state, even the largest states, was challenged by multinational corporations. . . . The decision-making of such corporations . . . could annul or threaten contrary decisions by governments. Whole sectors of world trade . . . are now managed by such faceless entities. . . . The power of nation-states is fixed at their own frontiers; the powers of corporations have ramified and stretched beyond single states. With manufacturing in many countries, financial operations directed from one country, marketing from another and with capital derived from a wide variety of sources, such corporations . . . . became . . . . as powerful as many governments and far more flexible. . . .[33]

According to economic theory, changes in relative prices shape the division of labor through trade. Yet as Scammell pointed out, "A considerable part of international trade is now intra-company trade, taking place at 'transfer' prices (i.e. accounting or imputed prices) which are internal to the firms themselves and are not determined by market forces."[34] Were a country to alter its taxation system or even devalue its currency, a large firm could minimize the consequences by adjusting internal pricing. The multinational corporation was becoming a "command system" in which prices were no longer directly related to costs of production.[35]

By 1968 "about 25 percent of British manufactured exports was by firms to their own subsidiaries."[36] In the case of the United States, the Soviet economist T.Ya. Belous reported in 1970 that approximately 20 percent of exports and 25 percent of imports occurred on an intrafirm basis. Multinationals were growing at 10 percent per year—twice the rate of capitalist world output—and were collectively responsible for 18 percent of all nonsocialist production. Sales abroad, by foreign affiliates and offshore companies controlled by American capital, were four times greater than total American exports. Half of the Fortune 500 companies had international operations, with IT&T in sixty countries, Standard Oil in forty-five, Colgate Palmolive in thirty-eight, Goodyear in thirty-five, Singer in twenty-eight, and Ford in twenty-seven.[37] When a parent company decided what its subsidiaries would produce and at what price,

Belous thought the effectiveness of national planning was necessarily suspect:

> Centralization of management on the part of American capital represents a serious threat to the economy of European countries, including their state programming. The condition of the economy of these countries is largely determined by . . . the affiliates of American enterprises. The activities of the latter are regulated from the headquarters of the parent company according to . . . [criteria] that are not under the control of West European states.[38]

Attributing the international character of production to a strategy of minimizing exposure both to local crises and to particular governments, A.A. Manukyan claimed in 1969 that "supermonopolies" viewed national frontiers as an "annoying nuisance."[39] Yu. Shishkov thought the taxation and credit incentives offered by indicative plans were of minor importance to "financial empires that have overstepped national frontiers and occupied tens of countries."[40] Industrial giants and their small-scale capitalist suppliers were like musicians in a multinational "orchestra"; they played "in unison" according to the will of "a single director."[41] If corporate plans added up to anarchy in the *domestic* economy—as Shishkov believed was still the case—the same must be all the more true in the *international* arena: "In the quest for monopolistically high profits these essentially supranational private economic complexes scorn the attempts by national authorities to regulate the balance of payments; they undermine the tariff regime as well as anti-inflationary and anticyclical measures."[42]

Trade liberalization and postwar changes in transportation and communications created conditions for the rise of multinational firms; the EEC accelerated the trend as American companies situated themselves within the common tariff wall to avoid exclusion from European markets. The spread of American capital also added a novel dimension to the international financial system by creating the trade in "Eurodollars," or deposits held in European banks but denominated in dollars rather than local currencies. In 1963 the volume of Eurodollars was estimated to be $5 billion, rising to as much as $91 billion by the end of 1972.[43]

This vast pool of liquid assets was not directly subject to the policies of any central bank and could respond instantly to minor differences between national interest rates. Flows of speculative short-term capital had the potential to topple currencies and even governments. If a country used high interest rates to stabilize internal prices, firms might borrow instead in the Eurodollar market, convert their dollars into the national currency, and thus defeat central bank policy.[44] If corporate treasurers suspected a currency to be overvalued, they could instantly transfer funds into some other currency. Describing attacks on the dollar and the pound from 1964 to 1971, Scammell wrote that "the sheer volume of with-drawals from a currency were now so great that official monetary authorities were unable to counter them with the reserves at their command. . . . [I]f it was widely considered that a currency would be devalued, then adverse speculation decreed it so."[45]

5. The Pound, the Mark, and the Franc

Dramatic evidence of the power of speculation came with the collapse of sterling in 1967. Great Britain was the textbook example of a country trapped between the requirements of domestic growth and the need to defend a weak currency. In order to finance the war, Britain had been compelled to liquidate a large volume of overseas assets, which traditionally generated much of the revenue needed to pay for imports of food and materials. After World War II, visible imports chronically exceeded exports. Because most Commonwealth countries, the remaining colonies, and some other important trading partners kept their reserves in sterling, whenever the British currency came under pressure, interest rates had to rise in order to prevent withdrawal of foreign deposits. Recurrent threats to the pound slowed Britain's postwar growth by creating the cycle known as "stop-go."

Britain experienced balance of payments crises in 1947, 1949, 1951, 1955-57, 1961, 1964, and 1966-67, culminating in a 14.3 percent devaluation in November 1967.[46] The pattern in each instance was for government to launch the "go" phase with expansionary policies. Given a high level of domestic employment, increased demand soon raised prices and incomes, drew in more imports, slowed exports, caused a deterioration of the payments balance, and ended with the pound having to be rescued through a fiscal and monetary "stop"; that is, deflationary measures aimed at restricting domestic growth. High interest rates discouraged investments needed to improve productivity and competitiveness; military expenditures and capital exports added to the balance of payments burden and transferred resources abroad that were needed in the domestic economy.[47]

While western writers interpreted the swings of British policy in terms of interactions between capital flows, trade volume, and domestic demand, Soviet commentators emphasized the class struggle. In 1964, E. Khesin published an article in the English-language journal *New Times* and attributed the "vicious circle" of stop-go to a conflict between lingering imperialist ambitions and Britain's diminished postwar resources:

> The natural thing to do . . . would be to cut down capital exports and overseas military spending. But that did not suit the Big Business interests. . . . And so a different line was adopted—that of choking the growth of imports by holding back the growth of production . . . . by "deflationary" measures. . . .
>
> Thus the balance of payments difficulties stem ultimately from solicitous protection of the monopolies' profits. And it is the working man that has been made to pay. The Number One method of restricting consumption has been by keeping down wages—under the "pay pause," "incomes policy," "regulated growth," etc.[48]

Election of Harold Wilson's Labour government in 1964 brought no change in British determination to resist devaluation, but it was followed by "the largest speculative attack ever mounted against a currency." George Brown, Wilson's economics minister, attributed sabotage of the new socialist government to malevolent speculation by the banking "gnomes of Zurich."[49] Brown hoped to launch a "national plan" inspired by the French system; an incomes policy was to hold back domestic consumption while incentives for investments and real growth corrected the underlying problem in the balance of payments.[50] Before the plan could be implemented, however, Britain faced another currency crisis. In the summer of 1966 planning was abandoned while incomes policy was retained in the form of a twelve-month wage freeze followed by "severe moderation."[51]

S.M. Men'shikov thought Labour's deflationary policies again illustrated his concept of "artificial" crises. In April 1967, Men'shikov attended a conference of western economists in London and condemned Labour for betraying working-class voters:

instances when bourgeois governments quite consciously accelerate the onset of a crisis are recently becoming frequent. . . . "[A]rtificial fabrication" of crises is becoming more widespread. The most striking examples are the Italian crisis of 1964, the French "stabilization plan" of 1963-1964, the English crisis of 1965-1966, and the West German crisis of 1966-1967.[52]

When Wilson appealed to British workers to show "personal restraint and readiness to accept some sacrifice," I.I. Kuz'minov remarked that "The imperialist state . . . puts the blame [for inflation] . . . on the workers. . . . This example testifies . . . to the class character of . . . state economic control, which is exercised . . . in the interest of the monopolies."[53] L. Sedin agreed that the real cause of the currency crisis was not wage-inspired inflation but monopoly pricing and British support for the American war in Vietnam and for Israeli aggression in the Suez Canal zone. Sedin applauded trade unionists for demanding repudiation of American foreign policy, cuts in British military spending, controls on prices and profits rather than on wages, and further nationalization:

> the Wilson government has oriented its entire economic policy on the interests of the City tycoons. . . . To this end the widely advertised National Development Plan drawn up by George Brown . . . was quickly jettisoned. . . . Many other Labour election promises were likewise sacrificed to the arms build-up and monopoly interests.[54]

A.V. Anikin (and two coauthors) thought the cycle of stop-go also illustrated divisions within the ruling class: banking circles called for "temporary" fiscal and monetary restraint in order to increase reserves and maintain London's role as a world financial center; industrialists replied that investments must be stimulated first in order to improve the country's competitive position in the market for manufactures.[55] When growing unemployment finally prompted new efforts to stimulate demand, sterling had to be devalued in November 1967 from $2.80 to $2.40. Fourteen other IMF members followed Britain by devaluing their own currencies within the next ten days.[56] Anikin attributed the crisis to structural contradictions inherent in the Bretton Woods system:

> Bourgeois states actively attempt to regulate foreign economic relations and the payments balance, but at the same time the

[postwar] easing of currency and trade restrictions has expanded the role of spontaneous factors. . . . [The result is] a contradiction between a significant measure of state economic regulation within separate countries and the limited possibilities for such regulation on an international scale. . . . The impossibility of simultaneously satisfying the basic objectives of modern economic policy—high rates of growth (and, consequently, a satisfactory employment level) together with a certain degree of price stability and equilibrium in the payments balance—often leads to . . . the payments balance being sacrificed.[57]

In West Germany the stresses of the 1960s took a form opposite to what occurred in Britain. Germany had combined a high rate of postwar accumulation with rapid productivity gains. From 1950 to 1966 the average rate of industrial growth was 9.2 percent. In 1959 Germany displaced Britain as the world's second largest industrial exporter and was also second to the United States in terms of total reserves of gold and foreign currency.[58] Germany's problem was not one of domestic inflation and a payments deficit, but rather of importing inflation through a chronic payments surplus, which in turn fueled speculation that the mark would have to rise in value relative to other currencies.

For holders of sterling or any under currency under threat, the mark represented a port in a gathering storm. From the German perspective, however, an influx of foreign capital threatened to be just as destabilizing as the British deficit. Bundesbank purchases of foreign currency tended to expand the domestic money supply. If interest rates were raised in order to slow growth, the differential between Germany and other countries would attract even more foreign deposits. In 1961 the mark had to be revalued upward by 5 percent in an effort to offset a continuing payments surplus. Despite the revaluation, Germany's currency remained undervalued throughout the 1960s.[59]

In 1966-67 the Bundesbank engineered Germany's first postwar recession in order to hold back prices and demand.[60] A modest decline of industrial production eased domestic pressures; but since inflation was rising more quickly in other countries, Germany's export surplus again grew. When trading partners urged that the imbalance be corrected through another revaluation, German industrialists objected that the result would be to discourage foreign sales. In the meantime, "a flood of liquidity coming in through the balance of payments and feeding domestic demand was the key element in the imported-inflation process."[61] Germany argued that its export surplus called for restraint on the part of those countries that were creating inflation: instead of the mark being revalued, weaker currencies should be devalued.[62] After the devaluation of sterling in 1967, the next currency to fall was the franc.

Shortly after coming to power in 1958, de Gaulle had devalued the franc and introduced currency reform with two goals in mind: to halt a cycle of domestic inflation and to increase French exports.[63] After further stabilization measures in 1963-64, the French improved their balance of payments and simultaneously launched a campaign to undermine the influence of the Anglo-Saxons. With the franc gaining in strength, de Gaulle announced in February 1965 that the solution to international currency instability was return to the gold standard and abandonment of the dollar and the pound as reserve currencies.[64] In the spring of 1965, France converted nearly $1 billion into gold by drawing from America's already declining reserves.[65]

Welcoming this new evidence of imperialist disunity, Soviet authors patronizingly encouraged the French. D.B. Smyslov thought de Gaulle was perfectly justified in condemning the Bretton Woods gold-exchange standard: "there is no valid justification for the dollar being used instead of gold."[66] The Soviet press supported French claims that the United States exploited the dollar's role in order to acquire assets in other countries. So long as foreign central banks were prepared to buy incoming dollars, America seemed to expand its global economic power merely by exporting *paper*. A.V. Anikin wrote in April 1965 that

> the United States can afford to maintain an adverse balance of payments . . . since other countries finance it. . . . Moreover, . . . the United States . . . continues to increase the export of capital to Western Europe, establishing its control over many key industries. . . . In other words, the West European countries themselves give the United States the money with which it buys up their companies and factories! . . . No wonder . . . de Gaulle remarked that the present state of affairs "in some countries leads to a kind of expropriation . . .", that is, . . . expropriation by American capital.[67]

V.A. Cheprakov remarked that "One must agree with President de Gaulle, who said that the United States, through generous investment abroad of the paper dollars 'which it itself issues', was virtually engaged in the 'expropriation' of enterprises in other countries."[68] N. Yuryev noted that "U.S. capital controls 90 per cent of the French production of synthetic rubber, 60 per cent of the production of agricultural machines, telephones and lifts, 50 per cent of electric bulbs, and 20 per cent of electrical equipment. . . . France has repeatedly appealed to the E.E.C. Council to take up the problem of limiting American investments. . . ."[69] In 1967 de Gaulle complained that America's payments deficit over the past eighteen years exactly equaled the sum of U.S. investments in Western Europe.[70]

Franco-American relations were further soured by differences over NATO strategy, trade with socialist countries, and the war in Vietnam.[71] When France called for neutralization of Indochina, the Soviet press eagerly approved. Victor Perlo, a "progressive" American economist, argued in one Soviet journal that America used the Bretton Woods system not only to buy up enterprises in other countries but also "to get allies to absorb the main financial burden of U.S. aggression—the ultimate cause of the [American] balance of payments deficit."[72] On the eve of a visit by de Gaulle to the USSR in 1966, N. Yuryev declared that "It is a long-standing tradition [for] France and the Soviet Union to . . . act jointly in politics."[73] While Washington opposed trade with the socialist countries, de Gaulle spoke of a Europe based on "concord and co-operation from the Atlantic to the Urals."[74] The Soviet Union, according to Yuryev, had always favored "a strong and independent France."[75]

The USSR looked upon France as the American government did Romania, Czechoslovakia, or Poland; that is, as an ally of the opposing system to be pried loose. France signed a long-term trade agreement with Moscow in 1965 and undertook to dismantle quotas on manufactured imports from the Soviet Union and Eastern Europe.[76] Michel Debre, the minister of economic affairs and finance, encouraged Soviet hopes of expanding trade with the EEC by referring to socialist countries as "the market of the future."[77] Between 1965 and 1968, French sales of machinery to the USSR rose from $28 million to $193 million.[78] The Soviet Union attached particular significance to a joint undertaking to develop the SECAM III system of colored television, seeing it as an opening for further technology transfers.[79] By 1967, Moscow and Paris had agreements extending from Soviet launches of French satellites to cooperation in nuclear physics. When France withdrew from the NATO military organization and required U.S. forces to leave her territory, I. Grigoryev remarked that French "independence and sovereignty naturally meet with the approval of the Soviet Union."[80]

The Gaullist hope of replacing the dollar with gold and restoring French stature in world affairs suffered a severe blow in the near-revolutionary crisis of the spring of 1968. Almost overnight the franc ceased to be one of the world's most stable currencies. The agreement that ended the strikes involved an increase of the minimum wage by 35 percent and of most other wages by 10-15 percent.[81] Fearing inflation, speculators fled the franc; French reserves plummeted in 1968 by 40 percent, dissipating the nearly $2 billion in gold recently acquired from the United States.[82] Most of the capital outflow went into marks, creating currency havoc that forced European exchange markets to close for several days in November. But instead of accepting the loss of prestige associated with devaluation, de Gaulle attempted to support the franc through foreign borrowing and severe domestic restraint. By April 1969 the French president lost a referendum on the reorganization of regional government and resigned from office.

In a dispatch from Paris, Yuri Bochkaryov assured Soviet readers that French workers had not voted "against the President's foreign policy, which objectively accorded with France's national interest, but against his domestic social policies, which did not answer to the needs and demands of the mass of the workers and petty bourgeois."[83] A.V. Anikin explained de Gaulle's defeat in terms of the political implications of deflation: when France was accumulating gold from America, it favored the gold standard; when the franc foundered, the French preferred "an unstable currency system to the risk of economic and social shocks."[84] In August 1969 the franc was devalued by 11.1 percent.[85] Despite its vaunted state-monopoly planning, France followed Britain into the vortex of the international monetary crisis. Germany was not far behind. To dam the tide of incoming short-term capital, especially from France, in October 1969 the newly elected Brandt government again had to raise the value of the mark, this time by more than 9 percent.[86]

6. The Dollar Crisis and Nixon's "Stop"

As Europeans struggled with the spreading currency crisis, Americans began to experience the long-term effects of Kennedy's growth policies and the escalating Vietnam war. Buoyant American demand attracted imports, while exports were slowed by European efforts to contain inflation. By March 1968 speculation against the dollar caused the end of the international gold pool, which central banks had operated since 1961 to maintain the price of $35 an ounce. Despite preserving formal convertibility in official transactions, the United States made it clear that henceforth gold would be provided even to other countries' central banks only on the basis of negotiation: "With convertibility at an end, the world was on a *de facto* dollar standard rather than on a genuine gold-exchange standard."[87]

In an article on "The Troubled Dollar," S.M. Men'shikov wrote that "The Western press considers the continuing escalation of aggression in Vietnam [to be] the main cause of the present currency crisis."[88] In January 1967, Lyndon Johnson called for an increase of both corporate and personal income taxes to finance military spending. I.I. Kuz'minov responded that the president was abandoning his "Great Society" and war on poverty in favor of his "criminal war against the freedom-loving Vietnamese people."[89] Predicting another "artificial crisis," Men'shikov thought that American workers would be victimized in the domestic struggle against inflation. Following a trip to the United States, Men'shikov wrote in March 1968 that

> Big Business . . . has been pressing for higher taxation. . . . Moreover the trade unions are putting forward—and at times winning—wage claims far in excess of the guide lines. . . . Many monopoly spokesmen believe that the time has come for an economic pause, perhaps even a slump, which would send unemployment up again and bring the labour market to "normalcy" from the standpoint of the capitalist class.[90]

Richard M. Nixon became president in January 1969. The Soviet journal *New Times* quoted the *New York Times* saying that Nixon's cabinet, "made up basically of bankers, corporation lawyers and millionaire businessmen, is clearly conservative."[91] However, Soviet writers thought the real inspirer of Nixon's economic policies remained outside the cabinet in the person of Milton Friedman, leading exponent of the new "monetarist" alternative to Keynesianism. Friedman opposed discretionary government policies, whether to promote growth or to cure past excesses; instead of imposing control over private incomes, he argued that inflation should be prevented through balancing the budget and limiting monetary expansion to the average rate of increase of real production.

Despite important theoretical differences between Keynesianism and monetarism, most Soviet economists saw Friedman's prescriptions as Keynesian demand management in a radically conservative form. A.G. Mileikovsky predicted that under Friedman's influence Nixon would precipitate a crisis to protect the dollar at the expense of American workers.

> In the 1960s, the forecasts of bourgeois economists painted the prospects of a [Keynesian] "policy of growth". Now . . . they have to abandon these illusions. . . . [T]he ruling circles of imperialist countries now put their stake on a policy of deflation. . . . Milton Friedman, a noted American economist close to President Nixon, even stated that there was no other way of controlling inflation except an economic crisis. . . . Friedman hopes the United States will have a recession in 1970 of about the same order as in 1960-1961, when production decreased by 10 per cent. . . . Friedman thinks it expedient to increase the scale of unemployment. . . . All this is explained by the need to raise the competitive position of exports . . . on the world markets.[92]

When the United States slipped into recession late in 1969, many authors held Nixon and Friedman jointly responsible. Whereas the budget deficit in 1967/68 had climbed to a postwar record of $25.2 billion, Nixon's first year in office produced a small surplus. Growth of the money supply was halted; by May 1970 the index of industrial production was 3.3 percent lower than in the previous July; and unemployment had risen to 5 percent.[93] I.M. Osadchaya wrote that the dollar crisis had compelled the United States to adopt the same "stop-go" cycle as Britain: "extraordinary rates of growth, . . . stimulated by the war in Vietnam . . . [and] the enormous growth of the budget deficit . . . caused an acute outbreak of inflationary price rises. As a result, the policy of growth had to be set aside under the pressure of circumstances that urgently demand use of traditional countercyclical measures to limit the rate of economic development and reduce state expenditures."[94]

7. The American Recession: "Artificial" or "Spontaneous"?

In July 1970, IMEMO held a conference to debate Nixon's policies and their implications for the theory of state-monopoly regulation. The participants faced an obvious dilemma. Most had recently argued that capitalist states were capable of regulation and even programming, yet now they saw that the currency crisis was contagious. Even if national plans restructured domestic proportions, there was no assurance that growth in *different countries* could be synchronized in order to ensure stability of relative prices and the balance of payments. Capitalist planning appeared to be creating self-negating disproportions at the international level.

Influenced by Men'shikov's theory of artificial crises, in his opening report to the conference A.V. Anikin argued that the Americans were searching for new methods of state-monopoly regulation in unprecedented circumstances: "Among American economists there is virtually no disagreement concerning the fact that the recession of 1969-1970 is a direct result of the conscious economic policy of the government, which is aimed at overcoming inflation. The prevailing view is that the recession is a price that the USA must pay for at least 4-5 years of using inflation to swell demand."[95] With downwardly inflexible prices set by monopolies, it was imperative to make adjustments elsewhere.[96] Since exchange rates were pegged, Anikin believed the alternative to currency devaluation must be a program of domestic "disinflation," which would transfer the burden of flexibility to the labor market as a way of reducing demand for both domestic and imported goods.[97]

The theory of artificial crises appeared to derive support from recent Keynesian literature in the west. The British economist A.W. Phillips claimed to have demonstrated a stable tradeoff between inflation and unemployment: the "Phillips curve" suggested that governments could deliberately choose either low unemployment together with high inflation, or the alternative of low inflation with high unemployment.[98] Although Phillips' theory implied the possibility of broad discretion in government policy, it left open the question of how quickly the economy might respond to monetary and fiscal changes.

In the case of America, Anikin thought the choice between inflation and unemployment had been complicated in two ways: first, Keynesian fiscal policy was too slow in reducing the rate of price increases, given the vulnerability of the dollar; second, Friedman's preferred instrument, tight monetary policy, was proving equally ineffective. Anikin described a new puzzle that contradicted the Phillips curve and seemed to refute the possibility of smooth adjustments: "A certain increase of unemployment was viewed as an inevitable stage in the transition from the present inflationary economy to one with a moderate rate of price increase. In reality, however, such a transition has become excessively prolonged, creating a dangerous combination of [high] inflation *and* unemployment."[99]

Notwithstanding doubts concerning the efficacy of government regulation, most participants at the conference agreed with Anikin that the Nixon administration bore much of the responsibility for America's domestic problems. A.G. Mileikovsky declared that Nixon had "artificially" created a recession in order to avoid a more acute cyclical crisis that would otherwise follow the Vietnam boom.[100] V.M. Usoskin, a specialist on monetary theory and policy, maintained that "putting the brakes on industrial output and the growth of employment was in large measure deliberately 'provoked' by the ruling Republican administration": "Nixon and his circle show a clear leaning to the philosophy of so-called monetarism, the main inspirer of which in the USA is Milton Friedman."[101]

In an article published after the conference, L.A. Leont'ev described Friedman as a representative of "the most reactionary section of the bourgeoisie."[102] The "mad gnome of Chicago" was being heralded as a "messiah" for denouncing Keynesian fine-tuning. Once inflation was beaten, Friedman wanted to neutralize both monetary and fiscal policy in favor of free markets. Leont'ev commented that "Genius is always simple . . . [and] Friedman's economic discoveries are certainly as simple as they come. . . . [A]ll the troubles of capitalist society spring from state intervention. . . . If only the state will refrain from meddling and let capitalism make people happy, everything will come right. Untrammelled capitalism—that is the panacea for all ills." Leont'ev thought Friedman's ideas "could fit into a thimble."[103]

While Soviet economists unanimously disdained Milton Friedman, many were reluctant to exaggerate the practical influence of his ideas. With West European precedents in mind, a number of conference speakers chose instead to emphasize the restraints imposed upon government by spontaneous forces. Yu. Chizhov pointed to an autonomous slowdown of investments beginning in 1967; although Nixon's anti-inflationary policy accelerated the course of events, the fall of production and employment resulted mainly from objective conditions and had not been "planned" in advance.[104] A.I. Kats likewise referred to excessive industrial capacity created during the Vietnam buildup.[105] V.M. Shamberg spoke of a combination of government measures and spontaneous cyclical forces.[106] A.A. Manukyan denied that government was responsible,[107] although he conceded that Nixon had worsened matters by overdoing restrictive measures.[108]

The IMEMO debate ended in a standoff when both S.M. Men'shikov and S.A. Dalin—two of the leading exponents of state regulation—unexpectedly sided with the skeptics. Since the mid-1960s Men'shikov had stressed moderation of the classical cycle, which in turn created the need for "artificial" crises. Yet contrary to his own predictions, he now told Anikin that in the American case it was "not true that the recession was caused by suspension in the growth of state expenditures." Nixon had attempted to cope with inflation by creating conditions for a moderate recession, but he had been overtaken by spontaneous forces: "Thus the slump of 1969-1970 was caused primarily by the action of cyclical forces in the economy, combined with inflationary forces resulting from the escalation of war in Vietnam."[109]

Elaborating the theory of monopoly "reserves," Men'shikov and Dalin had both warned of a possible overaccumulation of fixed capital.[110] By 1970 they thought the war had caused an investment boom, which in normal circumstances would have ended by 1967. State purchases in 1968-70 had delayed an inevitable slowdown; but they had also intensified inflation and eroded real incomes, thereby revealing excessive reserves of production capacity.[111] Dalin claimed that underutilization of capacity had reached 14.7 percent in 1967, rising to 15.4 percent in 1968 and more than 20 percent by 1970.[112] In his view, Nixon would have been foolish to provoke a recession in 1970 even if it had been within his power to do so:

> The Nixon government inherited from Johnson both the Vietnam war and a widespread antiwar movement, which has recently become even stronger. Let us ask ourselves, why would he want to intensify this dissatisfaction by increasing unemployment and reducing profits with congressional elections coming in November?[113]

8. The Dollar Crisis and Nixon's "Go"

It appears that Nixon had similar concerns in mind, at least with regard to his own forthcoming bid for reelection in 1972. With unemployment at 6 percent, in late 1970 and early 1971 the administration finally eased monetary policy and began to prime the economy for expansion. I.M. Osadchaya thought Nixon's reversal meant return to "traditional

Keynesian recipes . . . including a significant increase of government expenditures."[114] Associating Friedman with the "right extremist groups of American society," V.M. Usoskin agreed that monetary policy would once more be subordinated to Keynesian state-monopoly regulation.[115]

Although Nixon's anti-inflation program seemed to have brought some modest improvement in external accounts, the respite proved to be illusory. International movements of short-term capital soon added new strains to the world currency system and exacerbated financial tensions. Faced with higher U.S. interest rates, in 1969 American banks and corporations had borrowed Eurodollars. E. Grebennikova estimated that by the autumn of 1969 the sums involved amounted to $15 billion.[116] These short-term capital imports had shown as credits in the external accounts. When U.S. interest rates were subsequently lowered relative to those in Europe, this flow was reversed as borrowings were repaid.[117] At the same time, speculators converted "hot money" from dollars into safer currencies. Grebennikova described the consequences:

> in exchange for dollars, the European central banks issue additional amounts of national currency, thereby increasing the amount of money in circulation at home. This "imported" inflation makes it even harder to stop domestic inflation: thus, in late March 1971, the amount of money in circulation within the FRG [Federal Republic of Germany] was 22.5 percent above last year's level.[118]

The American capital outflow of 1971 was accompanied by the first deficit in merchandise trade since 1935; imports climbed by more than 14 percent, exports by a mere 2 percent.[119] "Thus . . . the US balance on reserve asset transactions swung wildly from a surplus in the late sixties to . . . enormous deficits . . . of the order of $10 billion in 1970 and $30 billion in 1971. . . ."[120] By the end of 1970 the gold drain reached a cumulative total of more than $13 billion since 1958.[121] With $11 billion left in reserves, by May 1971 the United States was theoretically obligated, upon request, to convert almost $30 billion in assets held by foreign central banks.[122]

9. America's "Sick Economy" and the General Crisis of Capitalism

Regardless of whether the upheavals in America and the world currency system were due to Keynesianism, monetarism, or spontaneous cyclical forces, official Moscow was coming to the view that capitalism had entered dangerous times. Economic deterioration amplified civil strife caused by the Vietnam war and encouraged hopes for a revolutionary crisis to parallel the crises of economic theory and government policy. In the spring of 1971, Leonid Brezhnev told the twenty-fourth congress of the Communist Party that "the ruling circles of the capitalist countries are afraid . . . of the class struggle developing into a mass revolutionary movement." Returning to themes dating from the 1920s, Brezhnev denied "that capitalism has been stabilised as a system. *The general crisis of capitalism has continued to deepen.*"[123]

Brezhnev was simply repeating advice coming from all quarters of Soviet economic opinion. Even when expectations of state-monopoly planning had been high, conservatives had not abandoned their view of intensifying contradictions. In 1968, S.L. Vygodsky had linked sterling's crisis and "inevitable" devaluation of the dollar with capitalist decay: "regardless of cyclical development and the greater or lesser intensity of economic crises of overproduction, the movement forward of the world capitalist system occurs in the context of the general crisis of capitalism, which, once begun, continues to deepen."[124] I.I. Kuz'minov insisted in 1968 that "according to the Marxist method it is necessary to proceed from the unity of the production process on the scale of the world capitalist system. . . . [T]he last world crisis occurred in 1957-1958. . . . [T]he second postwar cycle is [now] drawing near to completion."[125]

Referring to articles in the *New York Post,* by the spring of 1971 Kuz'minov was writing of "a nightmarish combination of growing unemployment, rapidly rising prices, stagnation in business activity, dwindling profits, and ever more frequent failures and financial crashes on Wall Street."[126] Criticizing those who claimed that planning had negated Marx's laws, he denied any significant difference between the 1970s and the 1950s: America still had a militarized economy, and Vietnam confirmed that "state anti-crisis 'regulation'" always consists of "replacing one crisis form of destruction of the productive forces by another one, namely, war."[127] If anything had changed by the early 1970s, it was the attitude of the American public:

> Under the impact of the crisis and the war and also their concomitants—inflation, rise in the cost of living, higher taxes and unemployment—the mistrust of Americans and their critical attitude to measures of state regulation of the economy are on the increase. This is strikingly displayed in public opinion polls,

anti-war demonstrations and a definite change of tone in press
comments on statements made by spokesmen of the ruling
circles.[128]

These conservative opinions sounded all the more plausible when
endorsed by more liberal authors. In July 1970, S.A. Dalin quoted a poll
in *Fortune* magazine showing that even the ruling class was becoming
disenchanted: 45 percent of "top executives" from three hundred major
corporations agreed that "they lived in a racist society, that wealth was
distributed unfairly, and that the nation needed spiritual regenera-
tion."[129] While Friedman referred to a recession on the scale of 1957-
58, Dalin noted that Galbraith thought a better analogy was with 1929.

As for the war economy, Dalin spoke in terms reminiscent of previous
debates over "one-sidedness": from August 1969 to May 1970, total
U.S. industrial production contracted by 3 percent; during roughly the
same period, output of consumer electronics fell by 32 percent,
automobiles by 26 percent, and agricultural machinery by 13
percent.[130] "Planned capitalism" had produced both the dollar crisis
and "America's sick economy":[131] "This is something new in the
history of U.S. capitalism, which so far has been immune to economic
crises when the country was at war."[132] Dalin thought that interaction
of economic, social, and political crises in America was creating a
replica of the French events of 1968:

> The sharpening of the internal and external contradictions of
> American imperialism has led to a profound social crisis . . . .
> expressed in growth of the strike movement, in racial conflicts
> that are becoming more acute, in the struggle against militarism
> and war in Vietnam, in a broad student movement, in the
> movement against rising prices and taxes. The object of the
> conflict has become the policies of both the monopolies and the
> state. The social crisis is . . . a result of the entire postwar
> development of American state-monopoly capitalism.[133]

For the first time since the Second World War, Soviet writers were
encouraged in the early 1970s to expect real social disintegration in the
United States. In an article on "The American Crisis and Nixon's
Policy," S. Vishnevsky exclaimed in July 1970 that "The word 'crisis'
never disappears from the pages of books, newspapers and magazines;
. . . the urban crisis, the racial crisis, the crisis in education and in

public health, the Administration's credibility crisis, the crisis in the electoral system, etc. All these different 'crises' . . . combine to form one great *American crisis*."[134]

Vishnevsky referred to poverty, the "programming" of unemployment, segregation, the Black Panthers, urban ghettos, police repression, the shooting of student demonstrators at Kent State University, and fears of a "new McCarthyism." Although America had passed through previous recessions with minimal social conflict, Vishnevsky thought Nixon's presidency had brought the country to a moral and political crisis greater than any since the 1930s. He ended with a quotation from Stewart Alsop: "Everywhere, even in the affluent suburbs, there is a restlessness and discontent such as this country has not known before, and for the first time large numbers of people question the validity of the country's basic institutions."[135]

By September 1971, A.G. Mileikovsky concluded that the entire capitalist world was experiencing "crisis processes of a new type": "The 'policy of growth' turned out to be a factor which considerably accelerates inflation. The increase in production secured at such a price has made it necessary to take anti-inflation measures that are actually directed against economic growth." Nixon's policies, like those of de Gaulle, had "advanced the economic struggle to the level of political demands and vigorous opposition of the masses to the reactionary economic policy of state-monopoly capitalism."[136] In Britain, circumstances were no better: a wave of unofficial strikes in 1969-70 led to replacement of Wilson's Labour government by Heath's Conservatives in June 1970. By that time, money wages were rising at an annual rate of 15 percent and unemployment was again growing rapidly.[137]

10. The End of the Postwar Expansion

Western historians confirm that by the late 1960s the postwar world was fundamentally changing. In all the leading capitalist countries the end of the decade brought slower growth, followed by mounting economic turmoil. Keynesian experiments in full employment were ending long before the oil, raw material, and food supply shocks of the early 1970s. In most countries there was a common pattern: national planning and macro-economic regulation created a tight labor market by the mid-1960s and threatened capital accumulation by changing income distribution in favor of labor. Given the system of pegged exchange rates, during the early 1960s the American dollar had placed a ceiling on inflation elsewhere;

when American inflation accelerated, the dollar became a floor. Other countries imported wage and price pressures to add to those generated domestically.[138] To contain inflation, economic restraints were imposed, causing a return of high unemployment. The result everywhere was social and political unrest.

Marx had seen the "disproportion between capital and exploitable labour power" as an important factor contributing to cyclical crises. Crises typically erupted in conditions of relatively full employment and rising wages. In a study of unionism and incomes policies for the Brookings Institution, R.J. Flanagan, D.W. Soskice, and L. Ulman summarized European experience during the 1960s in terms of a pattern Marx would have recognized:

> Memories of prewar unemployment . . . became less influential . . .; workers came increasingly to expect that real compensation would be raised . . . under collective bargaining and that full employment would be assured by official policy. It is interesting that the wildcat strikes at the end of the 1960s had typically been preceded by declines in the rate of increase in real wages, rather than in their absolute levels.[139]

Philip Armstrong, Andrew Glyn, and John Harrison wrote in *Capitalism Since 1945* that "Towards the end of the postwar boom, an imbalance between accumulation and the labour supply led to an increasingly severe labour shortage"[140] that pulled up real wages in several countries at the expense of a "profits squeeze."[141] From 1965 to 1973, the share of profits in American business output fell from 23.4 percent to 17.2 percent; in Europe, the profit share declined from 29.2 percent in 1960 to 24.5 percent in 1973.[142] European strikes against anti-inflation policies in the years 1968-70 developed parallel with the social unrest in America. In *The European Economy: Growth and Crisis*, Andrea Boltho described the effects of slower growth in terms of renewed animosity between labor and capital: "The achievement of virtual full employment conditions . . . was bound to lead . . . to a strengthening of labour power and to a shift in income distribution away from capital."[143]

Franco Bernabe, one of Boltho's collaborators, wrote that "gradual achievement of full employment in Western Europe . . . was, in some ways, carrying the seeds of its own destruction. At a highly aggregate level, the strengthening of labour's bargaining power . . . led, on the one hand, to a gradual decline in the share of profits in national income and, on the other, to an acceleration in the rate of wage inflation, particularly dramatic at the time of the wage explosions of the late 1960s."[144] Jacques Mazier gave the same interpretation from the perspective of a Western Marxist: although the rate of exploitation rose in the 1950s and early 1960s through improved technology and rising productivity, by the end of the decade "the rise in the share of labour . . . depressed profit rates and contributed to the deceleration of growth rates which began in the mid-1960s."[145]

Although historical turning points are easily discerned in retrospect, it was clear to Soviet observers at the time that novel forces were at work, undermining both their own preconceptions and those of Western Keynesians. A.I. Shapiro saw in the American recession of 1969-70 final refutation of theories of state "omnipotence."[146] Yu. N. Pokataev claimed that the role of the state had been overestimated: "At first its effect upon the economy was denied altogether, then individual comrades became so carried away that they began to assign to bourgeois governments achievements generally beyond their capacity."[147] A.A. Manukyan concluded that both Keynesianism and monetarism had failed: Nixon had been overtaken by the objective laws of Marx's economic cycle, which no state policies could fundamentally alter.[148]

Soviet writers discovered by the late 1960s that they had acknowledged the successes of state-monopoly capitalism at precisely the moment when the long era of postwar growth and consensus politics was ending. The early 1970s brought international turbulence on a scale unprecedented since the 1930s. In these circumstances, it was predictable that the theory of capitalism's deepening "general crisis" would return to displace thoughts of state-monopoly programming.

CHAPTER 10

DETENTE AND "DEEPENING OF THE GENERAL CRISIS"

From 1945 until the late 1960s, Soviet economists were preoccupied with disputes concerning the capitalist state. After World War II, Varga had thought the problem of markets might be alleviated by public works and American aid to Europe. Stalinists denounced both Varga and Keynes on the grounds that stabilization was impossible in the "general crisis." During the 1960s a new consensus emerged regarding the state's ability to plan. The problem of markets was set aside in the belief that aggregate demand could be regulated and that capitalism could coordinate restructuring and technological change within national economies. By the early 1970s the limitations of state-monopoly planning were obvious. The problem now was to explain why capitalist plans had failed.

Milton Friedman held governments accountable for the inflationary crisis. Instead of accepting a "natural" rate of unemployment consistent with stable prices, central banks were said to have allowed excessive monetary expansion. Rising prices and incomes might generate more activity in the short term, but Friedman argued that eventually employers and workers must see that nominal gains were being erased by inflation. Workers would then demand still higher wages, companies would raise prices, and recession would follow unless the money supply was increased even more rapidly. In the mid-1960s, Friedman warned that to yield to these pressures "would postpone a recession, but only at the cost of further price increases [and eventually] . . . a still more severe recession."[1] The only long-run alternative to accelerating inflation was a neutral monetary policy—even if slowing the rate of monetary expansion caused short-run unemployment.

John Kenneth Galbraith subscribed to a different theory of inflation. He argued that large firms had control over prices, allowing them to satisfy wage demands while passing on the increased costs to consumers. Galbraith's view of causality was the reverse of Friedman's. Whereas Friedman thought governments initiated inflation by creating excessive demand, Galbraith claimed that they increased the money supply merely to accommodate *prior* increases of prices that would otherwise reduce sales, production, and employment. According to Galbraith, the state had become "an extension of the power of the [private] planning system. . . . [S]hould demand be insufficient to clear markets at the higher prices, the state will sooner or later . . . make up the deficiency."[2]

By the early 1970s, Soviet writers thought both Galbraith and Friedman had overestimated the state. Recent turmoil in the world economy went beyond nation-states: international crises disrupted national plans; failure to coordinate national plans caused international crises. The destabilization of currencies was a *systemic crisis of world capitalism*. To comprehend it required an analysis not only of why state planning had failed, but also of the implications for the future. Critical reassessments of state-monopoly planning led to renewed emphasis upon "deepening of the general crisis" and hopes that it might be turned to Soviet advantage. The detente agreements between Richard Nixon and Leonid Brezhnev in 1972-74 were viewed as evidence of American weakness and Soviet ascendancy in the struggle between two systems.

1. Domestic Obstacles to Capitalist Planning

Until the American recession began late in 1969, Soviet economists were convinced that state policy could at least moderate cyclical fluctuations. Some had predicted that Nixon would cause an "artificial" crisis, but many others were taken unawares. At a conference organized by IMEMO in April 1969, not a single participant expected the recession that came later in the year. Business activity had slowed in 1967, coinciding with difficulties in Britain and Germany, but new investments at the end of 1968 suggested that capitalism could no longer be forced into what Yu.N. Pokataev called the "Procrustean bed" of Marx's four-phased cycle.[3] S.M. Nikitin remarked that the traditional phase of crisis was being replaced—as a result of state-monopoly practices—by "a simple decline in the rates of growth."[4] Thinking that the slowdown of 1967 had initiated a new world cycle, S.M. Men'shikov agreed that classical crises of overproduction were no longer necessary.[5]

Industrial production peaked in the United States in September 1969 and did not regain the prerecession level until April 1972.[6] While they quarreled over Nixon's role, Soviet commentators soon recognized that they had misjudged capitalist planning. In *The Leninist Analysis of Monopoly Capitalism and Modern Times*, M.S. Dragilev and N.I. Mokhov attacked S.A. Dalin in 1970 for exaggerating the role of the state. Dalin had claimed that principles of anarchy and planning limited each other.[7] Dragilev and Mokhov thought this view was "incorrect": "elements of planning (*planomernost'*) do not limit the anarchy of production, but only modify its manifestations in one manner or another."[8]

Because state measures could control neither international corporations nor the "millions" of small capitalists who worked with no prior knowledge of the market, Dragilev and Mokhov insisted that there remained a contradiction between "the organization of production within the firm and the anarchy of capitalist production as a whole."[9] Despite knowledge of the market, monopolies both overinvested in the hope of eliminating competitors and ignored state policies when they saw an opportunity to reap higher profits.[10] The result was excessive production capacity, which "certain bourgeois economists"—including Dalin—had "delicately" interpreted as "a reserve of production capacity provided for in advance."[11] Paraphrasing Stalin's comment to H.G. Wells, Dragilev and Mokhov wrote that "In the final analysis it is not the state that determines the economic life of society; on the contrary, the state's activity is . . . an effort to adapt to changes in economic development."[12]

Dalin replied in *The USA: Postwar State-Monopoly Capitalism*. Although he denied that anarchy was increasing, he also conceded that capitalism had proved to be incapable of solving its fundamental dilemma: production always tended to go "beyond the limits of consumption,"[13] and overaccumulation of capital remained "the direct cause of crises."[14] Marx had shown that crises are preceded by rising wages,[15] but growth of nominal consuming power could not prevent excess capacity when "inflation reduces the real content of wages."[16] Marx had also written that in capitalist society social reason asserts itself *post festum*. Dalin decided that capitalist planning was unworkable because "anticrisis measures . . . are [always] undertaken . . . after a crisis has begun."[17] Even Arthur F. Burns, Nixon's head of the Federal Reserve Board, had failed to anticipate the recession.[18] If the most highly placed American officials could not make accurate forecasts, the thesis of a "known market" had to be reconsidered.

In a major collective work on *The Political Economy of Modern Monopoly Capitalism*, S.M. Men'shikov similarly acknowledged in 1970 that effective countercyclical policies were improbable: "The main thing is that the monopolies . . . are guided first of all . . . by their own interests. . . . [W]hen the market conjuncture turns out to be better than foreseen by the program, the monopolies always increase production and capital investments. . . . Thus state-monopoly programming only changes and modifies—but does not eliminate—the cyclical character inherent in reproduction."[19] Like Dalin, Men'shikov now thought that western governments had placed excessive trust in computers:

> The bourgeois state does not possess the technical ability to foresee a change of the market conjuncture in good time. . . . [E]conometric models . . . are not sufficiently accurate and do not provide the necessary information quickly enough. Because of commercial secrecy, it is impossible in a capitalist economy to secure the flow of statistical information needed for really effective economic regulation.[20]

From 1970 onward, one economist after another disavowed the theory of state-monopoly planning. Notwithstanding his earlier enthusiasm for the French model, A.I. Pokrovsky wrote of a "crisis spiral" in all capitalist countries, marked by inflationary pressures, deflationary crises, and growing working-class unrest:

> Vivid examples of the social storms lashing imperialism are the powerful wave of strikes and demonstrations conducted by the French workers in the summer of 1968; the unprecedented general strike of millions of workers in Italy in February 1969; the dockers' and miners' strikes in Britain in 1971 and 1972; and the annual militant spring marches of millions of Japanese workers. These actions . . . . indicate the growing . . . militancy of the working class. . . . About two-thirds of the strikes are staged under political slogans or have some political shading.[21]

V.A. Cheprakov agreed that state-monopoly capitalism could never become an "organically unified system."[22] A.I. Shapiro, who in 1969 had referred to the longest expansion "in the entire epoch of imperialism,"[23] wrote one year later of state policy swinging like a pendulum between inflationary expansion and deflationary contraction.[24] By 1972, I.I. Kuz'minov described the new American crisis as "the longest in the postwar period. In duration (though not in extent) it really resembles the Great Depression of 1929-1933."[25]

A.G. Mileikovsky also repudiated his earlier work on state-coordinated restructuring: "while improving the organization and direction of production within the confines of one or another corporation, the capitalists are unable to extend the same efficiency standards to the whole of the national economy."[26] Mileikovsky saw a crisis of economic theory developing parallel to the general crisis of capitalism. Keynesian policies of full employment had led to "creeping" and then "galloping inflation."[27] Galbraith thought wage controls were the answer; Mileikovsky remarked that Galbraith had "'good' intentions, which can be used by reaction in order to 'pave the road to hell.'"[28]

In April 1973, IMEMO held another conference to consider "specific features of the modern capitalist cycle." The director, N.N. Inozemtsev, praised Varga, Trakhtenberg, Mendel'son, Mileikovsky, Manukyan, and Dalin for past contributions. He added, however, that "we cannot be satisfied with what has been accomplished."[29] Although more than thirty speakers took part in the conference, they produced about the same number of divergent interpretations.[30] V.I. Kuznetsov concluded that the difficulty of analyzing modern cycles resulted from spontaneous *global* forces: "The world cycle and world crisis, which previously arose from the spread of a cycle and crisis [outward] from separate countries . . . can now originate in the sphere of international economic relations and then spread [into] particular countries . . . [in the form of] national crises and cycles."[31]

I.I. Kuz'minov gave the same interpretation in more traditional language: the "omnipotence of the imperialist state" had suffered a "crushing blow"[32] because "the main problem . . . is the problem of the market."[33] Linking failure of domestic planning with global contradictions and return of a world economic cycle, Kuz'minov declared that Marx had been vindicated: "the 1969-1971 crisis . . . is a world cyclical crisis of overproduction. Consequently, not only [has] the cyclical nature of . . . development . . . been preserved . . . but also the duration of the cycle predicted by Marx, namely, 10-12 years."[34] To dramatize the plight of capitalist countries, Kuz'minov quoted an article in *La vie francaise*:

> We were told that in our day a crisis was inconceivable, that specialists were able to detect it and the government to prevent it.

. . . [W]e were also lulled with illusions. . . . The dollar blew up the entire mechanism. American deficits spread across the world.[35]

2. Global Disproportionality and the End of Bretton Woods

The problems of the early 1970s appeared to demonstrate conclusively the impossibility of state-monopoly planning. High levels of employment brought inflation; inflation caused destabilizing flows of short-term capital; to protect its balance of payments, each country tried to increase exports by turning sooner or later to domestic restraint and unemployment. At the center of the maelstrom was the United States. America had stabilized capitalism with the Marshall Plan after World War II; a quarter of a century later, America was destabilizing the world system and accelerating the general crisis. Collapse of the dollar was both cause and effect of international contradictions.

Following Nixon's decision to reflate, the American balance of payments deteriorated at an alarming pace. The deficit reached an unprecedented $9.8 billion in 1970 and then soared to $29.8 billion in 1971.[36] The German Bundesbank was forced to buy more than $1 billion of hot money on May 3-4, 1971, and another $1 billion during the first forty minutes of trading on May 5. At that point, Germany surrendered to speculation and allowed the mark to float upward. The United States lost a further $1.1 billion in reserve assets during the first two weeks of August. On August 15, 1971, President Nixon declared a national emergency, levied a 10 percent surcharge on imports, imposed a domestic price and income freeze for ninety days, and suspended dollar convertibility. World exchange markets closed for several days; when they reopened, almost all major currencies were temporarily floating.[37]

During 1971, American reserve liabilities grew from $23.78 billion to $50.65 billion—a greater increase in a single year than in all of previous history.[38] Were these liabilities to be presented for conversion, U.S. gold would cover approximately one-fifth of the total. In December 1971, a final effort was made to save the Bretton Woods system. The Group of Ten major industrial countries met in Washington and agreed to compromise: America would lift the import surcharge in exchange for general currency realignment. The dollar was devalued by raising the price of gold from $35 to $38 per ounce; returning to fixed parities, other countries revalued their currencies upward within a range of 7.5 percent (for Italy and Sweden) to 16.9 percent (for Japan).[39]

In the spring of 1972 pressure on the dollar temporarily abated as attention turned once more to sterling. Frightened by inflation and labor strife in mining and shipbuilding, speculators forced the pound to resume floating on June 23. In November, Prime Minister Heath backed his antiunion legislation of the previous year with another freeze on prices and wages.[40] By early 1973 the dollar came back into the spotlight. The United States announced that its trade deficit had worsened in spite of currency realignment. Exchange markets collapsed into chaos. In the first nine days of February, the Bundesbank purchased almost $6 billion in an attempt to resist further revaluation of the mark. On February 10, Japan closed its market to avoid absorbing more dollars. Two days later the dollar was devalued by a further 10 percent. When this second devaluation proved inadequate, the dollar came under renewed attack. On March 16, 1973, representatives of fourteen countries met in Paris and decided that exchange rates pegged to the dollar were impossible to sustain. The Paris agreement "ended the Bretton Woods system . . . and established floating exchange rates for the leading currencies covering 70 per cent of total world trade."[41]

E. Grebennikova exclaimed that "it is hardly possible to count on even relative currency stabilization in the Western world in the foreseeable future."[42] She attributed currency chaos to speculation by multinational firms, whose assets were estimated to be $300 billion by late 1973 —double the total reserves of all capitalist countries.[43] E.S. Shershnev emphasized the effects of foreign investments; American multinationals exacerbated the payments deficit first by exporting capital and then by serving the American market from plants located in other countries where labor costs were lower.[44] V.V. Motylev blamed military expansionism: "The chronic deficit in the balance of payments has been caused above all by implementation of the USA's aggressive policy, by the financing of military blocs, subsidization of reactionary regimes, [and] expenditures on waging the aggressive war in Vietnam. . . ."[45]

During the 1960s, Soviet writers had assumed that currencies mediated relations between national economies and that exchange rate stability was both a condition for and a result of planning. Conversely, disruption of fixed exchange rates in the early 1970s was attributed to failure to synchronize national policies, which in turn created uneven rates of inflation. E. Selikhov described currency conflicts as "an indicator of disproportions and crisis phenomena" in the world economy as a whole.[46] S. Safronov thought deficit countries were being driven to wage "total war for foreign markets."[47] Men'shikov described the world market as a "war of each against all"[48] in which no country could "protect itself against a deteriorating conjuncture if other countries are not taking measures in the same direction."[49] A.V. Anikin summarized these reactions in terms of a single contradiction:

> In its present form, the system of programming accommodates regulation within the limits of closed-in national economies and has no instruments whatever to affect processes developing on the world market. But it is precisely these processes that have become important factors of instability in the capitalist economic system. Internationalization of . . . production . . . [leads] to the need for regulation to go beyond national limits.[50]

3. The Theory of Two Systems in a Single World Market

When the capitalist countries failed to maintain international proportionality, Soviet analysts turned from state-monopoly planning to relations between the two systems. Prior to the dollar crisis, the USSR's trade with Western Europe had been growing impressively. From 1960 to 1968 the turnover with thirteen capitalist countries more than doubled. The outstanding exception was Soviet-American trade, which remained insignificant. In ruble values, trade with the United States represented just under 4 percent of the total (with the same thirteen countries) in 1965 and fell to 2.3 percent in 1968.[51] The eagerness of Western Europe to trade in socialist markets seemed to grow in proportion to America's relative decline as an imperialist center.

As Soviet trade initiatives began to yield results, the role of two systems in one world economy had to be redefined. In *Economic Problems*, Stalin had attributed "deepening of the general crisis" to replacement of the "single all-embracing world market" by "two parallel world markets."[52] Lenin, on the other hand, had said in 1921 that "There is a force more powerful than the wishes, the will and the decisions of any of the governments that are hostile to us. That force is *worldwide [vsemirnye] general economic relations*, which compel them to make contact with us."[53] Reinterpretation of the theory of two systems began with Lenin's concept of *vsemirnye* relations.

In 1964, S.A. Dalin claimed that Stalin had been mistaken. Capitalism had not contracted, nor could formation of "two parallel markets" mean "liquidation" of the single world market so long as "there continues to be an international division of labor and exchange between socialist and capitalist countries." Dalin evoked Lenin's authority to dispute that of Stalin: "V.I. Lenin, as is known, from the very beginning of Soviet Russia's existence supported development of trade and economic relations with the capitalist world and considered the world market to be indivisible, despite the opposition of two systems."[54]

The first thorough reassessment of East-West relations came in V.I. Stepanov's *The Economic Foundations of Peaceful Coexistence*, which also appeared in 1964. Stepanov used the same terms as Lenin: rise of the socialist system did not eliminate "general worldwide relations, the worldwide market or the international division of labor."[55] Lenin had described national economies as "links of a single world economy." Stepanov interpreted Lenin to mean that modern productive forces objectively entailed "internationalization of production and exchange."[56] The two systems could not lead an "isolated existence," for socialism was not "autarkic by nature."[57] Instead, the worldwide market represented a "contradictory unity"[58] whose parts were mediated through "the commodity, value, money, price [and] credit."[59]

In Stepanov's view the worldwide division of labor resulted from demands placed upon both systems by "the law of economy of labor time,"[60] or the need for continual technological and organizational improvements. In notes for *Capital* Marx had said that "Real economy—saving—consists of the saving of labour time. . . ."[61] Marx elaborated in *Capital* by referring to three types of economic organization: "the division of labour in general" (between sectors); division "in particular" (within individual sectors); and division "within the workshop . . . or in detail."[62] While trade between capitalist and socialist countries typically involved division of labor either in general or in particular, Stepanov saw no reason why ideology should prevent "production cooperation" and joint efforts to develop new branches of industry.[63]

Marking the fiftieth anniversary of Lenin's *Imperialism*, IMEMO declared in 1967 that Lenin had foreseen the "internationalization of economic life" and the impossibility of excluding the USSR from the system of world economic links. Marx had spoken of detailed division within a workshop, but IMEMO pointed out that the modern workshop was becoming global. Monopolies were creating patent pools, entering agreements on specialization and coordination of production, and forming international consortia to share the costs of research and development. "Imperialist integration"—within the EEC—created rivalry between opposing blocs; the alternative was cooperation on an all-European basis.

The creation of modern complexes and large-scale experiments increasingly demand the joint efforts of several countries in mobilizing human and material resources. A closer economic rapprochement (*sblizhenie*) of nations and states, the interweaving and interdependence of national economies, is an objective requirement for development of the modern productive forces.[64]

Engels had associated the state's role as "collective capitalist" with technologies whose costs were beyond individual firms. In November 1967, A.G. Mileikovsky called for a "global analysis" and applied a similar argument to international relations:[65] "World socialism does not in the least strive for autarky. . . . Besides trade, a vitally necessary form of the division of labor between countries of the two systems is becoming the exchange of patents, technological experience and scientific knowledge. In conditions of the modern scientific-technical revolution not even the greatest Power can assure itself of the possibility of independently resolving all of the new problems of science and technology while ignoring the achievements of other countries."[66] Mileikovsky noted that "certain economists"—Stalinists—had thought industrialization would lead to socialist self-sufficiency; in reality, conditions had been created "for even greater development of the worldwide division of labor, in which both the world socialist and the world capitalist economy participate."[67]

During the 1960s several East European countries had undertaken innovative forms of coproduction with western firms, in which the two sides entered licensing agreements and produced components for joint products. In Yugoslavia, capitalist investors were even allowed to own up to 49 percent of shares in joint enterprises. Under Khrushchev the USSR purchased entire chemical plants from Western Europe. In 1966 Fiat agreed to participate in building a $1.5 billion Soviet automobile plant capable of producing 600,000 units a year and involving machinery imports worth $600 million. In all such cases the socialist countries were responding to the problem cited by W.W. Rostow: imported technology was intended to alleviate the threat of domestic slowdown due to rising costs of research and development.

In 1968, M.V. Senin published *Development of International Economic Ties* and emphasized that purchase of factories and foreign licences accelerated introduction of new products and provided opportunities to learn western organization and management.[68] The "universal law of economy of time"[69] required a combination of world technology with capitalist experience in organizing production, reducing costs, and developing money and credit relations in order to determine the optimal combination of centralization and decentralization.[70]

G.M. Prokhorov also described trade expansion in terms of specialization and the "objective law of economy of labor and time."[71] From 1961 to 1969 world capitalist trade had more than doubled, compared to a 39 percent increase during the entire first half of the twentieth century.[72] Multinational corporations had internationalized the detailed division of labor, causing trade to grow far more rapidly than total production:

> An important part of modern world trade . . . is not trade in the strict sense (commodity exchange between independent sellers and buyers), but deliveries of materials, manufactures, machinery parts and items of equipment embodying specialized technical knowledge, from the main (or key) enterprises to their subsidiaries (operating abroad), shipments in the reverse direction, or else the movement of commodities between subsidiary enterprises.[73]

International firms had made science a direct productive force through global transmission of knowledge. According to Prokhorov, scientific research must be given the same priority in Soviet industry: "the economic effectiveness of expenditures on the development of science and incorporation of its results into production are 3-4 times higher than the effectiveness of [fixed-] capital investments. . . . More than a quarter of the national income of the USSR is created through investing resources in popular education and the corresponding improvement of labor skills."[74] In 1969 capitalists had approximately fifty thousand international patent and licensing agreements, demonstrating that the most effective way to accelerate labor productivity was to combine domestic research with technical cooperation and purchase of knowledge already developed elsewhere.[75]

Prokhorov noted that production cooperation could include several forms: participation of foreign firms in developing Soviet resources (as France, Italy, and Germany were already doing in natural gas); assistance in setting up new factories (as in the case of Fiat); and the licensed production of components for export. By adopting the latest technology, the Soviet Union might also increase sales of its own machinery and finished goods. In 1970 machinery and equipment represented only 3.8 percent of Soviet exports to developed capitalist countries, compared to 39 percent of imports.[76] The way to redress this imbalance was to enlist the capitalists themselves in improving the quality and promoting the sale of Soviet products. The standard of "international value"[77] must govern socialist as well as capitalist countries.[78]

In a study of *Theories and Methods of Capitalist Programming*, G.A. Shpil'ko cited Japan as the outstanding example of a country that accomplished structural change on the basis of "imported technical progress." By the mid-1960s, 77 percent of Japanese equipment met or exceeded world standards. Although Japan had paid the price of "a certain dependence" on other countries, it was now building on the imported technological base by spending more on domestic research and development. Shpil'ko quoted a Japanese government report describing the country's industrial strategy:

> We imported the leading technology from industrially developed countries and thus saved time in research and experimentation and were able to accomplish industrialization in a short time. The increase of labor productivity on the basis of imported technology led to creation of an ultramodern industrial structure and accelerated the process of expanding investment in equipment, which, in turn, made possible high rates of economic growth.[79]

In a book that he coedited with M.S. Dragilev, I.P. Faminsky sounded another common theme when he cautioned against becoming so dependent on foreign suppliers as to promote international "convergence."[80] Equalization of "levels" of development within Comecon promoted specialization, cooperation, and integration, but by 1970 all the socialist countries together had only some four hundred licensing agreements with capitalist firms.[81] While Faminsky thought that socialism and capitalism exerted a "mutual influence" and could not be "isolated from each other," he also condemned capitalist "bridge building"—or use of credits and other inducements to split the socialist camp.[82] If trade with capitalist countries was to grow, socialist integration must proceed even more rapidly.

4. From the Currency Crisis to Detente

In 1970 a definitive statement on trade and the Cold War appeared in a two-volume study edited by four of the most prominent economists specializing on capitalist countries: N.N. Inozemtsev, S.M. Men'shikov,

A.G. Mileikovsky, and A.M. Rumyantsev. A chapter by V.I. Gantman dealt with "Economic Development and the Foreign Policy of Imperialism" and argued that the world "relation of forces" had radically shifted: "Socialism is currently no longer on the defensive but is waging an historical offensive."[83] The result was "intensification of the general instability of the capitalist system."[84] Gantman quoted Brezhnev's Party Program of 1969: "the main content, the main direction and the main features of the historical development of mankind are determined by the world socialist system, by the forces struggling against imperialism and for the socialist reconstruction of society."[85] The EEC had thrown off American hegemony, Japan was emerging as a major industrial power, and the United States would have to seek accommodation with socialism in order to replace lost markets.

By the early 1970s it was widely believed that the USSR could profit from America's problems. Evidence of American decline, both at home and abroad, seemed overwhelming. The Vietnam war had reached a turning point in February 1968, when American forces suffered heavy casualties during the Tet offensive. The assassination of Martin Luther King, in April, sparked ghetto riots that left Washington in flames and troops stationed on the Capitol Hill lawn. Lyndon Johnson declined to seek reelection; Robert Kennedy was assassinated; the Democratic convention became a scene of antiwar riots—and all the while the dollar crisis intensified. As America went from crisis to crisis, Soviet leaders put their own house in order. In August 1968 they sent tanks into Czechoslovakia, overthrew the reformist government of Alexander Dubček, and ended western hopes of "building bridges" to Prague. After ensuring the "normalization" of Eastern Europe, Brezhnev was content to watch pressures grow in Washington.

In November 1969 a foreign trade convention, chaired by the head of General Motors and attended by two thousand business delegates, called upon the Nixon administration to liberalize trade with the Soviet bloc.[86] S.A. Dalin reported that recession and the Vietnam war had divided the ruling class: "not all American monopolies have profited . . . from the war. . . . It has enriched primarily the big military-industrial monopolies."[87] In December Congress modified the Export Control Act of 1949 with a new Export Administration Act intended to prevent sales of goods only with *military*—as opposed to "military or economic"—potential.[88] The law provided for reduction of the number of prohibited items from thirteen hundred to two hundred. Export licences could be issued even for "strategic commodities" if they were already available elsewhere.[89]

B.M. Pichugin wrote that "the United States . . . has been forced to review its policy by chronic unemployment, systematic balance-of-payment difficulties and production slumps which are more frequent and prolonged than in any other capitalist country."[90] E.S. Shershnev welcomed the new export rules as a victory for business circles who favored a "realistic approach."[91] He later recalled that "adoption of the 1969 Act was interpreted in the socialist countries as a symptom of America's willingness to . . . renounce its cold war strategy."[92] Attempts to continue the blockade would have been pointless. According to Shershnev, multinationals had been systematically evading controls long before the law was revised:

> the biggest US companies, such as General Motors, International Business Machines and Honeywell, which had no formal authorization to sell socialist countries goods manufactured . . . in the United States, had in fact been supplying them from their West European subsidiaries for a long time. . . . [T]he volume of such trade had reached 300-400 million dollars a year by the early seventies.[93]

In October 1971 it was announced that Nixon would travel to Moscow the following May for a summit meeting with Brezhnev. In November Maurice Stans, secretary of commerce, delivered a letter from the president suggesting expansion of trade. B. Dmitriev attributed Nixon's new realism to a "radically altered balance of strength" and "a considerable change . . . in the temper of the American public."[94] In fact, Nixon had his own strategy for manipulating Brezhnev. Before going to Moscow he first visited Peking, signed trade and friendship agreements with Mao Tse-tung, and threatened Soviet leaders with a Sino-American alliance.

In *Soviet-American Trade in the Cold War*, Philip J. Funigiello described the thinking of the Nixon administration: "detente was intended to compensate for the erosion of American military superiority"; it was also "the response to Russia's domestic economic weakness. Detente would give . . . the Kremlin a deal it could not refuse: entry into American (and global) markets of trade, investments, and credits; and 'legitimacy' in a consultative, coequal superpower relationship. . . ." In exchange, Nixon expected Brezhnev to broker a deal in Vietnam and cooperate in establishing "international equilibrium" through a new "balance of power."[95]

While Brezhnev wanted access to everything from American grain to advanced technology—most of it on credit—his own thoughts had nothing to do with a stable balance of power. On the contrary, the new relation of forces indicated that capitalism was "destabilized" and that the general crisis would continue to deepen through inflation, unemployment, and the global currency crisis.[96] Soviet leaders thought in terms of objective contradictions working against the United States. An editorial in *Kommunist* asserted that imperialists were forced to adopt more realistic policies because the "historical initiative" had passed to revolutionary forces throughout the world.[97] On the eve of Nixon's flight to Moscow, Foreign Minister A.A. Gromyko described "the real situation": Washington was afraid that America would be defeated on the Vietnam front by weakness in the "economic and social rear."[98]

5. From Detente to Cold War

From 1972 to 1974 Nixon and Brezhnev had three summit meetings: in Moscow in May 1972, in Washington in June 1973, and again in Moscow from late June to early July 1974. During this period the two countries signed twenty-nine treaties, agreements, interim agreements, and protocols. At their first meeting Nixon and Brezhnev initiated detente with a declaration of Basic Principles of Mutual Relations, a treaty to limit antiballistic missile systems, an interim agreement to limit strategic arms, an agreement to cooperate in environmental protection, and another concerning exploration and peaceful use of outer space.[99]

Even before Nixon arrived in Moscow, his statesmanship was compared to that of another American president—Franklin D. Roosevelt. In an English-language journal, *International Affairs*, A. Gorokhov flattered Nixon with this implicit comparison: "Franklin Roosevelt was the first American state leader to see that it is senseless and disadvantageous to the United States not to establish good relations with the Soviet Union. . . . He was concerned with the preservation of the capitalist system, but he had greater insight than the ordinary imperialist politicians."[100] On April 12, the anniversary of Roosevelt's death in 1945, a memorial service was held in Moscow. E.V. Ivanov credited Roosevelt with understanding "that development of economic cooperation of the USA with the USSR answers the interests of both states." G.A. Arbatov, director of the Institute of the USA, praised Roosevelt's capacity for "realistic decisions"—even though he was "a firm and convinced defender of capitalism."[101]

Roosevelt had extended diplomatic recognition in 1933; in 1934 the Export-Import Bank was created primarily to fund exports to the USSR; a first trade agreement was signed in 1935; in 1937 it was amended to include most-favored-nation (MFN) tariff treatment. Before current trade issues could be addressed, however, there was another matter inherited from the Roosevelt era that had to be resolved: the lend-lease debt. In October 1972 a joint trade commission struck a deal: the USSR would pay an amount less than originally demanded; in return, the U.S. administration would authorize long-term loans through the Export-Import Bank and ask Congress to grant MFN treatment.[102] *U.S. News and World Report* declared that "The cold war that has kept the United States and the Soviet Union hostile and at arm's length for 25 years officially ended on October 18, 1972."[103]

Once the irritant of lend-lease debt was removed, American business leaders flocked to Moscow in the hope of equipping new factories and opening up vast natural resources. In the forefront was Armand Hammer of Occidental Petroleum, whose dealings with the Soviet Union dated from an asbestos-mining agreement with Lenin in 1921. In July 1972, Occidental concluded a scientific-technical cooperation agreement with the Soviet government; less than a year later it negotiated one of the biggest contracts of the detente period, providing for joint production and export of fertilizers valued at $20 billion over two decades.[104]

A second focus of activity was the Kama Truck Works, in which more than eighty American firms eventually participated in building and equipping a plant designed to have twice the production capacity of the entire United States truck-building industry.[105] From 1972 to 1975 the Soviet Union purchased a wide range of other plants to manufacture such diverse products as acetic acid, iron ore pellets, cans, tableware, ammonia, engine bearings, and textiles. Equipment sales included computers, petroleum pumps, gas turbine compressors, electronic message-switching systems, tractors, road-building machinery, and heavy equipment to lay gas pipelines. Many of the largest American corporations were involved either in investment projects or in scientific-technical cooperation.[106]

Some of the most visionary projects broached in 1973-74 involved Soviet energy resources. France, Italy, Germany, and Austria were providing pipe in exchange for natural gas; the Soviet government urged American firms to help with construction of new trunk lines in order that gas could be transferred to the coasts, liquified, and exported in jointly owned tanker vessels. In view of American energy shortages and rising prices, E.S. Shershnev portrayed the two countries as ideal partners: American firms could provide equipment and technical services and be repaid with gas deliveries for sale in the United States.[107] Surveying "new horizons for economic links," N.P. Shmelev expressed a widely held Soviet opinion when he wrote in January 1973 that "It is possible that the world now finds itself on the threshold of essential changes in the relations between states that have been at loggerheads with each other for so long."[108]

Although Brezhnev insisted that peaceful coexistence meant no end to class struggle, both sides hoped that economic relations would produce beneficial political results. The Department of Commerce advised Nixon that "closer economic ties bear both cause and effect relationships to relaxation of political tension. . . . [O]nce in place, economic ties create a community of interest. . . ." Nixon told Congress that cooperative ventures would establish "an interdependence between our economies which provides a continued incentive to maintain a constructive relationship."[109] Brezhnev said it was "axiomatic" that the scientific-technical revolution required "long-term, large-scale economic cooperation."[110] G.A. Arbatov, one of Brezhnev's advisers, expected "mutually beneficial cooperation" to isolate the "military-industrial monopolies" and create "*mutual* dependence": "such relations stabilize the situation, promote normalization and make it difficult to return to the 'cold war.'"[111]

The high point of Soviet enthusiasm over detente came in 1974, when V.I. Stepanov published *East-West Economic Relations: Problems and Prospects*. Although he dismissed "global convergence,"[112] Stepanov in fact endorsed the concept by rephrasing it in more acceptable terms. "Internationalization of economic life" was to be regarded as an "economic law"[113] on the same plane as the law of value. Marx had said that the law of value governed sales of *all* commodities in the world market—even those produced by slaves, peasants, or state enterprises. Stepanov argued that "World value is a real category of the worldwide market. Around it prices are formed in trade between both socialist countries and countries of the capitalist world economy."[114]

The law of value created a "unity of opposites"[115] in which the "world socialist market" was already a "special sphere of the worldwide market."[116] The world capitalist economy had ceased to be merely a "sum of national economies,"[117] and socialist economies were likewise "parts of a whole—the world socialist economy."[118] Since the two systems together constituted the single "worldwide economy (*vsemirnoe khozyaistvo*),"[119] Stepanov treated rapprochement through detente as an objective step toward the final victory of socialism, when all national economies would be coordinated like a single factory.

> If one abstracts from social form, the process of international-ization of production . . . leads from *trade links* between closed-in, nationally isolated (even autarkic) economies to a *totality of national economic complexes* and the international binding together of national reproduction processes, and from there to *the interpenetration of national economic structures, to a single world and then worldwide economy, to general worldwide production* managed according to plan from a single center.[120]

Excitement over detente peaked while Stepanov was writing his book. By September 1973 more disruptive events began to intrude. In Chile, American efforts to undermine the Marxist government of Salvador Allende ended in a military coup. In October, Egypt and Syria attacked Israel. The Soviet Union mobilized troops for an airlift to the Middle East; the United States countered by putting nuclear strike forces on alert. When the Americans resupplied Israel from NATO bases in Europe, OPEC embargoed oil deliveries and quadrupled the price in world markets. In 1974, Angola gained independence from Portugal; the Soviet Union promptly flew in Cuban troops to support the pro-Marxist faction against its western-supported rivals. In August 1974, Nixon was driven from office by the Watergate scandal. Eight months later South Vietnam fell. As Cold War passions revived, anti-Soviet forces in Congress seized the opportunity to sabotage detente at a time when global energy, food, and materials shortages were creating the most severe crisis in the west since the Great Depression.

6. Return to the "General Crisis"

According to S.M. Men'shikov, world crises had been moderated until the 1970s by lack of synchrony between the leading capitalist countries: "crises of overproduction were less acute and in several cases less protracted than in the '20s and '30s. . . . [T]hey were more reminiscent of crises of the nineteenth century. . . ."[121] The result was world crises "of a special type," in which "cyclical" crises in some countries coincided with "intermediate" crises in others.[122] But government policies to control the domestic cycle had now deflected contradictions into the sphere of international relations: "The paradox is that a government, in combating an economic crisis, might bring on a monetary crisis."[123] When the currency crisis enveloped all countries, production cycles converged and reinforced the shocks of the mid-1970s.

The first postwar recession to occur more or less simultaneously in all capitalist countries was that of 1970-71. Governments responded by adopting expansionary policies and creating a synchronized "mini-boom" in 1972-73.[124] The increase of world liquidity, resulting from the continuing flood of dollars, supported a global rise of demand and generalized inflation. The boom also turned out to be the last before years of stagnation and unemployment. The end of the Keynesian era coincided with failure of detente and initiated an agonizing decade of global restructuring.

The synchronized upswing of 1972-73 resulted in global shortages of food and materials in 1973-75. Since the mid-1950s, countries producing food and raw materials for export had suffered from deteriorating terms of trade that discouraged investment in new production. Because of surpluses in the latter half of the 1960s, most wheat-producing countries had reduced their acreage. In 1972 poor weather in China, India, Africa, and the Soviet Union put unexpected pressure on world grain stocks. To protect livestock herds and avoid the political consequences of food shortages, the Soviet government turned to the United States. Accommodating Soviet needs in order to promote detente, the Nixon administration helped to ignite a spectacular rise in world food prices.

Within weeks of Nixon's return from his first meeting with Brezhnev, Soviet buyers used American credits to acquire $1.1 billion worth of grain, including one-quarter of the entire 1972 wheat crop.[125] The "Great Grain Robbery"—as Marshall Goldman called it—involved a subsidized price of $1.61 to $1.63 a bushel. The market became aware of these transactions when prices started to soar, reaching $5 a bushel by August 1973.[126] By 1974 wheat prices were three times above the levels of 1971, corn prices had more than doubled, and rice prices had more than quadrupled. From 1973 to 1974 the world price index for all food exports climbed by nearly 30 percent. In 1975 world grain inventories were 60 percent below 1970 levels.[127]

Food shortages occurred at the same time as the oil embargo drove up energy prices following the 1973 Arab-Israeli war. The cumulative effect was the greatest international inflation of the century together with the highest unemployment since World War II. From 1972 to 1974 prices on industrial materials rose by 73 percent, fibers by 59 percent, metals by

85 percent.[128] Because oil had to be paid for in dollars, the world dollar surplus was suddenly replaced by a shortage, creating new balance of payments crises in most oil-importing countries. In 1974 the combined expenditure on oil imports by the United States, Japan, France, Britain, and Italy came to $82.3 billion, compared to $21.4 billion in 1973.[129] This enormous transfer of income to OPEC reduced demand in the industrial countries and caused a decline of industrial production on the order of 10 percent from July 1974 to April 1975.[130] Yu.N. Pokataev described the crisis as one of global disproportionality:

> The crisis deepened as a result of the fact that proportions were destroyed between the volume of available energy resources and demands for energy, between raw material resources and manufacturing capacity, between agriculture and industry, and also because credit-monetary systems and state finances were shattered.[131]

Inflation and unemployment combined in the summer of 1974 to cause an economic crisis more acute than any since 1929.[132] Investments collapsed, gold prices skyrocketed, and stock markets panicked. The price of General Motors shares fell in 1973-74 by 66.4 percent, Peugeot by 72 percent, Volkswagen by 61 percent, British Leyland by 87 percent. General Electric, Anaconda Copper, Coca-Cola, Unilever, and IBM were all severely hit, with IBM shares losing 50 percent of their value.[133] In real terms, share prices in the United Kingdom fell to wartime levels.[134] Frustration of popular expectations generated acute social and political pressures in several countries. In Britain, public spending was slashed and a three-day work week was instituted to save energy. Following a bitter struggle with striking miners, Edward Heath's Conservatives were defeated in March 1974 and replaced by Labour. I.E. Gur'ev and A.G. Mileikovsky thought progressive forces were everywhere advancing:

> The social-political events of the 1970s, particularly of 1974— including the winning of almost half of the votes by the united left forces in the French presidential elections, defeat of the Conservatives in England, defeat of the clerical-fascist bloc in the Italian referendum, and the collapse of extreme reactionary dictatorships in Portugal and Greece—demonstrate that the

general-democratic movement in the capitalist countries, despite temporary setbacks of its individual detachments, is on the rise.[135]

One country to which this generalization did not apply was the United States. Richard Nixon, for whom Soviet observers had developed considerable grudging respect, resigned in August 1974. By 1975 detente was in disrepute and Gerald Ford even declined to use the term for fear of the negative responses it provoked. The issue upon which Nixon's arrangements with Brezhnev foundered was exactly the one that first made detente possible; that is, availability of credits guaranteed by the American government. Shortly after the first Moscow summit of 1972, Democratic Senator Henry Jackson had linked MFN status and export-import credits with the right of emigration for Soviet Jews. To aid passage of the Trade Reform Bill, in September 1974 Soviet leaders informally agreed to allow sixty thousand to emigrate annually. As signed by President Ford in January 1975, the bill gave MFN status for a period of eighteen months, after which time emigration policy would be reviewed. Having made the emigration concession, Moscow was furious when the Export-Import authorization bill set a limit of $300 million on credits for the next four years and specifically prohibited financing for energy projects.

The credit limitation was of greater importance than appeared on the surface. In most projects, 45 percent of the financing came from the Export-Import Bank, 45 percent from a private American bank, and 10 percent in cash.[136] With credits restricted and energy projects explicitly proscribed, on January 10, 1975, the Soviet government repudiated the trade agreement it had reached with the Nixon administration (including payment of remaining lend-lease obligations). Officially Moscow condemned America for violating the principle of noninterference in domestic affairs. Philip Funigiello summarized the issue in more practical terms: "the Soviets would be eligible for fewer credits over the period 1975-80 than had already been received over [the] past two years, before they had made any concessions at all! It appeared to Moscow as though Congress were putting a ceiling on trade rather than a floor under it."[137]

The Soviet interpretation of Washington's action could have been predicted. Since the mutual benefits of detente appeared to be self-evident, the only possible explanation of its failure was sabotage by Zionists, reactionaries, and the war monopolies, who alone had an interest in Cold War tensions. In July 1973 V.S. Alkhimov, deputy minister of foreign trade, had returned from Washington warning that "military-industrial concerns, various extreme right-wing forces and Zionist elements" would oppose normalization.[138] Yu.N. Kapelinsky claimed that Henry Jackson—the "Senator from Boeing"[139]—was an instrument in the hands of the "military-industrial complex and Zionist circles."[140] V. Korionov wrote of frantic opposition to detente on the part of the CIA, high-ranking Pentagon officers, Senator Barry Goldwater, Professor Zbigniew Brzezinski, "the reactionary AFL-CIO trade union bosses . . . the bigwigs of international Zionism, the nationalist emigre rabble, the neo-fascists and other obscurantists."[141]

In the Soviet view, America was hypocritically applying double standards. Korionov protested that "the cries . . . for 'liberty' and 'democracy' are intended to camouflage subversion against socialist states. . . . [T]he latter-day 'champions of human rights' have failed to condemn . . . the hideous crimes of the fascist generals who have drenched the soil of Chile with the blood of patriots."[142] E.S. Shershnev expressed the same indignation in more measured language:

> The position of the opponents [of detente] . . . is frankly motivated by the idea of using economic relations to put political pressure on the USSR and force it into a revision of certain legal standards and principles (for instance, its emigration policy), which belong to the sphere of its internal relations. This approach is not only a crying violation of the Basic Principles of Mutual Relations between the USSR and the USA agreed upon by the leaders of the two countries in May 1972 but also ignores the following fact: much of what exists or takes place in the United States is quite detestable to the USSR. This, however, has never been viewed as an obstacle to normalizing relations between the two countries.[143]

7. Two Systems and "Deepening of the General Crisis"

Seeing no rational justification for American policy, Soviet writers concluded that extremists had triumphed by exploiting anxieties resulting from the new intensification of capitalism's general crisis. In 1976 N.N. Inozemtsev, E.M. Primakov, and I.E. Gur'ev edited *The Deepening of the General Crisis of Capitalism*. The book revived themes from the 1950s and even the 1930s, but with one notable exception: intensification of capitalist contradictions was now associated with socialism's drive toward global ascendancy. V.A. Babak and B.M. Bolotin set the tone in the opening chapter: socialism had become the "leading force of world development." From 1971 to 1975 industry in the socialist countries had grown four times more quickly than in the west.[144] Collapse of the world capitalist economy had coincided with "failure of the American imperialist adventure in Indochina and the victory of the peoples of Vietnam, Laos and Cambodia."[145]

Describing "cardinal changes in international relations," O.N. Bykov and D.G. Tomashevsky maintained that the new "relation of forces" made it impossible to solve capitalism's problems "on the basis of a common hostility to socialism."[146] Since Stalin's time it had been assumed that imperialists react to crises by preparing war against the socialist camp. That threat now seemed remote: Nixon had accepted nuclear parity, Saigon had fallen, and West Germany had recognized postwar frontiers in Europe. Bykov and Tomashevsky thought "capitalism has had to surrender certain of its positions, to make concessions that go far beyond tactical changes."[147] Capitalism had originally forced the Cold War upon socialism; the "peace-loving policy of the Soviet Union"[148] had now imposed coexistence upon the west. Socialist containment of capitalism meant that contradictions would become steadily more acute *within* the world capitalist system:

> The increasing restriction of the possibilities of resolving interimperialist contradictions at the expense of socialism's interests must affect the internal processes of development in the capitalist world. Continuously reproducing its contradictions, and increasingly deprived of the possibility of resolving them in the broad international arena, monopoly capitalism is compelled to drive them inward—into its own system.[149]

In a chapter on "Intensification of the Contradictions of the World Capitalist Economy," R.N. Andreasyan, V.A. Morozov, E.M. Primakov, and Yu.B. Shishkov equated internalization of world contradictions with the synchronized crisis of 1974-75: "The states of the world capitalist system . . . are coming to resemble a group of mountain climbers, each one tied to the other by a rope: if any one of them stumbles, the security of all the others is threatened."[150] When the crises in energy, food, and materials forced most countries to turn again to anti-inflationary measures, any hope of moderating class struggle through domestic policy seemed futile.

Yu.N. Pokataev referred to an inflation without precedent in peacetime. In 1974 the cost of living rose by a stunning 24.5 percent in Japan, 19.4 percent in Italy, 16 percent in Britain, 13.7 percent in France, 11 percent in the United States, and 7 percent even in West Germany.[151] Industrial production fell from its precrisis peak by roughly the same extent as prices rose: 23 percent in Japan, 19 percent in Italy, 11 percent in Britain, 16 percent in France, 14 percent in America, and 12 percent in Germany. According to Pokataev, world capitalism had entered a catastrophic era in which "the crisis of state anticyclical regulation is an undoubted fact." Simultaneous inflation and unemployment proved

> the impotence of the theory and practice of state-monopoly regulation. In this sense the current crisis can be viewed as the event that completes the long historical period of postwar development of the capitalist economy and, thus, as the beginning of a new period that is inevitably connected with more acute and extensive shocks. . . . As a whole it signifies . . . deepening of . . . [capitalism's] general crisis.[152]

In 1973, A.A. Manukyan had predicted that the time of rapid growth through emergence of new industries was drawing to a close. Each capitalist country now had a "developed economy": "The inevitable result is . . . . [that] the center of gravity moves from problems of production to problems of realization."[153] S.A. Dalin also believed that "a definite stage of the scientific-technical revolution" had ended as early as 1969;[154] the 1970s would not see "the simultaneous rise of a series of new industries as in the '50s and '60s (synthetic fibers, materials, leather, rubber, plastics, electronics, jet aircraft, rockets, satellite communications, high-speed railway transportation, etc.), which served as the basis for the long phase of expansion."[155]

Since 1945 Keynesians and social democrats had regarded economic expansion as the alternative to class struggle. Social peace had been related to the welfare state, in which redistribution of incomes and steady growth replaced demands to socialize property. V.V. Lyubimova and K.G. Kholodovsky argued in *The Deepening of the General Crisis of Capitalism* that growth could no longer control social tensions;[156] the inflation of the 1970s had made any further increase of public spending impossible. Governments were now doing exactly the opposite of what Keynes had recommended, cutting social programs at the same time as they used incomes policies to suppress real wages. Whereas Varga had thought Roosevelt sustained capitalism in the 1930s by devising a new role for the state, Lyubimova and Kholodovsky claimed that the contradictions of state *economic* regulation had finally become *politically* destabilizing.

> The . . . intrusion of the bourgeois state into the sphere of social relations directly touches upon class interests, and for this reason it is difficult to give it the appearance of "impassive" and "impartial" mediation. . . . [T]he very policy that is intended to "regulate" class relations in fact makes them more acute. . . . [T]aking upon itself responsibility for . . . labor relations through "incomes policy", the government also draws upon itself the fire of criticism. "Incomes policy . . . by its very nature 'politicizes' the distribution of incomes. What was previously considered to result from the action of the 'invisible hand' now becomes a question of national policy."[157]

A.V. Anikin (and several coauthors) argued that the Great Depression had confronted capitalists with a choice: either assign regulation to the state or risk revolution. State involvement had delayed revolution, but the prestige of big business had been salvaged at the ultimate expense of the state's own legitimacy. If market forces were no longer held responsible for unemployment, inflation, and declining real incomes, it was to be expected that politicians would be. Anikin agreed with Lyubimova and Kholodovsky; state regulation had become a direct threat to the ruling class.

> When the full extent of the economic disasters of the early 1930s became apparent, it was customary to look for the "guilty parties" on the stock exchange or in the management of big corporations and banks. . . . Now matters are different. In developed capitalist countries the state has officially . . . taken responsibility. . . . It is not surprising . . . that governments are the first to be blamed. . . . The economic shocks of capitalism in the 1970s are inseparable from state activities. State regulation has been unable to prevent or moderate the crisis and in some respects has made it worse.[158]

Anikin saw capitalist governments trapped in a novel and menacing dilemma: anti-inflation measures caused unemployment and declining production; attempts to stimulate growth intensified inflation and jeopardized the social-political order.[159] The result was dramatic inconsistency both in government policies and in economic theory. The decline of Keynesianism had led to revival of "'old-fashioned' conservative conceptions, which look for a solution in return to the 'free market' and 'private initiative', in curtailment of state intervention"[160]—recipes espoused by "reactionary political forces" in some countries, by "fascist tendencies" in others. The only alternative, according to Anikin, was "genuine democratization" through return to a radicalized New Deal:

> The more moderate circles of the bourgeoisie support reforms. . . . The most important historical precedent . . . is the "New Deal" of Roosevelt. . . . In modern conditions the pressure of the broad masses on the ruling circles is stronger. . . . [B]ourgeois-democratic reforms . . . might turn out to be deeper and more radical. But the monopoly bourgeoisie is doing everything possible . . . [to preserve] its domination.[161]

In the 1930s, Varga had argued that Roosevelt's success resulted from divisions within the ruling class. In the mid-1970s, A.G. Mileikovsky thought the same divisions existed: "The right wing of the ruling bourgeoisie is looking for a way out along the lines of a more hardline policy, a sharp increase of executive power and reprisals against the revolutionary forces. . . . The other wing is trying to find the possibility of realizing its class goals in various projects of social reform." The difference between the 1930s and the 1970s was that workers would no longer be satisfied merely with "social maneuvering." The general crisis had deepened because socialist planned economies demonstrated that there was no need for either inflation or unemployment; the ruling classes of the capitalist countries could not "take any essential political decision without keeping in mind the existence of the socialist system" and its attraction for the toilers.[162]

While capitalists remained divided, workers appeared to be more restive than ever before. V.I. Borisyuk (together with several coauthors) thought the 1968 crisis in France had been "the first serious signal of the end of a comparatively 'peaceful' period of social-political life in the capitalist countries, of the onset of a period of storms and shocks."[163] In Britain the miners' struggle in 1974 had become "a clash with the government, the law and the state machine," ending in defeat of the

Heath government after "one of the most acute political crises in the history of the country."[164]

However, the problems of Britain paled beside those of America, where the Watergate affair had caused "loss of prestige for the entire political system."[165] "Defeat" in Vietnam was a crippling blow to institutions that were already in decay. Predicting a wave of "synchronized" social-political crises, Borisyuk portrayed America as a country racked by internal conflict, demoralized by spiritual decay, and incapable of effectively resuming the Cold War.

> Numerous symptoms of social-political instability, the inability of the ruling class . . . to maintain control of the situation, crisis phenomena in the economic, social, cultural and moral-ethical spheres of social life—all have merged into a single enormous complex of problems. Inflation, poverty, unemployment, economic recession, urban overcrowding, environmental pollution, race riots, the increase of crime, the mania over narcotics, the "rebellion of youth", the "hippy" movement, the spiritual impoverishment of society, constitutional conflicts, weakening of the two-party system, growth of the ultra-right danger, political murders, the omnipotence of the CIA, corruption in high places, the "Watergate" scandal, failure of the Vietnam adventure, the first resignation of a president in the history of the USA—all of these have befallen America practically simultaneously.[166]

When Soviet economists looked west from Moscow in the mid-1970s, they saw an America similar to the one Varga had described in the 1930s but also strikingly different. Although both decades had been characterized by severe crisis, modern America seemed prone to self-destruction. During the Great Depression, Americans had turned for solutions to elected authority. In the mid-1970s there was no Franklin Delano Roosevelt in the White House, the new monetarists denied the role Keynesians had ascribed to the state, and the country appeared no longer to have the resources needed to ensure social peace. Lyndon Johnson had referred to America as the "Great Society"; from Moscow it seemed to be a sick and degenerate society.

In terms of global relations between the two systems, Soviet economists and political leaders were convinced that the forces of "peace and democracy" were winning the Cold War. In Khrushchev's time the press had also claimed that socialism was the "decisive factor." When Sputnik demonstrated America's strategic vulnerability, Khrushchev even announced a new stage of the "general crisis." The *rhetoric* of the 1970s was not so novel as the *conviction* behind it. It was one thing to predict socialist victory when Kennedy was in power and America was pioneering the "scientific-technical revolution," quite another to make the same prediction after the collapse of the Bretton Woods system and the resignation of Nixon. In Khrushchev's time, America was criticized but still respected; a decade later, America was viewed with contempt.

After three decades of Cold War and Keynesianism, Soviet leaders had convinced themselves that capitalism was exhausted. Economists were quite aware that the Soviet Union had its own problems with falling growth rates and a technological gap. But compared to the "deepening of the general crisis," conditions in the socialist countries were at least stable after the "normalization" of Czechoslovakia. With the capitalist world imploding, it seemed to Brezhnev that final victory in the Cold War required nothing more than avoiding risks at home while exploiting capitalism's weaknesses when and where they appeared.

In the 1950s American leaders had been determined to "contain" communism and even to roll back the empire that Stalin created in Eastern Europe. Two decades later Soviet analysts thought peaceful coexistence represented the *containment of capitalism*, in which similar possibilities for rolling back the opposing system would surely occur—either through electoral victories on the part of "Eurocommunists" or through "national-liberation" struggles in the third world. When Brezhnev launched his own adventures in Angola, Ethiopia, and Afghanistan, he acted not out of fear of "capitalist encirclement,"[167] but rather in the conviction that capitalism was in historical decline. "Communists," he declared in 1976, "are by no means predicting the 'automatic collapse' of capitalism. It still has considerable reserves. However, events of recent years confirm all the more forcefully that capitalism is a society without a future."[168]

Believing that socialist prodding would accelerate deepening of capitalism's general crisis, Brezhnev continued the militarization of Soviet society and prevented any return to domestic reforms. When Mikhail Gorbachev took office in 1985, he launched *perestroika* with measures similar to those Kosygin had already attempted in the 1960s. Aleksandr N. Yakovlev, a member of the Politburo and adviser to Gorbachev, described *perestroika* in March 1990 as "a revolution through evolution."[169] Yakovlev thought the most fitting analogy was with Roosevelt's New Deal, which reformed the economy while leaving political institutions intact.[170]

Yakovlev's analogy was spurious. Had Varga been alive, he would have pointed out that Brezhnev's militarization deprived the Soviet Union of reserves of "idle" civilian production capacity of the kind that Roosevelt's New Deal helped to reactivate in the 1930s. Western historians would add that there was also a crucial difference in terms of *reserves of political legitimacy.* In the Soviet Union, the existing order collapsed in the minds of citizens long before it disintegrated economically. Rather than being similar, the two experiences were exact opposites.[171] At the close of 1991 the relation of forces changed for the last time. After failing in his effort to modernize the system created by Stalin, Mikhail Gorbachev "resigned" as president, the Soviet Union collapsed, and the coexistence of two systems ended with the terminal crisis of Soviet Marxism.

NOTES

Introduction

1. William Zimmerman, *Soviet Perspectives on International Relations, 1956-1967.* Cf. Morton Schwartz, *Soviet Perceptions of the United States*; Graham D. Vernon, ed., *Soviet Perceptions of War and Peace*; John Lenczowski, *Soviet Perceptions of U.S. Foreign Policy*; Stephen P. Gibert, *Soviet Images of America.*

2. Zbigniew K. Brzezinski, *Ideology and Power in Soviet Politics*, pp. 101-2.

3. The best account of Soviet institutes for research on foreign countries is found in Oded Eran, *The Mezhdunarodniki.*

Chapter 1. Origins of Postwar Soviet Debates

1. Joseph A. Schumpeter, *Capitalism, Socialism and Democracy*, p. 40.

2. Karl Marx, *Capital*, I, 633.

3. *Ibid.*, p. 626.

4. *Ibid.*, p. 631.

5. *Ibid.*, pp. 632-33.

6. *Ibid.*, III, 472; cf. p. 239.

7. *Ibid.*, II, 410-11 (my italics).

8. *Ibid.*, I, 619.

9. *Ibid.*, p. 637.

10. *Ibid.*, II, 467.

11. *Ibid.*, p. 186.

12. *Ibid.*, p. 170.

13. *Ibid.*, III, 251.

14. Marx, *Grundrisse*, p. 414.

15. Marx, *Capital*, II, 315.

16. *Ibid.*, p. 469.

17. *Ibid.*, I, 763.

18. *Ibid.*, III, 118.

19. *Ibid.*

20. *Ibid.*, p. 478.

21. See Engels' introduction to Marx, *The Poverty of Philosophy*, p. 18.

22. Marx, *Capital*, III, 478.

23. *Ibid.*, p. 428.

24. Marx and Engels, *Selected Correspondence*, p. 466.

25. Rosa Luxemburg, *The Accumulation of Capital*, p. 348.

26. *Ibid.*, pp. 351-52.

27. Luxemburg and Bukharin, *Imperialism and the Accumulation of Capital*, p. 58.

28. *Ibid.*, p. 59.

29. See Richard B. Day, "Rosa Luxemburg and the Accumulation of Capital," *Critique*, No. 12 (1979-1980), 81-96.

30. V.I. Lenin, *Collected Works*, I, 100.

31. *Ibid.*, pp. 498-99.

32. *Ibid.*, II, 167.

33. *Ibid.*, III, 66.

34. Engels, *Herr Eugen Duhring's Revolution in Science [Anti-Duhring]*, p. 313.

35. *Ibid.*

36. *Ibid.*, p. 312.

37. Rudolf Hilferding, *Finance Capital*, p. 225.

38. *Ibid.*, p. 230.

39. *Ibid.*, p. 296.

40. *Ibid.*, p. 297.

41. *Ibid.*, pp. 367-68.

42. N.I. Bukharin, "K teorii imperialisticheskovo gosudarstva," *Revolyutsiya prava, sbornik pervyi* (Moscow, 1925), p. 28.

43. *Ibid.*, p. 23.

44. Bukharin, *Ekonomika perekhodnovo perioda*, p. 34.

45. Lenin, *Selected Works*, I, 731.

46. *Ibid.*, p. 806. For a comparison of Lenin and Bukharin, see Day, "Dialectical Method in the Political Writings of Lenin and Bukharin," *Canadian Journal of Political Science*, 9, No. 2 (June, 1976), 244-60.

47. Leon Trotsky, *The First Five Years of the Communist International*, I, 200.

48. *Ibid.*, p. 202.

49. *Ibid.*, pp. 201-2.

50. *Ibid.*, p. 201.

51. *Ibid.*, p. 206.

52. *Ibid.*, pp. 206-7.

53. *Ibid.*, p. 211.

54. Marx, *Capital*, III, 244 (my italics).

55. N.D. Kondrat'ev, *Mirovoe khozyaistvo i evo kon'yunktury vo vremya i posle voiny*, p. 191.

56. See Day, "The Theory of the Long Cycle: Kondrat'ev, Trotsky, Mandel," *New Left Review*, No. 99 (September-October, 1976), 67-82.

57. Lenin, *Collected Works*, XXIX, 165.

58. Bukharin, *Ekonomika perekhodnovo perioda*, p. 39.

59. *Ibid.*, p. 46.

60. Bukharin, *Historical Materialism*, pp. 119-20.

61. Day, *The 'Crisis' and the 'Crash,'* p. 77.

62. *Ibid.*

63. Bukharin, *Imperializm i nakoplenie kapitala*, p. 82.

64. Bukharin, "Questions of International Politics," *International Press Correspondence* [hereafter *IPC*], 6, No. 72 (4 November, 1926), p. 1250.

65. Bukharin, "The World Situation and the Tasks of the Comintern," *IPC*, 6, No. 85 (3 December, 1926), p. 1464.

66. Bukharin, "The International Situation and the Tasks of the Comintern," *IPC*, 8, No. 41 (30 July, 1928), p. 727.

67. I.V. Stalin, *Sochineniya*, VII, 95.

68. *Ibid.*, p. 268.

69. *Ibid.*, X, 49.

70. E.S. Varga, "World Economics at the End of 1925," *IPC*, 6, No. 12 (11 February, 1926), p. 176.

71. *Ibid.*, p. 178.

72. Varga, *Problemy mirovovo khozyaistva i mirovoi politiki*, p. 30.

73. *Ibid.*, p. 54.

74. *Ibid.*, pp. 57-58.

75. Luxemburg, *Accumulation of Capital*, p. 334.

76. Bukharin, "Report on the Programme of the Communist International," *IPC*, 8, No. 56 (27 August, 1928), p. 986.

77. *Ibid.*, p. 985.

78. Bukharin, "Reply to the Debate on the Programme Question," *IPC*, 8, No. 59 (4 September, 1928), pp. 1034-35.

79. Bukharin, "Reply to the Discussion," *IPC*, 8, No. 49 (13 August, 1928), p. 871.

80. See Varga's comments in *IPC*, 8, No. 46 (25 July, 1928), pp. 817-18.

81. Engels' preface to *Capital*, I, 6.

82. See *Mirovoi ekonomicheskii krizis (kollektivnaya rabota Instituta Mirovoi Khozyaistva i Mirovoi Politiki)*, p. 9.

83. Varga, "Mirovoi krizis i evo problemy," *Problemy marksizma*, No. 4-6 (1930), p. 110.

84. Stalin, *Sochineniya*, XII, 235-36.

85. *Ibid.*, p. 240.

86. *Ibid.*, pp. 243-44.

87. Varga, "Economy and Economic Policy," *IPC*, 13, No. 27 (21 June, 1933), p. 587.

88. Varga, "Economy and Economic Policy in the Third Quarter of 1933," *IPC*, 13, No. 53 (6 December, 1933), p. 1198.

89. Varga, "Economy and Economic Policy," *IPC*, 13, No. 27 (21 June, 1933), p. 595.

90. Varga, "Economy and Economic Policy in the Second Quarter of 1933," *IPC*, 13, No. 40 (11 September, 1933), p. 876.

91. Varga, "Economy and Economic Policy in the Third Quarter of 1933," *IPC*, 13, No. 53 (6 December, 1933), p. 1203.

92. Varga, "Economics and Economic Policy in the Third Quarter of 1932," *IPC*, 12, No. 54 (3 December, 1932), p. 1157.

93. Varga, *Novye yavleniya v mirovom ekonomicheskom krizise*, p. 71.

94. Stalin, *Sochineniya*, XIII, 290-91.

95. Varga, "Economy and Economic Policy in the Second Quarter of 1934," *IPC*, 14, No. 49 (17 September, 1934), p. 1280.

96. *Ibid.*, p. 1281.

97. Varga, "Economy and Economic Policy in the Third Quarter of 1934," *IPC*, 14, No. 61 (5 December, 1934), p. 1634.

98. S. Dalin, *Ekonomicheskaya politika Ruzvel'ta*, p. 231.

99. Varga, "Kapitalisticheskoe khozyaistvo v pervoi polovine 1937g," *Mirovoe khozyaistvo i mirovaya politika* [hereafter *Mir.khoz.*], No. 8 (August, 1937), p. 57.

100. Varga, "K ekonomicheskomu polozheniyu v SShA," *Kommunisticheskii internatsional*, No. 5 (May, 1937), p. 44.

101. Varga, "Nachalo novovo ekonomicheskovo krizisa v stranakh kapitala," *Bol'shevik*, No. 23-24 (15 December, 1937), p. 61.

102. Varga, *Kapitalizm i sotsializm za 20 let*, p. 65.

103. *Ibid.*, pp. 80-81.

104. Varga, *Kapitalisticheskii mir na poroge novovo krizisa*, pp. 19-20.

105. Luxemburg, *Accumulation of Capital*, p. 454.

106. Varga, "Economy and Economic Policy in the Second Quarter of 1938," *World News and Views*, 18, No. 43 (9 September, 1938), pp. 988-89.

107. Stalin, "Report on the Activity of the CC of the CPSU," *World News and Views*, 19, No. 16 (29 March, 1939), p. 314.

108. Varga, "Economy and Economic Policy in the Second Half-Year 1938," *World News and Views*, 19, No. 13 (23 March, 1939), p. 254.

109. Varga, "Economy and Economic Policy in the First Half of 1939," *World News and Views*, 19, No. 48 (7 October, 1939), p. 1019.

110. Varga, "Economy and Economic Policy in the Second Half-Year 1938," *World News and Views*, 19, No. 13 (23 March, 1939), pp. 263-64.

111. J.M. Keynes, *The General Theory of Employment, Interest and Money*, p. 129.

Chapter 2. Postwar Capitalism: Fascism or a New Deal?

1. Robert C. Tucker, ed., *The Marx-Engels Reader*, p. 475.

2. Joseph Stalin, *Selected Interviews*, pp. 112-14.

3. Varga, "Protsess istoshcheniya khozyaistvennykh resursov Germanii," *Kommunisticheskii internatsional*, No. 8 (August, 1941), p. 18.

4. Varga, "Gitlerovskii rezhim priblizhaetsya k katastrofe," *Mir.khoz.*, No. 1-2 (January-February, 1942), p. 25.

5. Varga, "Oslablenie Germanii i ee armii v khode voiny," *Bol'shevik*, No. 11-12 (June, 1942), p. 70.

6. See the review by M. Myznikov in *Mir.khoz.*, No. 11 (1940), pp. 104-7.

7. S. Vishnev, "Voina lyudskikh i material'nykh rezervov," *Mir.khoz.*, No. 7 (July, 1941), p. 30.

8. A. Leont'ev, "Fashistskaya 'total'naya voina'," *Bol'shevik*, No. 19 (September, 1941), p. 31; cf. Vishnev, "Istoshchenie lyudskikh i material'nykh resursov Germanii," *Mir.khoz.*, No. 1-2 (January-February, 1942), p. 42.

9. I.M. Lemin, "Ekonomika Anglii na tret'em godu voiny," *Mir.khoz.*, No. 3-4 (March-April, 1942), p. 56.

10. Stalin, *Sochineniya*, 2 [XV], pp. 34-35.

11. *Ibid.*, p. 50.

12. *Ibid.*, p. 66; cf. p. 79.

13. Vishnev, "Tri goda voiny," *Mir.khoz.*, No. 9 (September, 1942), p. 14.

14. Vishnev, "Mobilizatsiya ekonomicheskikh resursov vpervoi i vo vtoroi mirovoi voine," *Bol'shevik*, No. 1 (January, 1943), p. 64.

15. Varga, ed., *Istoshchenie ekonomicheskikh resursov fashistskoi Germanii*, p. 9; cf. Varga, "Voennaya ekonomika Germanii ser'ezno oslablena," *Pravda* (28 June, 1943); also Varga, *Izmeneniya v ekonomike kapitalizma v itoge vtoroi mirovoi voiny*, pp. 77, 127, 162, 201.

16. Varga, "Voennyi potentsial Soedinennykh Shtatov Ameriki," *Pravda* (18 June, 1942).

17. E. Gurvich, "Voennaya ekonomika SShA," *Mir.khoz.*, No. 10-11 (October-November, 1943)), p. 45.

18. *Ibid.*, p. 49.

19. *Ibid.*, p. 40.

20. *Ibid.*, p. 49.

21. I. Trakhtenberg, "Imperialisticheskaya voina i finansy," *Mir.khoz.*, No. 4-5 (April-May, 1940), p. 50.

22. Varga, "Ob izmeneniyakh v kapitalisticheskom khozyaistve vo vremya voiny," *Kommunisticheskii internatsional*, No. 2 (February, 1941), p. 24.

23. *Ibid.*, p. 25.

24. *Ibid.*, p. 22.

25. *Ibid.*, p. 25.

26. Varga, *Izmeneniya v ekonomike kapitalizma*, p. 15.

27. *Ibid.*, pp. 253-54.

28. *Ibid.*, p. 38.

29. *Ibid.*, pp. 88-89.

30. *Ibid.*, p. 253.

31. *Ibid.*, p. 263.

32. *Ibid.*, p. 262.

33. *Ibid.*, p. 268.

34. *Ibid.*, pp. 269-70.

35. *Ibid.*, p. 300.

36. *Ibid.*, pp. 299-300.

37. *Ibid.*, p. 37.

38. *Ibid.*, p. 318.

39. Varga, "Demokratiya novovo tipa," *Mir.khoz.*, No. 3 (March, 1947), p. 5.

40. M. Smit, "Natsionalizatsiya angliiskovo banka i ugol'noi promyshlennosti," *Novoe vremya*, No. 2 (15 January, 1946), p. 7; cf. Smit, *Polozhenie rabochevo klassa SShA, Anglii i Frantsii posle vtoroi mirovoi voiny*, ch. 6; also Smit in L.N. Ivanov, O.V.Kuusinen, V.P. Glushkov, eds., *Pravye leiboristy na sluzhbe angliiskovo i amerikanskovo imperializma*, pp. 101-41.

41. D. Zorina, "Bor'ba vokrug natsionalizatsii promyshlennosti v Anglii," *Mir.khoz.*, No. 9 (September, 1946), p. 42.

42. L.A. Mendel'son, "Poslevoennye protivorechiya kapitalisticheskovo khozyaistva," *Mir.khoz.*, No. 5 (May, 1947), p. 38.

43. L.Ya. Eventov, *Voennaya ekonomika Anglii*, p. 153; cf. p. 95.

44. *Ibid.*, p. 211; cf. Eventov in I. Trakhtenberg, ed., *Voennoe khozyaistvo kapitalisticheskikh stran i perekhod k mirnoi ekonomike*, p. 60.

45. Eventov, *Voennaya ekonomika Anglii*, p. 6.

46. *Ibid.*, p. 7.

47. Sh. Lif in Trakhtenberg, ed., *Voennoe khozyaistvo kapitalisticheskikh stran*, p. 130.

48. E. Shifrin, "Apologetika kapitalizma pod vidom teorii 'planirovaniya,'" *Mir.khoz.*, No. 9 (September, 1946), p. 122.

49. See V. Cheprakov's review of K.E. Boulding, *The Economics of Peace*, in *Mir.khoz.*, No. 7-8 (July-August, 1946), p. 120.

50. Eventov, *Voennaya ekonomika Anglii*, p. 270.

51. Trakhtenberg, ed., *Voennoe khozyaistvo kapitalisticheskikh stran*, p. 33.

52. L. Mendel'son, "Burzhuaznaya nauka v poiskakh putei spaseniya kapitalizma ot krizisov," *Mir.khoz.*, No. 2 (February, 1947), p. 44.

53. I. Blyumin, "Problemy polnoi zanyatosti v sovremennoi angliiskoi ekonomicheskoi literature," *Mir.khoz.*, No. 4 (April, 1947), p. 82; cf. Blyumin, "Sovremennaya burzhuaznaya politicheskaya ekonomiya v Anglii," *Bol'shevik*, No. 10 (May, 1947), p. 42.

54. Blyumin, "Problemy polnoi zanyatosti . . .," p. 83.

55. Blyumin, " Sovremennaya burzhuaznaya politicheskaya ekonomiya . . .," p. 53.

56. See Varga's account of the European parties in "Osobennosti vnutrennei i vneshnei politiki kapitalisticheskikh stran v epokhu obshchevo krizisa kapitalizma," *Mir.khoz.*, No. 6 (June, 1946), pp. 12-13.

57. See Varga, *Izmeneniya v ekonomike kapitalizma*, p. 270.

58. M. Rubinshtein, "Ugroza massovoi bezrabotitsy v Soedinennykh Shtatakh," *Novoe vremya*, No. 3 [13] (1 July, 1945), p. 20.

59. V. Lan, "Rekonversiya i problema bezrabotitsy v SShA," *Mir.khoz.*, No. 12 (December, 1945), p. 37.

60. *Ibid.*, p. 46.

61. *Ibid.*, p. 44.

62. V. Lan, "Vnutripoliticheskoe polozhenie v SShA posle voiny," *Mir. khoz.*, No. 12 (December, 1946), p. 18.

63. *Ibid.*, p. 27.

64. *Ibid.*, p. 20.

65. *Ibid.*, pp. 24-25. According to Bert G. Hickman in *Growth and Stability of the Postwar Economy*, p. 70, inflation reduced the value of savings by 15 percent between the end of 1945 and 1947.

66. N. Sergeeva, "K itogam vyborov v Soedinennykh Shtatakh," *Novoe vremya*, No. 22 (15 November, 1946), p. 8.

67. *Ibid.*, p. 7.

68. *Ibid.*

69. See Stalin's interview of 21 December, 1946, with *Look* magazine reprinted in *Bol'shevik*, No. 1 (January, 1947), p. 3.

70. Walter LaFeber, *America, Russia, and the Cold War*, p. 39.

71. A. Georgiev, "O knige Elliota Ruzvel'ta 'Evo glazami,'" *Bol'shevik*, No. 4 (February, 1947), pp. 63-64.

72. I. Lemin, "Vneshnyaya politika SShA na sovremennom etape," *Mir.khoz.*, No. 4 (April, 1947), p. 7; cf. Lemin, "Mezhdunarodnye otnosheniya v 1945 godu," *ibid.*, No. 1-2 (January-February, 1946), 20-34; also Lemin, "Dva krizisa kapitalisticheskoi sistemy," *Ibid.*, No. 4-5 (April-May, 1946), 7-22.

73. Lemin, "Vneshnyaya politika SShA . . .," p. 10.

74. *Ibid.*, p. 8.

75. *Ibid.*, p. 11.

76. *Ibid.*, p. 12.

77. A. Leontyev, "American Expansion, Past and Present," *New Times*, No. 23 (6 June, 1947), pp. 3-8.

78. V. Cheprakov, "Sovremennoe ekonomicheskoe polozhenie SShA," *Bol'shevik*, No. 9 (May, 1947), p. 38.

79. *Ibid.*, pp. 39-40.

80. *Ibid.*, p. 43.

81. *Ibid.*, p. 46.

82. *Ibid.*, p. 44.

83. *Ibid.*, p. 46.

84. *Ibid.*, pp. 35-36.

85. Ibid., pp. 37-38; cf. M. Smit's review of Eventov, *Voennaya ekonomika Anglii* in *Sovetskaya kniga*, No. 1 (January, 1947), p. 96.

86. Cheprakov, "Sovremennoe ekonomicheskoe polozhenie SShA," p. 48.

87. Varga, "Demokratiya novovo tipa," *Mir.khoz.*, No. 3 (March, 1947), p. 13.

88. *Ibid.*, p. 9.

89. See "Diskussiya po knige E. Varga 'Izmeneniya v ekonomike kapitalizma v itoge vtoroi mirovoi voiny'," Mir.khoz., No. 11 (November, 1947), p. 3.

90. *Ibid.*, p. 4.

91. *Ibid.*, p. 6.

92. *Ibid.*, p. 34.

93. *Ibid.*, p. 19.

94. *Ibid.*, p. 13.

95. *Ibid.*, p. 50.

96. Lenin, *Selected Works*, I, 731.

97. See "Diskussiya po knige E. Varga . . .," p. 10

98. *Ibid.*, p. 44.

99. *Ibid.*, p. 33.

100. *Ibid.*, p. 23.

101. *Ibid.*, p. 24.

102. *Ibid.*, p. 39.

103. *Ibid.*, p. 48.

104. *Ibid.*, p. 53.

105. *Ibid.*, p. 18.

106. *Ibid.*, p. 56.

107. *Ibid.*

108. *Ibid.*

109. *Ibid.*, p. 60.

110. *Ibid.*

111. *Ibid.*, p. 61.

112. *Ibid.*, p. 60.

113. Stalin, *Sochineniya*, 3 [XVI], 3.

114. Lemin, "Dva krizisa kapitalisticheskoi sistemy," *Mir.khoz.*, No. 4-5 (April-May, 1946), p. 8.

115. *Ibid.*, p. 21.

116. See Day, *Leon Trotsky and the Politics of Economic Isolation*, p. 124.

117. Varga, *Plan Dauesa i mirovoi krizis 1924 goda*, p. 72.

118. See, for example, the unsigned editorial "Rehabilitation or a Dawes Plan for Europe," *New Times*, No. 28 (11 July, 1947), pp. 1-3.

119. *Ibid.*, p. 2.

120. A. Zhdanov, "O mezhdunarodnom polozhenii," *Bol'shevik*, No. 20 (October, 1947), p. 14.

121. *Ibid.*, p. 18.

122. *Ibid.*, p. 13.

123. *Ibid.*, p. 21.

124. Varga, "Bor'ba i sotrudnichestvo mezhdu SShA i Angliei," *Mir.khoz.*, No. 8 (August, 1947), p. 11.

125. *Ibid.*, p. 9.

126. Varga, *"Plan Marshalla" i ekonomika Anglii i SShA*, p. 12.

127. *Ibid.*, p. 14; cf. Varga, "The Marshall Plan and the Approaching Economic Crisis in America," *New Times*, No. 39 (24 September, 1949), pp. 5-7.

128. Varga, *"Plan Marshalla" i ekonomika Anglii i SShA*, p. 7.

129. Varga, "Sotsializm i kapitalizm za tridtsat' let," *Mir.khoz.*, No. 10 (October, 1947), pp. 5-6.

130. *Ibid.*, p. 21.

131. *Ibid.*, p. 19.

132. *Ibid.*, p. 10.

133. I. Gladkov, "Ob izmeneniyakh v ekonomike kapitalizma v rezul'tate vtoroi mirovoi voiny," *Bol'shevik*, No. 7 (15 September, 1947), p. 59.

134. *Ibid.*, p. 60.

135. *Ibid.*, p. 61.

136. *Ibid.*, p. 64.

137. K.V. Ostrovityanov, "Ob itogakh i napravlenii raboty Instituta Ekonomiki Akademii Nauk SSSR," *Voprosy ekonomiki*, No. 1 (March, 1948), pp. 88-89.

138. *Ibid.*, p. 89.

139. *Ibid.*, p. 91.

140. See L. Gatovsky, "V plenu burzhuaznoi ideologii," *Bol'shevik*, No. 15 (15 March, 1948), pp. 74-80.

141. See "Ot redaktsii," *Voprosy ekonomiki*, No. 1 (March, 1948), pp. 3-4.

142. N.V. Voznesensky, *Voennaya ekonomika SSSR v period otechestvennoi voiny*, p. 31.

143. *Ibid.*, p. 172.

144. See "Protiv antimarksistskovo osveshcheniya ekonomiki kapitalisticheskikh stran," *Voprosy ekonomiki*, No. 2 (April, 1948), p. 114.

145. *Ibid.*, p. 166.

146. See "O nedostatkakh i zadachakh nauchno-issledovatel'skoi raboty v oblasti ekonomiki," *Voprosy ekonomiki*, No. 8 (October, 1948), p. 71.

147. *Ibid.*, No. 9 (November, 1948), p. 56.

148. *Ibid.*, p. 57.

149. *Ibid.*, p. 96.

150. See "Rasshirennaya sessiya uchenovo soveta Instituta Ekonomiki Akademii Nauk SSSR," *Voprosy ekonomiki*, No. 3 (March, 1949), p. 116.

151. *Ibid.*

152. Varga, "Protiv reformistskovo napravleniya v rabotakh po imperializmu," *Voprosy ekonomiki*, No. 3 (March, 1949), p. 79.

153. *Ibid.*, p. 83.

154. *Ibid.*, p. 81.

155. *Ibid.*, p. 88.

156. Cheprakov, "Sovremennoe ekonomicheskoe polozhenie SShA," *Bol'-shevik*, No. 9 (May, 1947), p. 37.

157. Lif, "Finansovyi kapital i finansovaya oligarkhiya SShA," *Mir.khoz.*, No. 5 (May, 1947), p. 65.

158. A. Leontyev, "Economic Foundations of American Expansionism," *New Times*, No. 29 (16 July, 1947), p. 5.

159. M. Rubinshtein, "Kontsentratsiya ekonomicheskoi moshchi i protivorechiya amerikanskovo kapitalizma," *Mir.khoz.*, No. 6 (June, 1947), p. 85.

160. V. Lan, "Aktivizatsiya reaktsii v SShA," *Mir.khoz.*, No. 7 (July, 1947), pp. 19-20. For the Taft-Hartley Act of 1947 and U.S. labor law in the 1950s see Harold G. Vatter, *The U.S. Economy in the 1950's*, pp. 237-40.

161. Lan, "Aktivizatsiya . . .," p. 23.

162. *Ibid.*, p. 25.

163. Y. Minayev, "American Reaction and Its Struggle Against Democracy," *New Times*, No. 32 (6 August, 1947), p. 8.

164. I. Kuz'minov, "Kapitalisticheskie monopolii i voina (po povodu knigi Dzheimsa Allena 'Mezhdunarodnye monopolii i mir'," *Bol'shevik*, No. 20 (30 October, 1947), p. 81.

165. Lif, "Obnishchanie proletariata v usloviyakh obshchevo krizisa kapitalizma," *Mir.khoz.*, No. 10 (October, 1947), p. 73.

166. A. Shapiro, "Rost bezrabotitsy v kapitalisticheskikh stranakh v poslevoennyi period," *Voprosy ekonomiki*, No. 9 (September, 1949), p. 80.

167. N. Sergeyeva, "One Thousand Americans," *New Times*, No. 8 (18 February, 1948), pp. 24-25.

168. Smit, "Snizhenie real'noi zarabotnoi platy rabochevo klassa SShA posle vtoroi mirovoi voiny," *Voprosy ekonomiki*, No. 5 (May, 1949), p. 55.

169. *Ibid.*, p. 60.

170. Cheprakov, "Demokraticheskie sily SShA v bor'be protiv reaktsii," *Voprosy ekonomiki*, No. 5 (July, 1948), pp. 53-54.

171. Cheprakov, "Prinuditel'nyi trud v stranakh kapitala," *Bol'shevik*, No. 5 (15 March, 1949), p. 58.

172. *Ibid.*, pp. 62-63.

173. *Ibid.*, p. 64.

174. *Ibid.*, p. 61.

175. Cheprakov, "Narastanie novovo ekonomicheskovo krizisa v kapitalisticheskom mire," *Bol'shevik*, No. 13 (15 July, 1949), pp. 50-51.

176. See *Soveshchanie informatsionnovo byuro kommunisticheskikh partii v Vengrii vo vtoroi polovine noyabrya 1949 goda* (Moscow: Gosudarstvennoe Izdatel'stvo Politicheskoi Literatury, 1949), p. 54.

177. *Ibid.*, p. 47.

Chapter 3. Stalin's Legacy: Peaceful Coexistence or the Inevitability of War?

1. Quoted in Morton Schwartz, *Soviet Perceptions of the United States*, p. 2.

2. Hilferding, *Finance Capital*, p. 256.

3. *Ibid.*, p. 242.

4. Spektator, "Teoriya krizisov Marksa," *Pod znamenem marksizma*, No. 2 (February, 1928), p. 97.

5. *Ibid.*, p. 96.

6. *Ibid.*, p. 101.

7. *Ibid.*, p. 100.

8. See Lyusin's comments in *Problemy ekonomiki*, No. 3 (March, 1929), p. 127.

9. M.N. Smit, *Dinamika krizisov i polozhenie proletariata*, p. 124.

10. M. Gol'man, *Vseobshchii krizis kapitalizma v svete vzglyadov Marksa-Engel'sa i Lenina*, p. 37.

11. For Preobrazhensky's views see Day, *The 'Crisis' and the 'Crash,'* ch. 7; also Preobrazhensky, *The Decline of Capitalism*.

12. E.A. Preobrazhensky, *Zakat kapitalizma*, p. 38.

13. *Ibid.*, p. 8.

14. *Ibid.*, p. 24.

15. *Ibid.*, p. 110.

16. E. Gromov, "Reviziya Marksa i Lenina pod flagom teoreticheskovo 'sinteza'," *Mir.khoz.*, No. 4 (April, 1931), p. 68.

17. Gromov, "K probleme kapitalisticheskovo tsikla v epokhe vseobshchevo krizisa," *Problemy ekonomiki*, No. 9 (September, 1931), p. 93.

18. See Gurvich in G. Roginsky, ed., *Zakat kapitalizma v trotskistskom zerkale*, p. 67.

19. *Ibid.*, pp. 68-69.

20. I. Dvorkin, "Trotskistskaya teoriya krizisov i imperializma," *Pod znamenem marksizma*, No. 1-2 (January-February, 1932), p. 61.

21. A. Breitman, "Zakat kapitalizma v krivom trotskistskom zerkale," *Mir.khoz.*, No. 10-12 (October-December, 1931), p. 80.

22. See *Problemy mirovovo krizisa—Diskussiya v Institute Mirovovo Khozyaistva i Mirovoi Politiki Komakademii*, Moscow, 1932, pp. 47-48.

23. I.A. Trakhtenberg, *Kapitalisticheskoe vosproizvodstvo i ekonomicheskie krizisy*, p. 71.

24. *Ibid.*, p. 70.

25. *Ibid.*, p. 97.

26. *Ibid.*, p. 29.

27. Stalin, *Sochineniya*, XII, 243-44.

28. Trakhtenberg, *Kapitalisticheskoe vosproizvodstvo*, pp. 62-63.

29. *Ibid.*, p. 102.

30. *Ibid.*, p. 104.

31. *Ibid.*, p. 114.

32. P.K. Figurnov, *Kapitalisticheskoe vosproizvodstvo i ekonomicheskie krizisy*, p. 5 (Figurnov's book had the same title as Trakhtenberg's).

33. *Ibid.*, p. 16.

34. *Ibid.*, pp. 17-18.

35. *Ibid.*, p. 27.

36. *Ibid.*, p. 71.

37. *Ibid.*, p. 43.

38. *Ibid.*, p. 50.

39. Ibid., p. 53; cf. Lenin, *Collected Works*, II, 168.

40. L. Mendel'son, *Ekonomicheskie tsikly i krizisy XIX veka*, p. 12.

41. Mendel'son, "Poslevoennye protivorechiya kapitalisticheskovo khozyaistva," *Mir.khoz.*, No. 5 (May, 1947), p. 22; cf. Mendel'son, "Krizisy i tsikly v epokhu obshchevo krizisa kapitalizma," *Mir.khoz.*, No. 11 (October, 1947), p. 72.

42. Mendel'son, "Poslevoennye protivorechiya . . .," p. 20.

43. Mendel'son, "Krizisy i tsikly . . .," p. 61.

44. *Ibid.*, pp. 70-71.

45. *Ibid.*, p. 74.

46. F. Polyansky, "Protiv izvrashcheniya marksistsko-leninskoi teorii i istorii ekonomicheskikh krizisov," *Voprosy ekonomiki*, No. 8 (August, 1950), p. 121.

47. "O ser'eznykh oshibkakh v knigakh po teorii i istorii ekonomicheskikh krizisov," *Pravda* (29 September, 1950).

48. See "Za marksistsko-leninskuyu razrabotku voprosov teorii i istorii ekonomicheskikh krizisov," *Voprosy ekonomiki*, No. 11 (November, 1950), p. 86.

49. *Ibid.*, p. 92.

50. *Ibid.*, p. 102.

51. *Ibid.*, p. 105.

52. *Ibid.*, p. 98.

53. *Ibid.*

54. *Ibid.*, p. 105; cf. pp. 100-1.

55. *Ibid.*, p. 100.

56. *Ibid.*

57. Stalin, *Sochineniya*, XIII, 197.

58. Guttsait, "Fakty i tsifry ob 'Amerikanskom obraze zhizni'," *Voprosy ekonomiki*, No. 6 (June, 1950), pp. 127-28; cf. Smit, *Polozhenie rabochevo klassa*, pp. 120-33 on female and child labor in the U.S. and U.K.

59. Guttsait, "Novye svidetel'stva obostreniya protivorechiya amerikanskovo imperializma," *Voprosy ekonomiki*, No. 6 (August, 1948), p. 130.

60. Stalin, *Problems of Leninism*, pp. 749-50.

61. A. Manukyan, "The Economic Situation in the United States," *New Times*, No. 21 (18 May, 1949), p. 14.

62. *Ibid.*, p. 13.

63. *Ibid.*, p. 11.

64. Smit, "Snizhenie real'noi zarabotnoi platy rabochevo klassa SShA posle vtoroi mirovoi voiny," *Voprosy ekonomiki*, No. 5 (May, 1949), p. 50. By 1953 Smit recalculated the number of Americans unemployed in 1948 to be 12.888 million, rising to 16.064 million in 1950! See Smit, *Polozhenie rabochevo klassa*, p. 25.

65. Smit, "Snizhenie real'noi zarabotnoi platy . . .," p. 54. According to the same author, by 1951 U.S. real wages were at 59.6 percent of the 1939 level. See Smit, *Polozhenie rabochevo klassa*, p. 56.

66. Cheprakov, "Narastanie novovo ekonomicheskovo krizisa v kapitalisticheskom mire," *Bol'shevik*, No. 13 (15 July, 1949), p. 46.

67. *Ibid.*, p. 51.

68. *Ibid.*, pp. 54-55.

69. A. Shneerson, "Stalin o krizisakh kapitalisticheskoi sistemy mirovovo khozyaistva," *Voprosy ekonomiki*, No. 1 (January, 1950), p. 54.

70. *Ibid.*, p. 64.

71. *Ibid.*, p. 58.

72. *Ibid.*, p. 57.

73. *Ibid.*, p. 66.

74. Manukyan, "The Capitalist World Heads for a War Economy," *New Times*, No. 35 (30 August, 1950), p. 7.

75. Manukyan, "Rearmament Cannot Fend Off Crisis," *New Times*, No. 1 (1 January, 1952), p. 15.

76. *Ibid.*, p. 16 (my italics).

77. Harold G. Vatter, *The U.S. Economy in the 1950's*, p. 89.

78. Bert G. Hickman, *Growth and Stability of the Postwar Economy*, pp. 94-96.

79. Manukyan, "Rearmament Cannot Fend Off Crisis," p. 17.

80. Cheprakov, "Militarizatsiya ekonomiki SShA," Voprosy ekonomiki, No. 11 (November, 1950), p. 64.

81. *Ibid.*, p. 70.

82. Trakhtenberg, "Banki SShA na sluzhbe militarizma," *Voprosy ekonomiki*, No. 8 (August, 1951), p. 105.

83. B. Vronsky, "Fashizatsiya obshchestvenno-politicheskoi zhizni v SShA," *Voprosy ekonomiki*, No. 9 (September, 1950), p. 56.

84. *Ibid.*, p. 59.

85. *Ibid.*, p. 62.

86. *Ibid.*, p. 67.

87. Vronsky, "Obnishchanie trudyashchikhsya v Soedinennykh Shtatakh Ameriki," *Bol'shevik*, No. 20 (October, 1950), p. 56.

88. A. Bechin, "Razgul militarizma i obostrenie protivorechii v kapital-isticheskikh stranakh," *Voprosy ekonomiki*, No. 3 (March, 1951), p. 91.

89. *Ibid.*, p. 92.

90. *Ibid.*, p. 100.

91. According to Harold G. Vatter, from 1950 to 1953 the real net value of equipment in U.S. industry grew by 19 percent, of structures by 11 percent. See *The American Economy in the 1950's*, p. 86.

92. I. Kuz'minov, "Keins—ideolog imperialisticheskoi reaktsii i voiny," *Bol'shevik*, No. 19 (October, 1951), pp. 49-50.

93. Lenin, *Collected Works*, XXXI, 451.

94. Keynes, *The Economic Consequences of the Peace*, pp. 292-93.

95. See Stalin's resolution in *Chetyrnadtsatyi s'ezd Vsesoyuznoi Kommunisticheskoi Partii (Bol'shevikov)*, Moscow, 1926, p. 958; also his speech in the same volume, pp. 11 and 28.

96. Stalin, *Sochineniya*, XII, 255.

97. M. Litvinov, "Speech at the World Economic Conference," *IPC*, 13, No. 28 (23 June, 1933), p. 616.

98. Stalin, *Sochineniya*, XIII, 276-77. Roosevelt did set up the Export-Import Bank in 1934 primarily to finance trade with the USSR. See Marshall I. Goldman, *Detente and Dollars*, p. 41.

99. W.M. Scammell, *The International Economy Since 1945*, p. 41.

100. Quoted in Philip Armstrong, Andrew Glyn, and John Harrison, *Capitalism Since 1945*, p. 5.

101. Quoted in Thomas G. Paterson, *Soviet-American Confrontation*, p. 35.

102. *Ibid.*

103. *Ibid.*, p. 37. In January 1945 *Fortune* magazine estimated that for two to three years after the war, Soviet-American trade could amount to $5 billion, later settling at $2 billion per year. In 1945 Treasury Secretary Morgenthau proposed a $10 billion credit to the USSR. See E.S. Shershnev, *On the Principle of Mutual Advantage*, p. 51.

104. Varga, "Plans for Post-War Currency Stabilization," *Commercial and Financial Chronicle*, Vol. 159, No. 4260 (2 March, 1944), p. 919.

105. K. Velikanov, "Amerikanskie monopolii i vneshnyaya politika Soedinennykh Shtatov," *Novoe vremya*, No. 20 (15 October, 1946), pp. 9-10.

106. Varga, "Antiamerikanskie techeniya v angliiskoi politike," *Pravda* (15 February, 1947).

107. Varga, "The Geneva Trade Talks," *New Times*, No. 20 (16 May, 1947), p. 9.

108. *Izvestiya* (11 February, 1992).

109. Stalin, *Sochineniya*, 3 [XVI], 53.

110. "Zhurnal 'Luk' opublikoval interv'yu tovarishcha Stalina s Elliotom Ruzvel'tom," *Bol'shevik*, No. 1 (January, 1947), pp. 3-4.

111. Stalin, *Sochineniya*, 3 [XVI], 104.

112. *Ibid.*, p. 107.

113. "Beseda t. Stalina I.V. s korrespondentom 'Pravdy'," *Bol'shevik*, No. 4 (February, 1951), p. 4.

114. Quoted in Philip J. Funigiello, *American-Soviet Trade in the Cold War*, p. 41.

115. *Ibid.*, p. 78.

116. *Ibid.*, pp. 48-49.

117. Quoted in G, Parkhomenko, "East-West Trade," *New Times*, No. 3 (16 January, 1952), p. 15.

118. N. Osipenko, "What Normal International Trade Could Bring," *New Times*, No. 11 (12 March, 1952), p. 13.

119. *Ibid.*, p. 14.

120. *Ibid.*

121. R. Solodkin, "Some Aspects of Anglo-Soviet Trade," *New Times*, No. 13 (26 March, 1952), p. 5.

122. "Za vsestoronnee razvitie mezhdunarodnovo ekonomicheskovo sotrudnichestva," *Voprosy ekonomiki*, No. 3 (March, 1952), p. 7.

123. *Ibid.*, p. 6.

124. *Ibid.*, p. 10.

125. *Ibid.*, p. 16; cf. Goldman, *Detente and Dollars*, p. 18.

126. Ya. Kotkovsky, "Rasshirenie ekonomicheskikh svyazei i vozmozhnosti povysheniya zanyatosti v kapitalisticheskikh stranakh," *Voprosy ekonomiki*, No. 3 (March, 1952), p. 36.

127. A. Smirnov, "Normalizatisya mezhdunarodnykh ekonomicheskikh svyazei i valyutnaya problema," *Voprosy ekonomiki*, No. 3 (March, 1952), p. 47.

128. P. Yefanov, "International Economic Cooperation and Increased Employment," *New Times*, No. 14 (12 April, 1952), p. 11.

129. E. Shershnyov, "The Soviet Union and International Trade," *New Times*, No. 14 (12 April, 1952), pp. 4-5.

130. Stalin, *Sochineniya*, 3 [XVI], 305-6.

131. "Speech by M.V. Nesterov," *New Times* (supplement), No. 15 (9 April, 1952), p. 4.

132. See Nesterov's proposal for "reciprocal commodity deliveries," *ibid.*, p. 7.

133. "Communique of the International Economic Conference in Moscow," *New Times*, No. 16 (16 April, 1952), pp. 3-4.

134. G.V. Kozlov, "Obshchii krizis kapitalizma i evo obostrenie na sovremennom etape," *Voprosy ekonomiki*, No. 4 (April, 1952), pp. 74-75.

135. *Ibid.*, pp. 76-77.

136. *Ibid.*, p. 78.

137. *Ibid.*, p. 85.

138. *Ibid.*, p. 79.

139. *Ibid.*, pp. 83-84.

140. *Ibid.*, p. 85.

141. "Vazhnyi shag na puti razvertyvaniya mezhdunarodnoi torgovli," *Voprosy ekonomiki*, No. 5 (May, 1952), pp. 13-14.

142. A. Alekseev, "Usilenie parazitizma i zagnivaniya sovremennovo kapitalizma," *Voprosy ekonomiki*, No. 5 (May, 1952), p. 59.

143. Cheprakov, "Neravnomernost' razvitiya kapitalisticheskikh stran i obostrenie protivorechii mezhdu nimi," *Bol'shevik*, No. 9 (May, 1952), p. 40.

144. *Ibid.*, p. 43.

145. *Ibid.*

146. *Ibid.*, p. 39.

147. *Ibid.*, p. 53.

148. See Malenkov's report to the XIX party congress in *Pravda* (6 October, 1952).

149. *Ibid.* (my italics).

150. Stalin, *Sochineniya*, 3 [XVI], 230.

151. *Ibid.*, p. 228.

152. *Ibid.*, p. 231.

153. *Ibid.*, p. 224.

154. *Ibid.*, p. 223.

155. *Ibid.*, p. 225.

Chapter 4. Malenkov's "New Deal" and the "General Crisis" of Stalinism

1. Robert C. Tucker, ed., *Marx-Engels Reader*, p. 595.

2. Stalin, *Sochineniya*, 3 [XVI], 192.

3. *Ibid.*, p. 197.

4. *Ibid.*, p. 234.

5. *Ibid.*, p. 236.

6. *Pravda* (9 August, 1953).

7. *Pravda* (7 December, 1953).

8. *Pravda* (25 April, 1953).

9. *Pravda* (9 August, 1953).

10. Stalin, *Sochineniya*, 3 [XVI], 231.

11. A. Nikonov, "Vneshnyaya politika SSSR—politika mira i mezhdunarod-novo sotrudnichestva," *Kommunist*, No. 8 (May, 1953), p. 23.

12. *Ibid.*, pp. 28-29.

13. Yu. Pavlov, "Ideologicheskaya ekspansiya SShA v Zapadnoi Evrope terpit porazhenie," *Kommunist*, No. 14 (September, 1953), pp. 99-100.

14. I.S. Potapov, G.S. Roginsky, Yu.N. Kapelinsky, eds., *Mezhdunarodnaya torgovlya*, pp. 25-27.

15. M. Nesterov, "The Soviet Union and International Trade," *New Times*, No. 36 (2 September, 1953), p. 8.

16. Nesterov, "World Trade: Inexhaustible Potentialities," *New Times*, No. 6 (6 February, 1954), p. 13.

17. Nesterov, "International Trade: Partial Balance Sheet," *New Times*, No. 1 (1 January, 1955), p. 11.

18. Nesterov, "World Trade: Inexhaustible Potentialities," p. 11.

19. *Ibid.*, p. 12.

20. Nesterov, "International Trade: Partial Balance Sheet," p. 12.

21. Funigiello, *American-Soviet Trade*, p. 86.

22. *Ibid.*, p. 87.

23. Nesterov, "Necessary and Desirable," *New Times*, No. 51 (13 December, 1956), p. 4.

24. Paul R. Gregory and Robert C. Stuart, *Soviet Economic Structure and Performance*, 2d ed., p. 272. Soviet exports to developed capitalist countries rose from 347.6 million rubles in 1953 to 502.5 million rubles in 1955, imports from 399.8 million rubles to 401.8 million; see Yu.N. Kapelinsky, *Torgovlya SSSR s kapitalisticheskimi stranami posle vtoroi mirovoi voiny*, p. 51.

25. *Pravda* (3 February, 1955).

26. *Pravda* (27 March, 1955).

27. See Khrushchev's report to the XX congress in *Pravda* (15 February, 1956); cf. Michael Kaser, *Comecon*, ch. 5.

28. Kapelinsky, *Na vzaimovygodnoi osnove*, p. 89.

29. *Ibid.*, p. 91.

30. A.N. Manjulo, ed., *The USSR and International Economic Relations*, p. 48.

31. *Pravda* (24 April, 1956).

32. Nesterov, "Soviet Trade with the West," *New Times*, No. 27 (28 June, 1956), p. 4.

33. *Pravda* (18 February, 1956).

34. Nesterov, "Soviet Trade with the West," p. 4.

35. Z. Sviridova, "K voprosu ob osobennostyakh tsiklicheskovo vosproiz-vodstva v Anglii v poslevoennyi period," *Voprosy ekonomiki*, No. 6 (June, 1956), p. 133.

36. See Dan N. Jacobs, ed., *The New Communist Manifesto*, pp. 78-130.

37. *Pravda* (15 February, 1956).

38. Varga, "Protiv reformistkovo napravleniya v rabotakh po imperializmu," *Voprosy ekonomiki*, No. 3 (March, 1949), p. 79.

39. *Pravda* (15 February, 1956).

40. *Pravda* (18 February, 1956).

41. Stalin, *Sochineniya*, 3 [XVI], 240 (my italics).

42. Varga, *Osnovnye voprosy ekonomiki i politiki imperializma (posle vtoroi mirovoi voiny)*, p. 566.

43. Lenin, *Collected Works*, XXIX, 286.

44. A. Mileikovsky, "Tsennoe issledovanie o vazhneishikh izmeneniyakh v ekonomike i politike imperializma," *Voprosy ekonomiki*, No. 5 (May, 1954), p. 110.

45. *Ibid.*, p. 112 (my italics).

46. V. Zorin, "Predstoyashchie vybory i vnutripoliticheskaya obstanovka v SShA," *Kommunist*, No. 8 (May, 1954), p. 91.

47. *Ibid.*, p. 94.

48. Uil'yam Foster, "Usilenie fashistkikh tendentsii v SShA," *Kommunist*, No. 1 (January, 1955), p. 88.

49. *Ibid.*, p. 91.

50. Yu. Shvedkov, "V lagere finansovoi oligarkhii SShA," *Mezhdunarodnaya zhizn'*, No. 1 (January, 1955), p. 74.

51. *Ibid.*, p. 60.

52. S. Menshikov, "What Disarmament Would Bring the People," *New Times*, No. 21 (21 May, 1955), p. 13.

53. V. Solodovnikov, "Nalogi v kapitalisticheskikh stranakh—sredstvo ogrableniya rabochevo klassa monopoliyami," *Voprosy ekonomiki*, No. 5 (May, 1954), pp. 87-88.

54. Kuz'minov, "Burzhuaznoe gosudarstvo—orudie obogashcheniya monopolii," *Kommunist*, No. 9 (June, 1954), p. 61.

55. V. Glushkov, "Rost gosudarstvenno-monopolisticheskovo kapitalizma," *Voprosy ekonomiki*, No. 9 (September, 1955), p. 124.

56. Marx, *Capital*, III, 839-40.

57. V. Sushchenko, "Zakon konkurentsii i anarkhii proizvodstva v usloviyakh gospodstva monopolii," *Voprosy ekonomiki*, No. 8 (August, 1954), p. 109; cf. Lenin, *Selected Works*, I, 738.

58. Hilferding, *Finance Capital*, p. 231.

59. Stalin, *Sochineniya*, 3 [XVI], 234.

60. Vygodsky, "Osnovnoi ekonomicheskii zakon sovremennovo kapitalizma," *Kommunist*, No. 22 (December, 1952), p. 49.

61. *Ibid.*, p. 40.

62. Marx, *Capital*, I, 524.

63. Vygodsky, "Osnovnoi ekonomicheskii zakon . . .," p. 48.
64. V. Vladimirov, "Obnishchanie trudyashchikhsya v kapitalisticheskikh stranakh," *Kommunist*, No. 6 (April, 1953), p. 90 (my italics).
65. *Ibid.*, p. 96.
66. Smit, "Rost normy ekspluatatsii v SShA posle vtoroi mirovoi voiny," *Voprosy ekonomiki*, No. 7 (July, 1952), p. 99.
67. Smit, *Polozhenie rabochevo klassa*, p. 120.
68. Vatter, *The U.S. Economy in the 1950's*, p. 230.
69. Smit, "Polozhenie rabochevo klassa vo Frantsii, Anglii i SShA," *Mezhdunarodnaya Zhizn'*, No. 5 (May, 1956), p. 69; cf. Vatter, *The U.S. Economy in the 1950's*, pp. 229-30.
70. Smit, "Polozhenie rabochevo klassa . . .," p. 62.
71. *Ibid.*, p. 65.
72. *Ibid.*, p. 71.
73. M. Guttsait, "Khronicheskaya bezrabotitsa v epokhu obshchevo krizisa kapitalizma," *Voprosy ekonomiki*, No. 10 (October, 1953), p. 75.
74. *Ibid.*, p. 76.
75. *Ibid.*, p. 77.
76. *Ibid.*, p. 84.
77. This was a conceptual distinction. In fact, Marx thought intensification and rising productivity normally went together so that both tended to raise the rate of surplus value: see *Capital*, I, 530.
78. *Ibid.*, p. 629.
79. Kuz'minov, "Khronicheskaya massovaya bezrabotitsa v SShA," *Mezhdunarodnaya zhizn'*, No. 4 (April, 1956), p. 66.
80. In fact, U.S. unemployment averaged 4.2 percent of the civilian work force from mid-1955 to mid-1957, compared to 3.0 percent during the Korean war boom: see Vatter, *The U.S. Economy in the 1950's*, p. 73. Personal consumption grew in every year from 1950-1955, resulting in a total increase of 18 percent over the five-year period: Vatter, p. 89.
81. Ya. Segal, "O nekotorykh izmeneniyakh v promyshlennom proizvodstve kapitalisticheskikh stran," *Voprosy ekonomiki*, No. 5 (May, 1956), p. 92.
82. V. Antonov, "Amortizatsiya osnovnovo kapitala v SShA posle vtoroi mirovoi voiny," *Voprosy ekonomiki*, No. 6 (June, 1956), pp. 135-36.
83. E. Bregel', *Nalogi, zaimy i inflyatsiya na sluzhbe imperializma*, p. 63.
84. Stalin, *Selected Interviews*, p. 114; cf. Bregel', *Nalogi, zaimy i inflyatsiya*, p. 178.
85. Bregel', *Nalogi, zaimy i inflyatsiya*, p. 115.
86. *Ibid.*
87. *Ibid.*, p. 180.
88. *Ibid.*, p. 178.
89. Kuz'minov, *Gosudarstvenno-monopolisticheskii kapitalizm*, p. 384.

90. *Ibid.*, p. 381.
91. *Ibid.*, p. 389.
92. *Ibid.*, p. 383.
93. I.G. Blyumin, *Ocherki sovremennoi burzhuaznoi politicheskoi ekonomii SShA*, pp. 258-59.
94. *Ibid.*, p. 266.
95. Keynes, *The General Theory*, p. 113 *et seq.*
96. Manukyan, "Osobennosti tsiklicheskovo razvitiya ekonomiki SShA posle vtoroi mirovoi voiny," *Voprosy ekonomiki*, No. 1 (January, 1955), p. 92.
97. Bechin, "K voprosu ob osobennostyakh poslevoennovo kapitalisticheskovo tsikla," *Voprosy ekonomiki*, No. 9 (September, 1955), p. 119.
98. *Ibid.*, p. 116.
99. "Prezidium Akademii Nauk SSSR o nauchnoi deyatel'nosti i sostoyanii kadrov Instituta Ekonomiki i o razvertyvanii issledovanii v oblasti ekonomiki v AN SSSR," *Voprosy ekonomiki*, No. 12 (December, 1955), p. 151.
100. *Ibid.*, pp. 150-51.
101. "Chestvovanie akademika E.S. Varga," *Vestnik Kommunisticheskoi Akademii*, No. 1 (January, 1955), p. 97.
102. Cheprakov, "Nekotorye voprosy sovremennovo kapitalizma," *Kommunist*, No. 1 (January, 1956), p. 95.
103. *Ibid.*, p. 98.
104. *Ibid.*, pp. 105-8.
105. Bregel', "K voprosu o kapitalisticheskom vosproizvodstve v usloviyakh militarizatsii ekonomiki," *Voprosy ekonomiki*, No. 12 (December, 1955), p. 111.
106. *Ibid.*, p. 113.
107. *Ibid.*, p. 110.
108. *Ibid.*, p. 122.
109. G. Roginsky, "K voprosu o vozdeistvii militarizatsii khozyaistva na protsess kapitalisticheskovo vosproizvodstva," *Voprosy ekonomiki*, No. 10 (October, 1956), pp. 118-19.
110. Stalin, *Problems of Leninism*, pp. 749-50.
111. Roginsky, "K voprosu o vozdeistvii militarizatsii . . .," p. 120.
112. *Ibid.*, p. 124.
113. R. Khafizov, "Mif o 'reguliruemoi ekonomike' kapitalizma i neizbezhnost' ekonomicheskikh krizisov," *Voprosy ekonomiki*, No. 6 (June, 1957), p. 118.
114. *Ibid.*, p. 117.
115. A. Arzumanyan, "Voprosy marksistsko-leninskoi teorii obnishchaniya proletariata," *Kommunist*, No. 10 (July, 1956), p. 109.
116. Marx, *Capital*, I, 171.
117. Arzumanyan, "Voprosy marksistsko-leninskoi teorii . . .," pp. 112-13.

118. Arzumanyan, "Sotsialist Rember i marksistskaya teoriya obnishchaniya proletariata," *Kommunist*, No. 2 (February, 1957), p. 94.

119. Arzumanyan, "Velikaya oktyabr'skaya revolyutsiya i krizis kapitalizma," *Mirovaya ekonomika i mezhdunarodnye otnosheniya* [hereafter *MEMO*], No. 4 (October, 1957), pp. 25-26.

120. Quoted in "Peredovaya. Za tvorcheskuyu razrabotku problem mirovoi ekonomiki," *MEMO*, No. 3 (September, 1957), p. 6.

121. Manukyan, "Nekotorye yavleniya tsiklicheskovo razvitiya ekonomiki SShA," *Mezhdunarodnaya zhizn'*, No. 2 (February, 1957), pp. 46-47.

122. *Ibid.*, p. 40.

123. *Ibid.*, pp. 53-54.

124. Bechin, "Kapitalovlozhenie v poslevoennyi period," *MEMO*, No. 3 (September, 1957), p. 51.

125. *Ibid.*, p. 48.

126. *Ibid.*, p. 52,

127. Varga, *Osnovnye voprosy ekonomiki i politiki imperializma*, 2d ed., p. 22.

128. *Ibid.*, p. 45.

129. *Ibid.*, p. 532.

130. "Peredovaya . . .," p. 8.

131. *Ibid.*, p. 4.

132. *Ibid.*, p. 7.

133. *Ibid.*, p. 10.

134. *Ibid.*, p. 7.

135. *Ibid.*, p. 10.

136. *Ibid.*, p. 9.

137. Stalin, *Sochineniya*, 3 [XVI], 192.

Chapter 5. Reinterpreting Postwar America: A Normal Cycle or a "One-Sided" War Economy?

1. Varga, "Economy and Economic Policy in the Second Half-Year 1938," *World News and Views*, 19, No. 13 (23 March, 1939), pp. 263-64.

2. N.S. Khrushchev, *Control Figures for the Economic Development of the U.S.S.R.*, p. 77.

3. *Ibid.*, p. 104.

4. Vatter, *The U.S. Economy in the 1950's*, p. 86.

5. *Ibid.*, p. 1.

6. *Ibid.*, p. 221.

7. Bert G. Hickman, *Growth and Stability of the Postwar Economy*, p. 12.

8. Alvin H. Hansen, *The Postwar American Economy*, p. 3.

9. *Ibid.*, pp. 5-6.

10. *Ibid.*, pp. 6-7.

11. *Ibid.*, pp. 8-9.

12. *Ibid.*, p. 9.

13. *Ibid.*, p. 24.

14. *Ibid.*, p. 13.

15. Andrea Boltho, ed., *The European Economy: Growth and Crisis*, p. 11.

16. *Ibid.*, p. 292.

17. *Ibid.*, p. 19; cf. Armstrong, Glyn, Harrison, *Capitalism Since 1945*, p. 150.

18. Armstrong, Glyn, Harrison, *Capitalism Since 1945*, p. 84.

19. Andrew Shonfield, *Modern Capitalism*, pp. 11-12.

20. *Ibid.*, pp. 62-63.

21. Keynes, *The General Theory*, p. 161.

22. *Ibid.*, p. 49.

23. Shonfield, *Modern Capitalism*, p. 54.

24. Marx, *Capital*, II, 76.

25. *Ibid.*, pp. 185-86.

26. V. Maslennikov, "Nekotorye voprosy poslevoennovo promyshlennovo tsikla," *MEMO*, No. 8 (August, 1958), p. 81.

27. *Ibid.*, p. 86.

28. Marx, *Capital*, II, 185; cf. Manukyan in A.A. Rumyantsev, S.M. Men'shikov, G.B. Arbaev, eds., *Sovremennye tsikly i krizisy*, pp. 77-80.

29. Quoted in Varga, *Ocherki po problemam politekonomii kapitalizma*, p. 250.

30. Marx, *Capital*, I, 632 (my italics).

31. *Ibid.*, p. 637.

32. See Manukyan, "Nekotorye voprosy tsiklicheskovo razvitiya ekonomiki SShA," *Mezhdunarodnaya zhizn'*, No. 2 (February, 1957), p. 38.

33. *Ibid.*, p. 50; cf. Manukyan, "Ekonomicheskoe polozhenie kapitalis-ticheskikh stran v nachale 1958g," *MEMO*, No. 4 (April, 1958), p. 17.

34. Manukyan, "Ekonomicheskoe polozhenie . . .," p. 35.

35. Bechin, "Ob ekonomicheskom polozhenii v stranakh kapitalizma," *MEMO*, No. 5 (May, 1958), p. 56.

36. See "Nauchnaya zhizn'," *MEMO*, No. 4 (April, 1958), p. 152.

37. See "Sovremennoe ekonomicheskoe polozhenie kapitalisticheskikh stran," *Mezhdunarodnaya zhizn'*, No. 5 (May, 1958), pp. 102-3.

38. *Ibid.*, p. 105.

39. *Ibid.*, p. 106.

40. S.L. Vygodsky, *Ocherki teorii sovremennovo kapitalizma*, p. 274.

41. *Ibid.*, p. 252.

42. Kuz'minov, "Ekonomicheskii krizis v kapitalisticheskikh stranakh," *Mezhdunarodnaya zhizn'*, No. 9 (September, 1958), p. 48.

43. See "Sovremennoe ekonomicheskoe polozhenie kapitalisticheskikh stran," pp. 134-35.

44. Kats, "Burzhuaznaya ekonomicheskaya nauka i prognozy razvitiya ekonomiki SShA," *MEMO*, No. 8 (August, 1958), p. 51.

45. *Ibid.*

46. *Ibid.*, p. 55.

47. *Ibid.*, p. 53; cf. Bechin, "Ob ekonomicheskom polozhenii . . .," p. 60.

48. Kats, "Burzhuaznaya ekonomicheskaya nauka . . .," p. 57.

49. Kats, "Rol' militarizma v ekonomike SShA," *Mezhdunarodnaya zhizn'*, No. 9 (September, 1958), p. 98.

50. *Ibid.*, p. 100.

51. *Ibid.*, p. 92.

52. *Ibid.*, p. 102.

53. Mendel'son, "K voprosu ob osobennostyakh poslevoennovo tsikla," *MEMO*, No. 12 (December, 1958), p. 67.

54. *Ibid.*, p. 74.

55. Mendel'son in A.A. Arzumanyan, I.M. Lemin, E.L. Khmel'nitskaya, eds., *Problemy sovremennovo kapitalizma*, p. 136.

56. P. Figurnov, "K voprosu o nekotorykh osobennostyakh kapitalisticheskovo tsikla posle vtoroi mirovoi voiny," *MEMO*, No. 4 (April, 1959), pp. 83-84. See also Figurnov's criticism of Mendel'son, pp. 86-87; a similar criticism appeared in "Mezhdunarodnaya konferentsiya ekonomistov v Berline," *MEMO*, No. 12 (December, 1958), p. 136.

57. Figurnov, "K voprosu o nekotorykh osobennostyakh . . .," pp. 88-89.

58. *Ibid.*, p. 90.

59. *Ibid.*, p. 92.

60. Varga, "Problemy poslevoennovo promyshlennovo tsikla i novyi krizis pereproizvodstva," *Kommunist*, No. 8 (June, 1958), p. 140.

61. *Ibid.*, p. 141.

62. *Ibid.*, p. 140.

63. *Ibid.*, p. 141.

64. *Ibid.*, p. 143 (my italics).

65. "New Times Poll on the Crisis," *New Times*, No. 24 (June, 1958), p. 7.

66. Varga, "Problemy poslevoennovo promyshlennovo tsikla . . .," p. 156.

67. See "Nauchnaya zhizn'," *MEMO*, No. 7 (July, 1958), p. 148.

68. *Ibid.*, p. 150.

69. *Ibid.*

70. *Ibid.*

71. See "New Times Poll . . .," *New Times*, No. 24 (June, 1958), p. 3.

72. *Ibid.*, pp. 4-5.

73. See " New Times Poll . . .," *New Times*, No. 25 (June, 1958), pp. 8-10.

74. *Ibid.*, p. 10.

75. "New Times Poll . . .," *New Times*, No. 26 (June, 1958), p. 4.

76. *Ibid.*, p. 5.

77. Varga, "The Capitalist Economy in 1958," *New Times*, No. 5 (January, 1959), p. 12.

78. S. Dalin, "Ekonomicheskii krizis 1957-1958 gg. v SShA i evo osobennosti," *MEMO*, No. 6 (June, 1959), p. 84.

79. *Ibid.*, p. 72.

80. Manukyan, "U.S. Economy: New Developments," *New Times*, No. 33 (August, 1959), p. 11.

81. *Ibid.*, p. 10.

82. *Ibid.*

83. *Ibid.*, p. 13.

84. Kuz'minov, "Ekonomicheskoe polozhenie kapitalisticheskikh stran," *Mezhdunarodnaya zhizn'*, No. 3 (March, 1959), p. 45.

85. See Mendel'son quoted in S. Nikitin, "Fundamental'noe issledovanie," *MEMO*, No. 6 (June, 1966), p. 150.

86. Arzumanyan, "Reshayushchii etap ekonomicheskovo sorevnovaniya sotsializma i kapitalizma," *Voprosy ekonomiki*, No. 12 (December, 1959), p. 24.

87. See "Mezhdunarodnaya konferentsiya v Berline," *MEMO*, No. 12 (December, 1958), p. 138; cf. "Polozhenie i bor'ba rabochevo klassa kapitalisticheskikh stran v sovremennykh usloviyakh," *Mezhdunarodnaya zhizn'*, No. 6 (June, 1959), p. 90.

88. See "Mezhdunarodnaya konferentsiya . . .," p. 133.

89. Manukyan, "U.S. Economy: New Developments," p. 7.

90. Varga, "The Capitalist Economy in 1958," *New Times*, No. 5 (January, 1959), p. 11; cf. Varga, "Crisis and the Working Class," *World Marxist Review*, No. 8 (August, 1959), pp. 45-47.

91. D. Kostyukhin, "The U.S. Economy in 1959-1960," *New Times*, No. 17 (April, 1960), p. 20.

92. Quoted in "Sovremennoe ekonomicheskoe polozhenie kapitalisticheskikh stran," *Mezhdunarodnaya zhizn'*, No. 5 (May, 1958), p. 99.

93. Quoted in V.I. Stepanov, *Ekonomicheskie osnovy mirnovo sosushchestvovaniya*, p. 32. Stepanov gives *Vneshnyaya torgovlya*, No. 4 (1958), p. 11 as the original source. See also E. Menzhinsky, Yu. Sergeev, "Mirnoe sosushchestvovanie i perspektivy razvitiya evropeiskikh ekonomicheskikh svyazei," *MEMO*, No. 2 (February, 1960), p. 22.

94. Funigiello, *American-Soviet Trade*, p. 113.

95. Kostyukhin, "Vozmozhnosti razvitiya sovetsko-amerikanskoi torgovli," *MEMO*, No. 12 (December, 1959), pp. 32-33.

96. Funigiello, *American-Soviet Trade*, p. 111.

97. *Ibid.*, p. 113.

98. Louis J. Halle, *The Cold War as History*, p. 364.

99. "A Meeting of Benefit to the Whole World," *New Times*, No. 39 (September, 1958), p. 5.

100. The U.S. wanted payment for nonmilitary goods and for goods delivered after the war ended. For details see Goldman, *Detente and Dollars*, pp. 55-56.

101. I. Glagolev, Yu. Kapelinsky, "Razoruzhenie i ekonomicheskoe razvitie," *MEMO*, No. 11 (November, 1959), p. 33.

102. *Ibid.*, p. 35.

103. Kuz'minov, "Ekonomicheskii krizis v kapitalisticheskikh stranakh," *Mezhdunarodnaya zhizn'*, No. 9 (September, 1958), p. 51.

104. I. Mikuson, "Krizis v Soedinennykh Shtatakh i evo otrazhenie v politike," *Mezhdunarodnaya zhizn'*, No. 10 (October, 1958), pp. 74-76.

105. S. Menshikov, "U.S.A.: Pre-Election Winds," *New Times*, No. 41 (October, 1958), p. 15.

106. Menshikov, "The American Elections," *New Times*, No. 46 (November, 1958), p. 15.

107. *Ibid.*, p. 18.

108. Menshikov, "Post-Visit Views," *New Times*, No. 42 (October, 1959), p. 5.

109. Menshikov, "Who Will be America's Next President?" *New Times*, No. 30 (July, 1960), p. 13.

110. *Ibid.*, p. 14.

111. *Ibid.*, p. 116.

112. *Ibid.*, p. 9.

113. *Ibid.*, p. 10.

114. Kuzminov, "The Economic situation in the Capitalist world," *International Affairs*, No. 10 (October, 1960), p. 39.

115. Varga, "Crisis and the Working Class," *World Marxist Review*, No. 8 (August, 1959), p. 47.

116. Arzumanyan, "Novyi etap obshchevo krizisa kapitalizma," *MEMO*, No. 2 (February, 1961), p. 7.

117. Kats, "O nekotorykh ekonomicheskikh faktorov usileniya zagnivaniya amerikanskovo kapitalizma," *MEMO*, No. 2 (February, 1961), p. 47 (my italics).

118. *Ibid.*, p. 56.

119. See "Problemy poslevoennovo tsiklicheskovo razvitiya kapitalizma," *MEMO*, No. 4 (April, 1961), p. 94.

120. Varga, "Marksistskaya teoriya krizisov i izuchenie kon'yunktury," *MEMO*, No. 3 (March, 1961), p. 94.

121. *Ibid.*, p. 99.

122. *Ibid.*, p. 101.

123. *Ibid.*

124. *Ibid.*, p. 102 (my italics).

125. See "Problemy poslevoennovo tsiklicheskovo razvitiya kapitalizma," p. 94.

126. *Ibid.*, pp. 95-96.
127. *Ibid.*, p. 90.
128. *Ibid.*, p. 91.
129. *Ibid.*, p. 98.
130. Men'shikov, "Poslevoennyi tsikl i perspektivy kapitalisticheskoi eko-nomiki," *MEMO*, No. 9 (September, 1961), pp. 60-1.
131. *Ibid.*, p. 61; cf. "Exchange of Views: Crisis and the Working Class," *World Marxist Review*, No. 7 (July, 1961), p. 69.
132. Men'shikov, "Poslevoennyi tsikly i perspektivy . . .," p. 67.
133. *Ibid.*, p. 65 (my italics).
134. See "O zadachakh izucheniya sovremennovo kapitalizma," *MEMO*, No. 8 (August, 1959), pp. 6-7.
135. Varga, *Izmeneniya v ekonomike kapitalizma*, p. 318.
136. "Statement of the Meeting of Representatives of the Communist and Workers' Parties," *New Times*, No. 50 (December, 1960), p. 4.
137. *Ibid.*, p. 9.
138. *Ibid.*, p. 12.
139. "Programme of the CPSU," *New Times*, No. 48 (29 November, 1961), p. 19.
140. O. Kuusinen, "Modern Monopoly Capital and Its Perspectives," *World Marxist Review*, No. 4 (April, 1960), p. 11; cf. Kuusinen, ed., *Fundamentals of Marxism-Leninism*, pp. 500-1.
141. Kuusinen, "Modern Monopoly Capital . . .," p. 10 (my italics).
142. Arzumanyan, "Lenin i gosudarstvenno-monopolisticheskii kapitalizm," *Kommunist*, No. 7 (May, 1960), p. 23.
143. *Ibid.*, p. 26.
144. *Ibid.*, p. 29.
145. "The U.S. Presidential Election," *New Times*, No. 46 (November, 1960), p. 6.
146. *Ibid.*
147. S. Bol'shakov, "Presidentskie vybory v SShA: itogi i perspektivy," *MEMO*, No. 12 (December, 1960), p. 44.
148. *Ibid.*, p. 45.
149. *Ibid.*, p. 47.
150. *Ibid.*, pp. 50-51.
151. *Ibid.*, p. 46.

Chapter 6. New Frontiers of State-Monopoly Capitalism

1. *Documents of the 22nd Congress of the CPSU*, II, 23-24.
2. Marx, *Capital*, III, 429.
3. Marx and Engels, *Selected Correspondence*, pp. 251-52.

4. Marx, *Capital*, I, 39.

5. Marx, *Grundrisse*, pp. 137-38.

6. Marx, *Capital*, III, 192.

7. Vygodsky, "Osnovnoi ekonomicheskii zakon sovremennovo kapitalizma," *Kommunist*, No. 22 (December, 1952), p. 38.

8. Vygodsky, *Ocherki teorii sovremennovo kapitalizma*, p. 108.

9. *Ibid.*, pp. 98-99.

10. Hilferding, *Finance Capital*, p. 231.

11. Vygodsky, "Osnovnoi ekonomicheskii zakon . . .," p. 49.

12. Vygodsky, *Ocherki teorii*, p. 175.

13. *Ibid.*, p. 105.

14. *Ibid.*, p. 205.

15. *Ibid.*, p. 162.

16. *Ibid.*, p. 150.

17. *Ibid.*, p. 196.

18. *Ibid.*, p. 274.

19. *Ibid.*, p. 144.

20. *Ibid.*, p. 195. Bert G. Hickman calculated that the rate of utilization from 1954 to 1958 varied between 78 and 92 percent: see *Growth and Stability of the Postwar Economy*, p. 130.

21. Vygodsky, *Ocherki teorii*, p. 55.

22. *Ibid.*, p. 249.

23. *Ibid.*, p. 259.

24. *Ibid.*, pp. 285-86.

25. *Ibid.*, p. 252.

26. *Ibid.*, p. 302.

27. *Ibid.*, p. 212.

28. G.A. Kozlov, *Deistvie zakona stoimosti v usloviyakh sovremennovo kapitalizma*, p. 9.

29. *Ibid.*, p. 108.

30. *Ibid.*, p. 253.

31. *Ibid.*, pp. 235-36.

32. *Ibid.*, p. 225.

33. *Ibid.*, p. 251.

34. *Ibid.*, p. 264.

35. *Ibid.*, p. 352.

36. *Ibid.*, pp. 364-65.

37. *Ibid.*, p. 369.

38. *Ibid.*, p. 372.

39. *Ibid.*, p. 378.

40. *Ibid.*, p. 357.

41. *Ibid.*, p. 275.

42. *Ibid.*, pp. 390-1.

43. Walter W. Heller, *New Dimensions of Political Economy*, p. 2.

44. *Ibid.*, p. 9.

45. John Kenneth Galbraith, *The Affluent Society*, pp. 214-15.

46. Hansen, *The Postwar American Economy*, pp. 51-52.

47. S. Men'shikov, V. Shamberg, "Budet li ekonomika SShA razvivat'sya bystree?" *MEMO*, No. 1 (January, 1961), p. 102.

48. Men'shikov, ed., *Ekonomicheskaya politika pravitel'stva Kennedi, 1961-1963*, p. 31.

49. *Ibid.*, p. 34.

50. Seymour E. Harris, *Economics of the Kennedy Years*, p. 59.

51. LaFeber, *America, Russia, and the Cold War*, p. 215.

52. L. Leont'ev, "Krizis mirovovo kapitalizma," *Kommunist*, No. 15 (October, 1961), p. 123.

53. *Ibid.*, pp. 117-18.

54. Arzumanyan, "Krizis mirovovo kapitalizma," *MEMO*, No. 12 (December, 1961), pp. 9-10.

55. V. Lan, "God presidentsva Kennedi," *MEMO*, No. 3 (March, 1962), p. 99.

56. Harris, *Economics of the Kennedy Years*, pp. 141-42.

57. *Ibid.*, pp. 45-46.

58. Varga, "President Kennedy and the Steel Barons," *New Times*, No. 20 (16 May, 1962), p. 12.

59. *Ibid.*, p. 13.

60. *Ibid.*, p. 10.

61. See "XXII s'ezd KPSS o krizise mirovovo kapitalizma—nauchnaya sessiya v Institute Mirovoi Ekonomiki i Mezhdunarodnykh Otnoshenii Akademii Nauk SSSR," *MEMO*, No. 5 (May, 1962), p. 145.

62. Men'shikov, ed., *Ekonomicheskaya politika pravitel'stva Kennedi*, pp. 114-15.

63. Varga, "Wall Street's Black Monday," *New Times*, No. 24 (13 June, 1962), p. 13.

64. Harris, *Economics of the Kennedy Years*, p. 46.

65. *Ibid.*, p. 49.

66. Men'shikov, ed., *Ekonomicheskaya politika pravitel'stva Kennedi*, pp. 76-77.

67. Heller, *New Dimensions of Political Economy*, p. 36.

68. Vygodsky, "A Factor Deepening Capitalism's General Crisis," *International Affairs*, No. 4 (April, 1962), p. 30.

69. *Ibid.*, p. 31.

70. Arzumanyan, "Novyi etap obshchevo krizisa kapitalizma," *MEMO*, No. 2 (February, 1961), p. 8.

71. *Ibid.*, p. 15.

72. Kats, "O nekotorykh ekonomicheskikh faktorakh usileniya zagnivaniya amerikanskovo kapitalizma," *MEMO*, No. 2 (February, 1961), p. 59.

73. N. Ivanov, "Tekhnicheskii progress v kapitalisticheskikh stranakh i bez-rabotitsa," *MEMO*, No. 10 (October, 1961), p. 54.

74. G. Naidenov, "Voprosy vosproizvodstva i ispol'zovaniya osnovnovo kapitala obrabatyvayushchei promyshlennosti SShA," *MEMO*, No. 12 (December, 1962), p. 113.

75. Harris, *Economics of the Kennedy Years*, p. 176.

76. Heller, *New Dimensions of Political Economy*, p. 67.

77. Quoted in A. Kashkarov, "The American Economic Outlook," *New Times*, No. 14 (10 April, 1963), p. 18.

78. Harris, *Economics of the Kennedy Years*, p. 63.

79. V. Kur'erov, "Sostoyanie i perspektivy ekonomiki SShA," *MEMO*, No. 11 (November, 1963), p. 78.

80. *Ibid.*, p. 79.

81. *Ibid.*, p. 77.

82. Harris, *Economics of the Kennedy Years*, p. 238.

83. Kuzminov, "The Economic Situation in the Capitalist Countries," *International Affairs*, No. 4 (April, 1963), p. 18.

84. A. Kashkarov, "The American Economic Outlook," *New Times*, No. 14 (10 April, 1963), p. 20.

85. Valentin Zorin, "White House Grey Eminences," *New Times*, No. 15 (17 April, 1963), p. 9.

86. Men'shikov, ed., *Ekonomicheskaya politika pravitel'stva Kennedi*, p. 397. According to Harris, the U.S. provided $80 billion from 1946 to 1961, two-thirds for aid and one-third for defense: Harris, ed., *The Dollar in Crisis*, p. 6.

87. Men'shikov, ed., *Ekonomicheskaya politika pravitel'stva Kennedi*, p. 341.

88. *Documents of the 22nd Congress of the CPSU*, II, 25-26.

89. Varga, "The Dollar—Symbol of America's Policy Crisis," *New Times*, No. 48 (November, 1960), p. 10.

90. *Ibid.*

91. Harris, ed., *The Dollar in Crisis*, p. 224; cf. Robert Triffin, *Gold and the Dollar Crisis*.

92. Harris, ed., *The Dollar in Crisis*, p. 295.

93. Varga, "The Dollar—Symbol of America's Policy Crisis," p. 9; cf. Harris, ed., *The Dollar in Crisis*, pp. 79-80 .

94. Varga, "The Dollar . . .," p. 9; cf. S. Dalin, "'Kholodnaya voina' i ee ekonomicheskie posledstviya," *MEMO*, No. 12 (December, 1961), pp. 30-37.

95. Harris, ed., *The Dollar in Crisis*, pp. 97-113 and 295-307.

96. Funigiello, *American-Soviet Trade*, p. 126.

97. Harris, ed., *The Dollar in Crisis*, p. 94.

98. LaFeber, *America, Russia, and the Cold War*, p. 209. From 1960 to 1962 the share of socialist markets in British exports was 15 percent for textile equipment; 25 percent for equipment used in the paper industry; 25 percent of equipment exports for the food industry; and nearly one-third of complete sets of equipment for factories in the chemical industry. About 45 percent of British exports of synthetic materials also went to socialist markets: see V.I. Stepanov, *Ekonomicheskie osnovy mirnovo sosushchestvovaniya*, p. 91.

99. Funigiello, *American-Soviet Trade*, p. 136.

100. *Ibid.*, ch. 6.

101. Men'shikov, ed., *Ekonomicheskaya politika pravitel'stva Kennedi*, p. 356.

102. "'Obshchii rynok' i evo rol' v ekonomike i politike sovremennovo imperializma," *MEMO*, No. 7 (July, 1959), p. 111.

103. See Suslin's comments in "'Obshchii rynok' . . .," *MEMO*, No. 8 (August, 1959), p. 104; also V. Vetlanin in "'Obshchii rynok' . . .," *MEMO*, No. 9 (September, 1959), p. 94.

104. "'Obshchii rynok' . . .," *MEMO*, No. 8 (August, 1959), p. 107.

105. "'Obshchii rynok' . . .," *MEMO*, No. 9 (September, 1959), pp. 98-99.

106. *Ibid.*, p. 90.

107. *Ibid.*, No. 10 (October, 1959), p. 82.

108. Varga, "Teoreticheskie problemy ekonomiki 'obshchevo rynka,'" *MEMO*, No. 10 (October, 1962), p. 51.

109. *Ibid.*, p. 53.

110. *Ibid.*, pp. 55-56.

111. See "Exchange of Views," *World Marxist Review*, 5, No. 12 (December, 1962), p. 54.

112. *Ibid.*

113. See, "Imperialist 'Integration' in Western Europe," *New Times* (supplement), No. 36 (5 September, 1962), p. 38.

114. *Ibid.*, p. 41.

115. *Ibid.*, p. 36.

116. *Ibid.*, p. 37; cf. "'Integration' of Monopoly Capital—Some New Developments," *World Marxist Review*, 5, No. 7 (July, 1962), p. 16.

117. "Imperialist 'Integration' in Western Europe," p. 39.

118. *Ibid.*, pp. 41-42.

119. *Ibid.*, p. 35.

120. Stalin, *Sochineniya*, 3 [XVI], 223.

121. Day, *Leon Trotsky and the Politics of Economic Isolation*, p. 143.

122. P. Chernyshev, L. Lobanov, "Nasushchnie voprosy mezhdunarodnovo razdeleniya truda," *MEMO*, No. 6 (June, 1962), p. 38.

123. *Ibid.*, p. 40.

124. Suslin, "'Obshchii rynok'—orudie monopolii," *MEMO*, No. 8 (August, 1962), p. 34.

125. Cheprakov, "'Obshchii rynok'—orudie usileniya monopolisticheskovo gneta i agressii," *Kommunist*, No. 8 (May, 1962), p. 25.

126. *Ibid.*, p. 27.

127. E. Menzhinsky, "Sovremennaya vneshneekonomicheskaya politika imperializma," *MEMO*, No. 6 (June, 1963), p. 87.

128. A. Frumkin, "Mezhdunarodnoe razdelenie truda v burzhuaznykh teoriyakh i v zhizni," *MEMO*, No. 6 (June, 1963), p. 100.

129. A. Rumyantsev, "Nerazreshimye protivorechiya sovremennovo kapitalizma," *Kommunist*, No. 15 (October, 1962), p. 38.

130. "'Integration' of Monopoly Capital—Some New Developments," *World Marxist Review*, 5, No. 7 (July, 1962), p. 23.

131. Nesterov, "International Trade Conference," *New Times*, No. 4 (30 January, 1963), p. 13.

132. *Documents of the 22nd Congress of the CPSU*, II, 96.

133. Michael Kaser, *Comecon: Integration Problems of the Planned Economies*, p. 191.

134. *Ibid.*, p. 93.

135. I. Ivanov, "'Obshchii rynok' i sorevnovanie dvukh sistem," *MEMO*, No. 7 (July, 1963), pp. 11-12.

136. David Floyd, *Rumania: Russia's Dissident Ally*, p. 80.

137. Kaser, *Comecon*, p. 94.

138. Stalin, *Sochineniya*, 3 [XVI], 314.

139. "Programme of the CPSU," *New Times* (supplement), No. 48 (29 November, 1961), p. 18.

140. "Exchange of Views," *World Marxist Review*, 5, No. 3 (March, 1962), p. 79.

141. Menzhinsky, "Sovremennaya vneshneekonomicheskaya politika imperializma," p. 87.

142. Mileikovsky, "Sushchnost' i formy gosudarstvenno-monopolisticheskovo kapitalizma," *MEMO*, No. 1 (January, 1963), p. 94.

143. T. Timofeev, "O klassovoi bor'be na novom etape obshchevo krizisa kapitalizma," *MEMO*, No. 5 (May, 1961), p. 35.

144. Cheprakov, "Gosudarstvenno-monopolisticheskii kapitalizm i burzhuaznaya politicheskaya ekonomiya," *Voprosy ekonomiki*, No. 7 (July, 1962), pp. 88-89.

145. Arzumanyan, "Krizis mirovovo kapitalizma," *MEMO*, No. 12 (December, 1961), p. 22.

146. Arzumanyan, "Sovremennyi kapitalizm i klassovaya bor'ba," *MEMO*, No.2 (February, 1963), pp. 9-10.

147. *Ibid.*, p. 11.

148. See "Novye tendentsii v burzhuaznoi politicheskoi ekonomii," *Voprosy ekonomiki*, No. 9 (September, 1964), p. 149..

149. L. Al'ter, "O nekotorykh yavleniyakh v burzhuaznoi politicheskoi ekonomii," *Voprosy ekonomiki*, No. 1 (January, 1964), pp. 96-97.

150. Al'ter, "Teoriya i praktika kapitalisticheskovo regulirovaniya," *MEMO*, No. 3 (March, 1964), pp. 63-64.

151. *Ibid.*, p. 65.

152. Mileikovsky, "Sushchnost' i formy gosudarstvenno-monopolisticheskovo kapitalizma," pp. 88-89.

153. *Ibid.*, pp. 90-91.

154. Bechin, "Osobennosti vosproizvodstva v SShA," *MEMO*, No. 10 (October, 1962), p. 78.

155. *Ibid.*, p. 80.

156. Yu. Yudin, "Monopolii SShA i politika Vashingtona," *MEMO*, No. 8 (August, 1963), p. 37.

157. Quoted in Funigiello, *American-Soviet Trade*, p. 148.

158. Valentin Zorin, "What Course Will U.S. Policy Follow?" *New Times*, No. 51 (23 December, 1964), p. 5.

159. M.S. Arnoni, "The U.S. Military Junta," *New Times*, No. 47 (25 November, 1964), p. 11.

160. *Ibid.*, p. 14.

161. Boris Izakov, "The Kennedy Heritage," *New Times*, No. 48 (2 December, 1964), p. 10.

162. Men'shikov, "Pravitel'stvo Dzhonsona i politicheskie problemy SShA," *MEMO*, No. 6 (June, 1964), pp. 27-28.

163. Varga, *Ocherki po problemam politekonomii kapitalizma*, p. 55.

Chapter 7. Monopoly Planning and "Scientific-Technical Revolution"

1. Marx, *Capital*, I, 763.

2. Quoted by Lenin, *Selected Works*, II, 356.

3. Hilferding, *Finance Capital*, pp. 367-68.

4. Marx, *Capital*, II, 593.

5. Lenin, *Selected Works*, II, 438.

6. *Ibid.*, p. 384.

7. *Ibid.*, p. 814.

8. Cheprakov, "Sovremennoe ekonomicheskoe polozhenie SShA," *Bol'-shevik*, No. 9 (May, 1947), pp. 37-38.

9. *Ibid.*, p. 48.

10. Cheprakov, *Gosudarstvenno-monopolisticheskii kapitalizm*, pp. 11-12.

11. *Ibid.*, p. 93.

12. Marx and Engels, *Selected Works*, II, 147.

13. *Ibid.*, p. 496.

14. *Ibid.*, I, 604.

15. *Ibid.*, II, 492-93.

16. *Ibid.*, p. 492; cf. Marx and Engels, *Selected Correspondence*, p. 540.

17. Cheprakov, *Gosudarstvenno-monopolisticheskii kapitalizm*, p. 95.

18. *Ibid.*, p. 13.

19. *Ibid.*, p. 91.

20. *Ibid.*, pp. 91-92.

21. *Ibid.*, p. 345; cf. Engels, *Anti-Duhring*, p. 312.

22. Cheprakov, *Gosudarstvenno-monopolisticheskii kapitalizm*, p. 220.

23. *Ibid.*, p. 368.

24. Cheprakov's introduction to Varga, *Politico-Economic Problems of Capitalism*, p. 3.

25. *Ibid.*, pp. 5-6; cf. Cheprakov, "Vo imya tvorcheskovo marksizma," *MEMO*, No. 5 (May, 1965), pp. 144-49.

26. E. Varga, *Ocherki po problemam politekonomii kapitalizma*, p. 55.

27. *Ibid.*, p. 67.

28. Marx, *Capital*, III, 227.

29. Varga, *Ocherki po problemam*, p. 11. For Cheprakov's treatment of this question, see his article in V.N. Cherkovets, I.P. Faminsky, V.A. Kirov, eds., *Leninskii analiz imperializma i sovremennyi kapitalizm*, 207-24.

30. Marx, *Capital*, I, 644; cf. *Capital*, III, 229.

31. Varga, *Ocherki po problemam*, pp. 121-22.

32. *Ibid.*, p. 126.

33. *Ibid.*, p. 131.

34. *Ibid.*, p. 166.

35. *Ibid.*, p. 167.

36. *Ibid.*, p. 168.

37. *Ibid.* For an interpretation of Varga in light of Galbraith's view of corporate pricing, see Cherkovets *et al.*, eds., *Leninskii analiz imperializma*, pp. 81-96.

38. Varga, *Ocherki po problemam*, p. 190.

39. *Ibid.*, p. 211.

40. *Ibid.*, p. 187.

41. "Evgenii Samuilovich Varga," *Voprosy ekonomiki*, No. 10 (October, 1964), p. 159.

42. Bukharin, *Selected Writings on the State and the Transition to Socialism*, p. 40.

43. V. Maslennikov, "Gosudarstvo i monopolii v sisteme sovremennovo kapitalizma," *Voprosy ekonomiki*, No. 6 (June, 1965), p. 115 (my italics); cf. B. Denisov, "Rol' burzhuaznovo gosudarstva v sisteme gosudarstvenno-monopolisticheskovo kapitalizma," *Voprosy ekonomiki*, No. 7 (July, 1970), p. 99.

44. "Finance Capital Today," *World Marxist Review*, 7, No. 10 (October, 1964), p. 71.

45. Lemin, "Vneshnyaya politika SShA: dvizhushchie sily i tendentsii," *MEMO*, No. 6 (June, 1965), p. 25.

46. A. Mileikovsky, V. Shundeev, R. Entov, "O mnimykh i deistvitel'nykh izmeneniyakh v sovremennom kapitalizme," *Kommunist*, No. 11 (July, 1965), pp. 33-34.

47. Leont'ev, " Politicheskaya ekonomiya sovremennovo mira," *MEMO*, No. 7 (July, 1965), pp. 92-93.

48. *Ibid.*, p. 94.

49. Marx, *Capital*, II, 315.

50. Leont'ev, "Politicheskaya ekonomiya . . .," p. 94.

51. Ya. Pevzner, "Metodologiya 'Kapitala' i nekotorye voprosy izucheniya kapitalizma," *MEMO*, No. 11 (November, 1966), p. 27.

52. *Ibid.*, p. 30.

53. "Mezhdunarodnaya konferentsiya marksistov: k 50-letiyu vykhoda v svet knigi V.I. Lenina 'Imperializm, kak vysshaya stadiya kapitalizma'," *MEMO*, No. 6 (June, 1967), p. 72 (my italics).

54. "Uchenie V.I. Lenina ob imperializme i sovremennost'—k 50-letiyu vykhoda v svet raboty 'Imperializm, kak vysshaya stadiya kapitalizma,'" *MEMO*, No. 5 (May, 1967), p. 9.

55. "Mezhdunarodnaya konferentsiya . . .," *MEMO*, No. 7 (July, 1967), p. 72.

56. "Mezhdunarodnaya konferentsiya . . .," *MEMO*, No. 6 (June, 1967), pp. 76-77.

57. *Ibid.*, p. 90.

58. Ibid., p. 96; cf. Cheprakov, "Gosudarstvenno-monopolisticheskii kapitalizm i antimonopolisticheskaya bor'ba," *Kommunist*, No. 12 (August, 1966), p. 71; also V. Peshchansky, "Books and Journals: A Study of State-Monopoly Capitalism," *World Marxist Review*, 10, No. 3 (March, 1967), p. 50.

59. "Tvorcheskoe nasledie E.S. Vargi," *MEMO*, No. 1 (January, 1970), p. 124.

60. Men'shikov, "Sovremennye tsikly i krizisy," *MEMO*, No. 2 (February, 1966), p. 140; cf. Men'shikov, "O mekhanizme sovremennovo tsikla," *MEMO*, No. 4 (April, 1966), pp. 51-52. The summary of conference proceedings was not published until February 1966, but A.M. Rumyantsev indicated that it occurred in November 1965: A.M. Rumyantsev, S.M. Men'shikov, G.B. Arbaev, eds. *Sovremennye tsikly i krizisy*, p. 5.

61. Men'shikov, "Osobennosti sovremennykh kapitalisticheskikh tsiklov i krizisov," *Kommunist*, No. 4 (March, 1966), p. 111.

62. Men'shikov, "Sovremennye tsikly i krizisy," p. 142.

63. Men'shikov, "Osobennosti . . .," p. 115.

64. Men'shikov, "O mekhanizme sovremennovo tsikla," p. 57.

65. *Ibid.*, p. 54.

66. *Ibid.*, p. 58.

67. Men'shikov, "O mekhanizme sovremennovo tsikla," *MEMO*, No. 5 (May, 1966), p. 54.

68. *Ibid.*, p. 51.

69. *Ibid.*, p. 56.

70. *Ibid.*

71. Rumyantsev *et al.*, eds., *Sovremennye tsikly i krizisy*, p. 47.

72. Men'shikov, "O mekhanizme sovremennovo tsikla," *MEMO*, No. 5 (May, 1966), p. 51.

73. Rumyantsev *et al.*, eds., *Sovremennye tsikly i krizisy*, pp. 48-49.

74. *Ibid.*, p. 65.

75. *Ibid.*, p. 64.

76. *Ibid.*, p. 69.

77. *Ibid.*, p. 50.

78. Marx, *Capital*, II, 170 (my italics).

79. Men'shikov, "O mekhanizme sovremennovo tsikla," *MEMO*, No. 5 (May, 1966), p. 55; cf. Rumyantsev *et al.*, eds., *Sovremennye tsikly i krizisy*, p. 54.

80. Day, *The 'Crisis' and the 'Crash,'* pp. 235-36.

81. *Ibid.*, p. 243.

82. Rumyantsev *et al.*, eds., *Sovremennye tsikly i krizisy*, p. 61.

83. *Ibid.*, p. 62.

84. *Ibid.*, p. 54.

85. *Ibid.*, p. 116.

86. *Ibid.*, p. 124.

87. *Ibid.*

88. *Ibid.*, p. 137.

89. *Ibid.*, pp. 138-39.

90. *Ibid.*, p. 144.

91. *Ibid.*, p. 147.

92. *Ibid.*, p. 156.

93. *Ibid.*, pp. 147-48.

94. *Ibid.*, p. 156.

95. Marx, *Capital*, II, 469 (my italics).

96. Rumyantsev *et al.*, eds., *Sovremennye tsikly i krizisy*, p. 163 (my italics).

97. Marx, *Capital*, III, 258.

98. N.A. Tsagolov, V.A. Kirov, eds., *'Kapital' K. Marksa i problemy sovremennovo kapitalizma*, p. 323.

99. *Ibid.*, p. 325.

100. *Ibid.*

101. Rumyantsev *et al.*, eds., *Sovremennye tsikly i krizisy*, p. 143.

102. I. Dvorkin, "Kiberneticheskaya revolyutsiya," *Voprosy ekonomiki*, No. 5 (May, 1965), p. 103; cf. Dvorkin, "Burzhuaznye tekhnologicheskie teorii krizisov," *MEMO*, No. 12 (December, 1962), pp. 50-58.

103. N. Gauzner, "Nauchno-tekhnicheskaya revolyutsiya i ee sotsial'nye posledstviya," *MEMO*, No. 7 (July, 1969), p. 129.

104. Gauzner, "Rabochii klass SShA—strukturnye sdvigi," *MEMO*, No. 5 (May, 1963), p. 18.

105. Rumyantsev *et al.*, eds., *Sovremennye tsikly i krizisy*, p. 56.

106. L.S. Dubinsky, ed., *Ekonomicheskaya teoriya Marksa-Lenina i sovremennyi kapitalizm*, p. 226; cf. Manukyan, "Tendentsii i perspektivy kapitalisticheskoi ekonomiki," *MEMO*, No. 7 (July, 1964), pp. 30-31.

107. Arzumanyan, ed., *Burzhuaznaya politicheskaya ekonomiya o problemakh sovremennovo kapitalizma*, pp. 66-67.

108. Galbraith, *The Affluent Society*, p. 213.

109. Arzumanyan, ed., *Burzhuaznaya politicheskaya ekonomiya*, p. 51.

110. A. Mileikovsky, "Soedinennye Shtaty: tempy, zanyatost', rynki," *MEMO*, No. 6 (June, 1964), p. 47.

111. Bechin, "Struktura kapitalisticheskoi ekonomiki: metodologiya analiza i pokazateli izmenenii," *MEMO*, No. 12 (December, 1964), p. 60.

112. Marx, *Theories of Surplus Value*, I, 298.

113. Adam Smith, *Wealth of Nations*, p. 314.

114. Marx, *Surplus Value*, I, 171-72.

115. Marx, *Capital*, I, 509.

116. G.A. Kozlov, S.P. Pervushin, eds., *Kratkii ekonomicheskii slovar'*, p. 324 (my italics).

117. *Ibid.*, p. 350.

118. A. Koryagin, "Sfera uslug i problemy proizvoditel'novo truda," *MEMO*, No. 7 (July, 1968), p. 75.

119. A. Konovalov, "Povtornyi schet uslug sushchestvuet," *MEMO*, No. 3 (March, 1970), p. 92; cf. Marx, *Surplus Value*, I, 167.

120. D. Pravdin, "Ekonomicheskoe soderzhanie i otsenka poleznosti uslug," *MEMO*, No. 1 (January, 1970), p. 92.

121. *Ibid.*, p. 100.

122. E. Gromov, "Ekonomicheskaya rol' sfery uslug," *MEMO*, No. 11 (November, 1968), p. 79.

123. *Ibid.*, p. 78.

124. *Ibid.*, p. 80.

125. *Ibid.*, p. 82.

126. *Ibid.*, p. 84; cf. Gromov, "Sfera uslug i 'novoe obshchestvo' amerikanskikh sotsiologov," *MEMO*, No. 7 (July, 1969), pp. 121-27.

127. Marx, *Surplus Value*, I, 152 (my italics).

128. *Ibid.*, p. 157 (my italics).

129. As early as 1928 this fact was clear to I.I. Rubin. See his *Essays on Marx's Theory of Value*, pp. 259-75.

130. Marx, *Grundrisse*, p. 706.

131. *Ibid.*, p. 700.

132. *Ibid.*, p. 706.

133. *Ibid.*

134. *Ibid.*, p. 705.

135. *Ibid.*, p. 712.

136. S. Zagladina, "Sushchestvuet li edinaya sfera uslug?" *MEMO*, No. 5 (May, 1970), p. 98; cf. Zagladina, "'Ekonomika uslug' ili ekonomika korporatsii" *MEMO*, No. 11 (November, 1969), pp. 137-44.

137. P. Oldak, "Nakoplenie i vosproizvodimoe bogatsvo: problema proizvoditel'novo truda," *MEMO*, No. 11 (November, 1970), pp. 116-17.

138. N. Gauzner, "Rabochii klass SShA: strukturnye sdvigi," *MEMO*, No. 5 (May, 1963), p. 23; cf. E. Gromov, "Ekonomicheskaya rol' sfery uslug," pp. 85-86.

139. Gauzner, "Nauchno-tekhnicheskaya revolyutsiya i ee sotsial'nye posledstviya," *MEMO*, No. 7 (July, 1969), p. 128.

140. Ya. Pevzner, "Povtornovo scheta uslug ne sushchestvuet," *MEMO*, No. 3 (March, 1969), p. 94.

141. N. Inozemtsev, "Osobennosti sovremennovo imperializma i evo osnovnye protivorechiya," *MEMO*, No. 5 (May, 1970), p. 15.

142. Daniel Bell, *The End of Ideology*, p. 297.

143. *Ibid.*, p. 398.

144. Gauzner, "Rabochii klass SShA: strukturnye sdvigi," p. 16.

145. *Ibid.*, pp. 22-23.

146. *Ibid.*, p. 26.

147. E. Gromov, "Sfera uslug i 'novoe obshchestvo' amerikanskikh sotsiologov," *MEMO*, No. 7 (July, 1969), p. 122.

148. *Ibid.*, p. 127.

149. A. Mel'nikov, "Izmenenie struktury rabochevo klassa SShA," *MEMO*, No. 1 (January, 1969), p. 98.

150. Dalin, "Leninskaya teoriya imperializma i problemy sovremennovo imperializma," *Kommunist*, No. 7 (May, 1970), p. 78.

151. Dalin, "'Industrial'noe obshchestvo' i rabochii klass," *SShA*, No. 9 (September, 1970), p. 46.

152. *Ibid.*, p. 49.

153. E. Pletnev, "Rabochaya aristokratiya: mesto v proizvodtsve, rol' v politicheskoi i sotsial'noi zhizni," *MEMO*, No. 5 (May, 1969), pp. 92-93.

154. S. Nadel', "Klassovaya i sotsial'naya struktura razvitovo kapitalisticheskovo obshchestva," *MEMO*, No. 12 (December, 1970), p. 72.

155. Cheprakov, "O sotsial'no-ekonomicheskoi kontseptsii Gerberta Markuze," *MEMO*, No. 4 (April, 1969), p. 91.

156. *Ibid.*, pp. 93-94.

157. *Ibid.*, p. 91.

158. *Ibid.*, p. 93.

159. *Ibid.*, p. 94.

160. Rumyantsev *et al.*, eds., *Sovremennye tsikly i krizisy*, p. 73.

161. Boltho, ed., *The European Economy*, p. 512. Here wages are said to have risen by 14 percent in 1962 and by 20 percent in 1963.

162. *Ibid.*, p. 76.

163. *Ibid.*, p. 72; cf. Men'shikov, "O mekhanizme sovremennovo tsikla," *MEMO*, No. 4 (April, 1966), pp. 62-63.

164. Men'shikov, "Osobennosti sovremennykh kapitalisticheskikh tsiklov i krizisov," *Kommunist*, No. 4 (March, 1966), pp. 120-21.

165. Armstrong, Glyn, Harrison, *Capitalism Since 1945*, p. 192.

166. F. Burdzhalov, "'Politika dokhodov' i rabochii klass," *MEMO*, No. 9 (September, 1968), p. 48.

167. Leont'ev, ed., *Problemy sovremennovo imperializma*, p. 187.

168. Mileikovsky, "New Developments in the Economy of Capitalism," *International Affairs*, No. 5 (May, 1970), p. 64.

169. Inozemtsev, "Osobennosti sovremennovo imperializma i evo osnovnye protivorechiya," *MEMO*, No. 5 (May, 1970), p. 5.

170. *Ibid.*, p. 18.

171. N. Gauzner, R. Matveev, "Klassovaya bor'ba v usloviyakh gosudarst-venno-monopolisticheskovo kapitalizma," *MEMO*, No. 4 (April, 1968), p. 53.

172. *Ibid.*, p. 55.

173. Quoted in Armstrong, Glyn, Harrison, *Capitalism Since 1945*, p. 206.

174. E. Khmel'nitskaya, "Zapadnaya Evropa v sisteme mirovovo imperial-izma," *MEMO*, No. 10 (October, 1969), p. 33.

**Chapter 8. State-Monopoly Planning and Economic Restructuring
(Capitalist Perestroika)**

1. S.A. Dalin, *SShA: poslevoennyi gosudarstvenno-monopolisticheskii kapital-izm*, p. 481.

2. N.A. Tsagolov, V.A. Kirov, eds., *"Kapital" K. Marksa i problemy so-vremennovo kapitalizma*, p. 43.

3. *Ibid.*

4. A.G. Mileikovsky, ed., *Novye yavleniya v nakoplenii kapitala v impe-rialisticheskikh stranakh*, pp. 421-22.

5. Tsagolov, Kirov, eds., *"Kapital" K. Marksa*, p. 24 (my italics).

6. *Ibid.*, p. 16.

7. In *The New Industrial State* (p. 14), Galbraith wrote that "The five hundred largest corporations produce close to half of all the goods and services that are available annually in the United States."

8. Marx, *Capital*, II, 186.

9. Stalin, *Sochineniya*, 3 [XVI], 251.

10. *Ibid.*, pp. 214-15.

11. *Ibid.*, p. 215.

12. See I.M. Mrachkovskaya, *Razvitie V.I. Leninym marksistskoi teorii vosproizvodstva obshchestvennovo kapitala*, pp. 43-44 and 51-52; cf. Lenin, *Polnoe sobranie sochinenii*, III, 54-55.

13. L. Schapiro, P. Reddaway, eds., *Lenin: The Man, the Theorist, the Leader—a Reappraisal*, p. 197.

14. Marx, *Capital*, I, 612.

15. *Ibid.*

16. *Ibid.*, III, 231.

17. *Pravda* (7 November, 1957).

18. Quoted in Z. Brzezinski and S.P. Huntington, *Political Power: USA/USSR*, p. 275.

19. "Programme of the Communist Party of the Soviet Union," *New Times* (supplement), No. 48 (29 September, 1961), pp. 29-30.

20. *Documents of the 22nd Congress of the CPSU*, II, 42,

21. C.A. Linden, *Khrushchev and the Soviet Leadership, 1957-1964*, pp. 174-201.

22. Hickman, *Growth and Stability of the Postwar Economy*, p. 187.

23. *Ibid.*, p. 190.

24. *Ibid.*, pp. 187-89.

25. M. Golansky, "Vliyanie tekhnicheskovo progressa na kapitalisticheskoe vosproizvodstvo," *Voprosy ekonomiki*, No. 9 (September, 1961), p. 132.

26. Ibid., p. 133; cf. Marx, *Capital*, III, 231.

27. Arzumanyan, "Krizis mirovovo kapitalizma," *MEMO*, No. 12 (December, 1961), pp. 17-18.

28. Bechin, "Osobennosti vosproizvodstva v SShA," *MEMO*, No. 10 (October, 1962), p. 74.

29. I. Ivanov, "Sovremennyi kapitalizm i nauchno-tekhnicheskii progress," *MEMO*, No. 10 (October, 1962), p. 4.

30. S. Kheinman, "Ob izmeneniyakh v otraslevoi strukture promyshlennosti SShA," *Voprosy ekonomiki*, No. 2 (February, 1964), p. 78.

31. Ya. Kotkovsky, "Sovremennye usloviya ekonomicheskovo sorevnovaniya SSSR i SShA," *Voprosy ekonomiki*, No. 4 (April, 1967), pp. 74-75.

32. *Ibid.*, pp. 78-81.

33. *Ibid.*, p. 73.

34. W.W. Rostow, *The Stages of Economic Growth*, p. 93.

35. *Ibid.*, p. 99.

36. A. Bergson, H.S. Levine, eds., *The Soviet Economy: Toward the Year 2000*, pp. 180-83.

37. Mileikovsky, "Poleznyi analiz zarubeshnovo opyta," *MEMO*, No. 4 (April, 1963), p. 151.

38. *Ibid.*, p. 154.

39. See "Issledovanie problem ekonomicheskovo sorevnovaniya dvukh sistem," *Voprosy ekonomiki*, No. 6 (June, 1964), p. 153.

40. I. Osadchaya, "'Neoklassicheskaya' teoriya rosta v sovremennoi politicheskoi ekonomii," *MEMO*, No. 3 (March, 1967), p. 28.

41. S. Vygodsky, "Nekotorye tendentsii kapitalisticheskovo vosproizvodstva v sovremennykh usloviyakh," *MEMO*, No. 10 (October, 1965), p. 100.

42. *Ibid.*, p. 101.

43. *Ibid.*

44. *Ibid.*, p. 103.

45. S.M. Nikitin, *Strukturnye izmeneniya v kapitalisticheskoi ekonomike*, p. 4.

46. *Ibid.*, p. 6.

47. *Ibid.*, pp. 76-77.

48. *Ibid.*, p. 95.

49. Mileikovsky, ed., *Novye yavleniya*, p. 251.

50. Nikitin, *Strukturnye izmeneniya*, p. 100.

51. *Ibid.*; cf. N.N. Inozemtsev, S.M. Men'shikov, A.G. Mileikovsky, A.M. Rumyantsev, eds., *Politicheskaya ekonomiya sovremennovo monopolisticheskovo kapitalizma*, I, 332.

52. Nikitin, *Strukturnye izmeneniya*, pp. 154-55.

53. H.J. Sherman, *The Soviet Economy*, p. 109.

54. Nikitin, *Strukturnye izmeneniya*, p. 103.

55. Mileikovsky, ed., *Novye yavleniya*, p. 295.

56. Nikitin, *Strukturnye izmeneniya*, p. 239.

57. *Ibid.*, p. 242; cf. p. 246.

58. *Ibid.*, p. 237.

59. Mileikovsky, ed., *Novye yavleniya*, p. 319.

60. Marx, *Surplus Value*, I, 227; cf. Nikitin, *Strukturnye izmeneniya*, p. 119.

61. Mileikovsky, ed., *Novye yavleniya*, p. 230.

62. Galbraith, *The New Industrial State*, p. 32.

63. *Ibid.*, pp. 18-19.

64. *Ibid.*, p. 44.

65. *Ibid.*, p. 49.

66. *Ibid.*, p. 118.

67. *Ibid.*, p. 397.

68. *Ibid.*, p. 320.

69. Shonfield, *Modern Capitalism*, p. 121.

70. *Ibid.*, p. 86.

71. A.I. Pokrovsky, ed., *Ekonomicheskoe programmirovanie v stranakh Zapadnoi Evropy*, p. 6.

72. *Ibid.*, p. 8.

73. *Ibid.*, p. 40.

74. *Ibid.*, pp. 44-45.

75. *Ibid.*, p. 47.

76. *Ibid.*, pp. 48-49.

77. *Ibid.*, p. 50.

78. *Ibid.*, p. 11.

79. Mileikovsky, ed., *Novye yavleniya*, p. 5 (my italics).

80. *Ibid.*, pp. 11-14.

81. Mileikovsky, "State-Monopoly Capitalism," *New Times*, No. 41 (14 October, 1970), p. 20.

82. Mileikovsky, ed., *Novye yavleniya*, p. 43; cf. Mileikovsky, *Leninskaya teoriya imperializma i sovremennyi gosudarstvenno-monopolisticheskii kapitalizm*, pp. 39-40.

83. Mileikovsky, *Novye yavleniya*, p. 25.

84. Mileikovsky, "State-Monopoly Capitalism," *New Times*, No. 41 (14 October, 1970), p. 20.

85. Mileikovsky, ed., *Novye yavleniya*, p. 6.

86. Mileikovsky, "State-Monopoly Capitalism," *New Times*, No. 43 (28 October, 1970), p. 22.

87. Mileikovsky, "Burzhuaznaya politicheskaya ekonomiya i politika investitsii," *MEMO*, No. 4 (April, 1967), p. 25.

88. Mileikovsky, "State-Monopoly Capitalism," *New Times*, No. 46 (18 November, 1970), p. 20.

89. Mileikovsky, "State-Monopoly Capitalism," *New Times*, No. 43 (28 October, 1970, p. 20 (my italics).

90. Stalin, *Selected Interviews*, p. 113.

91. Tsagolov, Kirov, eds., *"Kapital" K. Marksa*, pp. 24-26.

92. Veblen, *The Theory of the Leisure Class: An Economic Study of Institutions*; also Veblen, *The Engineers and the Price System*.

93. A.A. Berle, G.C. Means, *The Modern Corporation and Private Property*, p. 94 *et seq.*

94. *Ibid.*, pp. 356-57.

95. Schumpeter, *Capitalism, Socialism and Democracy*, p. 142.

96. *Ibid.*, p. 134.

97. *Ibid.*, p. 156.

98. *Ibid.*, p. 132.

99. Galbraith, *New Industrial State*, p. 68.

100. *Ibid.*, p. 82.

101. *Ibid.*, pp. 100-1.

102. R.L. Heilbroner, *The Limits of American Capitalism*, pp. 132-33.

103. S. Khavina, "Lzhenauchnaya teoriya skhodstva dvukh sistem," *Voprosy ekonomiki*, No. 6 (June, 1963), pp. 79-85.

104. Cheprakov, "Teoriya konvergentsii i deistvitel'nost'," *Voprosy ekonomiki*, No. 1 (January, 1968), p. 92.

105. Vygodsky, "Ekonomicheskaya osnova krizisa mirovovo kapitalizma," *MEMO*, No. 11 (November, 1968), pp. 9-10.

106. K. Kozlova, "'Novoe industrial'noe obshchestvo' Dzhona Golbreisa," *MEMO*, No. 1 (January, 1968), p. 145.

107. *Ibid.*, p. 149.

108. S. Menshikov, *Millionaires and Managers*, p. 15.

109. S.L. Vygodsky, V.S. Afanas'ev, V.A. Matveev, eds., *Aktual'nye ekonomicheskie problemy sovremennovo kapitalizma*, pp. 152-53.

110. *Ibid.*, p. 159.

111. *Ibid.*, p. 161; cf. Yu. Shishkov, "Novye proyavleniya osnovnovo protivorechiya kapitalizma," *MEMO*, No. 5 (May, 1971), pp. 36-37.

112. Dalin, "Izmeneniya v strukture kapitalisticheskoi sobstvennosti," *MEMO*, No. 12 (December, 1965), p. 52.

113. Dalin, "Kritika burzhuaznykh kontseptsii sovremennoi korporatsii," *MEMO*, No. 6 (June, 1966), p. 34.

114. Dalin, "The Changing Structure of Capitalism," *New Times*, No. 37 (13 September, 1967), p. 9.

115. *Ibid.*, p. 10.

116. *Ibid.*, p. 7.

117. Marx, *Capital*, III, 427.

118. *Ibid.*, p. 428.

119. Engels, *Anti-Duhring*, p. 312.

120. L.A. Leont'ev, ed., *Problemy sovremennovo imperializma*, p. 48.

121. Dalin, "The Changing Structure of Capitalism," pp. 10-11.

122. N.N. Inozemtsev, A.G. Mileikovsky, V.A. Martynov, eds., *Politicheskaya ekonomiya sovremennovo monopolisticheskovo kapitalizma*, I, 55.

123. *Ibid.*, p. 49.

124. Nikitin, *Strukturnye izmeneniya*, p. 157; cf. Mileikovsky, ed., *Novye yavleniya*, p. 276.

125. Leont'ev, ed., *Problemy sovremennovo imperializma*, p. 95.

126. Inozemtsev, Men'shikov, Mileikovsky, Rumyantsev, eds., *Politicheskaya ekonomiya sovremennovo monopolisticheskovo kapitalizma*, I, 138.

127. Tsagolov, Kirov, eds., *"Kapital" K. Marksa*, p. 123.

128. "Monopolies Today," *International Affairs*, No. 5 (May, 1968), p. 86.

129. *Ibid.*, pp. 84-91; cf. M.V. Senin, *Razvitie mezhdunarodnykh ekonomicheskikh svyazei*, pp. 78-79 *et passim*.

130. Inozemtsev, Mileikovsky, Martynov, eds., *Politicheskaya ekonomiya sovremennovo monopolisticheskovo kapitalizma*, I, 57.

131. Paul R. Gregory, Robert C. Stuart, *Soviet Economic Structure and Performance*, 4th ed., p. 448.

132. E.G. Liberman, *Economic Methods and the Effectiveness of Production*, p. 43.

133. *Ibid.*, p. 52.

134. *Ibid.*, p. 87.

135. *Ibid.*, p. 116.

136. *Ibid.*, p. 97.

137. Galbraith, *The New Industrial State*, p. 41.

138. See Galbraith, *Economics and the Public Purpose*, pp. 55-77.

Chapter 9. National Plans and the International Monetary Crisis

1. Marx, *Capital*, I, 763.

2. Robert C. Tucker, ed., *Marx-Engels Reader*, p. 476.

3. *Ibid.*, p. 478.

4. *Ibid.*, p. 476.

5. *Ibid.*, p. 478.

6. See Martin Nicolaus' foreword to Marx, *Grundrisse*, p. 54; also pp. 108 and 264.

7. *Ibid.*, p. 101.

8. Lenin, *Collected Works*, I, 100.

9. Lenin, *Selected Works*, I, 764.

10. *Ibid.*, p. 780.

11. N. Bukharin, *Imperialism and World Economy*, p. 118.

12. Bukharin, *Selected Writings*, p. 41; cf. p. 51.

13. Day, *Leon Trotsky*, p. 13.

14. *Ibid.*, p. 14.

15. Lenin, *Selected Works*, I, 705; cf. 759.

16. Day, *Leon Trotsky*, p. 130.

17. "'Integration' of Monopoly Capital—Some New Developments," *World Marxist Review*, 5, No. 7 (July, 1962), p. 16.

18. E.L. Khmel'nitskaya, ed., *Ekonomicheskie problemy 'Obshchevo Rynka,'* p. 24.

19. Khmel'nitskaya, "Malaya Evropa—konflikty i kompromissy," *MEMO*, No. 2 (February, 1964), p. 99.

20. *Ibid.*

21. V.I. Stepanov, *Ekonomicheskie osnovy mirnovo sosushchestvovaniya*, p. 84.

22. Day, *Leon Trotsky*, p. 166 *et seq.*

23. Inozemtsev, Men'shikov, Mileikovsky, Rumyantsev, eds., *Politicheskaya ekonomiya sovremennovo monopolisticheskovo kapitalizma*, II, 65.

24. *Ibid.*, p. 70.

25. *Ibid.*, p. 69.

26. *Ibid.*, pp. 69-70.

27. *Ibid.*, p. 69. A.I. Mikoyan had made the same observation several years earlier in *Pravda* (30 November, 1959): "What is autarky? It means trying to produce everything at home, even items that are very costly, rather than buying them from others more cheaply."

28. Marx, *Capital*, III, 313.

29. From 1970 to 1972 the IMF also created new reserve assets in the form of SDRs (special drawing rights): see Brian Tew, *The Evolution of the International Monetary System 1945-77*, pp. 148-53.

30. Inozemtsev, Men'shikov, Mileikovsky, Rumyantsev, eds., *Politicheskaya ekonomiya sovremennovo monopolisticheskovo kapitalizma*, II, 94; cf. A.G. Mileikovsky, ed., *Burzhuaznye ekonomicheskie teorii i ekonomicheskaya politika imperialisticheskikh stran*, pp. 273-74.

31. Mileikovsky, ed., *Burzhuaznye ekonomicheskie teorii*, p. 266.

32. Inozemtsev, Men'shikov, Mileikovsky, Rumyantsev, eds., *Politicheskaya ekonomiya sovremennovo monopolisticheskovo kapitalizma*, II, 103.

33. W.M. Scammell, *The International Economy Since 1945*, p. 106.

34. *Ibid.*, p. 149.

35. *Ibid.*, p. 160.

36. *Ibid.*, p. 149.

37. Inozemtsev, Men'shikov, Mileikovsky, Rumyantsev, eds., *Politicheskaya ekonomiya sovremennovo monopolisticheskovo kapitalizma*, II, 119-20.

38. *Ibid.*, p. 121.

39. Manukyan, "Vyvoz kapitala i mezhdunarodnye monopolii," *MEMO*, No. 2 (February, 1970), p. 30.

40. Yu. Shishkov, "Novye proyavleniya osnovnovo protivorechiya kapitalizma," *MEMO*, No. 5 (May, 1971), p. 39.

41. *Ibid.*, p. 32.

42. *Ibid.*, p. 39.

43. Leland B. Yeager, *International Monetary Relations: Theory, History, and Policy*, p. 436.

44. *Ibid.*, p. 438.

45. Scammell, *The International Economy*, p. 161.

46. Motylev, *Teorii mirovoi kapitalisticheskoi ekonomiki*, p. 125.

47. Scammell, *The International Economy*, p. 94; cf. Yeager, *International Monetary Relations*, pp. 441-461; Boltho, ed., *The European Economy*, pp. 528-46; Felix Burdjalov, *State Monopoly Incomes Policy*, pp. 52-57.

48. E. Khesin, "Economic Clouds Over Britain," *New Times*, No. 42 (21 October, 1964), p. 19.

49. Yeager, *International Monetary Relations*, p. 456.

50. A. Sutulin, "The British National Plan," *New Times*, No. 49 (8 December, 1965), pp. 31-32; cf. V. Nekrasov, "The Labour Government's First Steps," *New Times*, No. 46 (18 November, 1964), pp. 12-14.

51. Burdjalov, *State Monopoly Incomes Policy*, pp. 124-26.

52. Men'shikov, "Ustarel li ekonomicheskii tsikl?" *MEMO*, No. 8 (August, 1967), p. 95.

53. Kuzminov, "Western Economy on the Threshold of 1967," *International Affairs*, No. 2 (February, 1967), p. 49.

54. L. Sedin, "Britain's Vicious Circle," *New Times*, No. 38 (20 September, 1967), p. 5.

55. Mileikovsky, ed., *Burzhuaznye ekonomicheskie teorii*, pp. 278-80.

56. Yeager, *International Monetary Relations*, pp. 460-61.

57. Mileikovsky, ed., *Burzhuaznye ekonomicheskie teorii*, p. 256.

58. V.A. Maslennikov, A.I. Medov, eds., *Mirovaya ekonomika*, pp. 204-10.

59. Boltho, ed., *The European Economy*, pp. 485-86.

60. *Ibid.*, p. 490.

61. Yeager, *International Monetary Relations*, p. 506.

62. *Ibid.*, p. 508.

63. Boltho, ed., *The European Economy*, pp. 456-57.

64. Dimitry Smyslov, "Gold Against the Dollar," *New Times*, No. 11 (17 March, 1965), p. 9; cf. N. Yuryev, "Franco-American Discord," *International Affairs*, No. 3 (March, 1965), pp. 51-55.

65. Yeager, *International Monetary Relations*, p. 481.

66. Dimitry Smyslov, "Gold Against the Dollar," p. 11.

67. A. Anikin, "Monetary Problems of the West," *International Affairs*, No. 4 (April, 1965), p. 28.

68. Cheprakov, "Rivalry in Partnership," *International Affairs*, No. 9 (September, 1965), p. 76.

69. N. Yuryev, "Franco-American Discord," p. 52; cf. Maslennikov, Medov, eds., *Mirovaya ekonomika*, pp. 225-56; Dalin, *SShA: poslevoennyi gosudarstvenno-monopolisticheskii kapitalizm*, p. 488.

70. O. Bogdanov, "Valyutnyi uzel mezhimperialisticheskikh protivorechii," *Kommunist*, No. 8 (May, 1968), p. 89.

71. Lyubov Vidyasova, "Paris and Washington—A Study in Disagreement," *New Times*, No. 36 (8 September, 1965), pp. 18-20.

72. Victor Perlo, "The U.S. Boom: Viet-Nam War Phase," *International Affairs*, No. 12 (December, 1965), p. 16; cf. Scammell, *The International Economy*, p. 143.

73. Yuryev, "Soviet-French Co-operation and European Security," *International Affairs*, No. 6 (June, 1966), p. 7.

74. *Ibid.*, p. 9.

75. *Ibid.*, p. 12.

76. Maslennikov, Medov, eds., *Mirovaya ekonomika*, p. 227.

77. I. Grigoryev, "France and the U.S.S.R.—Fruitful Co-operation," *International Affairs*, No. 7 (July, 1967), p. 19.

78. Goldman, *Detente and Dollars*, p. 34. French sales had been as high as $88 million in 1962.

79. Yuryev, "Soviet-French Co-operation . . .," p. 10.

80. Grigoryev, "France and the U.S.S.R. . . .," p. 23.

81. Boltho, ed., *The European Economy*, p. 462.

82. Motylev, *Teorii mirovoi kapitalisticheskoi ekonomiki*, p. 148.

83. Yuri Bochkaryov, "Background to de Gaulle's Resignation," *New Times*, No. 19-20 (May, 1969), p. 28.

84. Mileikovsky, ed., *Burzhuaznye ekonomicheskie teorii*, pp. 276-77.

85. Yeager, *International Monetary Relations*, pp. 481-83; cf. S. Ivashkevich, "Monetary Problems of the Capitalist World," *New Times*, No. 43 (October, 1968), pp. 7-9.

86. Yeager, *International Monetary Relations*, p. 510.

87. *Ibid.*, p. 575.

88. Menshikov, "The Troubled Dollar," *New Times*, No. 12 (27 March, 1968), p. 10.

89. Kuzminov, "Western Economy on the Threshold of 1967," *International Affairs*, No. 2 (February, 1967), p. 50.

90. Menshikov, "The U.S. Economic Maze," *New Times*, No. 9 (6 March, 1968), p. 10.

91. See "The Nixon Cabinet," *New Times*, No. 2 (13 January, 1969), p. 13.

92. Mileikovsky, "New Developments in the Economy of Capitalism," *International Affairs*, No. 5 (May, 1970), p. 68.

93. See "Ekonomika SShA: otsenka polozheniya i perspektivy," *MEMO*, No. 9 (September, 1970), pp. 85-87.

94. I.M. Osadchaya, *Sovremennoe keinsianstvo*, pp. 140-41.

95. "Ekonomika SShA . . .," *MEMO*, No. 9 (September, 1970), p. 87.

96. Mileikovsky, ed., *Burzhuaznye ekonomicheskie teorii*, p. 266.

97. "Ekonomika SShA . . .," *MEMO*, No. 9 (September, 1970), p. 87.

98. A.W. Phillips, "The Relation Between Unemployment and the Rate of Change of Money Wage Rates in the United Kingdom, 1861-1957," *Economica*, No. 25 (November, 1958), 283-99.

99. "Ekonomika SShA . . .," *MEMO*, No. 9 (September, 1970), p. 88 (my italics).

100. "Ekonomika SShA . . .," *MEMO*, No. 10 (October, 1970), p. 101; cf. Mileikovsky, "General Crisis of Capitalism: Further Aggravation," *International Affairs*, No. 9 (September, 1971), pp. 21-24.

101. "Ekonomika SShA . . .," *MEMO*, No. 10 (October, 1970), p. 98.

102. Leontyev, "The Discoveries of Milton Friedman," *New Times*, No. 2 (13 January, 1971), p. 28.

103. *Ibid.*, p. 27.

104. "Ekonomika SShA . . .," *MEMO*, No. 9 (September, 1970), p. 93.

105. *Ibid.*, p. 94.

106. "Ekonomika SShA . . .," *MEMO*, No. 10 (October, 1970), pp. 95- 96.

107. *Ibid.*, p. 93.

108. Manukyan, "Sovremennyi ekonomicheskii krizis v SShA," *SShA*, No. 2 (February, 1971), p. 3.

109. "Ekonomika SShA . . .," *MEMO*, No. 9 (September, 1970), pp. 90 and 96; cf. Dalin, *SShA: poslevoennyi gosudarstvenno-monopolisticheskii kapitalizm*, p. 474.

110. See "Kon'yunktura i tsikl," *MEMO*, No. 4 (April, 1969), p. 112.

111. "Ekonomika SShA . . .," *MEMO*, No. 9 (September, 1970), p. 90.

112. *Ibid.*, p. 97.

113. *Ibid.*, p. 96.

114. Osadchaya, *Sovremennoe keinsianstvo*, p. 173.

115. V. Usoskin, "Monetarizm v SShA: istoki, sushchnost', vliyanie na ekonomicheskuyu politiku," *MEMO*, No. 5 (May, 1971), pp. 69-70.

116. E. Grebennikova, "The Dollar Crisis and Monetary Contradictions in the West," *International Affairs*, No. 11 (November, 1971), p. 35.

117. Yeager, *International Monetary Relations*, p. 576; cf. Brian Tew, *The Evolution of the International Monetary System*, p. 162.

118. Grebennikova, "The Dollar Crisis . . .," p. 36.

119. Yeager, *International Monetary Relations*, p. 577.

120. Tew, *Evolution of the International Monetary System*, p. 164.

121. *Ibid.*, p. 114.

122. Grebennikova, "The Dollar Crisis . . .," p. 34.

123. Quoted in Mileikovsky, "General Crisis of Capitalism: Further Aggravation," *International Affairs*, No. 9 (September, 1971), p. 19.

124. Vygodsky, "Ekonomicheskaya osnova krizisa mirovovo kapitalizma," *MEMO*, No. 11 (November, 1968), p. 13.

125. Kuzminov, "The World Capitalist Economy: Present State and Prospects," *International Affairs*, No. 5 (May, 1968), p. 14.

126. Kuzminov, "Economic Situation in the Capitalist World," *International Affairs*, No. 5 (May, 1971), p. 38.

127. *Ibid.*, p. 41.

128. *Ibid.*, pp. 42-43.

129. Dalin, "A Sick Economy," *New Times*, No. 29 (22 July, 1970), p. 22.

130. *Ibid.*, p. 23.

131. Dalin, "A Sick Economy," *New Times*, No. 31 (5 August, 1970), p. 24.

132. Dalin, "A Sick Economy," *New Times*, No. 29 (22 July, 1970), p. 23.

133. Dalin, *SShA: poslevoennyi gosudarstvenno-monopolisticheskii kapitalizm*, p. 498.

134. S. Vishnevsky, "The American Crisis and Nixon's Policy," *International Affairs*, No. 7 (July, 1970), p. 37.

135. *Ibid.*, p. 43.

136. Mileikovsky, "General Crisis of Capitalism: Further Aggravation," pp. 22-23.

137. Robert J. Flanagan, David W. Soskice, Lloyd Ulman, *Unionism, Economic Stabilization, and Incomes Policies*, p. 397.

138. Armstrong, Glyn, Harrison, *Capitalism Since 1945*, p. 191; cf. p. 167.

139. Flanagan, Soskice, Ulman, *Unionism, Economic Stabilization, and Incomes Policies*, p. 651.

140. Armstrong, Glyn, Harrison, *Capitalism Since 1945*, p. 169.

141. *Ibid.*, p. 176.

142. *Ibid.*

143. Boltho, ed., *The European Economy*, p. 24.

144. Ibid., p. 184. See the table on profit shares in manufacturing, p. 372. On the same page, Karl-Olof Faxen speaks of "a general decline in the share of gross profits in manufacturing value added in Europe from at least the mid-1960s onwards."

145. *Ibid.*, p. 52.

146. A. Shapiro, "Ekonomicheskie problemy SShA 70-kh godov," *MEMO*, No. 3 (March, 1971), p. 27.

147. See "Kon'yunktura i tsikl," *MEMO*, No. 4 (April, 1969), p. 99.

148. Manukyan, "Sovremennyi ekonomicheskii krizis v SShA," *SShA*, No. 2 (February, 1971), pp. 4-6.

Chapter 10. Detente and "Deepening of the General Crisis"

1. Milton Friedman, *Dollars and Deficits*, p. 159.

2. Galbraith, *Economics and the Public Purpose*, p. 187.

3. See "Kon'yunktura i tsikl," *MEMO*, No. 4 (April, 1969), p. 112.

4. *Ibid.*, p. 110.

5. *Ibid.*

6. Dalin, *SShA: poslevoennyi gosudarstvenno-monopolisticheskii kapitalizm*, p. 463.

7. Rumyantsev *et al.*, eds., *Sovremennye tsikly i krizisy*, p. 122.

8. M.S. Dragilev, N.I. Mokhov, *Leninskii analiz monopolisticheskovo kapitala i sovremennost'*, p. 299.

9. *Ibid.*, p. 292.

10. *Ibid.*, pp. 294-95.

11. *Ibid.*, p. 297; cf. Dalin in Rumyantsev *et al.*, eds., *Sovremennye tsikly i krizisy*, p. 163.

12. Dragilev, Mokhov, *Leninskii analiz*, p. 300.

13. Dalin, *SShA: poslevoennyi gosudarstvenno-monopolisticheskii kapitalizm*, p. 419.

14. *Ibid.*, p. 424.

15. *Ibid.*, pp. 418 and 424.

16. *Ibid.*, p. 434.

17. *Ibid.*, p. 474.

18. *Ibid.*

19. Inozemtsev, Men'shikov, Mileikovsky, Rumyantsev, eds., *Politicheskaya ekonomiya sovremennovo monopolisticheskovo kapitalizma*, I, 367.

20. *Ibid.*, p. 368.

21. Pokrovsky, "The Capitalist Economy: A Crisis Spiral," *International Affairs*, No. 12 (December, 1972), p. 26.

22. V.N. Cherkovets, I.P. Faminsky, V.A. Kirov, eds., *Leninskii analiz imperializma i sovremennyi kapitalizm*, p. 211.

23. See "Kon'yunktura i tsikl," *MEMO*, No. 4 (April, 1969), p. 107.

24. Inozemtsev, Men'shikov, Mileikovsky, Rumyantsev, eds., *Politicheskaya ekonomiya sovremennovo monopolisticheskovo kapitalizma*, II, 7.

25. Kuzminov, "The Economy of Capitalism at the Beginning of 1972," *International Affairs*, No. 4 (April, 1972), p. 27.

26. Mileikovsky, "The Scientific-Technological Revolution and Capitalism," *New Times*, No. 13 (March, 1973), p. 18.

27. Mileikovsky, "O sovremennom etape krizisa burzhuaznoi politekonomii," *MEMO*, No. 12 (December, 1972), p. 45.

28. *Ibid.*, p. 54; cf. Mileikovsky, "Crisis of Bourgeois Economic Theory and Galbraith's 'New Ideas,'" *New Times*, No. 28 (July, 1972), pp. 18-21.

29. See "Osobennosti sovremennovo kapitalisticheskovo tsikla," *MEMO*, No. 6 (June, 1963), p. 63.

30. See M. Dragilev, "Sovremennyi tsikl: nekotorye teoreticheskie aspekty," *MEMO*, No. 6 (June, 1973), pp. 73-80; Yu. Pokataev, "Poslevoennye tsikly i krizisy v SShA," *Ibid.*, pp. 81-88; Ya. Pevzner, "Tsikly v poslevoennoi Yaponii," *Ibid.*, No. 7 (July, 1973), pp. 91-95.

31. V. Kuznetsov, "Tsiklicheskoe razvitie frantsuzskoi ekonomiki (1949-1972 gg.)," *MEMO*, No. 8 (August, 1973), p. 81.

32. Kuzminov, "The Economy of Capitalism at the Beginning of 1972," p. 26.

33. *Ibid.*, p. 29.

34. Kuzminov, "The 1969-1971 Economic Crisis, Its Character and Consequences," *International Affairs*, No. 9 (September, 1973), p. 39.

35. Kuzminov, "The Economy of Capitalism at the Beginning of 1972," p. 26.

36. Scammell, *The International Economy*, p. 181.

37. Yeager, *International Monetary Relations*, pp. 579-80.

38. *Ibid.*, pp. 580-81.

39. Tew, *Evolution of the International Monetary System*, p. 173; cf. Scammell, *The International Economy*, p. 183; A. Anikin, "Deval'vatsiya dollara i novaya sistema valyutnykh paritetov," *MEMO*, No. 2 (February, 1972), pp. 82-87.

40. Yeager, *International Monetary Relations*, p. 468.

41. Scammell, *The International Economy*, p. 185.

42. Grebennikova, "The West in Search of a New Currency System," *International Affairs*, No. 1 (January, 1973), p. 42.

43. Grebennikova, "Floating Monetary Crisis," *International Affairs*, No. 10 (October, 1973), p. 54.

44. E.S. Shershnev, "Torgovo-politicheskoe nastuplenie SShA," *SShA*, No. 1 (January, 1972), p. 13.

45. Motylev, *Teorii mirovoi kapitalisticheskoi ekonomiki*, p. 104.

46. E. Selikhov, "Anatomy of the Monetary Crisis," *New Times*, No. 34 (August, 1972), p. 20.

47. S. Safronov, "The Capitalist Economy, 1971," *New Times*, No. 52 (December, 1971), p. 20.

48. Inozemtsev, Men'shikov, Mileikovsky, Rumyantsev, eds., *Politicheskaya ekonomiya sovremennovo monopolisticheskovo kapitalizma*, I, 356.

49. *Ibid.*, p. 368.

50. N.N. Inozemtsev, E.M. Primakov, I.I. Gur'ev, eds., *Uglublenie obshchevo krizisa kapitalizma*, p. 139.

51. G. Stepanov, "East-West Trade Relations," *International Affairs*, No. 12 (December, 1969), p. 30; cf. Yu.N. Kapelinsky, *Na vzaimovygodnoi osnove*, p. 90.

52. Stalin, *Sochineniya*, 3 [XVI], 224.

53. Lenin, *Collected Works*, XXXIII, 155 (my italics).

54. Dalin, "Nekotorye voprosy sovremennoi bor'by za peredel mirovovo rynka," *MEMO*, No. 4 (April, 1964), p. 63.

55. Stepanov, *Ekonomicheskie osnovy mirnovo sosushchestvovaniya*, p. 4.

56. *Ibid.*, pp. 7-8.

57. *Ibid.*, p. 31.

58. *Ibid.*, p. 32.

59. *Ibid.*, p. 36.

60. *Ibid.*, p. 34.

61. Marx, *Grundrisse*, p. 711; cf. p. 139.

62. Marx, *Capital*, I, 351.

63. Stepanov, *Ekonomicheskie osnovy mirnovo sosushchestvovaniya*, p. 94.

64. "Uchenie V.I. Lenina ob imperializme i sovremennost'—k 50-letiyu vykhoda v svet raboty 'Imperializm, kak vysshaya stadiya kapitalizma,'" *MEMO*, No. 5 (May, 1967), p. 13.

65. Mileikovsky, "50 let Velikovo Oktyabrya i obshchii krizis kapitalizma," *MEMO*, No. 11 (November, 1967), p. 52.

66. *Ibid.*, p. 64.

67. *Ibid.*, p. 62.

68. M.V. Senin, *Razvitie mezhdunarodnykh ekonomicheskikh svyazei*, pp. 67-69.

69. *Ibid.*, p. 80.

70. *Ibid.*, pp. 76-77 *et seq.*

71. G.M. Prokhorov, *Vneshneekonomicheskie svyazi i ekonomicheskii rost sotsialisticheskikh stran*, p. 9.

72. *Ibid.*, p. 47.

73. *Ibid.*, p. 34.

74. *Ibid.*, p. 37.

75. *Ibid.*, p. 42.

76. *Ibid.*, p. 204.

77. *Ibid.*, p. 13.

78. *Ibid.*, p. 29.

79. G.A. Shpil'ko, *Teorii i metody regulirovaniya kapitalisticheskoi ekonomiki*, p. 161.

80. M.S. Dragilev, I.P. Faminsky, M.N. Os'mova, eds., *Problemy razvitiya ekonomicheskikh otnoshenii mezhdu sotsialisticheskimi i kapitalisticheskimi stranami*, p. 9.

81. *Ibid.*, p. 22.

82. *Ibid.*, p. 50

83. Inozemtsev, Men'shikov, Mileikovsky, Rumyantsev, eds., *Politicheskaya ekonomiya sovremennovo monopolisticheskovo kapitalizma*, II, 190.

84. *Ibid.*, p. 199.

85. *Ibid.*, p. 187.

86. Shershnev, "O sovetsko-amerikanskoi torgovle," *SShA*, No. 2 (February, 1970), p. 21; cf. Shershnev, *On The Principle of Mutual Advantage*, p. 82.

87. Dalin, "Ekonomicheskie posledstviya voiny vo V'etname," *SShA*, No. 2 (February, 1970), p. 50.

88. Funigiello, *American-Soviet Trade*, p. 179.

89. Shershnev, ed., *SSSR-SShA: Ekonomicheskie otnosheniya*, p. 186; cf. Shershnev, *Mutual Advantage*, p. 89.

90. B. Pichugin, "East-West Economic Relations," *International Affairs*, No. 11 (November, 1970), p. 46.

91. Shershnev, "O sovetsko-amerikanskoi torgovle," p. 19.

92. Shershnev, *Mutual Advantage*, p. 89; cf. Shershnev, ed., *SSSR-SShA*, p. 187.

93. Shershnev, *Mutual Advantage*, p. 91; cf. Goldman, *Detente and Dollars*, p. 73.

94. B. Dmitriev, "Policy of Detente," *New Times*, No. 43 (October, 1971), pp. 7-8.

95. Funigiello, *American-Soviet Trade*, p. 177; cf. LaFeber, *America, Russia, and the Cold War*, p. 264.

96. A.A. Gromyko, "Sovremennye tendentsii vneshnei politiki SShA," *SShA*, No. 4 (April, 1972), p. 42.

97. "Leninskii kurs vneshnei politiki KPSS," *Kommunist*, No. 9 (June, 1972), p. 78.

98. Gromyko, "Sovremennye tendentsii . . .," pp. 45-46; cf. Gromyko, "Leninskii revolyutsionnyi kurs vneshnei politiki," *Kommunist*, No. 1 (January, 1973), pp. 39-50.

99. Shershnev, *Mutual Advantage*, pp. 114-15.

100. A. Gorokhov, "Franklin Roosevelt on US-Soviet Relations," *International Affairs*, No. 6 (June, 1972), p. 67.

101. V.S. Chibisenkov, "Pamyati Franklina Delano Ruz'velta," *SShA*, No. 6 (June, 1972), p. 69.

102. For lend-lease negotiations see Goldman, *Detente and Dollars*, pp. 55-56.

103. Quoted in Funigiello, *American-Soviet Trade*, p. 183.

104. Shershnev, *Mutual Advantage*, p. 125; Goldman, *Detente and Dollars*, p. 132; V.I. Stepanov, *Ekonomicheskie otnosheniya Vostok-Zapad*, p. 168.

105. Shershnev, *Mutual Advantage*, p. 130; cf. Stepanov, *Ekonomicheskie otnosheniya*, p. 169.

106. Goldman, *Detente and Dollars*, pp. 292-97.

107. Shershnev, "Sovetsko-amerikanskie ekonomicheskie otnosheniya, ikh perspektivy," *SShA*, No. 1 (January, 1973), pp. 25-26.

108. N. Shmelev, "Novye gorizonty ekonomicheskikh svyazei," *MEMO*, No. 1 (January, 1973), p. 15.

109. Funigiello, *American-Soviet Trade*, pp. 182-83.

110. Stepanov, *Ekonomicheskie otnosheniya*, p. 192.

111. G.A. Arbatov, "Vneshnyaya politika SShA i nauchno-tekhnicheskaya revolyutsiya," *SShA*, No. 11 (November, 1973), p. 13. In his memoirs, Arbatov denies that the American side ever intended to end the arms race or the Cold War: see Georgi Arbatov, *The System*, pp. 188-89.

112. Stepanov, *Ekonomicheskie otnosheniya*, pp. 204-5; cf. p. 49.

113. *Ibid.*, pp. 29-30.

114. *Ibid.*, p. 129; cf. Marx, *Capital*, II, 110.

115. Stepanov, *Ekonomicheskie otnosheniya*, pp. 106-7.

116. *Ibid.*, p. 83.

117. *Ibid.*, p. 58.
118. *Ibid.*, p. 39.
119. *Ibid.*, p. 107.
120. *Ibid.*, pp. 39-40.
121. Inozemtsev, Mileikovsky, Martynov, eds., *Politicheskaya ekonomiya sovremennovo monopolisticheskovo kapitalizma*, I, 323; cf. Menshikov, *The Economic Cycle: Postwar Developments*, pp. 103-8.
122. Menshikov, *The Economic Cycle*, p. 100.
123. *Ibid.*, p. 179.
124. Armstrong, Glyn, Harrison, *Capitalism Since 1945*, p. 215.
125. Goldman, *Detente and Dollars*, p. 36.
126. *Ibid.*, p. 194.
127. Inozemtsev, Primakov, Gur'ev, eds., *Uglublenie obshchevo krizisa kapitalizma*, pp. 206-7.
128. Scammell, *The International Economy*, p. 195.
129. Inozemtsev, Primakov, Gur'ev, eds., *Uglublenie*, pp. 195-96.
130. Armstrong, Glyn, Harrison, *Capitalism Since 1945*, p. 225.
131. Inozemtsev, Primakov, Gur'ev, eds., *Uglublenie*, p. 179.
132. Armstrong, Glyn, Harrison, *Capitalism Since 1945*, p. 225.
133. Inozemtsev, Primakov, Gur'ev, eds., *Uglublenie*, p. 182.
134. Armstrong, Glyn, Harrison, *Capitalism Since 1945*, p. 227.
135. Inozemtsev, Mileikovsky, Martynov, eds., *Politicheskaya ekonomiya sovremennovo monopolisticheskovo kapitalizma*, I, 36.
136. Goldman, *Detente and Dollars*, p. 182.
137. Funigiello, *American-Soviet Trade*, p. 188; cf. Goldman, *Detente and Dollars*, p. 69.
138. V.S. Alkhimov, "Novyi etap kreditno-ekonomicheskikh otnoshenii," *SShA*, No. 7 (July, 1973), p. 8.
139. Yu. Kapelinsky, "Perspektivy sovetsko-amerikanskikh ekonomicheskikh otnoshenii," *MEMO*, No. 8 (August, 1973), p. 22.
140. Kapelinsky, *Na vzaimovygodnoi osnove*, p. 88.
141. V. Korionov, "Detente and Its Opponents," *New Times*, No. 47 (November, 1973), p. 18.
142. *Ibid.*, p. 19.
143. Shershnev, *Mutual Advantage*, p. 164.
144. Inozemtsev, Primakov, Gur'ev, eds., *Uglublenie*, p. 30.
145. *Ibid.*, p. 41.
146. *Ibid.*, p. 77.
147. *Ibid.*
148. *Ibid.*, p. 83.
149. *Ibid.*, p. 93.
150. *Ibid.*, p. 187.

151. *Ibid.*, p. 158; cf. Scammell, *The International Economy*, p. 195.

152. Inozemtsev, Primakov, Gur'ev, eds., *Uglublenie*, p. 184.

153. Manukyan, "Nekotorye izmeneniya v usloviyakh razvitiya ekonomiki kapitalisticheskikh stran," *MEMO*, No. 8 (August, 1973), p. 39.

154. Dalin, "Nauchno-tekhnicheskaya revolyutsiya i problema bezrabotitsy," *MEMO*, No. 8 (August, 1973), p. 53.

155. *Ibid.*, p. 61; cf. Dalin, *SShA: poslevoennyi gosudarstvenno-monopolisticheskii kapitalizm*, p. 502.

156. Inozemtsev, Primakov, Gur'ev, eds., *Uglublenie*, p. 261.

157. *Ibid.*, p. 269.

158. *Ibid.*, pp. 139-40.

159. *Ibid.*, p. 140.

160. *Ibid.*, p. 142.

161. *Ibid.*, p. 145.

162. Inozemtsev, Mileikovsky, Martynov, eds., *Politicheskaya ekonomiya sovremennovo monopolisticheskovo kapitalizma*, I, p. 36; cf. p. 21.

163. *Ibid.*, p. 21.

164. Inozemtsev, Primakov, Gur'ev, eds., *Uglublenie*, p. 307.

165. *Ibid.*, p. 311.

166. *Ibid.*, p. 289.

167. *Ibid.*, p. 309.

168. Some authors have described Soviet policy after detente as defensive in nature: see LaFeber, *America, Russia, and the Cold War*, p. 298; also Robert V. Daniels, *Russia: The Roots of Confrontation*, pp. 357-69.

169. *Pravda* (25 February, 1976).

170. A. Yakovlev, "Sotsializm: ot mechti k real'nosti," *Kommunist*, No. 4 (March, 1990), p. 10.

171. Aurel Braun and I made this argument when predicting Gorbachev's downfall in the spring of 1990: see "Gorbachevian Contradictions," *Problems of Communism*, 39 (May-June, 1990), pp. 36-50.

BIBLIOGRAPHY

Journals and Newspapers

Bol'shevik
International Press Correspondence (abbreviated as *IPC*)
Izvestiya
Kommunist (formerly *Bol'shevik*)
Kommunisticheskii internatsional
Mezhdunarodnaya zhizn' (*International Affairs*)
Mirovaya ekonomika i mezhdunarodnye otnosheniya (abbreviated as *MEMO*)
Mirovoe khozyaistvo i mirovaya politika (abbreviated as *Mir.khoz.*)
Novoe vremya (*New Times*)
Pravda
SShA: ekonomika, politika, ideologiya (abbreviated as *SShA*)
Vestnik Kommunisticheskoi Akademii
Voprosy ekonomiki
World Marxist Review
World News and Views (formerly *International Press Correspondence*)

Books

Adler-Karlsson, Gunnar. *Western Economic Warfare, 1947-1967.* Stokholm: lmqvist & Wiksell, 1968.

Akademiya Nauk SSSR. *Materialy mezhdunarodnovo simpoziuma 'Krizis i evolyutsiya mezhdunarodnoi valyutnoi sistemy kapitalizma.'* Moscow: mimeo, 1975.

Alekseev, A.M. *Voennye finansy kapitalisticheskikh gosudarstv.* Moscow: Gosudarstvennoe Izdatel'stvo Politicheskoi Literatury, 1949.

____, ed. *Ekonomicheskoe sorevnovanie dvukh mirovykh sistem.* Moscow: Gosudarstvennoe Izdatel'stvo Politicheskoi Literatury, 1957.

____, S.M. Ivanov, eds. *Polozhenie i bor'ba rabochevo klassa kapitalisticheskikh stran Evropy posle vtoroi mirovoi voiny.* Moscow: Izdatel'stvo Akademii Nauk SSSR, 1952.

____, ed. *Posledstviya militarizatsii ekonomiki SShA.* Moscow: Izdatel'stvo Inostrannoi Literatury, 1953.

____, L.P. Ivanova, eds. *Sovremennyi etap ekonomicheskovo sorevnovaniya dvukh mirovykh sistem.* Moscow: Izdatel'stvo 'Ekonomika,' 1964.

Al'ter, L.B. *Burzhuaznaya politicheskaya ekonomiya SShA.* Moscow: Izdatel'stvo Sotsial'no-Ekonomicheskoi Literatury, 1961.

____. *Izbrannye proizvedeniya.* Ed. A.M. Rumyantsev *et al.* Moscow: Izdatel'stvo 'Nauka,' 1971.

____. *Krushenie teorii 'planovovo kapitalizma.'* Moscow: Gosudarstvennoe Izdatel'stvo Politicheskoi Literatury, 1954.

Andreev, G. *Eksport Amerikanskovo kapitala.* Moscow: Gosudarstvennoe Izdatel'stvo Politicheskoi Literatury, 1957.

Arbatov, Georgi. *The System.* New York: Times Books, 1992.

____, G.A., ed. *SShA: Nauchno-tekhnicheskaya revolyutsiya i tendentsii vneshnei politiki.* Moscow: Izdatel'stvo 'Mezhdunarodnye Otnosheniya,' 1974.

Armstrong, Philip; Andrew Glyn; John Harrison. *Capitalism Since 1945.* Oxford: Basil Blackwell, 1991.

Arzumanyan, A.A. *Bor'ba dvukh sistem i mirovoe razvitie.* Moscow: Izdatel'stvo 'Nauka,' 1964.

____. *Krizis mirovovo kapitalizma na sovremennom etape.* Moscow: Izdatel'stvo Akademii Nauk SSSR, 1962.

____. *Problemy sovremennovo kapitalizma.* Moscow: Izdatel'stvo Ekonomicheskoi Literatury, 1963.

____, ed. *Burzhuaznaya politicheskaya ekonomiya o prolemakh sovremennovo kapitalizma.* Moscow: Izdatel'stvo 'Mysl',' 1965.

____; I.M. Lemin; E.L. Khmel'nitskaya, eds. *Problemy sovremennovo kapitalizma: k 80-letiyu akademika E.S. Varga.* Moscow: Izdatel'stvo Akademii Nauk SSSR, 1959.

Barghoorn, Frederick C. *The Soviet Image of the United States.* New York: Harcourt, Brace, 1950.

Bashkarov, E., Y. Kornilov. *Soviet-American Relations: New Prospects.* Moscow: Progress, 1975.

Bechin, A.I. *et al. Ekonomika kapitalisticheskikh stran (izmeneniya v strukture).* Moscow: Izdatel'stvo 'Mysl',' 1966.

Bell, Daniel. *The End of Ideology,* 2d ed. New York: Collier, 1962.

Belous, I.D., Yu.D. Laryushin. *Novye yavleniya v ekonomike sovremennovo kapitalizma (na primere SShA i Anglii).* Kishinev: Izdatel'stvo 'Shtiintsa,' 1972.

Bergson, Abram, Herbert S. Levine, eds. *The Soviet Economy: Toward the Year 2000.* London: Allen & Unwin, 1983.

Berle, Adolf A., Gardiner C. Means. *The Modern Corporation and Private Property.* New York: Macmillan, 1932.

Blyumin, I.G. *Kritika sovremennoi burzhuaznoi politicheskoi ekonomiki Anglii.* Moscow: Izdatel'stvo Akademii Nauk SSSR, 1953.

____. *Kritika burzhuaznoi politicheskoi ekonomii.* 3 vols. Moscow: Izdatel'stvo Akademii Nauk SSSR, 1962.

____. *Krizis sovremennoi burzhuaznoi politicheskoi ekonomii.* Moscow: Izdatel'stvo Instituta Mezhdunarodnykh Otnoshenii, 1959.

_____, I.N. Dvorkin. *Mif o 'narodnoi kapitalizme.'* Moscow: Gosudarstvennoe Izdatel'stvo Politicheskoi Literatury, 1957.

_____. *O sovremennoi burzhuaznoi politicheskoi ekonomii.* Moscow: Izdatel'stvo Sotsial'no-Ekonomicheskoi Literatury, 1958.

_____. *Ocherki sovremennoi burzhuaznoi politicheskoi ekonomii SShA.* Moscow: Gosudarstvennoe Izdatel'stvo Politicheskoi Literatury, 1956.

_____, ed. *Kritika teorii "reguliruemovo kapitalizma."* Moscow: Izdatel'stvo Sotsial'no-Ekonomicheskoi Literatury, 1959.

Bokshitsky, M.L. *Tekhniko-ekonomicheskie izmeneniya v promyshlennosti SShA vo vremya vtoroi mirovoi voiny.* Moscow: Gosplanizdat, 1947.

Boltho, Andrea, ed. *The European Economy: Growth and Crisis.* Oxford: Oxford University Press, 1982.

Bregel, E.Ya. *Kredit i kreditnaya sistema kapitalizma.* Moscow: Gosfinizdat, 1948.

_____. *Kritika burzhuaznykh uchenii ob ekonomicheskoi sisteme sovremennovo kapitalizma.* Moscow: Izdatel'stvo 'Mysl',' 1972.

_____. *Nalogi, zaimy i inflyatsiya na sluzhbe imperializma.* Moscow: Gosfinizdat, 1953.

_____. *Politicheskaya ekonomiya kapitalizma.* Moscow: Izdatel'stvo 'Mezhdunarodnye Otnosheniya,' 1966.

_____. *Revizionizm i reformizm v teorii obnishchaniya.* Moscow: Gosudarstvennoe Izdatel'stvo Politicheskoi Literatury, 1960.

_____, ed. *Imperializm i krizis mirovovo kapitalizma.* Moscow: Izdatel'stvo 'Mezhdunarodnye Otnosheniya,' 1964.

_____, ed. *Monopolisticheskii kapitalizm—imperializm.* Moscow: Izdatel'stvo IMO, 1961.

Brzezinski, Zbigniew K. *Ideology and Power in Soviet Politics.* New York: Praeger, 1962.

_____, Samuel P. Huntington. *Political Power: USA/USSR.* New York: Viking, 1964.

Bukharin, N.I. *Ekonomika perekhodnovo perioda.* Moscow: Gosudarstvennoe Izdatel'stvo, 1920.

_____, *Historical Materialism.* Ann Arbor: University of Michigan, 1969.

_____. *Imperialism and World Economy.* London: Merlin, 1972.

_____. *Imperializm i nakoplenie kapitala.* 3d ed. Moscow and Leningrad: Gosudarstvennoe Izdatel'stvo, 1928.

_____. *Selected Writings on the State and the Transition to Socialism.* Trans. & ed. Richard B. Day. Armonk, NY: M.E. Sharpe, 1982.

Burdjalov, Felix. *State Monopoly Incomes Policy.* Moscow: Progress, 1978.

Burlakov, M.I. *Voennoe potreblenie i kapitalisticheskoe vosproizvodstvo.* Moscow: Izdatel'stvo 'Mysl',' 1969.

Bunkina, M.K. *Razvitie mezhimperialisticheskikh protivorechii v usloviyakh bor'by dvukh sistem.* Moscow: Izdatel'stvo Moskovskovo Universiteta, 1966.

_____. *Tsentry mirovovo imperializma: itogi razvitiya i rasstanovka sil.* Moscow: Izdatel'stvo 'Mysl',' 1970.

Cheprakov, V.A. *Gosudarstvenno-monopolisticheskii kapitalizm.* Moscow: Izdatel'stvo Sotsial'no-Ekonomicheskoi Lliteratury 'Mysl',' 1964.

_____. *Osnovnye cherty gosudarstvenno-monopolisticheskovo kapitalizma.* Moscow: Izdatel'stvo VPSh i AON pri TsK KPSS, 1959.

Cherkasova, L.A. *Formy gosudarstvennovo regulirovaniya ekonomiki pri kapitalizme.* Moscow: Izdatel'stvo Moskovskovo Universiteta, 1972.

Cherkovets, V.N.; I.P. Faminsky; V.A. Kirov, eds. *Leninskii analiz imperializma i sovremennyi kapitalizm.* Moscow: Izdatel'stvo Moskovskovo Universiteta, 1969.

Cornwall, John. *Modern Capitalism.* New York: St. Martin's, 1977.

Dalin, S.A. *Ekonomicheskaya politika Ruzvel'ta.* Moscow: Gosudarstvennoe Sotsial'no-Ekonomicheskoe Izdatel'stvo, 1936.

_____. *SShA: poslevoennyi gosudarstvenno-monopolisticheskii kapitalizm.* Moscow: Izdatel'stvo 'Nauka,' 1972.

_____. *Voenno-gosudarstvennyi monopolisticheskii kapitalizm v SShA.* Moscow: Izdatel'stvo Akademii Nauk SSSR, 1961.

Daniels, Robert V. *Russia: The Roots of Confrontation.* Cambridge: Harvard University Press, 1985.

Day, Richard B. *The 'Crisis' and the 'Crash': Soviet Studies of the West (1917-1939).* London: NLB, 1981.

_____. "Dialectical Method in the Political Writings of Lenin and Bukharin." *Canadian Journal of Political Science* 9, no. 2 (June 1976): 244-60.

_____. *Leon Trotsky and the Politics of Economic Isolation.* Cambridge: Cambridge University Press, 1973.

_____. "Rosa Luxemburg and the Accumulation of Capital." *Critique* 12 (1979-1980): 81-96.

_____. "The Theory of the Long Cycle: Kondrat'ev, Trotsky, Mandel." *New Left Review* 99 (September-October 1976): 67-82.

Lemin, A.A.; N.V. Raskov; L.D. Shirokorad, eds. *Istoriya politicheskoi ekonomii kapitalizma.* Leningrad: Izdatel'stvo Leningradskovo Universiteta, 1989.

Demin, A.A., S.I. Tyulpanov. *Gosudarstvenno-monopolisticheskii kapitalizm FRG.* Leningrad: Izdatel'stvo Leningradskovo Universiteta, 1971.

Documents of the 22nd Congress of the CPSU. 2 vols. New York: Crosscurrents Press, 1961.

Dokunin, V.I. *Kritika sovremennykh antimarksistskikh ekonomicheskikh teorii,* 2d ed. Moscow: 'Vysshaya Shkola,' 1974.

_____, V.P. Trepelkov. *Obshchii krizis kapitalizma.* Moscow: Izdatel'stvo Sotsial'no-Ekonomicheskoi Literatury, 1963.

_____. *Sovremennaya burzhuaznaya politicheskaya ekonomiya na sluzhbe monopolii.* Moscow: Izdatel'stvo 'Vysshaya Shkola,' 1966.

Dragilev, M.S.; I.P. Faminsky *et al,* eds. *Gosudarstvenno-monopolisticheskii kapitalizm: obshchie cherty i osobennosti.* Moscow: Izdatel'stvo Politicheskoi Literatury, 1975.

Dragilev, M.S., N.I. Mokhov. *Leninskii analiz monopolisticheskovo kapitala i sovremennost'.* Moscow: Izdatel'stvo 'Vysshaya Shkola,' 1970.

_____. *Obshchii krizis kapitalizma.* Moscow: Gosudarstvennoe Izdatel'stvo Politicheskoi Literatury, 1957.

_____, G. Rudenko. *Monopolisticheskii kapitalizm.* Moscow: Izdatel'stvo Sotsial'no-Ekonomicheskoi Literatury, 1963.

_____, I.P. Faminsky, eds. *Mezhdunarodnye formy gosudarstvenno-monopolisticheskovo kapitalizma.* Moscow: Izdatel'stvo Moskovskovo Universiteta, 1971.

_____; I.P. Faminsky; M.N. Os'mova, eds. *Problemy razvitiya ekonomicheskikh otnoshenii mezhdu sotsialisticheskimi i kapitalisticheskimi stranami.* Moscow: Izdatel'stvo Moskovskovo Universiteta, 1974.

_____; N.I. Mokhov; P.A. Kashutin, eds. *Sovremennye voprosy politicheskoi ekonomii kapitalizma.* Moscow: Izdatel'stvo 'Vysshaya Shkola,' 1967.

_____, ed. *Voprosy gosudarstvennovo kapitalizma v imperialisticheskikh i razvivayushchikhsya stranakh na sovremennom etape.* Moscow: Izdatel'stvo Moskovskovo Universiteta, 1966.

Dubinsky, L.S., ed. *Ekonomicheskaya teoriya Marksa-Lenina i sovremennyi kapitalizm.* Moscow: Izdatel'stvo 'Mysl',' 1967.

Dvorkin, I. *Ideologiya i politika pravykh Leiboristov na sluzhbe monopolii.* Moscow: Gosudarstvennoe Izdatel'stvo Politicheskoi Literatury, 1953.

_____. *"Kapital" K. Marksa i sovremennaya burzhuaznaya politekonomiya.* Moscow: Izdatel'stvo 'Znanie,' 1968.

_____. *Kritika ekonomicheskikh teorii pravykh sotsialistov (Zapadnogermanskikh i Avstriiskikh).* Moscow: Izdatel'stvo Sotsial'no-Ekonomicheskoi Literatury, 1959.

_____. *Nauchno-tekhnicheskii perevorot i burzhuaznaya politicheskaya ekonomiya.* Moscow: Izdatel'stvo 'Nauka,' 1964.

_____. *O mirnom sosushchestvovanii kapitalisticheskoi i sotsialisticheskoi obshchestvennykh sistem.* Moscow: Gosudarstvennoe Izdatel'stvo Politicheskoi Literatury, 1955.

_____, ed. *Kritika sovremennykh burzhuaznykh ekonomistov.* Moscow: Izdatel'stvo 'Mysl',' 1966.

_____, ed. *Kritika teorii sovremennykh burzhuaznykh ekonomistov.* Moscow: Izdatel'stvo Ekonomicheskoi Literatury, 1963.

_____, ed. *Kritika teorii sovremennykh burzhuaznykh ekonomistov.* Moscow: Izdatel'stvo 'Mysl',' 1971.

Engels, F. *Herr Eugen Duhring's Revolution in Science [Anti-Duhring].* Trans. Emile Burns and ed. C.P. Dutt. London: Martin Lawrence, n.d.

Eran, Oded. *The Mezhdunarodniki.* Ramat Gan, Israel: Turtledove, 1979.

Eventov, L.Ya. *Voennaya ekonomika Anglii.* Gosudarstvennoe Izdatel'stvo Politicheskoi Literatury, 1946.

Faminsky, I.P. *Mirovoe kapitalisticheskoe khozyaistvo i uglublenie evo krizisa v sovremennykh usloviyakh.* Moscow: Izdatel'stvo Moskovskovo Universiteta, 1966.

Faramazyan, R.A. *SShA: Militarizm i ekonomika.* Moscow: Izdatel'stvo 'Mysl',' 1970.

Figurnov, P.K, *Kapitalisticheskoe vosproizvodstvo i ekonomicheskie krizisy.* Moscow: Voennoe Izdatel'stvo Ministerstva Vooruzhennykh Sil Soyuza SSR, 1949.

_____. *Marksistsko-leninskaya teoriya krizisov.* Moscow, 1948.

_____. *Sovremennyi kapitalizm (izbrannye raboty).* Moscow: Izdatel'stvo Sotsial'no-Ekonomicheskoi Literatury 'Mysl',' 1964.

Flanagan, Robert J.; David W. Soskice; Lloyd Ulman. *Unionism, Economic Stabilization, and Incomes Policies: European Experience.* Washington, DC: Brookings Institution, 1983.

Floyd, David. *Rumania: Russia's Dissident Ally.* New York: Praeger, 1965.

Friedman, Milton. *Capitalism and Freedom.* Chicago: University of Chicago, 1962.

_____. *Dollars and Deficits.* Englewood Cliffs, NJ: Prentice-Hall, 1968.

Funigiello, Philip J. *American-Soviet Trade in the Cold War.* Chapel Hill, NC: University of North Carolina, 1988.

Galbraith, John Kenneth. *The Affluent Society.* Toronto: Mentor, 1963.

_____. *Economics and the Public Purpose.* Boston: Houghton Mifflin, 1973.

_____. *The New Industrial State.* New York: Mentor, 1968.

Gauzner, N.D. *Nauchno-tekhnicheskii progress i rabochii klass SShA.* Moscow: Izdatel'stvo 'Nauka,' 1968.

_____. *Social Effects of the Scientific and Technological Revolution under Capitalism.* Moscow: Novosti, 1973.

Gibert, Stephen P. *Soviet Images of America.* New York: Crane, Russak, 1978.

Glagolev, I.S. *Vliyanie razoruzheniya na ekonomiku.* Moscow: Izdatel'stvo 'Nauka,' 1964.

_____, ed. *Ekonomicheskie problemy razoruzheniya.* Moscow: Izdatel'stvo Akademii Nauk SSSR, 1961.

Glushkov, V.P. *Korporatsii, gosudarstvo, ekonomika.* Moscow: Izdatel'stvo 'Nauka,' 1972.

Glyn, Andrew, Bob Sutcliffe. *British Capitalism, Workers and the Profit Squeeze*. Harmondsworth, Middlesex: Penguin, 1972.

Goldman, Marshall I. *Detente and Dollars*. New York: Basic Books, 1975.

Gol'dshtein, I., R. Levina. *Germanskii imperializm*. Moscow: Gosudarstvennoe Izdatel'stvo Politicheskoi Literatury, 1947.

Gol'man, M. *Vseobshchii krizis kapitalizma v svete vzglyadov Marksa-Engel'sa i Lenina*. Moscow: Izdatel'stvo Kommunisticheskoi Akademii, 1929.

Goilo, V.S. *Teoreticheskoe opravdanie bezrabotitsy*. Moscow: Izdatel'stvo 'Mysl',' 1966.

_____. *Sovremennye burzhuaznye teorii vosproizvodstva rabochei sily (kriticheskii ocherk)*. Moscow: Izdatel'stvo 'Nauka,' 1975.

Goncharov, A.N. *Voina kotoraya ne prekrashchaetsya*. Moscow: Izdatel'stvo 'Mezhdunarodnye Otnosheniya,' 1975.

Gregory, Paul R., Robert C. Stuart. *Soviet Economic Structure and Performance*, 2d ed. New York: Harper and Row, 1981.

_____. *Soviet Economic Structure and Performance*, 4th ed. New York: Harper Collins, 1990.

Gromyko, Anat. *1036 dnei prezidenta Kennedi*. Moscow: Izdatel'stvo Politicheskoi Literatury, 1968.

Guttsait, M.G. *Khronicheskaya bezrabotitsa i nedogruzka predpriyatii v SShA*. Moscow: Izdatel'stvo Sotsial'no-Ekonomicheskoi Literatury, 1961.

Halle, Louis J. *The Cold War as History*. New York: Harper and Row, 1975.

Hansen, Alvin H. *The Postwar American Economy: Performance and Problems*. New York: Norton, 1964.

Harris, Seymour E. *Economics of the Kennedy Years*. New York: Harper & Row, 1964.

_____, ed. *The Dollar in Crisis*. New York: Harcourt, Brace and World, 1961.

Heilbroner, Robert L. *The Limits of American Capitalism*. New York: Harper & Row, 1966.

Heller, Walter W. *New Dimensions of Political Economy*. New York: Norton, 1967.

Hickman, Bert G. *Growth and Stability of the Postwar Economy*. Washington, DC: Brookings Institution, 1960.

Hilferding, Rudolf. *Finance Capital: A Study of the Latest Phase of Capitalist Development*. Ed. Tom Bottomore, trans. Morris Watnick and Sam Gordon. London: Routledge & Kegan Paul, 1981.

Institut Mirovoi Ekonomiki i Mezhdunarodnykh Otnoshenii. *Uchenie V.I. Lenina ob imperializme i sovremennost'*. Moscow: Politizdat, 1967.

Inozemtsev, N.N. *Contemporary Capitalism: New Developments and Contradictions*. Moscow: Progress, 1974.

_____. *Vneshnyaya politika SShA v epokhu imperializma*. Moscow: Gosudarstvennoe Izdatel'stvo Politicheskoi Literatury, 1960.

_____; V.A. Martynov; S.M. Nikitin, eds. *Leninskaya teoriya imperializma i sovremennost'*. Moscow: Izdatel'stvo 'Mysl',' 1977.

_____, ed. *Mezhdunarodnye otnosheniya posle vtoroi mirovoi voiny*. 3 vols. Moscow: Gosudarstvennoe Izdatel'stvo Politicheskoi Literatury, 1962-1964.

_____; S.M. Men'shikov; A.G. Mileikovsky; A.M. Rumyantsev, eds. *Politicheskaya ekonomiya sovremennovo monopolisticheskovo kapitalizma*. 2 vols. Moscow: Izdatel'stvo 'Mysl',' 1970.

_____; A.G. Mileikovsky; V.A. Martynov, eds. *Politicheskaya ekonomiya sovremennovo monopolisticheskovo kapitalizma*, 2d ed. 2 vols. Moscow: Izdatel'stvo 'Mysl',' 1975.

_____; E.M. Primakov; I.E. Gur'ev, eds. *Uglublenie obshchevo krizisa kapitalizma*. Moscow: Izdatel'stvo 'Mysl',' 1976.

Ivanov, L.N.; O.V. Kuusinen; V.P. Glushkov, eds. *Pravye Leiboristy na sluzhbe Angliiskovo i Amerikanskovo imperializma*. Moscow: Gosplanizdat, 1950.

Jacobs, Dan N., ed. *The New Communist Manifesto and Related Documents*. New York: Harper & Row, 1962.

Kapelinsky, Yu.N. *Torgovlya SSSR s kapitalisticheskimi stranami posle vtoroi mirovoi voiny*. Moscow: Izdatel'stvo 'Mezhdunarodnye Otnosheniya,' 1970.

_____. *Na Vzaimovygodnoi osnove*. Moscow: Izdatel'stvo 'Mezhdunarodnye Otnosheniya,' 1975.

Kaser, Michael. *Comecon: Integration Problems of the Planned Economies*. London: Oxford University Press, 1965.

Kats, A.I. *Polozhenie proletariata SShA pri imperializme*. Moscow: Izdatel'stvo Akademii Nauka SSSR, 1962.

Katsenelenboigen, A. *Soviet Economic Thought and Political Power in the USSR*. New York: Pergamon, 1980

Keynes, John Maynard. *The Economic Consequences of the Peace*. New York: Harper & Row, 1971.

_____. *The General Theory of Employment, Interest and Money*. London: Macmillan, 1961.

Khafizov, R.Kh. *Kritika teorii gosudarstvennovo regulirovaniya kapitalisicheskoi ekonomiki*. Moscow: Izdatel'stvo 'Mezhdunarodnykh Otnoshenii,' 1961.

Khmel'nitskaya, E.L. *Izmeneniya v ekonomicheskoi strukture stran Zapadnoi Evropy*. Moscow: Izdatel'stvo 'Nauka,' 1965.

_____. *Monopolisticheskii kapitalizm zapadnoi Germanii*. Moscow: Izdatel'stvo IMO, 1959.

_____. *Ocherki sovremennoi monopolii*. Moscow: Izdatel'stvo 'Mysl',' 1971.

_____, ed. *Ekonomicheskie problemy 'Obshchevo Rynka.'* Moscow: Izdatel'stvo Sotsial'no-Ekonomicheskoi Literatury, 1962.

Kindleberger, Charles P. *Europe's Postwar Growth*. Cambridge: Harvard University, 1967.

_____. *International Economics*, 3rd ed. Homewood, IL: Irwin, 1963.

Kim, F.P. *Dialektika razvitiya protivorechii gosudarstvennovo-monopolistiches-kovo kapitalizma*. Moscow: Izdatel'stvo 'Mysl',' 1965.

Klepikov, V.F.; I.I. Kuz'minov; I.T. Nazarenko, eds. *O gosudarstvenno-mo-nopolisticheskom kapitalizme*. Moscow: Izdatel'stvo VPSh i AON pri TsK KPSS, 1963.

Kondrat'ev, N.D. *Mirovoe khozyaistvo i evo kon'yunktury vo vremya i posle voiny*. Vologda: Gosudarstvennoe Izdatel'stvo, 1922.

Kornienko, K. *K kritike sovremennykh teorii militarizatsii ekonomiki*. Moscow: Izdatel'stvo Ministerstva Oborony Soyuza SSR, 1960.

Kostecki, M. *East-West Trade and the GATT System*. London: Macmillan, 1978.

Kozlov, G.A. *Deistvie zakona stoimosti v usloviyakh sovremennovo kapitalizma*. Moscow: Izdatel'stvo Sotsial'no-Ekonomicheskoi Literatury 'Mysl',' 1964.

_____, S.P. Pervushin. *Kratkii ekonomicheskii slovar'*. Moscow: Gosudarsten-noe Izdatel'stvo Politicheskoi Literatury, 1958.

Khrushchev, N.S. *Control Figures for the Economic Development of the U.S.S.R. for 1959-1965*. Moscow: Foreign Languages Publishing House, 1959.

Kudrov, V.M. et al. *Sovremennaya nauchno-tekhnicheskaya revolyutsiya v razvitykh kapitalisticheskikh stranakh: ekonomicheskie problemy*. Moscow: Izdatel'stvo 'Mysl',' 1971.

_____, G. Shpil'ko. *Tempy i proportsii obshchestvennovo proizvodstva v SShA*. Moscow: Izdatel'stvo 'Mysl',' 1965.

Kuusinen, O.V. et al. *Fundamentals of Marxism-Leninism*. Moscow: Foreign Languages Publishing House, 1963.

Kuz'minov, I. *Gosudarstvenno-monopolisticheskii kapitalizm*. Moscow: Gos-udarstvennoe Izdatel'stvo Politicheskoi Literatury, 1955.

_____. *Obnishchanie trudyashchikhsya pri kapitalizme*. Moscow: Izdatel'stvo VPSh i AON pri TsK KPSS, 1960.

_____. *Poslevoennyi kapitalisticheskii tsikl*. Moscow: Izdatel'stvo Sotsial'no-Ekonomicheskoi Literatury, 1962.

LaFeber, Walter. *America, Russia and the Cold War, 1945-1980*. 4th ed. New York: Wiley, 1980.

Lavrichenko, M.V. *'Plan Marshalla' i razorenie sel'skovo khozyaistva Zapadnoi Evropy*. Moscow: Gosudarstvennoe Izdatel'stvo Politicheskoi Literatury, 1950.

Lemin, I.M. *Anglo-Amerikanskie protivorechiya posle vtoroi mirovoi voiny*. Moscow: Izdatel'stvo Akademii Nauk SSSR, 1955.

_____. *Bor'ba dvukh napravlenii v mezhdunarodnykh otnosheniyakh*. Moscow, 1947.

_____. *Obostrenie krizisa Britanskoi Imperii posle vtoroi mirovoi voiny*. Moscow: Izdatel'stvo Akademii Nauk SSSR, 1951.

_____. *Vneshnyaya politika Sovetskovo Soyuza v period velikoi otechestvennoi voiny*. Moscow, 1947.

_____, ed. *Dvizhushchie sily vneshnei politiki SShA*. Moscow: Izdatel'stvo 'Nauka,' 1965.

_____, ed. *Ekonomika i politika Anglii posle vtoroi mirovoi voiny*. Moscow: Izdatel'stvo Akademii Nauk SSSR, 1958.

Lenczowski, John. *Soviet Perceptions of U.S. Foreign Policy*. Ithaca, NY: Cornell University Press, 1982.

Lenin, V.I. *Collected Works*. 45 vols. Moscow: Progress, 1972-1974.

_____. *Polnoe sobranie sochinenii*. 55 vols. Moscow: Gosudarstvennoe Izdatel'stvo Politicheskoi Literatury, 1958-1965.

_____. *Selected Works*. 3 vols. Moscow: Foreign Languages Publishing House, 1960-1961.

Leontyev, L. *Are Socialism and Capitalism Drawing Closer Together? (The Theory of Convergence and What Is Behind It)*. Moscow: Novosti, 1972.

Leont'ev, L.A. *"Kapital" K. Marksa i sovremennaya epokha*. Moscow: Izdatel'stvo 'Nauka,' 1968.

_____. *Imperializm dollara v Zapadnoi Evropy*. Moscow: Gosudarstvennoe Izdatel'stvo Politicheskoi Literatury, 1949.

_____. *Leninskoe issledovanie imperializma*. Moscow: Izdatel'stvo 'Nauka,' 1964.

_____. *Leninskaya teoriya imperializma*. Moscow: Izdatel'stvo 'Nauka,' 1969.

_____. *Sotsializm v ekonomicheskom sorevnovanii s kapitalizmom*. Moscow: Gosudarstvennoe Izdatel'stvo Politicheskoi Literatury, 1958.

_____, ed. *Problemy sovremennovo imperializma*. Moscow: Izdatel'stvo Politicheskoi Literatury, 1968.

Levin, I.D. *Krakh burzhuaznoi demokratii i sovremennoe gosudarstvennoe pravo kapitalisticheskikh stran*. Moscow: Izdatel'stvo Akademii Nauk SSSR, 1951.

_____, V.A. Tumanov, eds. *Ideologicheskaya deyatel'nost' sovremennovo imperialisticheskovo gosudarstva*. Moscow: Izdatel'stvo 'Nauka,' 1972.

_____, ed. *Imperialisticheskoe gosudarstvo i kapitalisticheskoe khozyaistvo*. Moscow: Izdatel'stvo Akademii Nauk SSSR, 1963.

_____, ed. *Konstitutsionnyi mekhanizm diktatury monopolii*. Moscow: Izdatel'stvo 'Nauka,' 1964.

_____, ed. *Partii v sisteme diktatury monopolii*. Moscow: Izdatel'stvo 'Nauka,' 1964.

_____, V.A. Tumanov, eds. *Politicheskii mekhanizm diktatury monopolii*. Moscow: Izdatel'stvo 'Nauka,' 1974.

Liberman, E.G. *Economic Methods and the Effectiveness of Production*. Trans. Arlo Schultz. White Plains, NY: IASP, 1970.

Linden, Carl A. *Khrushchev and the Soviet Leadership, 1957-1964*. Baltimore: Johns Hopkins, 1966.

Lozyuk, N.I., et al. *Gosudarstvenno-monopolisticheskoe regulirovanie ekonomiki*. Kiev: "Naukova Dumka," 1972.

Luxemburg, R., *The Accumulation of Capital*. Trans. Agnes Schwarzschild. London: Routledge & Kegan Paul, 1963.

____, N. Bukharin. *Imperialism and the Accumulation of Capital*. Trans. Rudolf Wichmann, ed. Kenneth J. Tarbuck. London: Allen Lane the Penguin Press, 1972.

Lyubimova, V.V., ed. *Real'naya zarabotnaya plata v period obshchevo krizisa kapitalizma*. Moscow: Izdatel'stvo Sotsial'no-Ekonomicheskoi Literatury, 1962.

Maximova, M. *Economic Aspects of Capitalist Integration*. Moscow: Progress, 1973.

Maksimova, M.M. *Ekonomicheskie gruppirovki v Zapadnoi Evropy*. Moscow: Izdatel'stvo 'Nauka,' 1969.

Malin, V.N.; A.I. Malysh; N.R. Mironov; A.M. Rumyantsev; P.N. Fedoseev, eds. *Marks i sovremennost'*. Moscow: Izdatel'stvo Politicheskoi Literatury, 1968.

Manjulo, A.N., ed. *The USSR and International Economic Relations*. Moscow: Progress, 1985.

Manukyan, A.A. *Problemy poslevoennovo razvitiya ekonomiki kapitalisticheskikh stran*. Moscow: Izdatel'stvo 'Ekonomika,' 1966.

Markushina, V.I. *Mezhdunarodnye nauchno-tekhnicheskie svyazi v sisteme sovremennovo kapitalizma*. Moscow: Izdatel'stvo 'Mysl',' 1972.

Marx, Karl. *Capital*. 3 vols. Moscow: Foreign Languages Publishing House, 1957-1962.

____. *Grundrisse: Foundations of the Critique of Political Economy*. Trans. Martin Nicolaus. New York: Vintage, 1973.

____. *The Poverty of Philosophy*. New York: International Publishers, 1963.

____ and Frederick Engels. *Selected Correspondence*. Moscow: Foreign Languages Publishing House, n.d.

____ and Frederick Engels. *Selected Works*. 2 vols. Moscow: Foreign Languages Publishing House, 1962.

____. *Theories of Surplus Value*. 3 vols. Trans. Emile Burns, ed. S. Ryazanskaya. Moscow: Progress, 1963-1971.

Masal'sky, V.N. *Protiv fal'sifikatsii posledstvii tekhnicheskovo progressa pri kapitalizme*. Moscow: Izdatel'stvo 'Mysl',' 1965.

____. *Sotsial'no-ekonomicheskie problemy nauchno-tekhnicheskovo progressa pri kapitalizme*. Leningrad: Izdatel'stvo Leningradskovo Universiteta, 1975.

Maslennikov, V.A.; S.M. Ivanov; S.M. Vishnev, eds. *Amerikanskii plan zakabaleniya Evropy*. Moscow: Gosplanizdat, 1949.

_____, ed. *Mirovaya ekonomika.* Moscow: Izdatel'stvo 'Mezhdunarodnye Ot-nosheniya,' 1966.

_____, A.I. Medov, eds. *Mirovaya ekonomika.* Moscow: Izdatel'stvo 'Mezhdu-narodnye Otnosheniya,' 1969.

Mastny, Vojtech. *Russia's Road to the Cold War.* New York: Columbia Uni-versity Press, 1979.

Means, Gardiner C. *Pricing Power and the Public Interest.* New York: Harper & Brothers, 1962.

_____. *The Corporate Revolution in America.* New York: Collier, 1964.

Mendel'son, L. *Ekonomicheskie krizisy i tsikly XIX veka.* Moscow: Gosudarst-vennoe Izdatel'stvo Politicheskoi Literatury, 1949.

_____. *Teoriya i istorya ekonomicheskikh krizisov i tsiklov,* 3 vols. Moscow: Izdatel'stvo Sotsial'no-Ekonomicheskoi Literatury, 1959-1964.

Men'shikov, S.M. *Amerikanskie monopolii na mirovom kapitalisticheskom rynke.* Moscow: Izdatel'stvo Sotsial'no-Ekonomicheskoi Literatury, 1958.

_____. *The Economic Cycle: Postwar Developments.* Moscow: Progress, 1975.

_____. *Millionaires and Managers.* Moscow: Progress, 1969.

_____. *Sovremennyi kapitalizm: kratkaya politekonomiya.* Moscow: Izdatel'stvo 'Mysl',' 1974.

_____, ed. *Ekonomicheskaya politika pravitel'stva Kennedi, 1961-1963.* Moscow: Izdatel'stvo Sotsial'no-Ekonomicheskoi Literatury 'Mysl',' 1964.

Mikhalevsky, F.I. *Zoloto v sisteme kapitalizma posle vtoroi mirovoi voiny.* Moscow: Izdatel'stvo Akademii Nauk SSSR, 1952.

Mikulsky, K. *Lenin's Teaching on the World Economy and Its Relevance to Our Times.* Moscow: Progress, 1975.

Mileikovsky, A.G. *Leninskaya teoriya i sovremennyi gosudarstvenno-monopolisticheskii kapitalizm.* Moscow: Izdatel'stvo 'Znanie,' 1968.

_____, ed. *Burzhuaznye ekonomicheskie teorii i ekonomicheskaya politika imperialisticheskikh stran.* Moscow: Izdatel'stvo 'Mysl',' 1971.

_____, ed. *Novye yavleniya v nakoplenii kapitala v imperialisticheskikh stranakh.* Moscow: Izdatel'stvo 'Mysl',' 1967.

_____, ed. *Raspad Britanskoi Imperii.* Moscow: Izdatel'stvo 'Nauka,' 1964.

Mil'shtein, V.M. *Voenno-promyshlennyi kompleks i vneshnyaya politika SShA.* Moscow: Izdatel'stvo 'Mezhdunarodnye Otnosheniya,' 1975.

Motylev, V.V. *Mirovoe kapitalisticheskoe khozyaistvo: tendentsii razvitiya i protivorechiya.* Moscow: Izdatel'stvo 'Nauka,' 1973.

_____, *Teorii mirovoi kapitalisticheskoi ekonomiki.* Moscow: Izdatel'stvo 'Mysl',' 1971.

Mrachkovskaya, I.M. *Razvitie V.I. Leninym marksistskoi teorii vosproizvodstva obshchestvennovo kapitala.* Moscow: Izdatel'stvo Sotsial'no-Ekonomiches-koi Literatury, 1960.

Novikov, R.A. and Yu.V. Shishkov. *Mezhdunarodnaya kooperatsiya kapitalist-icheskikh stran.* Moscow: Izdatel'stvo 'Mysl',' 1972.

Nikolayev, A. *R & D in Social Reproduction.* Moscow: Progress, 1975.

Nikitin, S.M. *Kritika ekonometricheskikh teorii 'planirovaniya' kapitalisticheskoi ekonomiki.* Moscow: Gosstatizdat, 1962.

_____. *Problemy tsenoobrazovaniya v usloviyakh sovremennovo kapitalizma.* Moscow: Izdatel'stvo 'Nauka,' 1973.

_____. *Strukturnye izmeneniya v kapitalisticheskoi ekonomike.* Moscow: Izdatel'stvo 'Mysl',' 1965.

Novoselov, S.P. *Osnovnoe protivorechie kapitalizma i sovremennost'.* Moscow: Izdatel'stvo 'Mysl',' 1974.

Nukovich, E.S. *Ekonomicheskoe sotrudnichestvo i manevry antikommunistov.* Moscow: Izdatel'stvo 'Mezhdunarodnye Otnosheniya,' 1969.

Nutsubidze, Appolon G. *Imperializm ili 'transformirovannyi' kapitalizm.* Tbilisi: Izdatel'stvo 'Metsniereba,' 1970.

Osadchaya, I.M. *From Keynes to Neoclassical Synthesis.* Moscow: Progress, 1974.

_____. *Kritika sovremennykh burzhuaznykh teorii ekonomicheskovo rosta.* Moscow: Izdatel'stvo 'Mezhdunarodnykh Otnosheniya,' 1963.

_____. *Sovremennoe Keinsianstvo.* Moscow: Izdatel'stvo 'Mysl',' 1971.

Paterson, Thomas G. *Soviet-American Confrontation.* Baltimore: Johns Hopkins University Press, 1973.

Pevzner, Ya.A. *Gosudarstvenno-monopolisticheskii kapitalizm v Yaponii posle vtoroi mirovoi voiny.* Moscow: Izdatel'stvo Akademii Nauk SSSR, 1961.

_____, ed. *Vosproizvodstvo obshchestvennovo produkta v Yaponii.* Moscow: Izdatel'stvo 'Nauka,' 1970.

Pokrovsky, A.I., ed. *Ekonomicheskoe programmirovanie v stranakh Zapadnoi Evropy.* Moscow: Izdatel'stvo 'Nauka,' 1969.

Potapov, I.S.; G.S. Roginsky; Yu.N. Kapelinsky, eds. *Mezhdunarodnaya torgovlya.* Moscow: Vneshtorgizdat, 1954.

Preobrazhensky, E.A. *Zakat kapitalizma.* Moscow and Leningrad: Gosudarstvennoe Sotsial'no-Ekonomicheskoe Izdatel'stvo, 1931. (*The Decline of Capitalism.* Trans. & ed. Richard B. Day. Armonk, NY: M.E. Sharpe, 1985.)

Primakov, E.M.; L.M. Gromov; L.L. Lyubimov, eds. *Energeticheskii krizis v kapitalisticheskom mire.* Moscow: Izdatel'stvo 'Mysl',' 1975.

Prokorov, G.M. *Vneshneekonomicheskie svyazi i ekonomicheskii rost sotsialisticheskikh stran.* Moscow: Izdatel'stvo 'Mezhdunarodnye Otnosheniya,' 1972.

Raskov, N.V. *Gosudarstvenno-monopolisticheskii kapitalizm (ocherk teorii).* Leningrad: Izdatel'stvo Lerningradskovo Universiteta, 1974.

Roginsky, G., ed. *Zakat kapitalizma v Trotskistskom zerkale.* Moscow: Partiinoe Izdatel'stvo, 1932.

Rostow, W.W. *The Stages of Economic Growth: A Non-Communist Manifesto.* London: Cambridge University Press, 1960.

Rubin, I.I. *Essays on Marx's Theory of Value*. Montreal: Black Rose, 1973.

Rubinshtein, M.I. *If the Arms Race Were Stopped*. London: Soviet News, 1958.

_____. *Burzhuaznaya nauka i tekhnika na sluzhbe imperializma*. Moscow: Izdatel'stvo Akademii Nasyuk SSSR, 1951.

_____. *Militarizatsiya ekonomika SShA i ukhudshenie polozheniya trudyashchikhsya*. Moscow: Izdatel'stvo Akademii Nauk SSSR, 1953.

_____; I.M. Lemin; I.S. Glagolev; V.V. Sushchenko, eds. *Monopolisticheskii kapital SShA posle vtoroi mirovoi voiny*. Moscow: Izdatel'stvo Akademii Nauk SSSR, 1958.

Rumyantsev, A.M.; S.M. Men'shikov; G.B. Arbaev, eds. *Sovremennye tsikly i krizisy*. Moscow: Izdatel'stvo 'Mysl',' 1967.

_____; V.Ya. Aboltin; I.N. Dvorkin, eds. *Sovremennyi kapitalizm i burzhuaznaya politicheskaya ekonomiya*. Moscow: Izdatel'stvo 'Mysl',' 1967.

Santalov, A.A. *Imperialisticheskaya bor'ba za istochniki syr'ya*. Moscow: Izdatel'stvo Akademii Nauk SSSR, 1954.

Scammell, W.M. *International Monetary Policy*. 2d ed. London: Macmillan, 1962

_____. *The International Economy Since 1945*. London: Macmillan, 1980.

Schapiro, L., P. Reddaway, eds. *Lenin: The Man, the Theorist, the Leader—a Reappraisal*. London: Pall Mall, 1967.

Schumpeter, Joseph A. *Capitalism, Socialism and Democracy*. 3rd ed. New York: Harper & Row, 1962.

Schwartz, Morton. *Soviet Perceptions of the United States*. Berkeley: University of California Press, 1969.

Senin, M.V. *Razvitie mezhdunarodnykh ekonomicheskikh svyazei*. Moscow: Izdatel'stvo 'Mysl',' 1968.

Shein, A.I. *Kritika ekonomicheskikh teorii pravykh Leiboristov Anglii*. Moscow: Izdatel'stvo Moskovskovo Universiteta, 1975.

Sherman, Howard J. *The Soviet Economy*. Boston: Little, Brown, 1969.

Shershnev, E.S. *On the Principle of Mutual Advantage: Soviet-American Economic Relations*. Moscow: Progress, 1978.

_____, ed., *SSSR-SShA: Ekonomicheskie otnosheniya (problemy i vozmozhnosti)*. Moscow: Izdatel'stvo 'Nauka,' 1976.

_____, I. L. Sheidina. *Sovetsko-Amerikanskie nauchno-tekhnicheskie svyazi: problemy i vozmozhnosti*. Moscow: Izdatel'stvo 'Znanie,' 1974.

Shonfield, Andrew. *Modern Capitalism: The Changing Balance of Public and Private Power*. Oxford: Oxford University Press, 1970.

Shpil'ko, G.A. *Teorii i metody regulirovaniya kapitalisticheskoi ekonomiki*. Moscow: Izdatel'stvo 'Mysl',' 1975.

Shundeev, V.M. *Gosudarstvo i nakoplenie kapitala v SShA*. Moscow: Izdatel'stvo 'Nauka,' 1967.

Shvyrkov, Yu.M.; V.P. Aksenova; N.M. Kulagina. *Gosudarstvennoe programmirovanie v kapitalisticheskikh stranakh.* Moscow: Izdatel'stvo 'Mysl',' 1975.

Smit, M.N. *Dinamika krizisov i polozhenie proletariata.* Moscow: Izdatel'stvo Kommunisticheskoi Akademii, 1929.

_____. *Ocherki istorii burzhuaznoi politicheskoi ekonomii.* Moscow: Izdatel'stvo Sotsial'no-Ekonomicheskoi Literatury, 1961.

_____. *Polozhenie rabochevo klassa v SShA, Anglii i Frantsii posle vtoroi mirovoi voiny.* Gosudarstvennoe Izdatel'stvo Politicheskoi Literatury, 1953.

Smith, Adam. *The Wealth of Nations.* New York: Modern Library, 1937.

Solodovnikov, V. *Vyvoz kapitala.* Moscow: Gosudarstvennoe Izdatel'stvo Politicheskoi Literatury, 1957.

Stadnichenko, A. *Monetary Crisis of Capitalism.* Moscow: Progress, 1975.

Stalin, I.V. *Sochineniya.* 13 vols. Moscow: Gosudarstvennoe Izdatel'stvo Politicheskoi Literatury, 1953.

_____. *Sochineniya.* Ed. Robert H. McNeal. 3 vols. (XIV-XVI). Stanford: Hoover Institution, 1967.

Stalin, J. *Problems of Leninism.* Moscow: Foreign Languages Publishing House, 1954.

_____. *Economic Problems of Socialism in the U.S.S.R.* New York: International Publishers, 1952.

_____. *Selected Interviews.* Calcutta: Mass Publications, 1976.

Stepanov, V.I. *Ekonomicheskie osnovy mirnovo sosushchestvovaniya.* Moscow: Izdatel'stvo 'Ekonomika,' 1964.

_____. *Ekonomicheskie otnosheniya Vostok-Zapada: problemy, perspekitvy—ocherk teorii.* Khabarovsk: Khabarovskoe knizhnoe Izdatel'stvo, 1974.

Taubman, William. *Stalin's American Policy.* New York: Norton, 1982.

Tew, Brian. *The Evolution of the International Monetary System 1945-77.* London: Hutchinson, 1977.

Torkanovsky, V.S. *Novye yavleniya v razvitii monopolisticheskovo kapitalizma.* Leningrad: Izdatel'stvo Leningradskovo Universiteta, 1973.

Trakhtenberg, A.I. *Denezhnoe obrashchenie i kredit pri kapitalizme.* Moscow: Izdatel'stvo Akademii Nauk SSSR, 1962.

_____. *Finansovye itogi voiny.* Moscow: Gosfinizdat, 1946.

_____. *Kapitalisticheskoe vosproizvodstvo i ekonomicheskie krizisy.* Gosudarstvennoe Izdatel'stvo Politicheskoi Literatury, 1947

_____. *Kreditno-denezhnaya sistema kapitalizma posle vtoroi mirovoi voiny.* Moscow: Izdatel'stvo Akademii Nauk SSSR, 1954.

_____. *Voennoe khozyaistvo kapitalisticheskikh stran i perekhod k mirnoi ekonomike.* Moscow: Gosplanizdat, 1947.

Triffin, Robert. *Gold and the Dollar Crisis.* New Haven, CT: Yale University Press, 1961.

Trotsky, Leon. *The First Five Years of the Communist International.* 2 vols. (Vol. I) New York: Pioneer, 1945; (Vol. 2) London: New Park, 1953.

Tsagolov, N.A., V.A. Kudrov. *"Kapital" K. Marksa i problemy sovremennovo kapitalizma.* Moscow: Izdatel'stvo Moskovskovo Universiteta, 1968.

_____, ed. *Kritika sovremennykh burzhuaznykh, reformistskikh i revizionistskikh ekonomicheskikh teorii.* Moscow: Izdatel'stvo Sotsial'no-Ekonomicheskoi Literatury, 1960.

Tucker, Robert C., ed. *The Marx-Engels Reader,* 2d ed. New York: W.W. Norton, 1978.

Turchins, Ya.B. *Obostrenie neravnomernosti razvitiya kapitalizma v itoge vtoroi mirovoi voiny.* Moscow: Gosudarstvennoe Izdatel'stvo Politicheskoi Literatury, 1953.

Turner, C.B. *An Analysis of Soviet Views on John Maynard Keynes.* Duke University, 1969.

Tyulpanov, S.I., V.L. Sheinis. *Aktual'nye problemy politicheskoi ekonomii sovremennovo kapitalizma.* Leningrad: Izdatel'stvo Leningradskovo Universiteta, 1973.

Tyulpanov, S.I., ed. *Krizis mirovovo kapitalizma.* Leningrad: Izdatel'stvo Leningradskovo Universiteta, 1963.

_____, S.I. Ivanov, eds. *SShA: gosudarstvenno-monopolisticheskoe regulirovanie vosproizvodstva obshchestvennovo kapitala.* Leningrad: Izdatel'stvo Leningradskovo Universiteta, 1972.

_____, ed. *SShA: Nauchno-tekhnicheskii progress i vosproizvodstvo.* Leningrad: Izdatel'stvo Leningradskovo Universiteta, 1969.

_____; S.I. Ivanov; V.G. Onushkin; S.I. Yakovleva, eds. *SShA: nauchno-tekhnicheskii progress i vosproizvodstvo.* Leningrad: Izdatel'stvo Leningradskovo Universiteta, 1969.

Varga, E.S. *Anglo-Amerikanskie ekonomicheskie otnosheniya.* Moscow: Izdatel'stvo 'Pravda,' 1946.

_____. *Fashistskii 'novyi poryadok' v Evrope.* Leningrad: Izdatel'stvo Akademii Nauk SSSR, 1942.

_____. *Istoricheskie korni osobennosti Germanskovo imperializma.* Magadan: Izdatel'stvo 'Sovetskaya Kolyma,' 1943.

_____. *Izbrannye proizvedeniya,* 3 vols. Moscow: Izdatel'stvo 'Nauka,' 1974.

_____. *Izmeneniya v ekonomike kapitalizma v itoge vtoroi mirovoi voiny.* Gosudarstvennoe Izdatel'stvo Politicheskoi Literatury, 1946.

_____. *Kapitalisticheskii mir na poroge novovo krizisa.* Moscow: Gosudarstvennoe Izdatel'stvo Politicheskoi Literatury, 1938.

_____. *Kapitalizm dvadtsatovo vekha.* Moscow: Gosudarstvennoe Izdatel'stvo Politicheskoi Literatury, 1961.

_____. *Kapitalizm i sotsializm za 20 let.* Moscow: Partizdat, 1938.

_____. *Marxism and the General Crisis of Capitalism.* Bombay: People's Publishing House, 1948.

_____. *Novye yavleniya v mirovom ekonomicheskom krizise*. Moscow: Partizdat, 1934.

_____. *O budushchem Leiboristskom pravitel'stve Anglii*. Moscow: IMEMO, 1958.

_____. *Ocherki po problemam politekonomii kapitalizma*. Moscow: Izdatel'stvo Politicheskoi Literatury, 1964.

_____. *Osnovnye voprosy ekonomiki i politiki imperializma (posle vtoroi mirovoi voiny)*. Moscow: Gosudarstvennoe Izdatel'stvo Politicheskoi Literatury, 1953.

_____. *Osnovnye voprosy ekonomiki i politiki imperializma (posle vtoroi mirovoi voiny)*, 2d ed. Moscow: Gosudarstvennoe Izdatel'stvo Politicheskoi Literatury, 1957.

_____. *O vosmeshchenii ushcherba prichinennovo Gitlerovskoi Germaniei Sovetskomu Soyuzu*. Moscow: Lektsionnoe Byuro pri Komitete po Delam Vysshei Shkoly pri SNK SSSR, 1943.

_____. *Plan Dauesa i mirovoi krizis 1924 goda*. Moscow: Moskovskii Rabochii, 1925.

_____. *"Plan Marshalla" i ekonomika Anglii i SShA*. Moscow: Izdatel'stvo 'Pravda,' 1947.

_____. *Problems of the Post-War Industrial Cycle and the New Crisis of Overproduction*. New York: International Arts and Sciences Press, 1958.

_____. *Problemy mirovovo khozyaistva i mirovoi politiki*. Moscow: Izdatel'stvo Kommunisticheskoi Akademii, 1929.

_____. *Sovremennyi kapitalizm i ekonomicheskie krizisy*. Moscow: Izdatel'stvo Akademii Nauk SSSR, 1962.

_____, ed. *Istoshchenie ekonomicheskikh resursov fashistskoi Germanii*. Gosdarstvennoe Izdatel'stvo Politicheskoi Literatury, 1943.

_____ et al. *Mirovoi ekonomicheskii krizis (kollektivnaya rabota Instituta Mirovovo Khozyaistva i Mirovoi Politiki)*. Moscow: Izdatel'stvo Kommunisticheskoi Akademii, 1930.

Vatter, Harold G. *The U.S. Economy in the 1950's*. New York: Norton, 1963.

Veblen, Thorstein. *The Theory of the Leisure Class: An Economic Study of Institutions*. New York: Modern Library, 1934.

_____. *The Engineers and the Price System*. New York: A.M. Kelley, 1965.

Vereshchagin, I.K. *Zakon pribavochnoi stoimosti v usloviyakh sovremennovo kapitalizma*. Moscow: Izdatel'stvo 'Mysl',' 1966.

Vernon, Graham D., ed. *Soviet Perceptions of War and Peace*. Washington, DC: National Defense University Press, 1981.

Vishnev, S.M. *Ekonomicheskie resursy Germanii*. Moscow: Sotsekgiz, 1940.

_____. *Promyshlennost' kapitalisticheskikh stran vo vtoroi mirovoi voiny (tekhniko-ekonomicheskie sdvigi)*. Moscow: Izdatel'stvo Akademii Nauk SSSR, 1947

____. *Sovremennyi militarizm i monopolii*. Moscow: Izdatel'stvo Akademii Nauk SSSR, 1952.

Voinov, A.M.; V.Ya. Iokhin; L.A. Rodina. *Ekonomicheskie otnosheniya mezhdu sotsialisticheskimi i razvitymi kapitalisticheskimi stranami*. Moscow: Izdatel'stvo 'Nauka,' 1975.

Voznesensky, N. *Voennaya ekonomika SSSR v period otechestvennoi voiny*. Moscow: Gosudarstvennoe Izdatel'stvo Politicheskoi Literatury, 1948.

Vygodsky, S.L. *Ocherki teorii sovremennovo kapitalizma*. Moscow: Izdatel'stvo Ekonomicheskoi Literatury, 1961.

____. *Sovremennyi kapitalizm (opyt teoreticheskovo analiza)*, 2d ed. Moscow: Izdatel'stvo 'Mysl',' 1975.

____, *Usilenie zagnivaniya kapitalizma v usloviyakh novovo etapa obshchevo krizisa*. Moscow: Izdatel'stvo VPSh i AON pri TsK KPSS, 1961.

____; V.S. Afanas'ev; V.A. Matveev, eds. *Aktual'nye ekonomicheskie problemy sovremennovo kapitalizma*. Moscow: Izdatel'stvo 'Mysl',' 1973.

____; P.A. Zykov; V.A. Matveev, eds. *Nekotorye tendentsii razvitiya kapitalisticheskoi ekonomiki, 1917-1967*. Moscow: Izdatel'stvo 'Mysl',' 1968.

____, ed. *Novye yavleniya v ekonomike sovremennovo imperializma*. Moscow: Izdatel'stvo VPSh i AON pri TsK KPSS, 1963.

Watts, Nita G., ed. *Economic Relations Between East and West*. London: Macmillan, 1978.

Yeager, Leland B. *International Monetary Relations: Theory, History, and Policy*, 2d ed. New York: Harper & Row, 1976.

Zhamin, V.A., ed. *Ekonomicheskoe sorevnovanie sotsializma s kapitalizmom*. Moscow: Izdatel'stvo Sotsial'no-Ekonomicheskoi Literatury, 1962.

Zhurkov, A., I.P. Faminsky. *Velikobritaniya i problemy Zapadno-Evropeiskoi integratsii*. Moscow: Izdatel'stvo Moskovskovo Universiteta, 1970.

Zimmerman, William. *Soviet Perspectives on International Relations 1956-1967*. Princeton, NJ: Princeton University Press, 1969.

Zorin, Val. *Monopolii i politika SShA*. Moscow: Izdatel'stvo Instituta Mezhdunarodnykh Otnoshenii, 1960.

INDEX

ABOUT THE AUTHOR

Richard B. Day is professor of political economy at the University of Toronto, Canada. His articles on the history of Marxist theory have appeared in several journals, including *Soviet Studies, Canadian Journal of Political Science, International Journal, New Left Review, Critique, Studies in Comparative Communism, Labour/Le Travailleur, Comparative Economic Studies, History of European Ideas, Studies in Soviet Thought, Problems of Communism,* and *International Journal of Political Economy*. He is the author of *Leon Trotsky and the Politics of Economic Isolation,* and *The 'Crisis' and the 'Crash': Soviet Studies of the West (1917-1939)*. He is translator and editor of N.I. Bukharin, *Selected Writings on the State and the Transition to Socialism,* and E.A. Preobrazhensky, *The Decline of Capitalism*. He is co-editor of *Democratic Theory and Technological Society,* contributing editor to *International Journal of Political Economy,* and has also contributed to *Colliers Encyclopedia, The New Palgrave: A Dictionary of Economic Theory and Doctrine,* and the *Oxford Companion to Politics of the World*.